Praise for *Web Development with Clojure, 3rd Edition*

Luminus has been the go-to web development toolkit for Clojure for years, and its author, Dmitri Sotnikov (with Third Edition co-author Scot Brown), in *Web Development with Clojure*, has the go-to book on developing in Clojure for the web. Complete, comprehensive, accessible: don't go out there without it.

➤ **Simon Brooke**
   Chair, Standingstone Farm Ltd

Web Development with Clojure is a great, thorough introduction to this complex topic, which is as interesting as it can be confusing, especially when starting out. The possibilities are endless, so it really helps to be introduced to some best practices by an experienced Clojure developer. I also bought the previous editions and have found *Web Development with Clojure* to be invaluable in my quest to use Clojure for modern web applications!

➤ **Maximilian Gerlach**
   Senior Technical Architect, Ada Inc.

If you're new to Clojure, the Clojure community's "assemble-your-own-web-framework" culture can be frustrating, forcing you to guess at which libraries to use and patch together what you can from online tutorials. The Luminus "micro"-framework bundles together the community's preferred libraries and has become the recommended starting place for new Clojure developers. With the creator of Luminus as your guide, *Web Development with Clojure* provides a comprehensive and realistic walk-through of how to build a web application in the Clojure ecosystem in 2021.

➤ **Rafal Dittwald**
   Partner, Bloom Ventures

Web Development with Clojure, 3rd Edition is the book you need for learning to write single-page apps in Clojure/Script. Well-paced, interactive, and covering everything from basics to structuring and deploying real-life web projects. New tools, new libraries, and lots of new content. Highly recommended.

➤ **Tommi Reiman**
  CTO, Metosin

Web Development with Clojure, Third Edition

Build Large, Maintainable Web Applications Interactively

Dmitri Sotnikov
Scot Brown

The Pragmatic Bookshelf

Raleigh, North Carolina

For our complete catalog of hands-on, practical, and Pragmatic content for software developers, please visit *https://pragprog.com*.

The team that produced this book includes:

CEO: Dave Rankin
COO: Janet Furlow
Managing Editor: Tammy Coron
Development Editor: Michael Swaine
Copy Editor: L. Sakhi MacMillan
Indexing: Potomac Indexing, LLC
Layout: Gilson Graphics
Founders: Andy Hunt and Dave Thomas

For sales, volume licensing, and support, please contact *support@pragprog.com*.

For international rights, please contact *rights@pragprog.com*.

ISBN-13: 978-1-68050-682-2
Book version: P1.0—July 2021

Contents

Acknowledgments

In the case of this book, there's no false modesty. We genuinely have to thank a great many folk who have helped make it possible. The volume of feedback we received shaped the book and made it far more useful than it would have been otherwise.

Dmitri would like to thank his beautiful wife, Linda. She spent many hours helping him refine the book. It simply would not have been the same without her oversight.

Scot would like to thank his wonderful partner Christina for her support and patience through this journey. This book would not have been possible without her.

The Pragmatic Bookshelf team has our thanks for their guidance and insight. We'd like to call out Mike Swaine in particular for his suggestions and constant demand for quality throughout the process. We'd also like to thank Sakhi MacMillan for her thorough copyediting and valuable feedback on the drafts.

We were lucky to have a team of highly experienced technical reviewers who were willing to ask tough questions. Thank you, Tommi Reiman, Maximilian Gerlach, Rafal Dittwald, and Simon Brooke.

Finally, we owe a big thanks to the beta readers who chose to put their trust in us. Their feedback helped elevate this book to a higher standard.

We're proud to put our names on this book. Thank you to all the people who've taken this journey with us. Our sincere respect and gratitude goes out to all of you.

Introduction

The cover of this book has a bonsai tree on it. We chose it to represent elegance and simplicity because these qualities make Clojure such an attractive language. A good software project is like a bonsai. You have to meticulously craft it to take the shape you want, and the tool you use should make it a pleasant experience. We hope to convince you here that Clojure is that tool.

What You Need

This book is aimed at readers of all levels. While having some basic proficiency with functional programming will be helpful, it's by no means required to follow the material presented. If you're not a Clojure user already, this book is a good starting point since it focuses on applying the language to solve concrete problems. This means we'll focus on the small set of language features needed to build web applications.

Why Clojure?

Clojure is a small language whose primary goals are simplicity and correctness. As a functional language, it emphasizes immutability and declarative programming. As you'll see, these features make it easy and idiomatic to write clean and correct code.

Web development has many languages to choose from and as many opinions on what makes a language "good." Some languages are simple but verbose. You've probably heard people say that verbosity doesn't matter—that if two languages are Turing complete, anything that can be written in one language can also be written in the other with a bit of extra code. We think that's missing the point.

The real question isn't whether something can be expressed in principle; it's how well the language maps to the problem being solved. One language lets you think in terms of your problem domain, while another forces you to translate the problem to its constructs.

The latter is often tedious and rarely enjoyable. You end up writing a lot of boilerplate code and constantly repeating yourself. There's a certain irony in having to write repetitive code.

At the other extreme, some languages are concise because they provide many different tools for solving problems. Unfortunately, this vast array of tools brings different problems.

The more features a language has, the more things you have to keep in your head to work with the language effectively. Soon we find ourselves constantly expending mental overhead thinking about all the different features and how they interact with one another.

What really matters is whether you can use a language without thinking about it. When a language is lacking in expressiveness, you become acutely aware that you're writing code that you shouldn't be. On the other hand, when a language has too many features, it can feel overwhelming and it's easy to get distracted playing with them.

To make an analogy with mathematics, understanding a few fundamental theorems and their implications is far more useful than rote memorization of specific formulas.

This is where Clojure comes in. It allows us to easily derive a solution to a particular problem from a small set of general patterns. All you need to become productive is to learn a few simple concepts and a bit of syntax. These concepts can then be combined in myriad ways to solve all kinds of problems.

Why Make Web Apps in Clojure?

Clojure boasts tens of thousands of users across hundreds of companies; it's used in a wide range of settings, including banks and hospitals. Clojure is likely the most popular Lisp dialect today for starting new development. It has proven itself in serious production systems, and the feedback from users has been overwhelmingly positive.

Because web development is one of the major domains for using Clojure, several popular libraries and frameworks have sprouted and matured in this area. In this book we'll primarily focus on the Luminus stack. The following chapters will teach you how to use Clojure and Luminus to build web applications effectively.

Many platforms are available for doing web development, so why should you choose Clojure over other options?

Well, consider those options. Many popular platforms force you to make trade-offs. Some platforms lack performance, others require a lot of boilerplate, and others lack the infrastructure necessary for real-world applications.

Clojure addresses the questions of performance and infrastructure by being a hosted language. The Java Virtual Machine (JVM) is a mature and highly performant environment with great tooling and deployment options. Clojure brings expressive power akin to that of Ruby and Python to this excellent platform. When working with Clojure you won't have to worry about being limited by your runtime when your application grows.

Additionally, Clojure isn't limited to the server. It can be compiled into Java-Script that is on par with popular front-end frameworks. Most web platforms require to learn and write JavaScript as well. With Clojure, you have a common toolset for both client and server.

The most common way to handle the boilerplate in web applications is by using a framework. Examples include Ruby on Rails, Django, and Spring. The frameworks provide the canned functionality needed for building a modern site.

The benefits these frameworks offer also come with inherent costs. Since many operations are done implicitly, you have to memorize what effects any action might have. This opaqueness makes your code more difficult to reason about. When you need to do something that's at odds with the framework's design, it can quickly become awkward and difficult. You might have to dive deep into the internals of that framework and hack around the expected behaviors.

Instead of using frameworks, Clojure makes a number of powerful libraries available, and we can put these libraries together in a way that makes sense for our particular project. As you'll see, we manage to avoid having to write boilerplate, while retaining the code clarity we desire. As you read on, we think you'll agree that this model has clear advantages over the framework-based approach.

Our goal is to give you both a solid understanding of the Clojure web stack and the expertise to quickly and easily build web applications using it. The following chapters will guide you all the way from setting up your development environment to creating a complete real-world application. We'll show you what's available and then guide you in structuring your application using the current best practices.

How to Read This Book

Before you get started, we should cover some conventions used in this book.

Throughout the book, we iteratively improve the applications we're working on with instructiveness as our primary goal. You'll see the top-level directory of files change periodically. This is intentional and is done to provide different stages of development for a single app. We recommend working along with your own version of the application and trying different variations of the examples provided. This will help you to get a feel for how things work and what alternatives are possible to what we present here. If you encounter any issues, you can compare your code against our version. The source code used throughout the book can be found on the Pragmatic Programming website.[1]

We strongly recommend experimentation in the REPL. This is by far the best way to develop your skill with Clojure.

---

1. https://pragprog.com/titles/dswdcloj3/web-development-with-clojure-third-edition/

CHAPTER 1

Getting Your Feet Wet

In the Introduction, on page xi, we looked at some of the benefits of the functional style when it comes to writing applications. Of course, you can't learn a language by just reading about it. To really get a feel for it, you have to write some code yourself.

In this chapter you'll dive right in and build a guestbook application that allows users to leave messages for one another. You'll see the basic structure of a web application, set up necessary tools for effective Clojure development, and get a feel for how web development in Clojure works. If you're new to Clojure, we recommend you read through Appendix 1, Clojure Primer, on page 363, for a crash course on the basic concepts and syntax.

The material we'll cover in this book is based on our experience and personal preferences. It's worth noting that there are other equally valid approaches to structuring Clojure web applications. The libraries and methodologies that we'll cover each have alternatives, but the ones we use will provide you with a solid starting point. As your familiarity with the Clojure ecosystem grows, we encourage you to evaluate different libraries and choose the ones that best suit your needs.

Set Up Your Environment

Clojure is distributed as a JAR (Java Archive file) that you'll need on your project's classpath. Clojure requires the Java Virtual Machine (JVM) to run, and you'll need a working Java Development Kit (JDK), version 1.9 or higher.[1] You'll also need to have Leiningen installed in order to work with Clojure projects.[2]

---

1. https://openjdk.java.net/install/index.html
2. http://leiningen.org/

Managing Projects with Leiningen

Leiningen lets you create, build, test, package, and deploy your projects. In other words, it's your one-stop shop for all your project-management needs.

Leiningen is the Clojure counterpart of Maven,[3] a popular Java build tool. It uses a Maven-compatible dependency management system, so it has access to large and well-maintained repositories of Java libraries. In addition, Clojure libraries are commonly found in the Clojars repository.[4] This repository is enabled by default in Leiningen.

With Leiningen, you don't need to worry about manually downloading all the libraries for your project. Specifying the top-level dependencies will cause any libraries that they depend on to be pulled in automatically.

Leiningen is available as a package for many Linux distributions, as well, via Homebrew on MacOS. If Leiningen isn't packaged on your system, then it can be installed using the installation script found on the official project page:[5]

```
$ wget https://raw.github.com/technomancy/leiningen/stable/bin/lein
...
HTTP request sent, awaiting response... 200 OK
Length: 12463 (12K) [text/plain]
Saving to: 'lein'

lein 100%[==========================>]  12.17K  --.-KB/s    in 0s

yyyy-MM-dd HH:mm:ss (96.3 MB/s) - 'lein' saved [12463/12463]
$ chmod +x lein
$ mv lein ~/bin
$ lein new myapp
Generating a project called myapp based on the 'default' template.
The default template is intended for library projects, not applications.
To see other templates (app, plugin, etc), try `lein help new`.
```

Note that the preceding code expects that ~/bin is available on the shell path. Since we're running lein for the first time, it will install itself. If the installation was successful, we should now have a brand-new project in the myapp folder.

Let's take a moment to look at what we've created inside myapp/. Leiningen generated a skeleton application here based on the default template. The source code for the application can be found in the src folder. Here we have another folder called myapp containing a single source file named core.clj. This file has the following code inside:

---

3. http://maven.apache.org/
4. https://clojars.org/
5. http://leiningen.org/#install

myapp/src/myapp/core.clj
```
(ns myapp.core)

(defn foo
  "I don't do a whole lot."
  [x]
  (println x "Hello, World!"))
```

Note that the namespace declaration matches the folder structure. Since the core namespace is inside the myapp folder, its name is myapp.core.

What's in a Leiningen Project File?

Inside the myapp project folder, we have a project.clj file. This file contains the description of our application. The project configuration is represented declaratively using regular Clojure data structures. It contains the application name, version, URL, license, and dependencies.

myapp/project.clj
```
(defproject myapp "0.1.0-SNAPSHOT"
  :description "FIXME: write description"
  :url "http://example.com/FIXME"
  :license {:name "EPL-2.0 OR GPL-2.0-or-later WITH Classpath-exception-2.0"
            :url "https://www.eclipse.org/legal/epl-2.0/"}
  :dependencies [[org.clojure/clojure "1.10.1"]]
  :repl-options {:init-ns myapp.core})
```

The project.clj file allows us to manage many different aspects of our application. One thing we can try is adding :main. This option sets a function as the entry point for the application. Let's try setting the :main key to the foo function from the myapp.core namespace:

myapp/project.clj
```
(defproject myapp "0.1.0-SNAPSHOT"
  :description "FIXME: write description"
  :url "http://example.com/FIXME"
  :license {:name "EPL-2.0 OR GPL-2.0-or-later WITH Classpath-exception-2.0"
            :url "https://www.eclipse.org/legal/epl-2.0/"}
  :dependencies [[org.clojure/clojure "1.10.1"]]
  ;;this will set foo as the main function
  :main myapp.core/foo
  :repl-options {:init-ns myapp.core})
```

Let's run our application using lein run and see what happens. Remember that the foo function expects an argument, so we have to give it one.

```
$ cd myapp
$ lein run Obligatory
Obligatory Hello, World!
```

Our app runs! The :main key is just one of many configuration options in a Leiningen project. You'll encounter many more Leiningen options throughout this book.

Build Your First Web App

In the preceding example we used the default Leiningen template to create a very simple application that has only one dependency: the Clojure runtime. If you used this as the base for a web application, then you'd have to write a lot of boilerplate to get it up and running. Let's see how we can use a different Leiningen template to create a web-application project with all the boilerplate already set up.

Our primary goal here is to get a high-level understanding of the project structure and get something working. We'll gloss over some of the finer details to maintain our momentum. Don't worry if you don't fully understand all the steps at this point. We'll get into the details in subsequent chapters.

Creating an Application from the Luminus Template

A template is used to generate a skeleton project from certain parameters, such as the project name or which database to use. Many different templates exist to quickly create different kinds of projects. Later on we'll even see how we can create templates ourselves. The Luminus template[6] provides a good base, and we'll use it this time.

We can specify a template by placing it after lein new (for example, lein new my-template my-app). Any additional parameters will be passed in as the arguments to the selected template.

Let's create a new application by specifying luminus as the template name and guestbook as the project name. We add the +h2 parameter to indicate that we want to have an instance of the H2[7] embedded database initialized and the +http-kit parameter to indicate that we want to use the http-kit[8] web server. We also specify the version of the template that we want to use explicitly to ensure that the projects you generate are exactly the same as the ones used in this book. Otherwise, Leiningen will default to the latest available version of the Luminus template. You can find the version of Luminus used to generate a project in the generated README.md.

---

6. http://www.luminusweb.net/
7. http://www.h2database.com/html/main.html
8. http://http-kit.github.io

```
$ lein new luminus guestbook  --template-version 3.91 -- +h2 +http-kit
Generating a Luminus project.
```

To generate a new project using the latest version of the template, we'd simply omit --template-version 3.91 -- from the arguments.

What's in a Web App

This type of application needs to start up a web server in order to run. Since Clojure development is best done interactively, the first thing to do is open a terminal in our project's root directory and start the REPL:

```
$ cd ./guestbook
$ lein repl
Retrieving ...
```

The first run may take a while because Leiningen first has to retrieve all of its dependencies. Once downloaded, the dependencies are cached locally in the ~/.m2/repository folder and will be available on subsequent runs. After the dependencies are downloaded, you should see the following output in the console:

```
nREPL server started on port XXX on host 127.0.0.1 - nrepl://127.0.0.1:XXX
REPL-y 0.4.4, nREPL 0.8.3
Clojure 1.10.1
OpenJDK 64-Bit Server VM 11.0.8+10
    Docs: (doc function-name-here)
          (find-doc "part-of-name-here")
  Source: (source function-name-here)
 Javadoc: (javadoc java-object-or-class-here)
    Exit: Control+D or (exit) or (quit)
 Results: Stored in vars *1, *2, *3, an exception in *e

user=>
```

The REPL puts us in the user namespace by default. This namespace is located in env/dev/clj/user.clj. The user namespace, along with the rest of env/dev/, is reserved for any development code that we wouldn't want to package in our application. It contains helper functions for handling various development tasks, including start and stop functions that allow us to control the state of the application.

guestbook-base/env/dev/clj/user.clj

```clojure
(ns user
  "Userspace functions you can run by default in your local REPL."
  (:require
   [guestbook.config :refer [env]]
    [clojure.pprint]
    [clojure.spec.alpha :as s]
    [expound.alpha :as expound]
    [mount.core :as mount]
    [guestbook.core :refer [start-app]]
    [guestbook.db.core]
    [conman.core :as conman]
    [luminus-migrations.core :as migrations]))

(alter-var-root #'s/*explain-out* (constantly expound/printer))

(add-tap (bound-fn* clojure.pprint/pprint))

(defn start
  "Starts application.
  You'll usually want to run this on startup."
  []
  (mount/start-without #'guestbook.core/repl-server))

(defn stop
  "Stops application."
  []
  (mount/stop-except #'guestbook.core/repl-server))

(defn restart
  "Restarts application."
  []
  (stop)
  (start))

(defn restart-db
  "Restarts database."
  []
  (mount/stop #'guestbook.db.core/*db*)
  (mount/start #'guestbook.db.core/*db*)
  (binding [*ns* (the-ns 'guestbook.db.core)]
    (conman/bind-connection guestbook.db.core/*db* "sql/queries.sql")))

(defn reset-db
  "Resets database."
  []
  (migrations/migrate ["reset"] (select-keys env [:database-url])))

(defn migrate
  "Migrates database up for all outstanding migrations."
  []
  (migrations/migrate ["migrate"] (select-keys env [:database-url])))
```

```
(defn rollback
  "Rollback latest database migration."
  []
  (migrations/migrate ["rollback"] (select-keys env [:database-url])))

(defn create-migration
  "Create a new up and down migration file with a timestamp and `name`."
  [name]
  (migrations/create name (select-keys env [:database-url])))
```

The REPL is like a sandbox where we can control, inspect, and modify a running version of our application in real time. Before we do anything, we should start our application like so:

```
;;timestamp prefixes have been removed from log statements for brevity
user=> (start)
;INFO  guestbook.env -
;-=[guestbook started successfully using the development profile]=-
;INFO  luminus.http-server - starting HTTP server on port 3000
;{:started ["#'guestbook.config/env"
;           "#'guestbook.db.core/*db*"
;           "#'guestbook.handler/init-app"
;           "#'guestbook.handler/app-routes"
;           "#'guestbook.core/http-server"]}
user=>
```

You'll notice that the output from running the start function indicates that various components such as the environment configuration, database, and the HTTP server have been started. We can open a new browser window and navigate to http://localhost:3000 to see the home page of our application.

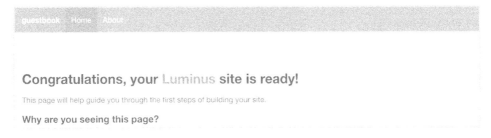

This is the default Luminus home page. It has some useful documentation on the structure of a Luminus application.

Now that we've created our application and tested that it's working, let's take a look at the directory structure that's been generated for us.

```
$ tree -d guestbook
guestbook
├── env
│   ├── dev
│   │   ├── clj
│   │   │   └── guestbook
│   │   └── resources
│   ├── prod
│   │   ├── clj
│   │   │   └── guestbook
│   │   └── resources
│   └── test
│       └── resources
├── resources
│   ├── docs
│   ├── html
│   ├── migrations
│   ├── public
│   │   ├── css
│   │   └── img
│   └── sql
├── src
│   └── clj
│       └── guestbook
│           ├── db
│           ├── middleware
│           └── routes
└── test
    └── clj
        └── guestbook
            └── db

XX directories

$
```

The project structure is significantly more complex this time around than what we had in the myapp project. We'll learn what all the pieces are for as we build different applications throughout the book. For now, we'll just take a quick overview of how the project is structured and what files go where.

The majority of our code lives under the src folder. This folder contains a clj folder that's reserved for Clojure source files. Since our application is called *guestbook*, this is the root namespace for the project. The application is further broken down into different namespaces based on function. We'll explore each of these in detail in Chapter 3, Luminus Architecture, on page 55. The namespace that is of immediate interest to us is the routes namespace.

The routes namespace is reserved for defining application routes. Each route is bound to a function that's responsible for processing the request and generating the response.

The db namespace houses database-related logic and serves as the model layer for the application. The guestbook.db.core namespace contains logic for defining queries and managing the database connection.

The other folder that's relevant for our application is the resources folder. It contains all the static assets associated with the application. These include HTML templates, CSS styles, and so on. Since we created a database for the app, it also contains a migrations folder with the SQL migration files.

Refine Your App

Okay, enough with the overview. Let's write some code.

Managing Database Migrations

The first thing we need to do is to initialize the database. The template generates two example migration files in the resources/migrations folder. Note the date on your files will be different since it's set to the date the application was instantiated. Let's delete the files generated by the template before proceeding.

```
$ rm resources/migrations/*
```

Next, let's see how to add migrations that are appropriate for our application. New pairs of migration files can be generated from the REPL by running the create-migration function:

```
user=> (create-migration "guestbook")
nil
user=>
```

A common beginner error that you may encounter is forgetting to start the database connection. If you do get this error, don't worry—just run (start) and try again. In fact, any error that mentions mount.core.DerefableState is probably due to forgetting to run (start).

The create-migration function creates a pair of migration files, one for updating the database and another for rolling back the changes. These files should look something like the following:

```
resources/migrations/20180903223633-guestbook.up.sql
resources/migrations/20180903223633-guestbook.down.sql
```

The generated migration files are prefixed with the timestamp, followed by the name we provided, and suffixed with the type of migration that they represent. Let's place the following SQL statement in the up migration file. We want to store the messages along with the name of the author and a timestamp indicating when the message was written. Let's also create an autogenerated ID column to keep track of the messages.

guestbook/resources/migrations/20180903223633-guestbook.up.sql
```
CREATE TABLE guestbook
(id INTEGER PRIMARY KEY AUTO_INCREMENT,
name VARCHAR(30),
message VARCHAR(200),
timestamp TIMESTAMP DEFAULT CURRENT_TIMESTAMP);
```

Put this statement to delete the guestbook table in the down migration file.

guestbook/resources/migrations/20180903223633-guestbook.down.sql
```
DROP TABLE guestbook;
```

Let's create the guestbook database table using the migrate function:

```
user=> (migrate)
;... INFO  migratus.core - Starting migrations
;... INFO  migratus.database - creating migration table 'schema_migrations'
;... DEBUG migratus.migrations - Looking for migrations in #object[...]
;... INFO  migratus.core - Running up for [20180903223633]
;... INFO  migratus.core - Up 20180903223633-guestbook
;... DEBUG migratus.migration.sql - found 1 up migrations
;... DEBUG migratus.database - marking 20180903223633 complete
;... INFO  migratus.core - Ending migrations
nil
user=>
```

Since H2 keeps the database in memory, we need to reload the state of the database connection after running the migrations:

```
user=> (restart)
;... INFO  luminus.http-server - HTTP server stopped
;... INFO  guestbook.env -
; -=[guestbook has shut down successfully]=-
;... INFO  guestbook.env -
; -=[guestbook started successfully using the development profile]=-
;... INFO  luminus.http-server - starting HTTP server on port 3000
{:started ["#'guestbook.config/env"
           "#'guestbook.db.core/*db*"
           "#'guestbook.handler/init-app"
           "#'guestbook.handler/app"
           "#'guestbook.core/http-server"]}
user=>
```

Our database is now ready to use, and we can start working with it. Our next step is to write the queries to create and read messages.

Querying the Database

Luminus defaults to using HugSQL[9] to interact with the database. SQL template files are used by the HugSQL library to automatically create database access functions.

Our project contains a file called resources/sql/queries.sql. This file is already populated with some sample query templates. The function names are specified using the -- :name comment followed by hints indicating the type of query, and the parameters are prefixed with a :. The -- :doc comment is used to generate the documentation metadata for the function. HugSQL has some advanced features not shown here, but otherwise, queries are written using regular SQL syntax.[10]

The generated queries aren't very useful to us, so let's replace them with new ones that allow us to work with the tables we just created. We'd like to be able to save messages in our database, so let's create a query called save-message!. Note that the name ends with !; by convention this indicates that it mutates data. We also need a query to retrieve stored messages. Let's call it get-messages.

```
guestbook/resources/sql/queries.sql
-- :name save-message! :! :n
-- :doc creates a new message using the name and message keys
INSERT INTO guestbook
(name, message)
VALUES (:name, :message)
-- :name get-messages :? :*
-- :doc selects all available messages
SELECT * from guestbook
```

Notice that the save-message! query name is followed by :! and :n flags. The first flag indicates the query is destructive. The second flag indicates that the query returns the number of affected rows.

The get-messages query uses the :? flag to indicate that the query does a select, and the :* flag indicates that multiple rows are returned.

The guestbook.db.core namespace contains a call to the conman.core/bind-connection macro. This macro reads the SQL queries that we defined and creates Clojure

---

9.   https://www.hugsql.org/
10.   https://www.hugsql.org/#detail

functions that perform the queries on the bound database connection using the name specified in the `-- :name` comment.

guestbook/src/clj/guestbook/db/core.clj
```
(conman/bind-connection *db* "sql/queries.sql")
```

Now that we have our data layer set up, we can try querying it to make sure that everything works correctly. The entirety of the guestbook.db.core namespace looks as follows:

guestbook/src/clj/guestbook/db/core.clj
```
(ns guestbook.db.core
  (:require
    [next.jdbc.date-time]
    [next.jdbc.result-set]
    [conman.core :as conman]
    [mount.core :refer [defstate]]
    [guestbook.config :refer [env]]))

(defstate ^:dynamic *db*
          :start (conman/connect! {:jdbc-url (env :database-url)})
          :stop (conman/disconnect! *db*))
(conman/bind-connection *db* "sql/queries.sql")

(extend-protocol next.jdbc.result-set/ReadableColumn
  java.sql.Timestamp
  (read-column-by-label [^java.sql.Timestamp v _]
    (.toLocalDateTime v))
  (read-column-by-index [^java.sql.Timestamp v _2 _3]
    (.toLocalDateTime v))
  java.sql.Date
  (read-column-by-label [^java.sql.Date v _]
    (.toLocalDate v))
  (read-column-by-index [^java.sql.Date v _2 _3]
    (.toLocalDate v))
  java.sql.Time
  (read-column-by-label [^java.sql.Time v _]
    (.toLocalTime v))
  (read-column-by-index [^java.sql.Time v _2 _3]
    (.toLocalTime v)))
```

The database connection is specified using a map that's passed to the con-man/connect! function. It is populated with the database connection specification. The :database-url environment variable is used to provide the connection URL for the database. This variable is populated in the dev-config.edn file found in the root of the project.

The dev-config.edn file contains information about the local environment that's not meant to be checked into the shared code repository. Database connection parameters are an example of such environment variables. The contents of the file look as follows:

```
guestbook/dev-config.edn
{:dev true
 :port 3000
 ;; when :nrepl-port is set the application starts the nREPL server on load
 :nrepl-port 7000
 :database-url "jdbc:h2:./guestbook_dev.db"}
```

The :database-url environment URL specifies that the database is stored in a file called guestbook_dev.db in the path where the application is run. In our case, this will be the root folder of the project.

Back in the guestbook.db.core namespace, the state of the database is stored in the *db* variable. The state of the database is managed by the Mount library.[11] We'll take a closer look at managing the life cycle of stateful resources in Chapter 3, Luminus Architecture, on page 55.

The queries that we just wrote are bound to functions using the bind-connection macro when the namespace is loaded. The generated functions will automatically use the connection stored in the *db* variable.

The functions generated by the macro accept the parameter map representing the dynamic query variables as their arguments. Since the queries are parameterized, any variables we pass in are sanitized to prevent SQL injection.

As we learned earlier, the REPL starts in the user namespace. So switch to the guestbook.db.core namespace, where the query functions are defined:

```
user=> (in-ns 'guestbook.db.core)
#namespace[guestbook.db.core]
guestbook.db.core=>
```

Next, reload the query functions by running the following command:

```
guestbook.db.core=> (conman/bind-connection *db* "sql/queries.sql")
{:snips {},
 :fns
 {:save-message!
  {:meta
   {:doc "creates a new message using the name and message keys",
    :command :!,
    :result :n,
    :file "sql/queries.sql",
    :line 1},
   :fn #function[conman.core/try-query/fn--14027/fn--14028]},
```

---

11. https://github.com/tolitius/mount

```
  :get-messages
  {:meta
   {:doc "selects all available messages",
    :command :?,
    :result :*,
    :file "sql/queries.sql",
    :line 6},
   :fn #function[conman.core/try-query/fn--14027/fn--14028]}}}
guestbook.db.core=>
```

We can see that the output from running conman/bind-connection is a map keyed on the names that we used to define the queries in the queries.sql file earlier. The database should now be ready to use, and we can try running the queries we just wrote:

```
;;Let's check if we have any existing data:
guestbook.db.core=> (get-messages)
()
;;We don't have any messages, so let's create one:
guestbook.db.core=> (save-message! {:name "Bob" :message "Hello, World"})
1
;;Finally, let's check that our message was created:
guestbook.db.core=> (get-messages)
({:id 1, :name "Bob", :message "Hello, World", :timestamp "..."})
guestbook.db.core=>
```

As you can see, it's possible to do most tasks against the running instance of the application. While you used the REPL from the terminal in this instance, we highly recommended that you use a Clojure editor that allows you to connect to the REPL going forward. That way you'll be able to evaluate any code as you're writing it.

In a few cases, you'll need to restart the application. The most common reason is when you're adding new dependencies to the project, as those can't be loaded dynamically by the JVM. Restarting may be slow sometimes, but it also gives you a clean slate. If you feel like you've gotten your REPL into a bad state and things are behaving unexpectedly, restarting is a good sanity check.

Creating Tests

Now that we've tested the database operations in the REPL, it's a good idea to create some tests for them. The project already comes with some default test operations defined. These are found in the test folder of the application. The database tests are in the test/clj/guestbook/db/core_teset.clj file.

The current tests are defined with the generated users table in mind. Since we've changed our table structure, let's replace it with the following test:

guestbook/test/clj/guestbook/db/core_test.clj

```
(ns guestbook.db.core-test
  (:require
   [guestbook.db.core :refer [*db*] :as db]
   [java-time.pre-java8]
   [luminus-migrations.core :as migrations]
   [clojure.test :refer :all]
   [next.jdbc :as jdbc]
   [guestbook.config :refer [env]]
   [mount.core :as mount]))

(use-fixtures
  :once
  (fn [f]
    (mount/start
     #'guestbook.config/env
     #'guestbook.db.core/*db*)
    (migrations/migrate ["migrate"] (select-keys env [:database-url]))
    (f)))

(deftest test-messages
  (jdbc/with-transaction [t-conn *db* {:rollback-only true}]
    (is (= 1 (db/save-message!
               t-conn
               {:name "Bob"
                :message "Hello, World"}
               {:connection t-conn})))
    (is (= {:name "Bob"
            :message "Hello, World"}
           (-> (db/get-messages t-conn {})
               (first)
               (select-keys [:name :message]))))))
```

Run this command in the project folder to ensure our tests are passing:

```
$ lein test
```

```
lein test guestbook.db.core-test
INFO  migratus.core - Starting migrations
INFO  migratus.database - creating migration table 'schema_migrations'
DEBUG migratus.migrations - Looking for migrations in #object[...]
INFO  migratus.core - Running up for [20180903223633]
INFO  migratus.core - Up 20180903223633-guestbook
DEBUG migratus.migration.sql - found 1 up migrations
DEBUG migratus.database - marking 20180903223633 complete
INFO  migratus.core - Ending migrations

lein test guestbook.handler-test

Ran 2 tests containing 4 assertions.
0 failures, 0 errors.
$
```

You might have noticed the project folder contains two configuration files called dev-config.edn and test-config.edn. As you may have guessed, the dev-config.edn file is used for the development configuration, while test-config.edn is used for testing. When Leiningen runs the tests, the program will use the test configuration so that the development database won't be affected. Configuration is selected using the :jvm-opts flag found in :project/dev and :project/test profiles in the project.clj file. When deploying applications to a production environment, a similar pattern is used to prevent development from altering production data.

Now that we have some tests, we can use a Leiningen plugin called *lein-test-refresh*[12] to run them automatically anytime we update the code in the project. This plugin is part of the Luminus template, so all we have to do is open a new terminal and run the following command:

```
$ lein test-refresh
*********************************************
*************** Running tests ***************
...
Ran 2 tests containing 4 assertions.
0 failures, 0 errors.

Passed all tests
Finished at HH:mm:ss.SSS (run time: 0.596s)
```

We can now keep an eye on this terminal to make sure that all our tests are passing whenever we make changes to the code or add new tests. This provides us with an automated sanity check that we haven't broken anything.

Developing functionality using the REPL and then generating tests is a common workflow in Clojure. This approach provides a faster feedback loop than test-driven development (TDD) since we don't have to constantly switch between tests and code while developing a feature. Instead, the development can be done interactively using the REPL. Once the feature works as intended, we can take the code from the REPL session and turn it into unit tests for this feature to ensure future changes don't break intended behavior.

Defining HTTP Routes

We've now confirmed that we're able to store and retrieve the messages from the database, and we've written tests to make sure we don't have any regressions. Next, we'll need to write a user interface that calls these functions. We'll create HTTP endpoints and have these call the function that corresponds to the user's intended action. The endpoints are commonly referred to as

---

12. https://github.com/jakemcc/lein-test-refresh

routes, and the route that renders the home page for our application is found in the guestbook.routes.home namespace.

guestbook-base/src/clj/guestbook/routes/home.clj
```
(ns guestbook.routes.home
  (:require
   [guestbook.layout :as layout]
   [guestbook.db.core :as db]
   [clojure.java.io :as io]
   [guestbook.middleware :as middleware]
   [ring.util.response]
   [ring.util.http-response :as response]))

(defn home-page [request]
  (layout/render request "home.html" {:docs (-> "docs/docs.md"
                                                io/resource
                                                slurp)}))

(defn about-page [request]
  (layout/render request "about.html"))

(defn home-routes []
  [""
   {:middleware [middleware/wrap-csrf
                 middleware/wrap-formats]}
   ["/" {:get home-page}]
   ["/about" {:get about-page}]])
```

You can see that the / route calls the home-page function that in turn renders the home.html template. You can also see that we're passing a map of parameters to the render function; currently the only parameter being passed is the :docs key. These parameters indicate dynamic content that is injected into our template before it's sent to the client. Let's take a quick look at the contents of the resources/html/home.html file:

guestbook-base/resources/html/home.html
```
{% extends "base.html" %}
{% block content %}
  <div class="content">
  {{docs|markdown}}
  </div>
{% endblock %}
```

You can see that this file extends a template called base.html and renders a block called *content*. The parent template provides a common layout for the pages in our application, and each individual page can render the portion of the page relevant to it. If you're familiar with Rails or Django templates, then this syntax should look very familiar. You'll also note that the templates are set up to use Bulma CSS[13] as the default scaffolding for the page layout.

The templates use a context map to populate the dynamic content. The keys in the map are used as template variables. For example, the {{docs|markdown}} statement corresponds to the :docs key in the map that was passed to the layout/render function by the home-page function.

Let's update our resources/html/home.html template to display our messages.

First, let's replace {{docs|markdown}} with a wrapper that will center and format our page nicely:

```
guestbook/resources/html/home.html
{% block content %}
<div class="content">
    <div class="columns is-centered">
        <div class="column is-two-thirds">
            <!-- Content -->
        </div>
    </div>
</div>
{% endblock %}
```

Then let's add some HTML inside our wrapper that displays a list of existing messages. Just like with docs, our messages are supplied using a variable called messages. Each item in messages is a map containing keys called timestamp, message, and name. We iterate over the messages and create an li tag for each message inside a ul tag, like so:

```
guestbook/resources/html/home.html
<div class="columns">
    <div class="column">
        <h3>Messages</h3>
        <ul class="messages">
            {% for item in messages %}
            <li>
                <time>
                    {{item.timestamp|date:"yyyy-MM-dd HH:mm"}}
                </time>
                <p>{{item.message}}</p>
                <p> - {{item.name}}</p>
            </li>
            {% endfor %}
        </ul>
    </div>
</div>
```

---

13. https://bulma.io/documentation/

Okay, let's go back to the guestbook.routes.home namespace and add the code to render the existing messages. Note we already have a reference to the guestbook.db.core namespace in the ns declaration at the top of the home namespace.

We can now update the home-page function to associate the messages with the :messages key when rendering the template.

guestbook/src/clj/guestbook/routes/home.clj
```
(defn home-page [request]
  (layout/render
    request "home.html" {:messages (db/get-messages)}))
```

Since we've already populated a message in our database during earlier testing, we should see it when we reload the page. We can now take a look at adding a form to create new messages from the page.

Now we need to create another div that contains a form for submitting new messages. Note that we need to provide a {% csrf-field %} in our form.[14] Luminus enables anti-forgery protection by default, and any POST requests that don't contain the anti-forgery token are rejected by the server.

guestbook/resources/html/home.html
```
<div class="columns">
    <div class="column">
        <form method="POST" action="/message">
            {% csrf-field %}
            <div class="field">
                <label class="label" for="name">
                    Name
                </label>
                <input class="input"
                       type="text"
                       name="name"
                       value="{{name}}" />
            </div>
            <div class="field">
                <label class="label" for="message">
                    Message
                </label>
                <textarea
                    class="textarea"
                    name="message">{{message}}</textarea>
            </div>
```

---

14. http://en.wikipedia.org/wiki/Cross-site_request_forgery

```
                    <input type="submit"
                            class="button is-primary"
                            value="comment" />

            </form>
        </div>
    </div>
</div>
```

Our final template should look as follows:

guestbook/resources/html/home.html
```
{% extends "base.html" %}
{% block content %}
<div class="content">
    <div class="columns is-centered">
        <div class="column is-two-thirds">
            <!-- Content -->
            <div class="columns">
                <div class="column">
                    <h3>Messages</h3>
                    <ul class="messages">
                        {% for item in messages %}
                        <li>
                            <time>
                                {{item.timestamp|date:"yyyy-MM-dd HH:mm"}}
                            </time>
                            <p>{{item.message}}</p>
                            <p> - {{item.name}}</p>
                        </li>
                        {% endfor %}
                    </ul>
                </div>
            </div>
            <div class="columns">
                <div class="column">
                    <form method="POST" action="/message">

                        {% csrf-field %}
                        <div class="field">
                            <label class="label" for="name">
                                Name
                            </label>
                            <input class="input"
                                    type="text"
                                    name="name"
                                    value="{{name}}" />
                        </div>

                        <div class="field">
                            <label class="label" for="message">
                                Message
                            </label>
```

```
              <textarea
                class="textarea"
                name="message">{{message}}</textarea>
          </div>
          <input type="submit"
                class="button is-primary"
                value="comment" />
        </form>
      </div>
    </div>
  </div>
</div>
</div>
{% endblock %}
```

We now need to create a new route on the server, called /*message*, to respond to the HTTP POST method. The route should call the function save-message! with the request to create a new message.

guestbook/src/clj/guestbook/routes/home.clj
```
["/message" {:post save-message!}]
```

The route handler calls the save-message! function that follows. This function grabs the params key from the request. This key contains a map of parameters that were sent by the client when the form was submitted to the server.

guestbook/src/clj/guestbook/routes/home.clj
```
(defn save-message! [{:keys [params]}]
  (db/save-message! params)
  (response/found "/"))
```

Since we named our fields *name* and *message*, they match the fields we defined in our table: to create a new record all we have to do is call the save-message! function from the db namespace with the params map. Once the message is saved, we redirect back to the home page. The final code in the namespace should look as follows:

guestbook/src/clj/guestbook/routes/home.clj
```
(ns guestbook.routes.home
  (:require
    [guestbook.layout :as layout]
    [guestbook.db.core :as db]
    [clojure.java.io :as io]
    [guestbook.middleware :as middleware]
    [ring.util.response]
    [ring.util.http-response :as response]))

(defn home-page [request]
  (layout/render
    request "home.html" {:messages (db/get-messages)}))
```

```
(defn save-message! [{:keys [params]}]
  (db/save-message! params)
  (response/found "/"))

(defn about-page [request]
  (layout/render
    request "about.html"))

(defn home-routes []
  [""
   {:middleware [middleware/wrap-csrf
                 middleware/wrap-formats]}
   ["/" {:get home-page}]
   ["/message" {:post save-message!}]
   ["/about" {:get about-page}]])
```

At this point our guestbook should display existing messages as well as allow the users to post new messages. As a last touch, we'll add some CSS to style our app. Static assets such as CSS, images, and JavaScript are found in the resources/public folder and are served without the need to define routes for them. Let's add the following CSS in the resources/public/css/screen.css file:

```
guestbook/resources/public/css/screen.css
ul.messages {
        list-style: none;
}

ul.messages li {
        padding: 0.5em;
        border-bottom: 1px dotted #ccc;
}

ul.messages li:last-child {
        border-bottom: none;
}

li time {
        font-size: 0.75em;
    color: rgba(0, 0, 0, 0.5);
}
```

The guestbook page should now look like the figure on page 23.

Validating Input

What else should we do? Currently, our guestbook doesn't do any validation of user input. That's weak. Let's see how we can ensure that user messages contain the necessary information before trying to store them in the database.

Luminus defaults to using the Struct library[15] to handle input validation. The library provides a straightforward way to check that our parameter map contains the required values.

Struct uses struct.core/validate function for handling validation. This function accepts a map containing the parameters followed by the validation schema. The schema is used to validate the input and return error messages for any invalid fields.

Many common validators such as required, email, matches, and so on are provided by Struct out of the box. These validators can be used individually or chained together to validate different aspects of the input value. Also, we can easily create custom validators for situations where the default ones won't do.

Before we see how validation works, we want to include struct.core in our guestbook.routes.home namespace.

```
(ns guestbook.routes.home
  (:require
  ...
  [struct.core :as st]))
```

We can now use the st/validate function to check that the input values are valid and to produce an error message when they're not. In our case, we need to ensure both that the username is not empty and that the message has at least ten characters before we persist them to the database. Our validation schema looks as follows:

---

15. http://funcool.github.io/struct/latest

guestbook-validation/src/clj/guestbook/routes/home.clj
```clojure
(def message-schema
  [[:name
    st/required
    st/string]
   [:message
    st/required
    st/string
    {:message "message must contain at least 10 characters"
     :validate (fn [msg] (>= (count msg) 10))}]])
```

The validation schema specifies that both the :name and the :message keys are required, that they're strings, and that the message must be more than 9 characters in length. The validation function then calls the st/validate function, passing it the params along with the schema to validate the message.

guestbook-validation/src/clj/guestbook/routes/home.clj
```clojure
(defn validate-message [params]
  (first (st/validate params message-schema)))
```

The result of the validate function is a vector where the first element is either nil when the validation passes or a map of errors. The keys in the map are the parameters that failed validation and the values are the error messages.

The next step is to hook up the validation function into our workflow. Currently, the save-message! function attempts to store the message and then redirects back to the home page. We need to add the ability to pass back the error message along with the original parameters when validation fails.

A common approach for this is to use a flash session to track the errors. Flash sessions have a lifespan of a single request, making them ideal storage for this purpose. The save-message! function validates the input and checks for errors. If it finds errors, it associates a :flash key with the response that contains the parameters along with the errors. If no errors are generated, it saves the message to the database and redirects as it did before.

guestbook-validation/src/clj/guestbook/routes/home.clj
```clojure
(defn save-message! [{:keys [params]}]
  (if-let [errors (validate-message params)]
    (-> (response/found "/")
        (assoc :flash (assoc params :errors errors)))
    (do
      (db/save-message! params)
      (response/found "/"))))
```

We can now update the home-page function to check for the :flash key. Let's select the name, message, and errors keys from the flash session and merge them with our parameter map.

guestbook-validation/src/clj/guestbook/routes/home.clj

```clojure
(defn home-page [{:keys [flash] :as request}]
  (layout/render
   request
   "home.html"
   (merge {:messages (db/get-messages)}
          (select-keys flash [:name :message :errors]))))
```

Finally, let's update our page to render the errors when they're present (also see figure on page 26).

guestbook-validation/resources/html/home.html

```html
<div class="columns">
    <div class="column">
        <form method="POST" action="/message">
            {% csrf-field %}
            <div class="field">
                <label class="label" for="name">
                    Name
                </label>
                {% if errors.name %}
                <div class="notification is-danger">
                    {{errors.name|join}}
                </div>
                {% endif %}
                <input class="input"
                       type="text"
                       name="name"
                       value="{{name}}" />
            </div>

            <div class="field">
                <label class="label" for="message">
                    Message
                </label>
                {% if errors.message %}
                <div class="notification is-danger">
                    {{errors.message|join}}
                </div>
                {% endif %}
                <textarea
                    class="textarea"
                    name="message">{{message}}</textarea>
            </div>
            <input type="submit"
                   class="button is-primary"
                   value="comment" />

        </form>
    </div>
</div>
```

Running Standalone

Up to now, we've been running our app using the lein run command. This starts an embedded server in development mode so that it watches files for changes and reloads them as needed. To package our application for deployment, we can package it into a runnable JAR as follows:

```
$ lein uberjar
```

The archive will be created in the target folder of our application, and we can run it using the java command.

Since we're using a database, we also have to make sure that the connection is specified as an environment variable. When we ran our application in development mode, the connection variable was provided in the dev-config.edn file. However, now that the application has been packaged for production, this variable is no longer available. Let's create a connection variable and then run our application as follows:

```
$ export DATABASE_URL="jdbc:h2:./guestbook_dev.db"
$ java -jar target/uberjar/guestbook.jar
```

What You've Learned

Okay, that's the whirlwind tour. By this point you should be getting a feel for developing web applications with Clojure, and you should be comfortable with some of the Clojure basics. You saw how to use Leiningen to create and manage applications. You learned about HTTP routing and some basic HTML templating. While we didn't explore many aspects of the skeleton application that was generated for us, you saw how the basic request life cycle is handled.

We'll be diving deeper and writing more code in upcoming chapters. If you aren't already, you should start using one of the popular Clojure-aware editor plugins, such as Cursive (IntelliJ), Calva (VSCode), Cider (Emacs), Fireplace (Vim), or Counterclockwise (Eclipse). We can't overstate the value of these tools, and we strongly recommend taking the time to set one up. See Appendix 2, Editor Configuration, on page 387, for guides on setting up a few popular Clojure editors.

In the next chapter, we'll delve into the details of the Clojure web stack to understand some of the details of how our application works.

CHAPTER 2

Luminus Web Stack

Now that we've gone through the process of building a web application using Clojure, let's take a look at what the Luminus template set up for us.

Many popular platforms, such as Rails or Django, take the approach of providing a monolithic framework for building web applications. The Clojure community has avoided this approach, using modular components instead. This means that you can structure your projects according to each one's needs.

Of course, to do that you have to know what libraries exist, what they are for, and how to put them together effectively. Even if you know the libraries that you wish to use, every project needs a certain amount of boilerplate.

The Clojure community tackles this problem by using project templates. These generate the necessary boilerplate for specific types of projects in a way that is readable and explicit, so you can get started quickly and change any of the generated code if necessary. In this book we're primarily using the Luminus template. The web application generated by Luminus is ready for deployment out of the box. The only missing part is your domain logic.

Two libraries are at the core of the application we developed in the previous chapter. Ring provides a basic API for handling HTTP requests and responses, and Reitit provides routing on top of Ring.

Let's take a look at how to handle HTTP requests and responses using Ring, and how to structure routes using Reitit, by building a web app from scratch.

Route Requests with Ring

Ring abstracts the details of HTTP into a concise and modular API that can be used as a base for any web application. If you've developed web applications in Python or Ruby, you'll find it similar to the WSGI and Rack libraries found in those languages.[1,2] Ring has adapters for many popular HTTP servers. The most common choices are embedded HTTP servers such as Jetty or HTTP Kit.[3,4]

Since Ring is the de facto standard HTTP library, many mature web development tools and libraries are built on top of it. Even though you'll rarely use Ring directly, it's the backbone of Clojure web applications. Knowing how it works is crucial to understanding Clojure web development.

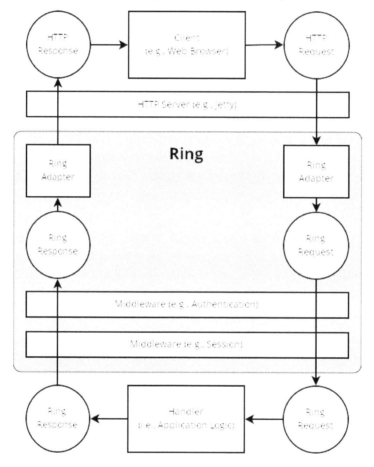

Ring applications consist of four basic components: the *handler*, the *request*, the *response*, and the *middleware*. When an HTTP request is received from

1.   http://wsgi.readthedocs.org/en/latest/

2.   http://rack.github.io/

3.   http://www.eclipse.org/jetty/

4.   http://http-kit.github.io/

the client via the HTTP server, it is transformed into a *Ring request* by the adapter. This request is passed down the *middleware stack*, being modified as necessary, until it reaches the *handler*. The handler generates a *Ring response* from the request. It's then passed back up the *middleware stack*, being modified as necessary, until it reaches the adapter. The adapter converts the response map into an HTTP response to be sent back to the client. Let's see this in action.

Creating a Web Server

First, let's create a new project called *ring-app* by running the following command:

```
$ lein new ring-app
```

Next let's open the project.clj file to add the dependency for Ring and specify the :main key that points to the namespace that has the -main function. This function is used as the entry point for starting the application.

ring-app-1/project.clj
```
(defproject ring-app "0.1.0-SNAPSHOT"
  :description "FIXME: write description"
  :url "http://example.com/FIXME"
  :license {:name "EPL-2.0 OR GPL-2.0-or-later WITH Classpath-exception-2.0"
            :url "https://www.eclipse.org/legal/epl-2.0/"}
  :dependencies [[org.clojure/clojure "1.10.1"]
                 [ring "1.8.2"]]
  :repl-options {:init-ns ring-app.core}
  :main ring-app.core)
```

We're now ready to update the ring-app.core namespace with the code to create a web server and handle HTTP requests.

Handling Requests

Ring uses standard Clojure maps to represent requests and responses. The handler is a function that processes incoming requests and generates corresponding responses. A very basic Ring handler might look like this:

ring-app-1/src/ring_app/core.clj
```
(defn handler [request-map]
  {:status 200
   :headers {"Content-Type" "text/html"}
   :body (str "<html><body> your IP is: "
              (:remote-addr request-map)
              "</body></html>")})
```

As you can see, the handler function accepts a map representing an HTTP request and returns a map representing an HTTP response. Ring takes care of generating the request map from the incoming HTTP request and converting the map returned by the function into the corresponding HTTP response that will be sent to the client. Let's open the ring-app.core and add the handler there.

Now we need to start a web server with our handler attached. We can use Ring's jetty adapter to configure and start an instance of jetty. To do so, we require it in the namespace declaration and then call run-jetty from our -main function. Our namespace should look like this:

ring-app-1/src/ring_app/core.clj
```clojure
(ns ring-app.core
  (:require [ring.adapter.jetty :as jetty]))

(defn handler [request-map]
  {:status 200
   :headers {"Content-Type" "text/html"}
   :body (str "<html><body> your IP is: "
              (:remote-addr request-map)
              "</body></html>")})

(defn -main []
  (jetty/run-jetty
    handler
    {:port 3000
     :join? false}))
```

The run-jetty function accepts the handler function we just created, along with a map containing options such as the HTTP port. The :join? key indicates whether the server thread should block. Let's set it to false so that we're able to work in the REPL while it's running.

Now, we can open up the terminal and start our application using the lein run command.

```
$ cd ring-app
$ lein run
...:main: Logging initialized @783ms ...
...oejs.Server:main: jetty-9.4.12.v20180830; ...
...oejs.AbstractConnector:main: Started ServerConnector ... {0.0.0.0:3000}
...oejs.Server:main: Started @833ms
```

At this point our server is ready to handle requests, and we can navigate to http://localhost:3000 or use curl to see our app in action. You should see "your IP is: 0:0:0:0:0:0:0:1" since we're accessing it from localhost and the server is listening on all of the available interfaces.

The handler that we wrote serves an HTML string with the client's IP address with a response status of 200. Since this is a common operation, the Ring

API provides a helper function for generating such responses found in the ring.util.response namespace. Let's reference it and update our handler as follows.

```
ring-app-2/src/ring_app/core.clj
(ns ring-app.core
  (:require [ring.adapter.jetty :as jetty]
            [ring.util.response :as response]))

(defn handler [request-map]
  (response/response
   (str "<html><body> your IP is: "
        (:remote-addr request-map)
        "</body></html>")))
```

We should now be able to restart the app in the terminal and see the same page displayed as before. If you want to create a custom response, you'll have to write a function that accepts a request map and returns a response map representing your custom response. Let's look at the format for the request and response maps.

Request and Response Maps

The request and response maps contain information such as the server port, URI, remote address, and content type, plus the body with the actual payload. The keys in these maps are based on the servlet API and the official HTTP RFC.[5,6]

What's in the Request Map

The request defines the following standard keys. Note that not all of these keys, such as :ssl-client-cert, are guaranteed to be present in a request.

- :server-port—the port on which the server is handling the request.

- :server-name—the server's IP address or the name it resolves to.

- :remote-addr—the client's IP address.

- :query-string—the request's query string.

- :scheme—the specifier of the protocol, which can be either :http or :https.

- :request-method—the HTTP request method, such as :get, :head, :options, :put, :post, or :delete.

- :content-type—the request body's MIME type.

---

5.   https://tools.ietf.org/html/rfc7230

6.   https://tools.ietf.org/html/rfc7231

- :content-length—the number of bytes in the request.

- :character-encoding—the name of the request's character encoding.

- :headers—a map containing the request headers.

- :body—an input stream for the body of the request.

- :context—the context in which the application can be found when not deployed as root.

- :uri—the request URI path on the server; this string will have :context prepended when available.

- :ssl-client-cert—the client's SSL certificate.

As you can see, the standard keys from the Ring specification are spartan and are still very close to regular HTTP. Middleware functions are often used to extend the request map with other application-specific keys and to make the request map easier to work with. Later in this chapter we'll cover how to accomplish this.

What's in the Response Map

The response map contains three keys needed to describe the HTTP response:

- :status—the response's HTTP status.
- :headers—any HTTP headers to be returned to the client.
- :body—the response's body.

The status is a number representing one of the status codes specified in the HTTP RFC. The lowest allowed number is 100.

The :headers key is a map containing the HTTP-header key/value pairs. Header values may either be strings or a sequences of strings. When the value is a sequence, then a name/value header is sent for each string in the sequence.

The response body can contain a string, a sequence, a file, or an input stream. The body must correspond appropriately with the response's status code.

When the response body is a string, it is sent back to the client as is. If it's a sequence, then a string representing each element is sent to the client. Finally, if the response is a file or an input stream, then the server sends its contents to the client.

```
{:status  404
 :headers {"content-type" "text/html"}
 :body    "<html><body>NOT FOUND</body></html>"}
```

```
{:status  200
 :headers {"content-type" ["text/plain" "text/html"]}
 :body     "<html><body>OK</body></html>"}
```

Adding Functionality with Middleware

Middleware allows wrapping the handlers in functions that can modify the way the request is processed, modify the generated response, or both. Middleware functions are often used to extend the base functionality of Ring handlers to match your application's needs.

A middleware handler is a function that accepts an existing handler with some optional parameters and then returns a new handler with some added behavior. Here's an example of a middleware function:

ring-app-2/src/ring_app/core.clj
```
(defn wrap-nocache [handler]
  (fn [request]
    (-> request
        handler
        (assoc-in [:headers "Pragma"] "no-cache"))))
```

The wrapper in our example accepts a handler and returns a function that in turn acts as a handler. When the returned handler function is invoked, it calls the original handler with the request and adds Pragma: no-cache to the headers of the response map the original handler returns. Wrapper functions like this one are called *closures* because they close over their parameters and make them accessible to the function they return, even if the returned function is invoked much later.

Before we try wrapping our handler with our new middleware, let's see what headers we get back:

```
$ curl -I localhost:3000
HTTP/1.1 200 OK
Date: ...
Content-Length: 54
Server: Jetty(9.4.12.v20180830)
```

Now let's wrap our handler with wrap-nocache, restart our app, and confirm that the headers change:

ring-app-2/src/ring_app/core.clj
```
(defn -main []
  (jetty/run-jetty
    (-> handler
        wrap-nocache)
    {:port 3000
     :join? false}))
```

```
$ curl -I localhost:3000
HTTP/1.1 200 OK
Date: ...
Pragma: no-cache
Content-Length: 54
Server: Jetty(9.4.12.v20180830)
```

We've updated our response without modifying our handler. Using middleware allows us to create small functions, each dealing with a particular aspect of our application. Because middleware functions both accept and return a handler function, we can easily chain together as many as we need to provide complex behaviors needed for real-world applications.

Many libraries provide middleware functions for modifying request and response maps. Ring itself comes with a number of such middleware helpers. For example, you may have noticed that we didn't have to keep restarting the guestbook app to see the changes. Instead, the code on the server was automatically reloaded by the wrap-reload middleware function found in the ring.middleware.reload namespace. Let's add this piece of middleware to our app.

ring-app-3/src/ring_app/core.clj
```
(ns ring-app.core
  (:require
   ;;...
   [ring.middleware.reload :refer [wrap-reload]]))

(defn -main []
  (jetty/run-jetty
   (-> handler
       var
       wrap-nocache
       wrap-reload)
   {:port 3000
    :join? false}))
```

Note that we have to create a var from the handler for this middleware to work.[7] This is necessary to ensure that the var object containing the current handler function is returned. If we use handler, then the first time this middleware is called it will resolve handler to the initial function and ignore any subsequent changes we might want to reload.[8] A more common way to create a var is to use the #' prefix as follows:

```
(-> #'handler
    wrap-nocache
    wrap-reload)
```

---

7.   https://clojure.org/reference/vars
8.   https://clojure.org/reference/evaluation

With the wrap-reload middleware in place, you'll have to restart the server one more time for it to take effect. After the server is restarted you should be able to modify the handler function, save the file, and reload the page to see the changes.

```
(defn handler [request-map]
  (response/response
   (str "<html><body>Hello, your IP is: "
        (:remote-addr request-map)
        "</body></html>")))
```

```
$ curl http://localhost:3000
<html><body>Hello, your IP is: 0:0:0:0:0:0:0:1</body></html>
```

What Are the Adapters?

Adapters sit between the handlers and the underlying HTTP protocol. They provide any necessary configuration, such as port mappings, and they parse HTTP requests into request maps and construct HTTP responses from the handler response maps. The adapters allow Ring to run on a number of different containers, such as Jetty and HTTP Kit. You'll generally not need to interact with adapters directly in your application.

Extend Ring

Ring provides a simple base for handling the HTTP request and response cycle. We'll now look at several libraries that provide many additional utility functions that extend the functionality of Ring.

As we saw earlier, the Ring stack consists of a chain of middleware functions. Each function accepts the request map, modifies it in some way, and then passes it on to the next function in the chain. The middleware functions have to be wrapped in order of dependency. For example, session-based authentication relies on the presence of a session, and the session middleware must run before it to make the session available.

A library called *ring-defaults* provides a standard set of middleware that's useful for typical web applications. The middleware is split into API middleware and site middleware. The configuration *api-defaults* is meant to be used for web service APIs, and its counterpart, *secure-api-defaults*, extends it with SSL redirects and enables HSTS. Conversely, *site-defaults* provide the middleware stack for a typical website, while *secure-site-defaults* provide security extensions such as SSL and secure cookies. Luminus defaults to using the site-defaults middleware.

Ideally, the responses returned by the server should follow the HTTP status codes whenever appropriate. When an operation is successful, we return a status of 200, when we have an internal error we return a status of 500, and so on. The ring-http-response library provides a set of handler functions that map to HTTP codes.[9]

Using this library, we can return meaningful responses that map to specific HTTP status codes, such as *ok*, *found*, *internal-server-error*, and so on.

Let's add the library to the dependencies in project.clj and update the handler function in the project.

```
ring-app-3/project.clj
:dependencies [[org.clojure/clojure "1.10.1"]
               [metosin/ring-http-response "0.9.1"]
               [ring "1.8.2"]]
```

Note that if the project is currently running, then we have to restart it for the changes to take effect. While Clojure namespaces can be reloaded dynamically, any changes on the classpath require the JVM to be restarted to take effect. Since adding a new library updates the classpath, the project needs to be reloaded for it to be found.

We can now replace the ring.util.response reference with a reference to ring.util.http-response and update the handler as follows.

```
ring-app-3/src/ring_app/core.clj
(ns ring-app.core
  (:require
   [ring.adapter.jetty :as jetty]
   [ring.util.http-response :as response]
   [ring.middleware.reload :refer [wrap-reload]]))

(defn handler [request-map]
  (response/ok
   (str "<html><body> your IP is: "
        (:remote-addr request-map)
        "</body></html>")))
```

You might encounter another common REPL problem here if you restarted *before* editing src/ring-app/core.clj. Since we were already using the response alias for ring.util.response, you'll get an IllegalStateException. To remedy this, simply call ns-unalias from the REPL before reloading your file, like so:

---

9.   https://github.com/metosin/ring-http-response

```
ring-app.core=> (ns ring-app.core
         #_=>    (:require [ring.adapter.jetty :as jetty]
         #_=>              [ring.util.http-response :as response]
         #_=>              [ring.middleware.reload :refer [wrap-reload]]))
IllegalStateException Alias response already exists in namespace...

ring-app.core=> (ns-unalias *ns* 'response)
nil
ring-app.core=> (ns ring-app.core
         #_=>    (:require [ring.adapter.jetty :as jetty]
         #_=>              [ring.util.http-response :as response]
         #_=>              [ring.middleware.reload :refer [wrap-reload]]))
nil
```

Now that we've got our namespace loaded, try out some different response types. Here are some examples:

```
ring-app.core=> (response/continue)
{:status 100,
 :headers {},
 :body ""}
ring-app.core=> (response/ok "<h1>hello, world</h1>")
{:status 200,
 :headers {},
 :body "<h1>hello, world</h1>"}
ring-app.core=> (response/found "/messages")
{:status 302,
 :headers {"Location" "/messages"},
 :body ""}
ring-app.core=> (response/internal-server-error "failed to complete request")
{:status 500,
 :headers {},
 :body "failed to complete request"}
```

When exposing a service API, it's often necessary to communicate with external clients that use different encoding formats. Most of the time, Clojure web apps will use EDN or Transit.[10] (See Appendix 3, Working with EDN and Transit, on page 391, for details.) The Muuntaja library provides middleware for automatically serializing and deserializing different data formats based on the Accept and Content-Type request headers. The library handles common formats, such as JSON and YAML, as well as Clojure-specific formats such as EDN and Transit. Let's add this library.

---

10. https://github.com/cognitect/transit-format

ring-app-4/project.clj

```
:dependencies [[org.clojure/clojure "1.10.1"]
               [metosin/muuntaja "0.6.7"]
               [metosin/ring-http-response "0.9.1"]
               [ring "1.8.2"]]
```

The library provides a middleware wrapper function called *muuntaja.middle-ware/wrap-format*. This function accepts the handler and an optional muuntaja instance. Let's reference the wrap-format middleware function and change the handler to accept a request containing a JSON-encoded request body. We rename our old handler, create a new one called json-handler that accepts and returns a map, and define handler to be json-handler.

ring-app-4/src/ring_app/core.clj

```
(ns ring-app.core
  (:require
   [muuntaja.middleware :as muuntaja]
   [ring.adapter.jetty :as jetty]
   [ring.util.http-response :as response]
   [ring.middleware.reload :refer [wrap-reload]]))

(defn html-handler [request-map]
  (response/ok
   (str "<html><body> your IP is: "
        (:remote-addr request-map)
        "</body></html>")))

(defn json-handler [request]
  (response/ok
   {:result (get-in request [:body-params :id])}))

(def handler json-handler)

(defn wrap-nocache [handler]
  (fn [request]
    (-> request
        handler
        (assoc-in [:headers "Pragma"] "no-cache"))))

(defn wrap-formats [handler]
  (-> handler
      (muuntaja/wrap-format)))

(defn -main []
  (jetty/run-jetty
   (-> #'handler
       wrap-nocache
       wrap-formats
       wrap-reload)
   {:port 3000
    :join? false}))
```

To parse our request body, the *wrap-format* middleware uses the *Content-Type* and *Accept* HTTP headers to determine how the request and response data should be handled. It optionally takes a second argument to specify options such as default response format, custom parsing and encoding per format, and so on. We'll use Muuntaja's defaults for now.

Let's test it out using cURL:

```
$ curl -H "Content-Type: application/json" \
-X POST -d '{"id":1}' localhost:3000
{"result":1}
```

It works! Since we specified that we're supplying a JSON encoded request, and we accept JSON in the response, the middleware deserializes the JSON into Clojure EDN data structure and automatically serializes the response data structure as a JSON string. However, we're not limited to working strictly with JSON. We can just change the headers to use a different encoding:

```
$ curl -H "Content-Type: application/edn" -H "Accept: application/edn" \
-X POST -d '{:id 1}' localhost:3000
{:result 1}
```

This time around we passed EDN encoded parameters and got an EDN encoded result back. You can mix and match request and response types as well. If you like, try turning an EDN request into a JSON response and vice versa to see how Muuntaja converts between the two formats.

Muuntaja supports JSON, EDN, and Transit by default and provides additional modules for YAML and Messagepack if you need them. This multitude of formats can become a problem, especially since they don't all share the same features. As we saw earlier, in EDN we get the keyword *:result* but in JSON we get the string *"result"*. This gets even more complex when you consider timestamps and other EDN extensions. To deal with this, Muuntaja provides an encoder/decoder API with a default instance, and the ability to specify a custom instance to be used by your middleware stack. We won't get into providing our own custom muuntaja instance here, but we'll see it later on.

Using middleware like this is a common pattern for capturing ordinary tasks, such as data encoding, in a centralized fashion. The alternative would be to have each handler function handle its own serialization and deserialization logic. The latter approach is both error prone and repetitive, so it should be avoided whenever possible. As a rule, patterns that are not specific to a particular request are good candidates for middleware functions.

It's also worth noting that different sets of handlers can be wrapped with their own middleware. For example, CSRF protection makes sense for routes that are called by the pages generated within the same session, as you saw with the guestbook application. But if you were creating a public service API, then you wouldn't want the routes to require a CSRF token.

Define the Routes with Reitit

Reitit is a general purpose routing library that can be used to provide routing on top of Ring as well as for client-side routing, as we'll see later on. It provides a way to associate handler functions with a URL and an HTTP method.

We already saw some examples of routing using Reitit when we built our first application in Chapter 1, Getting Your Feet Wet, on page 1. Now let's take a closer look at the functionality it provides. First, add it as a dependency in the ring-app project.

ring-app-5/project.clj
```
:dependencies [[org.clojure/clojure "1.10.1"]
               [metosin/muuntaja "0.6.7"]
               [metosin/reitit "0.5.11"]
               [metosin/ring-http-response "0.9.1"]
               [ring "1.8.2"]]
```

With the dependency in place, let's update the namespace to reference reitit.ring and add a route for the / URI.

ring-app-5/src/ring_app/core.clj
```
(ns ring-app.core
  (:require
   [reitit.ring :as reitit]
   [muuntaja.middleware :as muuntaja]
   [ring.adapter.jetty :as jetty]
   [ring.util.http-response :as response]
   [ring.middleware.reload :refer [wrap-reload]]))

;;...

(def routes
  [["/" {:get html-handler}]])

(def handler
  (reitit/ring-handler
   (reitit/router routes)))

(defn -main []
  (jetty/run-jetty
   (-> #'handler
       wrap-nocache
       wrap-formats
       wrap-reload)
   {:port 3000
    :join? false}))
```

We're using our html-handler to generate responses, and it's being called when the / route is called with the HTTP GET method. As you can see, Reitit uses plain Clojure data structures to declare routes. Each route is declared using a vector where the first item is a string representing the route path. The path is followed by a map describing the supported operations. In this case, the map indicates that the route responds to the :get operation and the request will be handled by the html-handler function.

We can test that our routing works correctly by restarting the application and using cURL to send a request to it:

```
$ curl http://localhost:3000
<html><body> your IP is: 0:0:0:0:0:0:0:1</body></html>
```

Currently, the route only responds to GET requests; if we try to send it a POST request, then we won't get a response:

```
$ curl -X POST http://localhost:3000
```

As you might have guessed, all we have to do to handle the POST method is to add the :post key in the route map:

```
(def routes
  [["/" {:get html-handler
         :post html-handler}]])
```

The server will now handle the POST method for the route:

```
$ curl -X POST http://localhost:3000
<html><body> your IP is: 0:0:0:0:0:0:0:1</body></html>
```

Alternatively, you can simply provide a handler function instead of a map, and it will accept any HTTP method.

```
(def routes
  [["/" html-handler]])
```

Reitit also supports dynamic paths with embedded parameters. These parameters are specified using a :.

Let's add another route to our handler that accepts an :id and displays its value on the page.

```
(def routes
  [["/" html-handler]
   ["/echo/:id"
    {:get
     (fn [{{:keys [id]} :path-params}]
       (response/ok (str "<p>the value is: " id "</p>")))}]])
```

Let's try it out:

```
$ curl http://localhost:3000/echo/5
<p>the value is: 5</p>
```

Another useful Reitit feature is the ability to selectively apply middleware for specific routes. Currently, the wrap-formats middleware is being applied to all the routes since it's wrapping the entire handler. Since this middleware introduces additional overhead, we want to only apply it to the routes that actually need it. Let's update the -main function to remove the wrap-formats middleware.

ring-app-6/src/ring_app/core.clj
```
(defn -main []
  (jetty/run-jetty
   (-> #'handler
       wrap-nocache
       wrap-reload)
   {:port 3000
    :join? false}))
```

Next, create a context path called /api that declares the middleware using the :middleware key in its configuration map. This middleware will be applied to any routes under this context path. Finally, add a route called /multiply.

ring-app-6/src/ring_app/core.clj
```
(def routes
  [["/" html-handler]
   ["/echo/:id"
    {:get
     (fn [{{:keys [id]} :path-params}]
       (response/ok (str "<p>the value is: " id "</p>")))}]
   ["/api" {:middleware [wrap-formats]}
    ["/multiply"
     {:post
      (fn [{{:keys [a b]} :body-params}]
        (response/ok {:result (* a b)}))}]]])
```

We can test it out using cURL as follows:

```
$ curl -H "Content-Type: application/json" -X POST \
  http://localhost:3000/api/multiply  -d '{"a": 3, "b": 2}'
{"result":6}
```

Using Reitit routes, we can easily map functionality to each URL of our site to provide much of the core functionality needed in a web application. We can then group these routes together using vectors, as we did previously. Reitit, in turn, creates the Ring handler for us.

Reitit Defaults

Now that you know how the basics of Reitit work, let's take a look at some other useful features that it provides. For example, we might wish to set some default handlers. We can accomplish that by adding a default handler as follows:

ring-app-6/src/ring_app/core.clj
```
(def handler
  (reitit/ring-handler
   (reitit/router routes)
   (reitit/create-default-handler
    {:not-found
     (constantly (response/not-found "404 - Page not found"))
     :method-not-allowed
     (constantly (response/method-not-allowed "405 - Not allowed"))
     :not-acceptable
     (constantly (response/not-acceptable "406 - Not acceptable"))})))
```

The reitit/ring-handler function accepts an optional default handler as a second argument. We've passed it a handler generated by the reitit.ring/create-default-handler function. This function creates a default handler from a configuration map that specifies the handler functions for 404, 405, and 406 client errors. With this change in place, we should get an informative error when the client accesses a route incorrectly. For example, if we call a route that doesn't exist, we'll see the following response:

```
$ curl http://localhost:3000/foo
404 - Page not found
```

Another useful handler would be one for serving static resources. Once again, Reitit provides a helper function for doing that called create-resource-handler. The function accepts a configuration map that can contain the following options:

- :parameter—optional name of the wildcard parameter; defaults to unnamed keyword :.

- :root—optional resource root; defaults to *public*.

- :path—optional path to mount the handler to; works only if mounted outside of a router.

- :loader—optional class loader to resolve the resources.

- :index-files—optional vector of index-files to look in a resource directory; defaults to ["index.html"].

We'll update our default handler to try the resource handler first, then to fall back on our original default handler. To accomplish this, wrap the two handlers in the reitit.ring/routes function, which will evaluate each handler in order, returning the first match. This means that the resource handler must be declared before the default handler in order not to be masked by it.

ring-app-6/src/ring_app/core.clj

```clojure
(def handler
  (reitit/ring-handler
   (reitit/router routes)
   (reitit/routes
    (reitit/create-resource-handler {:path "/"})
    (reitit/create-default-handler
     {:not-found
      (constantly (response/not-found "404 - Page not found"))
      :method-not-allowed
      (constantly (response/method-not-allowed "405 - Not allowed"))
      :not-acceptable
      (constantly (response/not-acceptable "406 - Not acceptable"))}))))
```

Next, let's create a resources/public folder with a file called index.html with the following contents:

ring-app-6/resources/public/index.html

```html
<html>
  <body>
    <h1>Hello from Reitit</h1>
  </body>
</html>
```

We can now check that the resource is being served:

```
$ curl http://localhost:3000/index.html
<html>
  <body>
    <h1>Hello from Reitit</h1>
  </body>
</html>
```

You should now be comfortable accomplishing basic routing tasks using Reitit. In the next section, we'll take a closer look at server-side HTML templating using Selmer.

HTML Templating Using Selmer

Selmer is a general-purpose templating engine that's content-agnostic. While it's primarily geared toward working with HTML, it can be used to transform any kind of text. If you're already familiar with Django or similar templating languages, you should feel right at home using Selmer.

When applied to generating HTML templates, Selmer encourages a clean separation between the presentation and the business logic. On top of that, the templates can be maintained by someone who has no knowledge of Clojure. Let's create a new project where we'll learn to use different features of Selmer. We'll use the default Leiningen template for this purpose.

```
$ lein new html-templating
```

Once the project is created, add the Selmer dependency in the project.clj file.

```
[selmer "1.12.31"]
```

We're now ready to take a look at what Selmer has to offer using the REPL. Open up the html-templating.core namespace and add a reference to Selmer there.

```
(ns html-templating.core
  (:require [selmer.parser :as selmer]))
```

Once we've added the reference, we should be able to load the namespace and test that everything is working by evaluating this command in the REPL:

```
(selmer/render "Hello, {{name}}" {:name "World"})
```

When the code runs we should see the Hello, World text printed. The render function accepts the template string followed by a context map containing the dynamic content. This map contains any variables that we'd like to render in our template. In our case, we're populating the name tag using the :name key in the map.

In most real-world applications, we want to keep the templates as separate files instead of using strings directly in code. Selmer is optimized for this use case and memoizes the file templates when it parses them. Let's take a look at how Selmer works with files.

Creating Templates

The templates are expected to be found on the resource path. Let's create a new template called hello.html and place it in the resources folder in our project. The template consists of HTML with additional template tags.

```
<html>
  <head>
    <meta http-equiv="Content-Type" content="text/html; charset=UTF-8"/>
    <title>My First Template</title>
  </head>
  <body>
    <h2>Hello {{name}}</h2>
  </body>
</html>
```

With the file created, we can run the render-file function to render it.

```
(selmer/render-file "hello.html" {:name "World"})
```

The result once again has the {{name}} tag replaced with the string World.

The render-file function accepts a string pointing to a resource that's expected to be found relative to the resource path of the application. Since we placed our template file in the resources folder, the path consists of its name.

Selmer also provides us with the ability to set a custom resource path using the selmer.parser/set-resource-path! function. For example, we could run the following code to specify the templates should be found in the /var/html/templates folder.

```
(selmer.parser/set-resource-path! "/var/html/templates/")
```

In the preceding code we passed in a string as the value for the variable name. However, we're not restricted to strings and can pass in any type we like. For example, if we pass in a collection, we can iterate over it using the for tag. Let's add the following content to our hello.html template.

```
<ul>
  {% for item in items %}
    <li> {{item}} </li>
  {% endfor %}
</ul>
```

When we run the render-file function, we pass it a range of numbers keyed on the :items key.

```
(selmer/render-file "hello.html" {:items (range 10)})
```

Note that since we passed no value for the {{name}} tag, its content is left blank. If an item happens to be a map, we can access the keys by name, as follows.

```
(selmer/render "<p>Hello {{user.first}} {{user.last}}</p>"
       {:user {:first "John" :last "Doe"}})
```

When no special processing is specified in the template, the parameter's default str representation will be used.

Using Filters

Filters allow for postprocessing the variables before they are rendered. For example, you can use a filter to convert the variable to uppercase, compute a hash, or count its length. Filters are specified by using a pipe symbol (|) after the variable name, as seen here:

```
{{name|upper}}
```

Selmer comes with a number of handy filters, such as upper, date, and pluralize, out of the box. On top of that we can easily define new filters using the selmer.filters/add-filter! function. Try this in the REPL by adding a reference to selmer.filters and creating a filter to check if a collection is empty.

```
(ns html-templating.core
  (:require [selmer.parser :as selmer]
            [selmer.filters :as filters]))

(filters/add-filter! :empty? empty?)

(selmer/render "{% if files|empty? %}no files{% else %}files{% endif %}"
  {:files []})
```

By default the content of the filters is escaped; we can override this behavior as follows:

```
(filters/add-filter! :foo
  (fn [x] [:safe (.toUpperCase x)]))

(selmer/render "{{x|foo}}" {:x "<div>I'm safe</div>"})
```

You should only unescape content that's generated by the server and known to be safe. You should always escape any user input because it can contain malicious content.

Using Template Tags

Selmer provides two types of tags. The first is inline tags such as extends and include. These tags are self-contained statements and don't require an end tag. The other type is the block tags. These tags have a start and an end tag, with the tag content in-between. An example of this is the if … endif block.

Defining Custom Tags

In addition to tags already provided, you can also define custom tags using the selmer.parser/add-tag! macro. Let's look at an example to see how it works:

```
(selmer/add-tag!
 :image
 (fn [args context-map]
   (str "<img src=" (first args) "/>")))

(selmer/render "{% image \"http://foo.com/logo.jpg\" %}" {})
```

We can also define a block tag by using the overloaded add-tag! definition. In this case we provide the opening tag, followed by the handler function and any closing tags. The handler accepts an additional parameter that holds the content of each block. The content is keyed on the name of the block, as in the following example:

```
(selmer/add-tag!
 :uppercase
 (fn [args context-map block]
   (.toUpperCase (get-in block [:uppercase :content])))
 :enduppercase)

(selmer/render
  "{% uppercase %}foo {{bar}} baz{% enduppercase %}"
  {:bar "injected"})
```

Inheriting Templates

Selmer templates can refer to other templates. We have two ways to refer to a template. We can either extend templates using the extends tag or include templates with the include tag.

Extending Templates

When we use the extends tag, the current template will use the template it's extending as the base. Any block tags in the base template with the names matching the current template will be overwritten.

Let's look at a concrete example. First, we define our base template, called base.html, and place it in the resources folder alongside the hello.html template we already have.

```
<!DOCTYPE html>
<html>
  <head>
    <link rel="stylesheet" href="style.css" />
    <title>{% block title %}My amazing site{% endblock %}</title>
  </head>
  <body>
    <div id="content">
        {% block content %}default content{% endblock %}
    </div>
  </body>
</html>
```

We then update the hello.html to extend base.html as follows:

```
{% extends "base.html" %}

{% block content %}
  <h2>Hello {{name}}</h2>

  <ul>
    {% for item in items %}
      <li> {{item}} </li>
    {% endfor %}
  </ul>
{% endblock %}
```

When the hello.html is rendered, the content block displays the entries defined there. But since we didn't define a block for the title, the base template—base.html—is used.

Optionally, we can include the parent content in the child block by using the {{block.super}} tag. It's replaced by the content of the parent when the template is rendered.

```
{% extends "base.html" %}

{% block content %}
  {{block.super}}
  <h2>Hello {{name}}</h2>

  <ul>
    {% for item in items %}
      <li> {{item}} </li>
    {% endfor %}
  </ul>
{% endblock %}
```

Note that you can chain extended templates together. In this case the latest occurrence of a block tag is the one that's rendered.

One caveat is that the templates are memoized by default. This means that a final version of the template is compiled once and kept in memory. This can be toggled with the selmer.parser/cache-on! and selmer.parser/cache-off! functions. You'd likely want to turn caching off during development.

Including Templates

The include tag allows us to include content from other templates in the current template. Let's look at an example. Say we want to include some additional content in our hello.html template. Let's create another template called register.html with the following content:

```
<form action="/register" method="POST">
    <label for="id">user id</label>
    <input id="id" name="id" type="text">
    <input pass="pass" name="pass" type="text">
    <input type="submit" value="register">
</form>
```

Then update the hello.html template to include register.html.

```
{% extends "base.html" %}

{% block content %}
  {% include "register.html" %}
  <h2>Hello {{name}}</h2>
```

```
<ul>
    {% for item in items %}
        <li> {{item}} </li>
    {% endfor %}
</ul>
{% endblock %}
```

Note that the hello.html template extends the base.html template. Any content in the template must be placed inside the block tags. When the template is compiled, the parser looks for the matching blocks in the parent and injects the content from the child. Any content outside the blocks is therefore ignored.

When hello.html is rendered, it replaces the include tags with the content from the included template.

Error Handling

Selmer attempts to provide meaningful errors when the templates contain syntax errors. For example, if we try to run the following code, we get an exception informing us that "safea" is not a valid tag.

```
(selmer/render "{{content|safea}}" {})
```

Selmer also provides a middleware function called selmer.middleware/wrap-error-page. This function captures errors and generates a page that can be rendered in the browser to notify you that a template compilation error has occurred.

Template Compilation Error

Unrecognized filter content|safea found inside the tag.

In file:/Users/Yogthos/src/tmp/book-code/guestbook-validation/resources/templates/home.html on line 4.

4 {{content|safea}}

You can try out this middleware in the REPL yourself. Let's create a template file called error.html with the following content:

```
{{content|safea}}
```

Middleware functions accept a handler function as a parameter and return a function that accepts the request map. Let's create a renderer function that returns a handler that accepts the template name as its input and returns a 200 status response.

We start by adding a reference for the selmer.middleware/wrap-error-page function.

```clojure
(ns html-templating.core
  (:require [selmer.parser :as selmer]
            [selmer.filters :as filters]
            [selmer.middleware :refer [wrap-error-page]]))
```

Then we proceed to write a renderer function that looks like this:

```clojure
(defn renderer []
  (wrap-error-page
    (fn [template]
      {:status 200
       :body (selmer/render-file template {})})))
```

We can now call it with different template files to see the result. First let's call it with a proper template, such as hello.html. The result is the response from calling the handler.

```clojure
((renderer) "hello.html")
```

However, if we call it with the error.html template, then we get a response of 500 with the body containing the error page.

```clojure
((renderer) "error.html")
```

This middleware for development is set up by default in Luminus, providing feedback right in the browser when a template fails to compile.

Revisiting Guestbook Templates

Now that we're familiar with the basics of HTML templating using Selmer, let's see how it's used in our guestbook application. As we saw, Luminus places HTML templates in the resources/html folder. Here we have four files, about.html, base.html, home.html, and error.html.

The error.html template is used for displaying general purpose error pages such as when the page isn't found or a server error occurs. For example, guestbook.middleware namespace defines a function called wrap-internal-error that will catch any unhandled errors and serve a 500 error page:

```clojure
guestbook/src/clj/guestbook/middleware.clj
(defn wrap-internal-error [handler]
  (fn [req]
    (try
      (handler req)
      (catch Throwable t
        (log/error t (.getMessage t))
```

```
(error-page {:status 500
             :title "Something very bad has happened!"
             :message "We've dispatched a team of highly trained
                       gnomes to take care of the problem."})))))
```

The wrap-internal-error function in turn calls the error-page function from the guestbook.layout namespace to render the error page:

guestbook/src/clj/guestbook/layout.clj
```
(defn error-page
  "error-details should be a map containing the following keys:
   :status - error status
   :title - error title (optional)
   :message - detailed error message (optional)

   returns a response map with the error page as the body
   and the status specified by the status key"
  [error-details]
  {:status  (:status error-details)
   :headers {"Content-Type" "text/html; charset=utf-8"}
   :body    (parser/render-file "error.html" error-details)})
```

As we saw earlier, home.html and about.html files are used to render the home and about pages, respectively. The base template is extended by both these templates and provides all the common elements for each page. The base template is where we declare common assets, such as JavaScript, CSS, or ClojureScript, as well as common UI elements, such as navbars, headers, and footers. Both home and about page templates extend the base and override its content block.

When the browser requests a particular page, the route calls the handler for the page. It in turn handles any business logic and then calls guestbook.layout/render to generate the page. The render function accepts the name of the template along with an optional context map containing dynamic content to be rendered. This is then passed to Selmer and the rendered page is returned.

What You've Learned

In this chapter we saw how to handle requests using Ring, how to structure routes using Reitit, and how to template HTML using Selmer. In the following chapter we'll take a deeper look at overall application structure and how all the pieces fit together.

CHAPTER 3

Luminus Architecture

At the start of the book, we jumped right into building a simple application. This let us get comfortable with the development environment and provided a glimpse of what to expect in terms of project structure. We looked at the directory layout as well as at the purpose of some of the files found in the project. But we didn't focus very closely on the code in these files. In this chapter, you'll learn the background necessary to fully understand our guestbook application.

Manage the Project

As we already saw working on the guestbook application, the project is managed using the configuration specified in the project.clj file.

Leiningen uses the concept of profiles to identify different build scenarios for the project. The dev and the test profiles are used for development and testing, respectively.

The UberJar profile is used to package the application for deployment. When the production build happens, the compiled bytecode is emitted into the resulting JAR. This results in a self-contained application that can be run using the standard Java Runtime Environment (JRE).

Profile-Specific Resources

Profiles can contain any configuration options that can be specified in the global scope. For example, we can add specific dependencies or plugins that are only necessary for development. Since we wouldn't want to package those for production, we don't specify them at the top level.

Each profile also specifies its own paths for source files and resources. The :dev profile has the :resource-paths ["env/dev/resources"] resource path. This path is used in addition to the global resources. This allows us to provide environment-specific settings for the app.

The profiles are also responsible for deciding what additional source paths should be used the same way as the resources. The :uberjar profile sets the :source-paths key to point to ["env/prod/clj"], while the :dev profile points to ["env/dev/clj"]. These paths become available in addition to the default src path, where the compiler looks for the application code.

Running Code Selectively

Commonly, some code in the application will need to behave differently between development and production modes. For example, we may want to disable HTML template caching while developing the application. Then once we put it in production, we would like to default to settings optimized for performance.

One common approach to this problem is to use an environment variable to indicate the mode that the application runs in and use conditional logic to select what code should be executed at runtime. This approach has a number of drawbacks. The conditional logic is error prone, it can add runtime overhead, and we end up having to package all the libraries used for development in our production build.

A better approach is to decide what code should be included at build time. This way, only the code that's necessary ends up being packaged for production, and we don't have to worry about checking what mode the application is in at runtime. This is the approach that Luminus takes.

The development code includes a guestbook.env namespace with the configuration optimized for development use.

guestbook/env/dev/clj/guestbook/env.clj
```clojure
(ns guestbook.env
  (:require
    [selmer.parser :as parser]
    [clojure.tools.logging :as log]
    [guestbook.dev-middleware :refer [wrap-dev]]))

(def defaults
  {:init
   (fn []
     (parser/cache-off!)
     (log/info
       "\n-=[guestbook started successfully using the development profile]=-"))
   :stop
```

```
  (fn []
    (log/info
      "\n-=[guestbook has shut down successfully]=-"))
  :middleware wrap-dev})
```

The namespace consists of the defaults map that contains keys called :init, :stop, and :middleware. The first key points to a function that should be run during startup. The second points to a function that's called when the application shuts down. And the last one specifies some additional development middleware for live code reloading and error reporting. The middleware itself is found in the guestbook.dev-middleware namespace.

Contrast this with the production version of guestbook.env, which contains the following code.

guestbook/env/prod/clj/guestbook/env.clj
```
(ns guestbook.env
  (:require [clojure.tools.logging :as log]))

(def defaults
  {:init
   (fn []
     (log/info "\n-=[guestbook started successfully]=-"))
   :stop
   (fn []
     (log/info "\n-=[guestbook has shut down successfully]=-"))
   :middleware identity})
```

As you can see, the version found in the prod source path doesn't disable the HTML template caching or wrap any development middleware.

Think in Terms of Application Components

The approach that a typical Clojure web application takes is probably different from what you're used to. Most frameworks favor using the model-view-controller (MVC) pattern for partitioning the application logic, with strong separation between the view, the controller, and the model.

Luminus doesn't enforce any strict separation between the view and the controller portion of the application. Instead, Luminus encourages organizing the application to keep related code in the same namespace. The route handler functions are typically responsible for processing HTTP requests from the client and dispatching actions based on them. This approach provides a clean separation between the domain logic and the presentation layer of your application without introducing any unnecessary indirection.

But since the Clojure web stack is designed to be flexible, it will let you build your applications any way you like. If you do feel strongly about using a traditional MVC architecture, nothing will stop you from doing that.

A typical application is broken up into several logical components.

Let's look at these in more detail. A Luminus application is typically composed of the following core namespaces:

- core—the core manages the life cycle of the HTTP server.

- config—the config manages the map containing the configuration variables used by the application.

- handler—the handler namespace is the root handler for the requests and responses that aggregates all the routes.

- routes—the routes namespace contains the namespaces that are responsible for handling different types of client requests.

- db—the db namespace is reserved for the data model of the application and the persistence layer.

- layout—the layout namespace contains common logic for generating the application layout.

- middleware—the middleware namespace contains any custom middleware we want to use in our application.

Application Core

The core namespace is used to start the application. Most importantly, this is where the -main function is found. The -main function is the entry point for the application, and the - in front of the function name indicates that it should be compiled to a Java method. This is necessary for the JVM to be able to start our application. The compilation of the namespace into a class is triggered by the :gen-class hint in its declaration.

The two functions that control the life cycle of the application are start-app and stop-app.

The start-app function is called by the -main function when the application is run, and it's responsible for running any initialization tasks.

guestbook/src/clj/guestbook/core.clj
```
(defn start-app [args]
  (doseq [component (-> args
                        (parse-opts cli-options)
                        mount/start-with-args
                        :started)]
    (log/info component "started"))
  (.addShutdownHook (Runtime/getRuntime) (Thread. stop-app)))
```

The life cycle of these resources is managed by the Mount library. It provides a defstate macro that allows us to declare something which can be started and stopped, such as a database connection, a thread-pool, or an HTTP server. These are sometimes referred to as resources or components. We provide :start and :stop keys that specify the code that should run when the resource is started and stopped, respectively. Once a resource is started, the return value of the :start function is bound to the symbol we used in our defstate. We can see an example of this by looking at how the HTTP and the nREPL servers are defined.[1]

guestbook/src/clj/guestbook/core.clj
```
(mount/defstate ^{:on-reload :noop} http-server
  :start
  (http/start
    (-> env
        (assoc :handler (handler/app))
        (update :port #(or (-> env :options :port) %))
        (select-keys [:handler :host :port])))
  :stop
  (http/stop http-server))

(mount/defstate ^{:on-reload :noop} repl-server
  :start
  (when (env :nrepl-port)
    (nrepl/start {:bind (env :nrepl-bind)
                  :port (env :nrepl-port)}))
  :stop
  (when repl-server
    (nrepl/stop repl-server)))
```

The template defaults to using the Jetty HTTP server unless otherwise specified.[2] The server is passed the guestbook.handler/app function to handle the incoming client requests. When our http-server resource is started, we call http/start with parameters taken from our env resource. This creates and starts our HTTP server. Furthermore, when we call mount/start or mount/start-with-args, Mount automatically determines the order in which our resources need to be

---

1. https://github.com/tolitius/mount
2. http://www.eclipse.org/jetty/

initialized. This saves us a lot of effort as our app grows. In the case of http-server, we've added some metadata for Mount: {:on-reload :noop}. By default, Mount tries to restart any resources, and any resources that depend on them, when their namespaces are reloaded. This metadata tells Mount that it shouldn't do this for http-server, since it would be incredibly disruptive if our server restarted unintentionally.

The start-app function calls the mount/start-with-args function. This function is responsible for starting stateful components defined using the defstate macro. It also sets the stop-app function as a shutdown hook so that it will be called when the JVM runtime is shutting down. This function is responsible for handling any cleanup that needs to be done when the app stops, such as gracefully shutting down the HTTP server.

guestbook/src/clj/guestbook/core.clj
```
(defn stop-app []
  (doseq [component (:stopped (mount/stop))]
    (log/info component "stopped"))
  (shutdown-agents))
```

That's all there is to bootstrapping the application. Now let's see how we can add some routes to provide the functionality specific to our application.

Application Configuration

The configuration is managed by the guestbook.config namespace. This namespace contains a defstate definition for the env variable. This variable contains the configuration aggregated from the config.edn file found on the resources path, the optional EDN config file pointed to by the conf Java parameter, the Java parameters, and the environment variables. The entirety of the namespace looks like this:

guestbook/src/clj/guestbook/config.clj
```
(ns guestbook.config
  (:require
    [cprop.core :refer [load-config]]
    [cprop.source :as source]
    [mount.core :refer [args defstate]]))

(defstate env
  :start
  (load-config
    :merge
    [(args)
     (source/from-system-props)
     (source/from-env)]))
```

The configuration management is handled by a library called *cprop*. This library provides intelligence for massaging the environment variables into a Clojure-friendly format.[3]

The guestbook.config namespace calls the load-config function to create the configuration. Different configuration sources are merged explicitly to produce the final configuration using the :merge flag. Note that the cprop library does a deep merge of the configurations that it finds. This merge allows us to specify a base configuration and then overwrite specific parts of it later on.

As we've already seen, dev-config.edn and test-config.edn files are used to specify environment variables used during development and testing. The cprop library looks for a configuration file specified using the -Dconf JVM environment variable. This is how the dev-config.edn file is loaded at development time. If you look at the :dev profile in project.clj, you'll notice the following flag there: :jvm-opts ["-Dconf=dev-config.edn"].

Application Handler

The guestbook.handler namespace is responsible transforming all of our route declarations into a single ring handler and wrapping them with shared middleware using the middleware/wrap-base in the app definition. The base middleware provides common functionality such as session and cookie management.

The ring/router function aggregates the routes for handling all the requests to our application into a reitit Router. Below ring/router we define our default ring handler, which serves application resources, WebJars, and error pages. The ring/ring-handler function creates the top-level ring handler from our application router and our default handler.

guestbook/src/clj/guestbook/handler.clj
```
(ns guestbook.handler
  (:require
    [guestbook.middleware :as middleware]
    [guestbook.layout :refer [error-page]]
    [guestbook.routes.home :refer [home-routes]]
    [reitit.ring :as ring]
    [ring.middleware.content-type :refer [wrap-content-type]]
    [ring.middleware.webjars :refer [wrap-webjars]]
    [guestbook.env :refer [defaults]]
    [mount.core :as mount]))

(mount/defstate init-app
  :start ((or (:init defaults) (fn [])))
  :stop  ((or (:stop defaults) (fn []))))
```

---

3.   https://github.com/tolitius/cprop

```
(mount/defstate app-routes
  :start
  (ring/ring-handler
    (ring/router
      [(home-routes)])
    (ring/routes
      (ring/create-resource-handler
        {:path "/"})
      (wrap-content-type
        (wrap-webjars (constantly nil)))
      (ring/create-default-handler
        {:not-found
         (constantly
          (error-page
           {:status 404, :title "404 - Page not found"}))
         :method-not-allowed
         (constantly
          (error-page
           {:status 405, :title "405 - Not allowed"}))
         :not-acceptable
         (constantly
          (error-page
           {:status 406, :title "406 - Not acceptable"}))})))))
(defn app []
  (middleware/wrap-base #'app-routes))
```

The app state is the core of the routing logic in the application, and any new routes that you add to the application must be included inside its Router.

Application Middleware

The guestbook.middleware namespace is reserved for any wrapper functions that are used to modify the requests and responses. The main purpose of the middleware is to provide a central place for handling common tasks such as CSRF protection.

If you recall, we had to specify an anti-forgery token when submitting forms in our guestbook application. This token is checked by the wrap-csrf middleware function. It checks each request to see if it contains a valid token and returns an error page if it doesn't. This way we don't have to remember to check for a CSRF token in each handler function, eliminating potential errors.

The wrap-base function is used to tie all the common middleware together in the order of dependency. It also adds the ring-defaults middleware that we discussed earlier.

Routing Requests

As we discussed before, application routes represent URIs that a client can call to perform an action or retrieve some data. Each route has a corresponding map that defines handler functions for allowed request methods and includes any route-specific configuration. When we identify a specific workflow in our application, it makes sense to group all routes related to this workflow in a single namespace. These namespaces are typically placed in the routes package. Our guestbook app only has one workflow, which is defined in the guestbook.routes.home namespace.

```clojure
guestbook/src/clj/guestbook/routes/home.clj
(ns guestbook.routes.home
  (:require
   [guestbook.layout :as layout]
   [guestbook.db.core :as db]
   [clojure.java.io :as io]
   [guestbook.middleware :as middleware]
   [ring.util.response]
   [ring.util.http-response :as response]))

(defn home-page [request]
  (layout/render
   request "home.html" {:messages (db/get-messages)}))

(defn save-message! [{:keys [params]}]
 (db/save-message! params)
 (response/found "/"))

(defn about-page [request]
  (layout/render
   request "about.html"))

(defn home-routes []
  [""
   {:middleware [middleware/wrap-csrf
                 middleware/wrap-formats]}
   ["/" {:get home-page}]
   ["/message" {:post save-message!}]
   ["/about" {:get about-page}]])
```

In home-routes, we have three separate routes, each performing a distinct action. The / route is responsible for displaying a list of messages along with a form to write new messages. The /message route is responsible for handling the creation of new messages. The /about route displays an image included in the Luminus template by default.

When we add a new workflow to our app, we will create a corresponding namespace in the routes package to keep the code manageable and to bundle together any workflow-specific configuration. Then we'll add these routes to our router in the guestbook.handler namespace.

Application Model

All but the most trivial applications need some sort of a model. The model describes the data stored by the application and the relationships between individual data elements.

When we use a relational database, it can often become the model for our application. Unlike object-oriented languages, Clojure doesn't require us to define a separate model in code and map it to the one defined in the database. Instead, the query results are represented by sequences of maps, where the keys correspond to the column names in the tables being queried.

All namespaces dealing with the model and the persistence layer traditionally live under the application's db package. This is a topic that warrants further discussion, and we'll revisit it later.

The guestbook database connection resides in the *db* variable. Note that the connection URL is populated using an environment variable called :database-url. This ensures that we're not hardcoding our connection in the application or checking it into our repository.

In development mode, the connection variable is populated in the dev-config.edn file that's used to keep the local configuration.

guestbook/dev-config.edn
```
{:dev true
 :port 3000
 ;; when :nrepl-port is set the application starts the nREPL server on load
 :nrepl-port 7000
 :database-url "jdbc:h2:./guestbook_dev.db"}
```

When you run the application in production, the database connection URL should be provided either in a separate production configuration file, such as prod-config.edn, or as an environment variable, like so:

```
export DATABASE_URL="jdbc:h2:./guestbook.db"
```

Keeping all the environment configuration outside the application ensures that the application is environment-agnostic. The same UberJar artifact build using the :uberjar profile can be put in different environments (for example, development, staging, production) without any changes.

Application Layout

The layout namespace is reserved for providing the visual layout as well as other common elements for our pages.

guestbook/src/clj/guestbook/layout.clj

```clojure
(ns guestbook.layout
  (:require
    [clojure.java.io]
    [selmer.parser :as parser]
    [selmer.filters :as filters]
    [markdown.core :refer [md-to-html-string]]
    [ring.util.http-response :refer [content-type ok]]
    [ring.util.anti-forgery :refer [anti-forgery-field]]
    [ring.middleware.anti-forgery :refer [*anti-forgery-token*]]
    [ring.util.response]))

(parser/set-resource-path! (clojure.java.io/resource "html"))

(parser/add-tag!
 :csrf-field
 (fn [_ _]
   (anti-forgery-field)))

(filters/add-filter!
 :markdown
 (fn [content]
   [:safe (md-to-html-string content)]))

(defn render
  "renders the HTML template located relative to resources/html"
  [request template & [params]]
  (content-type
    (ok
      (parser/render-file
        template
        (assoc params
          :page template
          :csrf-token *anti-forgery-token*)))
    "text/html; charset=utf-8"))

(defn error-page
  "error-details should be a map containing the following keys:
   :status - error status
   :title - error title (optional)
   :message - detailed error message (optional)

   returns a response map with the error page as the body
   and the status specified by the status key"
  [error-details]
  {:status  (:status error-details)
   :headers {"Content-Type" "text/html; charset=utf-8"}
   :body    (parser/render-file "error.html" error-details)})
```

The resource path is set to the resources/html/ folder. This sets the base template directory for the Selmer HTML templating library. Without setting the variable, we'd have to prefix all template names with html/.

Following the parser/set-resource-path! call, a custom tag is defined for the CSRF field. We already saw this tag in action when we submitted the form in the last chapter.

Next, a filter is added for processing Markdown content in the HTML templates. We'll take a closer look at how tags and filters work shortly.

The render function sets some default keys on the context map used to generate the HTML from the template. Since these keys are common to all pages, it makes sense to keep them centralized in one place. The result of the function is a regular response map with the rendered template string set as the body.

We call it when we render our page in the guestbook.routes.home/home-page function. It accepts the name of the template file located under resources/html/ and an optional map of context variables that will be used to inject dynamic content in the template.

Finally, we have the error-page function that provides a common layout for rendering error pages in our application. This function is used to generate the 404 page in the handler, the 500 page for server errors, and the 403 page by the anti-forgery middleware.

The function accepts a map that contains the :status, the :title, and the :message keys. These are passed to the resources/html/error.html template in order to generate the error page.

Defining Pages

The pages are defined by creating routes that accept the request parameters and generate the appropriate response. A route can return HTML markup, perform a server-side operation, redirect to a different page, or return a specific type of data, such as a JSON string or a file.

In many cases a page will have multiple route components. One route responds to GET requests and returns HTML to be rendered by the browser. The rest handle events such as Ajax requests or form submissions generated by the client when the user interacts with the page.

The page body can be generated by any means we choose, since Clojure architecture is highly modular. This leaves us with the option of using any templating library we like. The most popular choices are Hiccup and Selmer.[4,5]

Hiccup uses Clojure data structures to define the markup and generates the corresponding HTML from it. Selmer is modeled on the Django template system from Python and uses template tags to inject dynamic content into the page.[6]

In this book we'll start off with server-side templates written with Selmer. Then we'll cover single-page applications (SPAs) where most of the markup is generated on the client.[7] The SPA approach nicely separates your application's client and server components. Keeping the UI logic out of the server simplifies creating additional clients, such as native mobile applications, without the need to update the server.

Regardless of your favorite templating strategy, it's good practice not to mix domain logic with representation. In a properly designed application, it should be relatively easy to swap out one client for another.

Managing Stateful Components

Most applications rely on stateful external resources, such as database connections and queues. These resources often have a life cycle associated with them. Typically, we'd like to start such resources when our application initializes and stop them when it shuts down.

To facilitate a REPL-driven workflow, Luminus uses the Mount library to manage the life cycle of stateful resources in the application. This library treats resources as variables bound to namespaces—an approach that allows Mount to automatically infer the order that the components need to be started from the namespace hierarchy. Naturally, this means that we should be careful with how we access these variables.

Conceptually, Mount takes the approach of encapsulating stateful resources using namespaces. This leads to a natural separation between the code that deals with state from the pure core of the application business logic.

It helps to treat the core business logic as you would a library. It should be completely independent from where the data is coming from and where it's going. As a rule, we should avoid passing resources directly to our business

---

4.   https://github.com/weavejester/hiccup

5.   https://github.com/yogthos/Selmer

6.   https://docs.djangoproject.com/en/dev/ref/templates/

7.   http://en.wikipedia.org/wiki/Single-page_application

logic. Instead, we should create a thin layer that deals with external resources and calls the business logic to process the data.

Keeping the logic that deals with IO at the edges of our application allows us to keep most of our code pure. This is valuable because pure code can be tested without needing to access the external resources or create mocks in their place. Pure code is also much easier to factor out into libraries when you find yourself wanting to share it across applications or with other developers.

Luminus encourages keeping related logic close together. So in cases where we have functions that must rely on an external resource, the management of the state for that resource should ideally be handled in the same namespace where the functions using it are defined. A namespace that contains a stateful resource with the functions that operate on it is analogous to an instance of a class in object-oriented languages.

Mount uses the defstate declarations to identify stateful resources. It then leverages the Clojure compiler to infer the order for starting and stopping the resources based on the namespace hierarchy. This approach allows us to use the Clojure compiler itself as the dependency injection mechanism.

For example, if namespace A contains a resource and depends on namespace B, which contains another resource, then state B will be started before state A. Conversely, the resources are stopped in the reverse order of the one they're started in. Let's take a closer look at how the state of the HTTP server in the guestbook.core namespace is managed.

guestbook/src/clj/guestbook/core.clj
```clojure
(mount/defstate ^{:on-reload :noop} http-server
  :start
  (http/start
    (-> env
        (assoc  :handler (handler/app))
        (update :port #(or (-> env :options :port) %))
        (select-keys [:handler :host :port]))))
  :stop
  (http/stop http-server))
```

The server instance is defined as the http-server var that's declared using the defstate macro. The :start key calls the http/start function. This function returns an instance of the running server. The :stop key calls the http/stop function and passes it the http-server. These two functions are called by Mount when the mount.core/start and mount.core/stop functions are called, respectively.

Finally, note that the ^{:on-reload :noop} annotation is used to indicate that the component should not be restarted on reload. This allows the server to retain its state when namespaces are reloaded during development.

As you can see, the defstate macro provides an elegant way to manage resource life cycle. It doesn't require us to manage the dependencies manually or to pass a dependency graph around by hand. However, it can be useful to see the generated graph visually. We can do this by running the states-with-deps function found in the mount.tools.graph namespace.

```
user=> (require '[mount.tools.graph :as graph])
user=> (graph/states-with-deps)
({:name "#'guestbook.config/env",
  :order 1,
  :status #{:started},
  :deps #{}}
 {:name "#'guestbook.db.core/*db*",
  :order 2,
  :status #{:started},
  :deps #{"#'guestbook.config/env"}}
 {:name "#'guestbook.core/http-server",
  :order 3,
  :status #{:started},
  :deps #{"#'guestbook.config/env"}}
 {:name "#'guestbook.core/repl-server",
  :order 4,
  :status #{:started},
  :deps #{"#'guestbook.config/env"}})
```

Here we see that the env state is started first and has no dependencies, *db* is started second since it depends on env, and so on.

Mount lets us start only the specified states, as seen in the guestbook.test.db.core namespace. Since we only need the env and the *db* resources for testing the database, we omit starting other resources, such as the HTTP server.

guestbook/test/clj/guestbook/db/core_test.clj
```
(use-fixtures
  :once
  (fn [f]
    (mount/start
     #'guestbook.config/env
     #'guestbook.db.core/*db*)
    (migrations/migrate ["migrate"] (select-keys env [:database-url]))
    (f)))
```

Conversely, we can choose to start and stop Mount with specific states omitted, as seen in the user namespace.

guestbook/env/dev/clj/user.clj
```clojure
(defn start
  "Starts application.
  You'll usually want to run this on startup."
  []
  (mount/start-without #'guestbook.core/repl-server))

(defn stop
  "Stops application."
  []
  (mount/stop-except #'guestbook.core/repl-server))

(defn restart
  "Restarts application."
  []
  (stop)
  (start))

(defn restart-db
  "Restarts database."
  []
  (mount/stop #'guestbook.db.core/*db*)
  (mount/start #'guestbook.db.core/*db*)
  (binding [*ns* (the-ns 'guestbook.db.core)]
    (conman/bind-connection guestbook.db.core/*db* "sql/queries.sql")))
```

This covers all the basics of how Mount is used in Luminus, but we encourage you to explore its other features at a later time.

What You've Learned

In this chapter, you learned about the general layout of a Luminus application and how different pieces interact with one another. Hopefully, you're now comfortable reading and understanding the code in the guestbook project we created in Chapter 1, Getting Your Feet Wet, on page 1. If this isn't the case, reread this chapter and try the examples yourself using the REPL. Using the REPL to explore and experiment is often the most effective way to learn, and is a valuable skill itself.

So far we've focused on building a traditional application, where all the logic lives on the server and the client simply renders the HTML generated by the back end. In the next chapter, we'll revisit our guestbook project and see how it could be implemented as a single-page application (SPA) using ClojureScript for client-side scripting.[8]

---

8.   https://en.wikipedia.org/wiki/Single-page_application

CHAPTER 4

Introducing ClojureScript

In the preceding chapters, we wrote a typical server-side web application and learned how its components interact with one another. In this chapter, we'll look at ClojureScript and see how to use it to improve the way we write web applications.

As you've probably noticed, the separation between the client and the server portions of the application is not enforced. If we're not careful, we could easily end up with tightly coupled client and server components. This could become a problem if we want to add a different client later on—for example, if we decided to create a native mobile version of our application.

Up to now, we've only been using Clojure on the back end. In this chapter we'll look at ClojureScript, a dialect of Clojure that compiles to JavaScript. ClojureScript will allow us to bring Clojure to the browser. Let's look at reasons why you might want to use ClojureScript for front-end development.

Understand ClojureScript

If you've worked with JavaScript, you've probably noticed that it has a few shortcomings. Still, JavaScript does have the advantage of being a standard programmable environment for all of the modern browsers. JavaScript has become an essential part of front-end development as the demand for rich client-side applications continues to grow.

It would be nice to leverage this platform with a robust programming language like Clojure, wouldn't it? This is precisely where ClojureScript comes into play. Much like its cousin Clojure, ClojureScript embraces its hosting platform and allows seamless interoperability with JavaScript. We can continue leveraging mature JavaScript libraries while enjoying the benefits of Clojure language semantics.

And if you're using Clojure on the server, then it's possible to share code between the server and the client. One example where this is useful is validation logic that can now be written in a single place.

You should be aware of a few details when using ClojureScript. Since Clojure-Script runs in the browser, you can't leverage any code that relies on interfacing with Java. The syntax for interop with JavaScript is also slightly different from that for interacting with Java. Keep those facts in mind, though, and you'll be fine.

JavaScript Interop

Interacting with JavaScript is remarkably straightforward. You can access any standard JavaScript objects using the js namespace and use (.method js/obj ...) notation to invoke a method of an object, just as in Java. For example, if you want to make a logger that logs in to the console, you can write something like the following:

```
(defn log [& items]
  (.log js/console (apply str items)))
```

One thing that's less obvious is the interaction with JavaScript object properties. To access these, we use (.-property obj) notation, where the hyphen (-) indicates that we're referencing a property and not a method. We update properties by using set!. Here's an example:

```
(defn init []
  (let [canvas (.createElement js/document "canvas")
        ctx    (.getContext canvas "2d")]
    ;;set properties
    (set! (.-width canvas) 500)
    (set! (.-height canvas) 500)
    (set! (.-fillStyle ctx) "black")
    (.fillRect ctx 0 0 (.-width canvas) (.-height canvas))))
```

In the preceding example we call the createElement and the getContext methods the same way we would call Java methods in Clojure. However, we access the width and height properties using the ClojureScript-specific .- interop syntax. We set the .-fillStyle property to the "black" string by calling set!.

Google Closure

ClojureScript leverages the Google Closure compiler.[1] The compiler can perform a number of optimizations, such as dead code pruning, to produce lean JavaScript output.

---

1. https://github.com/google/closure-compiler

You can leverage the Google Closure library's[2] rich API for common tasks, such as handling Ajax requests, managing cookies, currency formatting, and so on. This means that you don't need to include any additional JavaScript libraries, such as jQuery, to accomplish these tasks.

Macros

Another way ClojureScript differs from Clojure is that you can't mix macros with regular ClojureScript source inside .cljs files. You have to place them inside .clj or .cljc files for them to be compiled by the Clojure compiler.

You can access macros two ways in ClojureScript. If a macro is defined in a Clojure namespace with the same name as a ClojureScript namespace, you can require them just like in Clojure. But if there is not a corresponding ClojureScript namespace, you have to explicitly specify that you're requiring macros, like so:

```
(ns my.app
  (:require-macros [app.macros :refer [fancy-macro]]))
```

Concurrency

While ClojureScript supports atoms, it has no software transactional memory and therefore no refs or agents. The binding semantics are slightly different, as well, because there are no vars or runtime reification.

Aside from these differences, development in ClojureScript is very similar to that in regular Clojure. However, if you're new to Clojure and ClojureScript, then we recommend exploring the official ClojureScript documentation[3] before moving on.

Add ClojureScript Support

Currently, our guestbook application uses server-side rendering and the browser simply displays a static page.

Let's modify our project from Chapter 1, Getting Your Feet Wet, on page 1, to be a single-page application (SPA) using ClojureScript.

---

2. https://github.com/google/closure-library
3. https://clojurescript.org/

Using lein-cljsbuild

The easiest way to add ClojureScript support to a Clojure project is by using the lein-cljsbuild plugin.[4] The plugin compiles the ClojureScript sources and outputs the resulting JavaScript in the specified location.

The first thing we have to do is to add the ClojureScript runtime dependency to our project. Note that it's scoped as "provided". Since we're outputting compiled JavaScript, it only needs to be present for development.

```
:dependencies
[...
 [org.clojure/clojurescript "1.10.764" :scope "provided"]]
```

Next, let's update our project.clj to add the plugin, provide a default configuration for it, and include the generated javascript in our :resource-paths.

guestbook-reagent/project.clj
```
:resource-paths ["resources" "target/cljsbuild"]
:target-path "target/%s/"
:main ^:skip-aot guestbook.core

:plugins [[lein-cljsbuild "1.1.8"]]

:cljsbuild
{:builds
 {:app {:source-paths ["src/cljs"]
        :compiler {:output-to "target/cljsbuild/public/js/app.js"
                   :output-dir "target/cljsbuild/public/js/out"
                   :main "guestbook.core"
                   :asset-path "/js/out"
                   :optimizations :none
                   :source-map true
                   :pretty-print true}}}}

:clean-targets
^{:protect false}
[:target-path
 [:cljsbuild :builds :app :compiler :output-dir]
 [:cljsbuild :builds :app :compiler :output-to]]
```

The compiler configuration has the following options and compiler hints:

- :source-paths—specifies where to find ClojureScript source files.

- :resource-paths—specifies the paths to static assets, such as the generated JavaScript files produced by the ClojureScript build.

- :main—used by the compiler to find the entry point for the compiled app.

---

4.   https://github.com/emezeske/lein-cljsbuild

- :asset-path—used to specify where to look for supporting JavaScript assets.

- :output-to—outputs the name of the resulting JavaScript file.

- :output-dir—specifies where the temporary JavaScript files will be generated.

- :source-map—used to map from the compiled JavaScript to the original ClojureScript source.

Also, we added a :clean-targets key below the :cljsbuild key. This tells Leiningen that we'd like to delete any JavaScript that is generated in the target/cljsbuild folder when lein clean is run.

Now we're ready to create a new source folder and a ClojureScript namespace called guestbook.core in src/cljs/guestbook/core.cljs. Note that the ClojureScript extension is .cljs, as opposed to the .clj extension for Clojure files. If the file ends with .clj, it will still compile, but it won't have access to the JavaScript runtime.

We'll start with the obligatory Hello, World! to make sure everything is working correctly. First, let's add the following code to our guestbook.core namespace:

```clojure
(ns guestbook.core)

(-> (.getElementById js/document "content")
    (.-innerHTML)
    (set! "Hello, World!"))
```

When the script runs, it will find the tag with the ID content on the page and set its inner HTML to Hello, World!.

Then let's update our resources/html/home.html template as follows:

```
guestbook-reagent-start/resources/html/home.html
{% extends "base.html" %}
{% block content %}
<input id="token" type="hidden" value="{{csrf-token}}" />
<div id="content"></div>
{% endblock %}
{% block page-scripts %}
    {% script "/js/app.js" %}
{% endblock %}
```

We added a div with the ID content, and included our compiled JavaScript.

We're now ready to see if our setup works. Let's run the ClojureScript compiler to generate the app.js file we're referencing in the template, and then start the server:

```
$ lein cljsbuild once
Compiling ClojureScript...
...
Compiling ["target/cljsbuild/public/js/app.js"] from ["src/cljs"]...
Successfully compiled ["target/cljsbuild/public/js/app.js"] in ... seconds
$ lein run
...
```

If everything went well, you should now see the Hello, World! text displayed when the page loads.

Automatic Recompilation

This is the simplest way to compile ClojureScript, but it requires us to compile everything anytime we make a change. We can use a few other ways to compile ClojureScript during development that give us some nice features. The simplest approach is to use the incremental compilation feature by running lein cljsbuild auto. Using this approach, the compiler will watch for changes in the source and recompile JavaScript as needed. However, we still need to refresh our browser to see the changes.

Let's try this out. Open a new terminal and run the following command:

```
$ lein cljsbuild auto
Watching for changes before compiling ClojureScript...
...
```

cljsbuild now waits for you to make changes before recompiling the relevant source files. Note that the compiler uses incremental compilation. Once the compiler finishes the initial compilation, any further changes are recompiled nearly instantly.

Let's confirm that our code is automatically compiling by changing our text.

```
(ns guestbook.core)

(-> (.getElementById js/document "content")
    (.-innerHTML)
    (set! "Hello, Auto!"))
```

Now, take a look at the terminal where cljsbuild is running. It should look like this:

```
$ lein cljsbuild auto
...
Compiling "target/cljsbuild/public/js/app.js" from ["src/cljs"]...
Successfully compiled "target/cljsbuild/public/js/app.js" in ... seconds.
```

This indicates that a recompilation of ClojureScript was triggered, and when we reload the page we should see the Hello, Auto! text rendered.

Now that we've got our code compiling automatically, let's take a look at how to build UIs. The ClojureScript ecosystem offers a number of libraries. The majority of these libraries are built on top of React.[5] The specific library we recommend is called Reagent.[6] This library is both simple and widely used.

Build the UI with Reagent

Reagent is more opinionated than React regarding component life cycle. While React is agnostic about the strategy used to trigger component updates; Reagent makes this decision for us. Reagent uses a data-driven approach where components observe the state of reactive atoms. Components just specify the state they're concerned with, and Reagent handles the life cycle for us. As a result, we typically only need to implement the render functions of our components.

Before we can build our UI, we need to add the Reagent dependency to our project:

```
:dependencies
[...
 [reagent "1.0.0"]]
```

Since our dependencies have changed, we also need to restart cljsbuild.

```
...
Successfully compiled "target/cljsbuild/public/js/app.js" in ... seconds.
^C
$ lein cljsbuild auto
Watching for changes before compiling ClojureScript...
...
```

To use Reagent, we have to require it in our namespace just like in Clojure. Let's open up the guestbook.core ClojureScript namespace. Recall that it's found in the src/cljs source folder and not the src folder that contains the Clojure source files. Update the namespace declaration to include the following require form:

```
(ns guestbook.core
  (:require [reagent.core :as r]
            [reagent.dom  :as dom]))
```

---

5.   https://reactjs.org/
6.   http://reagent-project.github.io/

Reagent Components

Reagent bases its UI component syntax on the popular templating library called Hiccup.[7] Hiccup uses plain data structures to represent HTML, so you don't have to learn a separate domain-specific language. Let's render a component by calling the reagent.dom/render function, like so:

```
(dom/render
  [:h1 "Hello, Reagent"]
  (.getElementById js/document "content"))
```

reagent.dom/render takes two arguments: a component and the target DOM node.

At this point our namespace should look like this:

```
(ns guestbook.core
  (:require [reagent.core :as r]
            [reagent.dom :as dom]))

(dom/render
  [:h1 "Hello, Reagent"]
  (.getElementById js/document "content"))
```

The HTML nodes are represented using a vector with the structure corresponding to that of the resulting HTML tag, as shown in the following example:

```
[:tag-name {:attribute-key "attribute value"} tag body]
```

```
<tag-name attribute-key="attribute value">tag body</tag-name>
```

Let's put our h1 inside a div with id hello and class content.

```
[:div {:id "hello", :class "content"} [:h1 "Hello, Auto!"]]
```

```
<div id="hello" class="content"><h1>Hello, Auto!</h1></div>
```

Since setting the id and the class attributes for elements is a common operation, Reagent provides CSS-style shorthand for these actions. Instead of what we wrote earlier, we could simply write our div as follows:

```
[:div#hello.content [:h1 "Hello, Auto!"]]
```

Reagent also provides shorthand for collapsing nested tags into a single tag. The preceding code could be rewritten this way:

```
[:div#hello.content>h1 "Hello, Auto!"]
```

The > indicates that the h1 tag is nested inside the div tag. This notation is very helpful with CSS frameworks, such as Bulma and Bootstrap, that rely on deeply nested tags to style elements.

---

7. https://github.com/weavejester/hiccup

As you can see, creating Reagent components takes very little code and produces markup that's easy to correlate back to the template definitions.

Reimplementing the Form

By this point you should have an understanding of how you can create different kinds of HTML elements using Reagent. Now let's take a look at what makes Reagent truly special: how you can connect elements to data. We'll bind the form that allows the user to input their name and a message to a Reagent atom that contains the entered values. Also, thanks to Reagent, this binding goes both ways—if the data changes, so will the UI.

So far we've only looked at components that directly represent HTML. However, Reagent allows you to treat any function as a component. The function simply has to return either a Reagent vector or a component that can be rendered by React directly. The latter becomes useful when you want to use React libraries or create your own custom components. Let's not worry about that just yet, though.

In our case, let's create a function called message-form. The function uses a let statement to create a binding for the atom that contains the form data. It then returns a function that generates the form and references the previously defined atom in the input fields of the following component:

```
guestbook-reagent-start/src/cljs/guestbook/core.cljs
(defn message-form []
  (let [fields (r/atom {})]
    (fn []
      [:div
       [:div.field
        [:label.label {:for :name} "Name"]
        [:input.input
         {:type :text
          :name :name
          :on-change #(swap! fields
                             assoc :name (-> % .-target .-value))
          :value (:name @fields)}]]
       [:div.field
        [:label.label {:for :message} "Message"]
        [:textarea.textarea
         {:name :message
          :value (:message @fields)
          :on-change #(swap! fields
                             assoc :message (-> % .-target .-value))}]]
       [:input.button.is-primary
        {:type :submit
         :value "comment"}]])))
```

Here, we're using a closure to create a local state for the fields binding and then returning a function that references it. Reagent first calls the outer function, then calls the returned function whenever it renders the component. This preserves our local state and protects it from any external code, for better or worse. Also note that any arguments referenced in the outer function will retain the value they have when it is first called. This is sometimes useful for initialization tasks, but more often than not, you should get the arguments from the inner function instead. This is *the* most common bug with Reagent, so be careful with your component arguments.

Note that we're using the r/atom from Reagent instead of using the regular ClojureScript atom. Reagent atoms behave the same way as regular atoms, with one important difference: any UI components that reference Reagent atoms will be repainted whenever the value of the atom is changed. When we want to create state, we create an atom to hold it.

This approach automates the process of keeping the UI in sync with the model. With Reagent, we're able to write our UI in a declarative fashion and have it automatically render the current state of our model. Let's see exactly how all this works by implementing the form in our guestbook application using Reagent.

Aside from that, the content of the form should look familiar, since it closely mimics the HTML we used previously. The changes to note are that we've changed the form element to a div, and in addition we've added the :on-change key to bind the input and the textarea elements to functions that are responsible for updating the fields atom with the current values entered by the user. These functions accept the DOM event object as their input and grab the value from its target.

Now, let's create a home function that uses our message-form component:

```
(ns guestbook.core
  ...)

(defn message-form []
  ...)

(defn home []
  [:div.content>div.columns.is-centered>div.column.is-two-thirds
   [:div.columns>div.column
    [message-form]]])
```

Note that we place the message-form in a vector instead of calling it as a function. This allows Reagent to decide when the function needs to be evaluated in case the component has to be repainted. Components can now be recomputed and repainted as the state of their corresponding atoms changes. We'll see how this becomes important shortly.

Finally, let's change our render call to use our home function:

```
(ns guestbook.core
  ...)
(defn message-form []
  ...)
(defn home []
  ...)
(dom/render
  [home]
  (.getElementById js/document "content"))
```

We should now be able to reload the page and see the form rendered there looking very much like the form we had previously. We can even type text in the fields, but we obviously can't see if it's being stored anywhere. Let's modify the form to convince ourselves that the inputs are actually writing the data to our fields atom by adding the following elements to it:

```
guestbook-reagent-start/src/cljs/guestbook/core.cljs
[:p "Name: " (:name @fields)]
[:p "Message: " (:message @fields)]
```

Now we can clearly see that whenever the value of the name or the message field changes, it's immediately reflected in the atom. Once the value of the atom changes, then the component is repainted and we see the new values displayed on the screen.

Talking to the Server

At this point we'd like to take the values of the fields and send them to the server when we click the comment button. We'll use the cljs-ajax[8] library to communicate with the server. The first thing we need to do is to add a dependency for it in our project.clj file.

```
guestbook-reagent/project.clj
[cljs-ajax "0.8.1"]
[org.clojure/clojurescript "1.10.764" :scope "provided"]
[reagent "1.0.0"]
```

Now that we've added the cljs-ajax library, we have to clean out the existing generated JavaScript and restart the ClojureScript compiler. Let's do that by running the following commands:

---

8.   https://github.com/JulianBirch/cljs-ajax

```
$ lein clean
$ lein cljsbuild auto
Watching for changes before compiling ClojureScript...
```

Now, let's add the following reference in our namespace declaration [ajax.core :refer [GET POST]]:

```
(ns guestbook.core
  (:require [reagent.core :as r]
            [reagent.dom  :as dom]
            [ajax.core :refer [GET POST]]))
```

This provides GET and POST functions that we'll use to talk to our server. Let's write a function that submits our form and prints the response:

```
(defn send-message! [fields]
  (POST "/message"
        {:params @fields
         :handler #(.log js/console (str "response:" %))
         :error-handler #(.error js/console (str "error:" %))}))
```

This function attempts to POST to the /message route using the value of the fields atom as the params. The function uses the :handler and the :error-handler keys to handle the success and the error responses, respectively. We're just logging the response for now to see how it behaves. Let's hook this function up to our submit comment button by using the :on-click key so we can test it out:

```
[:input.button.is-primary
  {:type :submit
   :on-click #(send-message! fields)
   :value "comment"}]
```

Let's check the terminal to see that our ClojureScript recompiled successfully and then reload the browser window. When the page reloads, open up the browser console and click the comment button.

```
error:{:status 403,
       :status-text "Forbidden",
       :failure :error,
       :response "<h1>Invalid anti-forgery token</h1>"}
```

We got an error response! This error indicates that we didn't supply the anti-forgery token in our request. If you recall, the server has anti-forgery protection enabled and requires the client to submit the generated token along with any POST request. Previously, we used the {% csrf-field %} tag in our template to supply the token. Since we're now using an Ajax call instead of a form submission, we have to provide this field another way.

First, let's update our home.html template to create a hidden field with the value of the token:

guestbook-reagent/resources/html/home.html
```
{% extends "base.html" %}
{% block content %}
<input id="token" type="hidden" value="{{csrf-token}}">
<div id="content"></div>
{% endblock %}
{% block page-scripts %}
    {% script "/js/app.js" %}
{% endblock %}
```

Now we set the token as an x-csrf-token header on our request. While we're at it, let's also set the Accept header to application/transit+json:

```
(defn send-message! [fields]
  (POST "/message"
        {:format :json
         :headers
         {"Accept" "application/transit+json"
          "x-csrf-token" (.-value (.getElementById js/document "token"))}
         :params @fields
         :handler #(.log js/console (str "response:" %))
         :error-handler #(.log js/console (str "error:" %))}))
```

We set the Accept header to tell the server we'd like to get the response encoded using Transit.[9] With Transit, Clojure data structures are tagged when they're encoded. This means that we can send data structures like keywords, sets, and dates without worrying about them being converted to strings, vectors, or numbers. We can also extend Transit with our own readers and writers, but we won't get into that here.

Let's reload our page and give it another try.

We're no longer getting an error, but we're getting an HTML response instead of data. Our original code for the /message route used the redirect function to display the page after attempting to add the message. This means it's sending us the HTML for the redirect page. This time around, we want to return a Transit response indicating success or failure.

Let's update our save-message! function as follows:

guestbook-reagent/src/clj/guestbook/routes/home.clj
```
(defn save-message! [{:keys [params]}]
  (if-let [errors (validate-message params)]
    (response/bad-request {:errors errors})
```

---

9. https://github.com/cognitect/transit-format

```
(try
  (db/save-message! params)
  (response/ok {:status :ok})
  (catch Exception e
    (response/internal-server-error
     {:errors {:server-error ["Failed to save message!"]}})))))
```

The updated function returns a 400 response when validation fails, a 200 response when it's saved successfully, and a 500 response in case of errors.

Note that we don't have to manually deserialize the request nor serialize the response in our route. This is handled by the Muuntaja library.[10] The library checks the Content-Type header in the request and deserializes the content based on that. The response is serialized to the format specified in the Accept header. The cljs-ajax library defaults to using the Transit format. If you recall, we explicitly set the Accept header to Transit as well. No additional work is needed on your part.

Let's reload the page and try it out. When we try to POST invalid parameters, we should see a response in the console that looks similar to the following:

```
error:{:status 400,
       :status-text "Bad Request",
       :failure :error,
       :response {:errors {:message ("message is less than the minimum")}}}
```

When we submit a valid request, we should see the following printed instead:

```
response:{:status :ok}
```

Notice that in the first case our error-handler was triggered, while in the second case our success handler function is triggered. The cljs-ajax library uses the status code in the response to select the appropriate handler.

Now that we're communicating with the server, let's update our code to display the errors on the page. We'll use the clojure.string namespace's join function, so let's add it to our namespace's require statement first:

```
(ns guestbook.core
  (:require ...
            [clojure.string :as string]))
```

Then let's update our code like so:

---

10. https://github.com/metosin/muuntaja

guestbook-reagent-start/src/cljs/guestbook/core.cljs
```clojure
(defn send-message! [fields errors]
  (POST "/message"
        {:format :json
         :headers
         {"Accept" "application/transit+json"
          "x-csrf-token" (.-value (.getElementById js/document "token"))}
         :params @fields
         :handler (fn [r]
                    (.log js/console (str "response:" r))
                    (reset! errors nil))
         :error-handler (fn [e]
                          (.log js/console (str e))
                          (reset! errors (-> e :response :errors)))}))

(defn errors-component [errors id]
  (when-let [error (id @errors)]
    [:div.notification.is-danger (string/join error)]))

(defn message-form []
  (let [fields (r/atom {})
        errors (r/atom nil)]
    (fn []
      [:div
       [:p "Name: " (:name @fields)]
       [:p "Message: " (:message @fields)]
       [errors-component errors :server-error]
       [:div.field
        [:label.label {:for :name} "Name"]
        [errors-component errors :name]
        [:input.input
         {:type :text
          :name :name
          :on-change #(swap! fields
                             assoc :name (-> % .-target .-value))
          :value (:name @fields)}]]
       [:div.field
        [:label.label {:for :message} "Message"]
        [errors-component errors :message]
        [:textarea.textarea
         {:name :message
          :value (:message @fields)
          :on-change #(swap! fields
                             assoc :message (-> % .-target .-value))}]]
       [:input.button.is-primary
        {:type :submit
         :on-click #(send-message! fields errors)
         :value "comment"}]])))
```

The updated code uses a second atom called errors to store any errors received from the server. We pass the errors to the send-message! function. The function now either clears the errors on success or sets the errors from the response.

We also created a new component called errors-component that accepts the errors and the field ID. It checks if any errors are associated with the ID and returns an alert with the message if that's the case. This component requires the clojure.string library, so remember to require [clojure.string :as string] in your namespace declaration. If the component sees no errors, we simply return a nil. Reagent will handle this intelligently and omit the component in that case. You can see that with the new approach the errors are showing up just as they did in the previous version.

Share Code with the Client

Using the same language on the client and the server allows us to share code between them. Doing so avoids duplication and reduces the chance for errors and unexpected behaviors. Also, we'll be able to run validation client-side and avoid calling the server entirely if the input data is invalid.

Let's update our project to extract validation into a namespace that will be cross-compiled to both Clojure and ClojureScript. The first step is to create a new source folder called src/cljc and update the source paths in project.clj to include it.

```
guestbook-cljc/project.clj
;;Clojure Source Paths
:source-paths ["src/clj" "src/cljc"]
;;...
;;ClojureScript Source Paths
:cljsbuild {:builds
            {:app
             {:source-paths ["src/cljs" "src/cljc"]
              :compiler «compiler options»}}}
```

With the new source folder in place, let's create a new namespace called validation in src/cljc/guestbook/validation.cljc. Note that the file extension is cljc—this hints the compiler that this file will be cross-compiled to both Clojure and Clojure-Script.

Next, let's move the validation code from the guestbook.routes.home namespace to the guestbook.validation namespace:

```
guestbook-cljc/src/cljc/guestbook/validation.cljc
(ns guestbook.validation
  (:require
   [struct.core :as st]))
```

```
(def message-schema
  [[:name
    st/required
    st/string]
   [:message
    st/required
    st/string
    {:message "message must contain at least 10 characters"
     :validate (fn [msg] (>= (count msg) 10))}]])

(defn validate-message [params]
  (first (st/validate params message-schema)))
```

The updated guestbook.routes.home namespace will now require the validate-message function from the guestbook.validation namespace:

guestbook-cljc/src/clj/guestbook/routes/home.clj
```
(ns guestbook.routes.home
  (:require
    [guestbook.layout :as layout]
    [guestbook.db.core :as db]
    [clojure.java.io :as io]
    [guestbook.middleware :as middleware]
    [ring.util.response]
    [ring.util.http-response :as response]
    [guestbook.validation :refer [validate-message]]))
```

Let's restart the application to confirm that server-side code still works correctly. Now we can turn our attention to the client, where we can start using the validate-message function to ensure that the message content is valid before sending it to the server.

We require the guestbook.validation namespace the same way we did earlier:

guestbook-cljc/src/cljs/guestbook/core.cljs
```
(ns guestbook.core
  (:require [reagent.core :as r]
            [reagent.dom :as dom]
            [ajax.core :refer [GET POST]]
            [clojure.string :as string]
            [guestbook.validation :refer [validate-message]]))
```

Then we add the validation check in the send-message! function:

guestbook-cljc/src/cljs/guestbook/core.cljs
```
(defn send-message! [fields errors]
  (if-let [validation-errors (validate-message @fields)]
    (reset! errors validation-errors)
    (POST "/message"
        ;;...
        )))
```

The updated code will attempt to validate the message before making the Ajax call. If any errors are returned by the validate-message function, those will be set in the errors atom, shortcutting the need for server-side validation.

The advantage of this approach is that we're able to reduce server load by avoiding making Ajax calls with invalid data. Of course, the server will still have the final say since it's using the same validation logic.

Reimplementing the List

Now that our form is working as expected, let's turn our attention to displaying the messages on the page. To do that, we have to add a route on the server to return the list of messages, create a component to display the messages, and add a function on the client to fetch them.

Since we're no longer baking the messages in our page, let's update our home-page function to render the HTML on load without any parameters.

guestbook-reagent/src/clj/guestbook/routes/home.clj
```
(defn home-page [request]
  (layout/render
   request
   "home.html"))
```

Next, we add a route that returns the message list:

guestbook-reagent/src/clj/guestbook/routes/home.clj
```
(defn message-list [_]
  (response/ok {:messages (vec (db/get-messages))}))

(defn home-routes []
  [""
   {:middleware [middleware/wrap-csrf
                 middleware/wrap-formats]}
   ["/" {:get home-page}]
   ["/messages" {:get message-list}]
   ["/message" {:post save-message!}]
   ["/about" {:get about-page}]])
```

Let's write a function called get-messages that calls our route and retrieves the messages. The function accepts an atom as a parameter and populates it with the retrieved messages in the handler.

guestbook-reagent/src/cljs/guestbook/core.cljs
```
(defn get-messages [messages]
  (GET "/messages"
       {:headers {"Accept" "application/transit+json"}
        :handler #(reset! messages (:messages %))}))
```

Note that we're not required to pass the anti-forgery header for the GET requests, and we can safely omit it when retrieving messages from the server.

Now let's write a component that uses the messages atom to render the messages in the same format we had in our server-side template:

guestbook-reagent/src/cljs/guestbook/core.cljs
```
(defn message-list [messages]
  (println messages)
  [:ul.messages
   (for [{:keys [timestamp message name]} @messages]
     ^{:key timestamp}
     [:li
      [:time (.toLocaleString timestamp)]
      [:p message]
      [:p " - " name]])])
```

The only thing to note in this function is that we're using the ^{:key timestamp} annotation for each element in the ul. This allows Reagent to efficiently check if a particular element needs to be re-rendered. We could safely omit the annotation in this case, but it could result in loss of performance for big lists.

The ^{} notation is used to supply metadata in Clojure.[11] The metadata is a map that can contain annotations for a symbol or a collection. In our case the metadata is used to provide a unique identifier key for each item in the collection.

Finally, let's update our home component function to use an atom called messages to store the state of the message list.

guestbook-reagent-start/src/cljs/guestbook/core.cljs
```
(defn home []
  (let [messages (r/atom nil)]
    (get-messages messages)
    (fn []
      [:div.content>div.columns.is-centered>div.column.is-two-thirds
       [:div.columns>div.column
        [:h3 "Messages"]
        [message-list messages]]
       [:div.columns>div.column
        [message-form]]])))
```

We've changed home to be a closure like our form component, but there's something extra. The component calls the get-messages function on the messages when it's first mounted, then returns its render function. Reagent will render home, including message-list, while the value of messages is still nil. When the

---

11. http://clojure.org/reference/metadata

get-messages function finishes, the messages atom is reset with the messages from the server and the message-list component is then repainted automatically.

This provides us with an extremely powerful mechanism for connecting producers and consumers of data in our application. The get-messages and the message-list functions have no direct coupling between them and aren't aware of each other. The Reagent atoms provide a way for any component to observe the current value in the model without having the knowledge of how and when it's populated.

One last thing we need to do is to add the message we submit to the server to the list of messages on the page. We can do that in the handler of the send-message! function. The function currently accepts the fields and the errors as its parameters. Let's update it to also accept the messages atom and append our message to it if the server returns a success:

guestbook-reagent/src/cljs/guestbook/core.cljs
```
(defn send-message! [fields errors messages]
  (POST "/message"
        {:format :json
         :headers
         {"Accept" "application/transit+json"
          "x-csrf-token" (.-value (.getElementById js/document "token"))}
         :params @fields
         :handler (fn [_]
                    (swap! messages conj (assoc @fields
                                                :timestamp (js/Date.)))
                    (reset! fields nil)
                    (reset! errors nil))
         :error-handler (fn [e]
                          (.log js/console (str e))
                          (reset! errors (-> e :response :errors)))}))
```

Our handler now can swap! the messages atom and append the fields the user entered and the timestamp set to the current date. If necessary, we could update our server to return the newly created message, but we'll skip this for the sake of simplicity.

Finally, let's update the form function to accept the messages and pass it to save-message!, and the home function to pass the messages to it as a parameter:

guestbook-reagent/src/cljs/guestbook/core.cljs
```
(defn message-form [messages]
  (let [fields (r/atom {})
        errors (r/atom nil)]
    (fn []
      [:div
       [errors-component errors :server-error]
```

```clojure
     [:div.field
      [:label.label {:for :name} "Name"]
      [errors-component errors :name]
      [:input.input
       {:type :text
        :name :name
        :on-change #(swap! fields
                           assoc :name (-> % .-target .-value))
        :value (:name @fields)}]]
     [:div.field
      [:label.label {:for :message} "Message"]
      [errors-component errors :message]
      [:textarea.textarea
       {:name :message
        :value (:message @fields)
        :on-change #(swap! fields
                           assoc :message (-> % .-target .-value))}]]
     [:input.button.is-primary
      {:type :submit
       :on-click #(send-message! fields errors messages)
       :value "comment"}]]))))
(defn home []
  (let [messages (r/atom nil)]
    (get-messages messages)
    (fn []
      [:div.content>div.columns.is-centered>div.column.is-two-thirds
       [:div.columns>div.column
        [:h3 "Messages"]
        [message-list messages]]
       [:div.columns>div.column
        [message-form messages]]])))
```

Let's refresh the browser and see what we've got.

It looks mostly correct, but we have this ugly [TaggedValue: LocalDateTime, ...]. This is because we're encoding a java.time.LocalDateTime, and Transit doesn't know how to decode it by default. We could write an encoder and decoder for this type, but for the sake of simplicity we'll just use java.util.Date objects, since they're supported by default.

To do this, we need to change how we extend the next.jdbc.result-set/ReadableColumn protocol for java.sql.Timestamp to return a java.util.Date instead of a java.time.LocalDate-Time. Currently, we just have the default implementation provided by the Luminus template. We'll leave the implementation of the protocol for other classes unchanged, since we only need to worry about timestamps for now.

The first thing we need to do is write a function to convert a java.sql.Timestamp into a java.util.Date. Luckily, Luminus includes the clojure.java-time[12] library by default. This library has a bunch of helpers for working with Java time classes.

First, let's require java-time and refer the java-date helper:

guestbook-reagent/src/clj/guestbook/db/core.clj
```clojure
(ns guestbook.db.core
  (:require
   [java-time :refer [java-date]]
   [next.jdbc.date-time]
   [next.jdbc.result-set]
   [conman.core :as conman]
   [mount.core :refer [defstate]]
   [guestbook.config :refer [env]]))
```

Next, let's write a helper function to convert a java.sql.Timestamp into a java.util.Date, like so:

guestbook-reagent/src/clj/guestbook/db/core.clj
```clojure
(defn sql-timestamp->inst [t]
  (-> t
      (.toLocalDateTime)
      (.atZone (java.time.ZoneId/systemDefault))
      (java-date)))
```

Finally, let's update our extend-protocol form for next.jdbc.result-set/ReadableColumn to use our new function for its two methods, like so:

guestbook-reagent/src/clj/guestbook/db/core.clj
```clojure
(extend-protocol next.jdbc.result-set/ReadableColumn
  java.sql.Timestamp
  (read-column-by-label [^java.sql.Timestamp v _]
    (sql-timestamp->inst v))
  (read-column-by-index [^java.sql.Timestamp v _2 _3]
    (sql-timestamp->inst v))
  java.sql.Date
  (read-column-by-label [^java.sql.Date v _]
    (.toLocalDate v))
  (read-column-by-index [^java.sql.Date v _2 _3]
    (.toLocalDate v))
  java.sql.Time
  (read-column-by-label [^java.sql.Time v _]
    (.toLocalTime v))
  (read-column-by-index [^java.sql.Time v _2 _3]
    (.toLocalTime v)))
```

---

12. https://github.com/dm3/clojure.java-time

There we go. Now all timestamps returned from database queries will be instances of java.util.Date. This will make serialization and conversion much more straightforward.

It's worth noting that use of java.util.Date instead of the java.time classes isn't generally recommended. A lot of nuance to do with time isn't captured by java.util.Date, and that can lead to a lot of trouble in the long run. But since these nuances aren't relevant to the app in its current state, and since proper handling of java.time classes and their corresponding goog.date JavaScript classes is tedious and not very instructive, we'll skip it for now. See Appendix 3, Working with EDN and Transit, on page 391, if you'd like to read about encoding and decoding java.time and goog.date classes.

Now that we've switched to Reagent, submitted messages are appended to the list of displayed messages when the server confirms that it is saved successfully. Unlike with the previous version of the app, we don't have to reload the entire page or even the list of messages. We simply add the new message to the list, and Reagent takes care of repainting the component for us.

Reagent is built on UI components responding reactively to changes in some dereffable state. It provides many different tools, including atoms, to create and manage state effectively. As we continue with ClojureScript, we'll discover many other tools Reagent gives us to manage state.

State in Reagent

The fact that Reagent can automatically re-render the UI when necessary is powerful, but it doesn't give us any guidance on how to actually organize state. Atoms can either be created as global variables or within closures for individual components, or we can choose to pass data from an atom that has already been dereferenced. All of these options have benefits and drawbacks, so it can be difficult to choose correctly. Moreover, an incorrect choice can make applications significantly harder to maintain.

State is where most, if not all, of your application's complexity lives. Most components care about very specific pieces of state. This means any changes to application state can be complex and far-reaching. For example, consider a sortable, searchable, paged message inbox. We're viewing the second page of messages that contain the word "foo", sorted by most recent, with a page size of 20, and we clear the search. We should go back to page 1, refresh our message list, and display a loading icon until we get our refreshed message list, all while maintaining our page size of 20 and sort order. We need to be careful not to bake our sorting choice into our message list, as it should be sorted when we reload it. We also need to be careful to make sure our paging accounts for changes in page size sensibly. This already sounds fairly complex, and it's just a list of messages with some common features.

A good rule of thumb is to keep the application state in a global atom and to use local atoms with caution, only where performance or isolation demands it. Reagent provides some basic tools like cursors and tracks[13] to preserve isolation or reusability even when everything shares a single global atom, but this is often not enough. Most large applications will use a framework built on top of Reagent that uses these tools to provide a nice API for managing state.

Managing State with Re-Frame

The most popular Reagent-based framework is re-frame. Re-frame places all its state in one global atom which it calls the app-db. The only way to read from the app-db is using re-frame subscriptions, and the only way to write to the app-db is by dispatching re-frame events. Note that even though the app-db can only be accessed this way, we can still include regular Reagent atoms in a re-frame application and manage them ourselves.

Let's get re-frame set up in our guestbook application so we can see how it works. First, just like we did with cljs-ajax, let's add it to our project's dependencies:

guestbook-rf-intro/project.clj
```
[cljs-ajax "0.8.1"]
[org.clojure/clojurescript "1.10.764" :scope "provided"]
[reagent "1.0.0"]
[re-frame "1.1.2"] ;add re-frame
```

Restart the ClojureScript compiler:

```
$ lein clean
$ lein cljsbuild auto
Watching for changes before compiling ClojureScript...
```

And require it in our namespace declaration:

guestbook-rf-intro/src/cljs/guestbook/core.cljs
```
(ns guestbook.core
  (:require [reagent.core :as r]
            [reagent.dom :as dom]
            [re-frame.core :as rf]
            [ajax.core :refer [GET POST]]
            [clojure.string :as string]
            [guestbook.validation :refer [validate-message]]))
```

---

13. http://reagent-project.github.io/docs/master/ManagingState.html

Now we're ready to get started with re-frame. Let's upgrade our Reagent app into a re-frame app.

Introducing Re-Frame

One of the main goals of re-frame is to, wherever possible, remove state and logic from UI components. This has many benefits. Having all of your application logic operate independent of how it renders allows you to write front-end tests based on data rather than UI. It allows you to more easily port your client to different platforms like React Native or Electron. And it makes writing and reusing UI components easier, as they're just pure functions from data to hiccup. We'll see many more benefits as we continue on, so let's get started.

Since the only way to write to the app-db is through events, the first thing we need to do is write an initialize event. Let's add an initialize event to guest-book.core:

guestbook-rf-intro/src/cljs/guestbook/core.cljs
```
(rf/reg-event-fx
 :app/initialize
 (fn [_ _]
   {:db {:messages/loading? true}}))
```

This is what a re-frame event looks like. An event is composed of a handler function and a keyword that identifies it (:app/initialize). An event handler is a function that takes two arguments and returns an effects map. Here, our event handler ignores its arguments and returns a map with one effect—:db. This effect tells re-frame to set the app-db to the returned value. There are many different effects, and you can even define your own, but for now we'll only be using the :db effect.

Note that with our initialize event, we've set :messages/loading? to true. Let's add a subscription that checks if our messages are loading and update our home component to trigger the initialize event and to only display our message list once it's fully loaded.

guestbook-rf-intro/src/cljs/guestbook/core.cljs
```
(rf/reg-sub
 :messages/loading?
 (fn [db _]
   (:messages/loading? db)))

(defn home []
  (let [messages (r/atom nil)]
    (rf/dispatch [:app/initialize])
    (get-messages messages)
    (fn []
```

```clojure
(if @(rf/subscribe [:messages/loading?])

  [:div>div.row>div.span12>h3
   "Loading Messages..."]
  ;;...
  ))))
```

We never set loading to false! Let's add an event to save our messages and clear the loading flag, and then add a dispatch to our get-messages callback. While we're at it, let's add a subscription to our message list and use it instead of an atom in home.

guestbook-rf-intro/src/cljs/guestbook/core.cljs
```clojure
(rf/reg-event-db
 :messages/set
 (fn [db [_ messages]]
   (-> db
       (assoc :messages/loading? false
              :messages/list messages))))

(rf/reg-sub
 :messages/list
 (fn [db _]
   (:messages/list db [])))

(defn get-messages []
  (GET "/messages"
       {:headers {"Accept" "application/transit+json"}
        :handler #(rf/dispatch [:messages/set (:messages %)])}))

(defn home []
  (let [messages (rf/subscribe [:messages/list])]
    ;;...
    ))
```

Notice, we've used rf/reg-event-db. This is a helper function for events which only use the db effect. It unwraps the db from the co-effects map (the first argument) and wraps your return with {:db ...}. Now our messages are display-ing after they're loaded, but we've missed a step. Loading isn't the only way we modify our message list. If we try to add a new message, we'll get an error like this in the web console:

```
Error: Assert failed: Reaction is read only; on-set is not allowed
(fn? (.-on-set a)) ratom.cljs:360:4
```

Why is this? We changed messages from an atom to a subscription, but we're still trying to use swap! in send-message! to update it. Let's register another event handler to address this and update our send-message! function.

guestbook-rf-intro/src/cljs/guestbook/core.cljs
```clojure
(rf/reg-event-db
 :message/add
 (fn [db [_ message]]
   (update db :messages/list conj message)))

(defn send-message! [fields errors]
  (if-let [validation-errors (validate-message @fields)]
    (reset! errors validation-errors)
    (POST "/message"
        {:format :json
         :headers
         {"Accept" "application/transit+json"
          "x-csrf-token" (.-value (.getElementById js/document "token"))}
         :params @fields
         :handler (fn [_]
                    (rf/dispatch
                     [:message/add (assoc @fields :timestamp (js/Date.))])
                    (reset! fields nil)
                    (reset! errors nil))
         :error-handler (fn [e]
                          (.log js/console (str e))
                          (reset! errors (-> e :response :errors)))})))
```

Since our form doesn't read messages, let's also remove messages from its arguments and its call to send-message!.

guestbook-rf-intro/src/cljs/guestbook/core.cljs
```clojure
(defn message-form []
  (let [fields (r/atom {})
        errors (r/atom nil)]
    (fn []
      [:div
       [errors-component errors :server-error]
       [:div.field
        [:label.label {:for :name} "Name"]
        [errors-component errors :name]
        [:input.input
         {:type :text
          :name :name
          :on-change #(swap! fields
                             assoc :name (-> % .-target .-value))
          :value (:name @fields)}]]
       [:div.field
        [:label.label {:for :message} "Message"]
        [errors-component errors :message]
        [:textarea.textarea
         {:name :message
          :value (:message @fields)
          :on-change #(swap! fields
                             assoc :message (-> % .-target .-value))}]]
```

```clojure
        [:input.button.is-primary
         {:type :submit
          :on-click #(send-message! fields errors)
          :value "comment"}]]))))
(defn home []
  (let [messages (rf/subscribe [:messages/list])]
    (rf/dispatch [:app/initialize])
    (get-messages)
    (fn []
      [:div.content>div.columns.is-centered>div.column.is-two-thirds
       (if @(rf/subscribe [:messages/loading?])
         [:h3 "Loading Messages..."]
         [:div
          [:div.columns>div.column
           [:h3 "Messages"]
           [message-list messages]]
          [:div.columns>div.column
           [message-form]]])])))
```

Now that we've finished moving our message list into re-frame, let's take a look back at what we've done and why. We've replaced our messages atom with a :messages/list subscription for reading, and two events, :messages/set and :message/add, for modifying. Our components haven't changed much. Our message-list is still parameterized, and just as reusable. Our message-form can now only save to one place, but this could easily be changed by passing the submit function as an argument.

Overall, re-frame has given us several benefits with no substantial drawbacks. Since any updates must pass through events, we have a single place to add validation and preprocessing. Since our view now uses subscriptions, we can easily change displayed messages without touching components or changing how data is stored. These are significant advantages, especially for the maintenance of large front-end applications.

This is just a small taste of what re-frame can do. In later chapters we'll learn about interceptors, effects, subscription chaining, and much more.

What You've Learned

In this chapter, you've learned how using ClojureScript can make your app cleaner and more feature rich. You've learned about how Reagent manages components via dereffables to allow views to be specified declaratively without sacrificing performance. And you've learned about re-frame's event-subscription model for managing application state and seen how it makes apps more flexible, robust, and manageable.

In the next chapter, we'll look at setting up professional ClojureScript development tools and how to use them to improve the architecture and features of our guestbook. We'll set up a Swagger service API, a REPL connected to the browser, and a re-frame debugger. Then we'll connect to our server using WebSockets to facilitate bidirectional communication and live message updates. In the process, we'll explore more of the design philosophy behind re-frame and learn some of its more advanced features.

CHAPTER 5

Setting Up for Success

Our guestbook concept is working well, but we aren't getting much value over our original server-rendered version. In fact, you could argue that we've added unnecessary complexity. Let's talk about some of the reasons why the new design provides a better foundation for growth and enhancement.

Users interact with the application via the interface rendered by the browser. Anytime a user performs an action, such as clicking a button or entering data in a field, they're updating the state of the application. Web applications typically track this state via user sessions. The more features an application has, the more complicated this session state will be. We could manage this state three ways.

The first approach we could take is to manage sessions entirely on the server and reload the page on each request. This approach is only practical when our state rarely changes, as the entire page has to be sent to the browser and rendered to reflect the outcome of a user action.

This problem can be addressed by the second approach: adding code that runs in the browser to dynamically update parts of the page based on user actions. Unfortunately, this approach introduces a new problem: client-side logic now also has to track its own version of the session state. Keeping the state in sync between the client and the server is an additional challenge that often leads to elusive bugs and user frustration.

The logical extension of the second approach is to handle session state management entirely on the client, supported by a lightweight set of stateless services. With this third approach, we're back to having state managed in one place, but we don't have to compromise on features or responsiveness. This is commonly referred to as the single-page application (SPA) style.

In addition to simplifying state management, the SPA style provides some other significant benefits. Having a clear separation between client and server code makes it easier to compartmentalize work and allows for alternative clients such as Android, iOS, or desktop. These clients will be able to leverage the same API that's already being used by the existing web client.

Since the rendering and session state management become the responsibility of the client, we end up freeing up the server, directly leading to handling larger concurrent client loads.

Finally, keeping the server stateless provides a clear path to horizontal scaling as your application usage grows.

As you can see, the nature of web applications has evolved over the years toward the thick client model where the user interface and application state are managed on the client. Clojure is a relatively new language, and its web ecosystem evolved to embrace the SPA approach as opposed to traditional server-side rendering. This may be the reason why server-side frameworks haven't gained traction in the Clojure ecosystem. Much of the complexity moved from the server to the client, and so did the frameworks.

Now that we've discussed some of the reasons for why it's desirable to build our application using SPA style, let's formalize this approach in our architecture. We've already refactored our original server-rendered guestbook to handle user interface to the client with ClojureScript, and we have an informal Ajax API between the client and the server. The next step is to create an explicit service API on the server.

Services

We'll factor out the API endpoints from the guestbooks.routes.home into a separate guestbook.routes.services namespace. The endpoints in the home namespace will be responsible for serving HTML and related assets to be used by the web browser to render the page. Meanwhile, the services namespace will provide a data API (for example, JSON, EDN, and others) to be used by the client over Ajax.

The key motivation for separating our page rendering code and the API endpoints is to facilitate maintainability. Keeping all of our logic in one place has been manageable so far, but it will require discipline to keep things organized as our application grows. We should separate our model logic early so that it doesn't become entangled with our routing going forward. We should also separate our API routes (endpoints responsible for querying and modifying data) from our application routes (our webpages). As our app grows, having a well-documented, validated, and tested API to build against will be invaluable.

The ability to interact with our data independently of a heavyweight client allows us to tailor our views to the needs of our users as they evolve. This approach also makes it easier to work on tasks independently. New service endpoints can be implemented and tested independent of the client UI development. Conversely, we can mock out the data that we expect to receive on the client and develop the UI independent of the server.

Guestbook Messages

Let's create a new namespace called guestbook.messages that's dedicated to managing guestbook messages. We want this to be separate from guestbook.routes.home so that it can be used by any type of service we expose, not just HTTP.

guestbook-services-1/src/clj/guestbook/messages.clj
```
(ns guestbook.messages
  (:require
   [guestbook.db.core :as db]
   [guestbook.validation :refer [validate-message]]))

(defn message-list []
  {:messages (vec (db/get-messages))})

(defn save-message! [message]
  (if-let [errors (validate-message message)]
    (throw (ex-info "Message is invalid"
                    {:guestbook/error-id :validation
                     :errors errors}))
    (db/save-message! message)))
```

We moved most of this code from guestbook.routes.home, but we've left behind anything that is related to HTTP. We changed validation to throw an error if it fails. Any handling of errors and reporting to users should be managed externally.

Now let's update our guestbook.routes.home namespace to use our new functions in guestbook.messages and handle validation errors:

guestbook-services-1/src/clj/guestbook/routes/home.clj
```
(ns guestbook.routes.home
  (:require
   [guestbook.layout :as layout]
   [guestbook.messages :as msg]
   [guestbook.middleware :as middleware]
   [ring.util.http-response :as response]))
;;...
(defn save-message! [{:keys [params]}]
  (try
    (msg/save-message! params)
```

```clojure
    (response/ok {:status :ok})
    (catch Exception e
      (let [{id      :guestbook/error-id
             errors :errors} (ex-data e)]
        (case id
          :validation
          (response/bad-request {:errors errors})
          ;;else
          (response/internal-server-error
           {:errors {:server-error ["Failed to save message!"]}}))))))))
;;...
(defn message-list [_]
  (response/ok (msg/message-list)))
```

Finally, let's check the browser and make sure we didn't break anything.

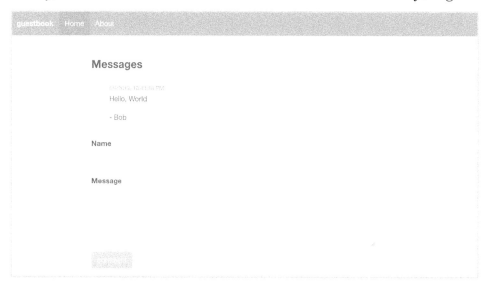

Configuring a Service API

Now that we have our model separated from our web server, we'll separate our web services from our web application.

Let's move the GET /messages and POST /message endpoints to guestbook.routes.services under the /api/ route:

guestbook-services-2/src/clj/guestbook/routes/services.clj
```clojure
(ns guestbook.routes.services
  (:require
   [guestbook.messages :as msg]
   [guestbook.middleware :as middleware]
   [ring.util.http-response :as response]))
```

```clojure
(defn service-routes []
  ["/api"
   {:middleware [middleware/wrap-formats]}
   ["/messages"
    {:get
     (fn [_]
       (response/ok (msg/message-list)))}]

   ["/message"
    {:post
     (fn [{:keys [params]}]
       (try
         (msg/save-message! params)
         (response/ok {:status :ok})
         (catch Exception e
           (let [{id      :guestbook/error-id
                  errors :errors} (ex-data e)]
             (case id
               :validation
               (response/bad-request {:errors errors})
               ;;else
               (response/internal-server-error
                {:errors
                 {:server-error ["Failed to save message!"]}})))))}]])
```

And remove them from guestbook.routes.home:

guestbook-services-2/src/clj/guestbook/routes/home.clj

```clojure
(ns guestbook.routes.home
  (:require
   [guestbook.layout :as layout]
   [guestbook.middleware :as middleware]))

(defn home-page [request]
  (layout/render
   request
   "home.html"))

(defn about-page [request]
  (layout/render
   request "about.html"))

(defn home-routes []
  [""
   {:middleware [middleware/wrap-csrf
                 middleware/wrap-formats]}
   ["/" {:get home-page}]
   ["/about" {:get about-page}]])
```

For our service routes to show up, we need to connect them to our handler, like so:

guestbook-services-2/src/clj/guestbook/handler.clj

```
(ns guestbook.handler
  (:require
   ;;...
   [guestbook.routes.services :refer [service-routes]]
   ;;...
   ))
;;...
(mount/defstate app-routes
  :start
  (ring/ring-handler
    (ring/router
      [(home-routes)
       (service-routes)])
    ;;...
    ))
```

And finally, we need to update our URLs on the client to reflect our changes:

guestbook-services-2/src/cljs/guestbook/core.cljs

```
(defn get-messages []
  (GET "/api/messages"
      {:headers {"Accept" "application/transit+json"}
       :handler #(rf/dispatch [:messages/set (:messages %)])}))
;;...
(defn send-message! [fields errors]
  (if-let [validation-errors (validate-message @fields)]
    (reset! errors validation-errors)
    (POST "/api/message"
        ;;...
        )))
```

Now we have all of our services in one place. This allows us to use service-specific tools, like Swagger, more easily.

Swagger Tools

Our routing library, Reitit, has first-class support for a very popular service API tool called Swagger. Swagger gives us plenty of benefits, like a generated JSON schema, but the most tangible at the moment is Swagger UI. Swagger UI will give us the ability to visualize and interact with our services through an auto-generated web UI.

Let's get it set up and see what it can do for us:

guestbook-swagger-1/src/clj/guestbook/routes/services.clj

```clojure
(ns guestbook.routes.services
  (:require
   [reitit.swagger :as swagger]
   [reitit.swagger-ui :as swagger-ui]
   [guestbook.messages :as msg]
   [guestbook.middleware :as middleware]
   [ring.util.http-response :as response]))

(defn service-routes []
  ["/api"
   {:middleware [middleware/wrap-formats]
    :swagger {:id ::api}}

   ["" {:no-doc true}
    ["/swagger.json"
     {:get (swagger/create-swagger-handler)}]
    ["/swagger-ui*"
     {:get (swagger-ui/create-swagger-ui-handler
            {:url "/api/swagger.json"})}]]
   ;;...
   ])
```

As you can see, Swagger endpoints are regular routes that point to handler functions generated by calling swagger/create-swagger-handler and swagger-ui/create-swagger-ui-handler, respectively. At this point we can navigate to the /api/swagger-ui/ route in the browser and see our service endpoints. But we're not quite ready to use it. Swagger needs some information about the *type* of data that each endpoint expects and returns in order to function properly.

Let's see what we've got. First, let's try out the GET /api/messages endpoint by clicking to expand, pressing Try it out!, and then pressing Execute as shown in the figure on page 108.

Great! We can see a cURL command that this request corresponds to, the request URL, the response body we got back from the server, the response code, and the response headers. Our route is working as expected.

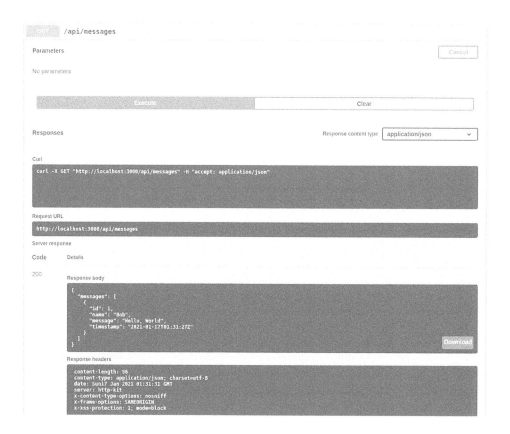

Next let's try out our POST /api/message route. When we expand it, all we see is Try it out!, just like our other endpoint—but something isn't right. We know that we have to specify a message to POST, but there's no way to input this information. If we try clicking the button, we see that we get an error back as shown in the figure on page 109.

This is because our handlers are just functions. For Swagger to know what the route expects, we need some way to specify that information when the route is declared. Thankfully, Reitit provides a way to specify the shape of our requests and responses that can be used by Swagger, Muuntaja, and Spec Coercion.

Coercion and Validation with Reitit

Now that we have Swagger UI showing up, let's get it configured properly.

When server and client communicate, data must be encoded somehow (for example, with JSON). Since we're working with full-stack Clojure, it would be nice to use Clojure data structures. But what if we wanted to have other

clients? This is what Muuntaja does. Muuntaja decodes the request body based on the Content Type header and encodes the response body using the Accept headers.

Unfortunately, many data formats, such as JSON, represent only a subset of EDN. When we're dealing with these formats, we'll often need to coerce from one type to another. This is handled by coercion middleware that tries to coerce the value based on the type specified in the endpoint specs. Our handlers won't need to be concerned with this, since all they'll see is a Clojure data structure, and their return value will be coerced into whatever response format was requested.

As we discussed in Define the Routes with Reitit, on page 42, middleware can be specified for a specific context. Reitit provides a suite of Ring middleware[1] for accomplishing common tasks. This middleware also has richer features that leverage Reitit itself. Let's replace middleware/wrap-formats with the middleware that Reitit provides. Although it's more complex, it provides functionality essential to real-world web services, such as declarative coercion and validation of parameters.

First, let's require the necessary Reitit namespaces:

---

1. https://metosin.github.io/reitit/ring/ring.html

guestbook-swagger-2/src/clj/guestbook/routes/services.clj
```clojure
(ns guestbook.routes.services
  (:require
    [reitit.swagger :as swagger]
    [reitit.swagger-ui :as swagger-ui]
    [reitit.ring.coercion :as coercion]
    [reitit.coercion.spec :as spec-coercion]
    [reitit.ring.middleware.muuntaja :as muuntaja]
    [reitit.ring.middleware.exception :as exception]
    [reitit.ring.middleware.multipart :as multipart]
    [reitit.ring.middleware.parameters :as parameters]
    [guestbook.messages :as msg]
    [guestbook.middleware :as middleware]
    [ring.util.http-response :as response]
    [guestbook.middleware.formats :as formats]))
```

Then let's update the options map for our "/api/" context, like so:

guestbook-swagger-2/src/clj/guestbook/routes/services.clj
```clojure
{:middleware [;; query-params & form-params
              parameters/parameters-middleware
              ;; content-negotiation
              muuntaja/format-negotiate-middleware
              ;; encoding response body
              muuntaja/format-response-middleware
              ;; exception handling
              exception/exception-middleware
              ;; decoding request body
              muuntaja/format-request-middleware
              ;; coercing response bodys
              coercion/coerce-response-middleware
              ;; coercing request parameters
              coercion/coerce-request-middleware
              ;; multipart params
              multipart/multipart-middleware]
 :muuntaja formats/instance
 :coercion spec-coercion/coercion
 :swagger {:id ::api}}
```

Notice that we added some additional attributes: :muuntaja and :coercion. This is how Reitit enriches middleware. As we mentioned in Extend Ring, on page 37, we can provide a custom muuntaja instance. Luminus actually provides an instance by default in <project-name>.middleware.formats. With Reitit's version of the Muuntaja middleware stack, we can specify which instance to use with the :muuntaja key. The :coercion key is similar but is used by Reitit's coercion middleware.[2]

---

2.   https://metosin.github.io/reitit/ring/coercion.html

We've also added a :swagger attribute. This will be inherited by all child routes of /api/ and designate them as part of the swagger API with ID ::api. If we wanted to, we could have as many apis as we like, or we could omit the ID to include all routes on our ring-handler. We'll use the single ::api ID so that our home-routes aren't included in our API.

Now that our context is updated, we have to update our individual routes to make use of the middleware we just added. For coercion, we'll use Clojure Spec[3] along with the Spec Tools[4] library. This allows us to provide a specification for each route's parameters and responses. Let's add a data-spec[5] to our GET /api/messages endpoint for our 200 OK response, like so:

guestbook-swagger-2/src/clj/guestbook/routes/services.clj
```
["/messages"
 {:get
  {:responses
   {200
    {:body ;; Data Spec for response body
     {:messages
      [{:id pos-int?
        :name string?
        :message string?
        :timestamp inst?}]}}}
   :handler
   (fn [_]
     (response/ok (msg/message-list)))}}]
```

Data-specs are maps shaped like our data, but with predicates instead of values. Our response body must be a map where the :messages key contains a vector of maps that each have :id as a positive integer, :name and :message as strings, and a :timestamp as an instant. We declare the shape of our data as regular Clojure data structures and the types of the leaves as predicates.

Next, let's add a data-spec for the parameters passed to POST /api/message:

guestbook-swagger-2/src/clj/guestbook/routes/services.clj
```
["/message"
 {:post
  {:parameters
   {:body ;; Data Spec for Request body parameters
    {:name string?
     :message string?}}
```

---

3.   https://clojure.org/guides/spec
4.   https://github.com/metosin/spec-tools
5.   https://github.com/metosin/spec-tools/blob/master/docs/02_data_specs.md

```
  :responses
  {200
   {:body map?}

   400
   {:body map?}

   500
   {:errors map?}}
  :handler
  (fn [{{params :body} :parameters}]
    (try
      (msg/save-message! params)
      (response/ok {:status :ok})
      (catch Exception e
        (let [{id      :guestbook/error-id
               errors :errors} (ex-data e)]
          (case id
            :validation
            (response/bad-request {:errors errors})
            ;;else
            (response/internal-server-error
             {:errors
              {:server-error ["Failed to save message!"]}}))))))}}]
```

The :parameters map looks very similar to the :responses map we wrote before. One subtle change is the shape of the request map passed to our handler function. Before, the guestbook.middleware/wrap-formats middleware placed our parameters under :body-params, but reitit-ring's parameter middleware stack places parameters based on where they originate. In this case, our parameters are under [:parameters :body], so we've changed how we destructure the request accordingly.

Debugging Reitit Middleware

We've added a bunch of middleware for incrementally transforming our request and response maps. This is a very powerful and effective way to add functionality that cuts across our application, such as validation and coercion. But it does have a drawback. As your middleware stack gets larger, it can become very hard to debug due to the sheer number of separate functions modifying every request map. Fortunately, Reitit allows us to specify our middleware as a vector so we can easily inspect between each step. Furthermore, it provides the :reitit.middleware/transform option to allow endpoints to specify a transformation function to apply to the middleware stack. This is fairly advanced, and we won't go into advanced use cases, but we'll highlight a useful trans-formation function provided by Reitit: reitit.ring.middleware.dev/print-request-diffs.

To use the print-request-diffs tool, do the following inside the guestbook.handler namespace:

```
(ns guestbook.handler
  (:require
    ;;...
    [reitit.ring.middleware.dev :as dev]))

(mount/defstate app-routes
  :start
  (ring/ring-handler
    (ring/router
      [(home-routes)
       (service-routes)]
      {:reitit.middleware/transform dev/print-request-diffs})
    ;;...
    ))
```

We recommend doing this manually when debugging is neccessary, as it's quite noisy.

When an HTTP request is received by the ring/router, it logs a diff for each middleware so that you can identify where each change to the request map is happening.

Try it out and see what's logged.

If you post a new message, you should get something like the following:

```
--- :request---

  {:async-channel #<org.httpkit.server.AsyncChannel...>,
   :body #<org.httpkit.BytesInputStream@23f41560 BytesInputStream[len=50]>,
   :character-encoding "utf8",
   :content-length 50,
   :content-type "application/json",
   :cookies {<cookies removed for brevity>},
   :flash nil,
   :form-params {},
   :headers {<headers removed for brevity>},
   :multipart-params {},
   :params {},
   :path-params {},
   :query-params {},
   :query-string nil,
```

```
   :remote-addr "0:0:0:0:0:0:0:1",
   :request-method :post,
   :scheme :http,
   :server-name "localhost",
   :server-port 3000,
   :session {:ring.middleware.anti-forgery/anti-forgery-token
             "<anti-forgery-token>"},
   :uri "/api/message",
   :websocket? false,
   :session/key "d537399a-a066-4172-ae54-6d8968a2dbf9"}

--- :request :reitit.ring.middleware.parameters/parameters ---

<map unchanged, removed for brevity>

--- :request :reitit.ring.middleware.muuntaja/format-negotiate ---

<unchanged keys removed for brevity>

  {+:muuntaja/request #muuntaja.core.FormatAndCharset
   {:charset "utf-8",
    :format "application/json",
    :raw-format "application/json"},
   +:muuntaja/response #muuntaja.core.FormatAndCharset
   {:charset "utf-8",
    :format "application/transit+json",
    :raw-format "application/transit+json"}}

--- :request :reitit.ring.middleware.muuntaja/format-response ---

<map unchanged, removed for brevity>

--- :request :reitit.ring.middleware.exception/exception ---

<map unchanged, removed for brevity>

--- :request :reitit.ring.middleware.muuntaja/format-request ---

<removed unchanged keys for brevity>

  {+:body-params {:message "This is a test message!", :name "Foo"}}

--- :request :reitit.ring.coercion/coerce-response ---

<map unchanged, removed for brevity>

--- :request :reitit.ring.coercion/coerce-request ---

<removed unchanged keys for brevity>

  {+:parameters {:body {:message "This is a test message!",
                        :name "Foo"}}}

--- :response :reitit.ring.coercion/coerce-request ---

  {:body {:status :ok}, :headers {}, :status 200}
```

```
--- :response :reitit.ring.coercion/coerce-response ---

{:body {:status :ok}, :headers {}, :status 200}

--- :response :reitit.ring.middleware.muuntaja/format-request ---

{:body {:status :ok}, :headers {}, :status 200}

--- :response :reitit.ring.middleware.exception/exception ---

{:body {:status :ok}, :headers {}, :status 200}

--- :response :reitit.ring.middleware.muuntaja/format-response ---

{:body {:status :ok}, :headers {}, :status 200}

--- :response :reitit.ring.middleware.muuntaja/format-negotiate ---

{:body -{:status :ok} +#<java.io.ByteArrayInputStream@4ddcf7f2>,
 :headers {+"Content-Type" "application/transit+json; charset=utf-8"},
 :status 200}

--- :response :reitit.ring.middleware.parameters/parameters ---

{:body #<java.io.ByteArrayInputStream@4ddcf7f2>,
 :headers {"Content-Type" "application/transit+json; charset=utf-8"},
 :status 200}

--- :response---

{:body #<java.io.ByteArrayInputStream@4ddcf7f2>,
 :headers {"Content-Type" "application/transit+json; charset=utf-8"},
 :status 200}
```

Notice that we have :request at the start and :response at the end. These are the maps received by and returned from the router, respectively. Since we have some middleware being applied *outside* of Reitit, our :request map already has some parsed keys on it. Be aware that this tool won't help with debugging those middlewares.

In between, we have a :request printed for each middleware in order and then a :response printed in reverse order. We can see annotations with + and/or - to denote the change, addition, or removal of a value in the request and response maps.

It isn't often that you'll have to use this tool, but it's invaluable when you need it.

Using Swagger UI

Now that we have Swagger properly configured, let's open Swagger UI in the browser again and see what's changed as shown in the figure on page 116.

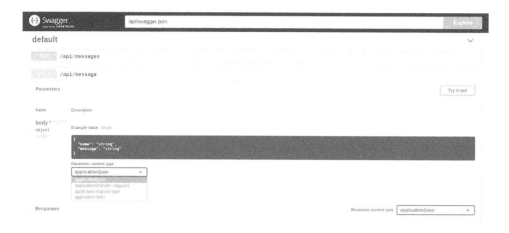

Swagger has read our data-specs and now provides us with example requests and responses. We can now select Try it out and Swagger UI will provide us with a JSON Skeleton to fill in.

Then, if you click Execute to submit your request, you should get something like the figure on page 117 in the Responses section.

You might have noticed that we didn't try to send an EDN request. A bug in Swagger UI v3.44.0 (the latest version available when this book was published)

prevents sending an application/edn request. Since we'll be using EDN fairly extensively throughout this book, we'll downgrade to Swagger UI v2.x. However, if this bug has since been resolved, feel free to continue on with the latest version of Swagger UI.

Luckily, the process for downgrading is straightforward. Simply add the following dependency to your project.clj:

```
[metosin/ring-swagger-ui "2.2.10"]
```

Now restart the application and take a look at Swagger UI:

It looks and behaves a bit differently, but it's more or less the same. Click the POST /api/message endpoint to expand it, and switch the parameter and response content type dropdowns to application/edn.

Now we should be able to fill in our request like the figure on page 118.

When we click Try it out!, we should get a response like this:

```
Curl

curl -X POST --header 'Content-Type: application/edn' --header 'Accept: application/edn' -d '{:name "Jane" \
    :message "Hello There"}' 'http://localhost:3000/api/message'
```

```
Request URL

http://localhost:3000/api/message
```

```
Response Body

    {:status :ok}
```

```
Response Code

200
```

```
Response Headers

{
    "content-length": "13",
    "content-type": "application/edn; charset=utf-8",
    "date": "Sat, 27 Feb 2021 23:07:50 GMT",
    "server": "http-kit",
    "x-content-type-options": "nosniff",
    "x-frame-options": "SAMEORIGIN",
    "x-xss-protection": "1; mode=block"
}
```

We now have a way to organize our service endpoints in a structured way and an interactive API documentation page. Let's move on to tools for our front end.

ClojureScript Development Tools

We have a REPL set up on the back end, but all we have on the front end is recompilation. We can do better. To this end we'll introduce two tools: shadow-cljs and re-frame-10x.

Shadow-cljs

Several tools other than lein-cljsbuild are available for adding ClojureScript support to a Clojure project. Let's update our project to use shadow-cljs[6] to compile ClojureScript. Note that you'll need to have NPM[7] installed before following along with this section. By switching to shadow-cljs, we'll gain seamless integration with NPM modules and ClojureScript hot loading. Shadow-cljs watches your ClojureScript files and sends compiled changes to the browser through a WebSocket without requiring the browser to refresh. It also provides us with a ClojureScript REPL connected to the browser. This is invaluable because it allows us to make incremental changes to our application without losing any built-up state.

Other similar tools, such as Figwheel[8] and Figwheel Main,[9] don't require NPM, but we'll use shadow-cljs because we'll be using NPM modules later on. While it's possible to use NPM with other tools, shadow-cljs is by far the simplest in this regard.

Let's get shadow-cljs configured and see what it can do. Shadow-cljs can be installed via NPM by running the following command:

```
$ npm install -g shadow-cljs
```

Next, we need to create a configuration file for shadow-cljs called shadow-cljs.edn. This file has the following content:

```
guestbook-shadow/shadow-cljs.edn
{:nrepl {:port 7002}
 :builds {:app {:target :browser
                :output-dir "target/cljsbuild/public/js"
                :asset-path "/js"
                :modules {:app {:entries [guestbook.app]}}
                :devtools {:watch-dir "resources/public"}}
          :test {:target :node-test, :output-to "target/test/test.js"
                 :autorun true}}
 :lein true}
```

---

6. https://github.com/thheller/shadow-cljs
7. https://www.npmjs.com/
8. https://github.com/bhauman/lein-figwheel
9. https://figwheel.org/

The configuration hints shadow-cljs that it's being used within a Leiningen project with the :lein key being set to true. Using this flag hints shadow-cljs to read the ClojureScript source path information from project.clj. The :nrepl specifies the port that nREPL will be started on; this port can be used to connect the editor to the browser REPL. Take a look at Appendix 2, Editor Configuration, on page 387, for details if you wish to set this up. Finally, the :builds key specifies different build configurations. The :app configuration is used to compile the application for running in the browser, while the :test key specifies an alternative test configuration that compiles the tests and runs them using Node.js. We won't get into configuring ClojureScript tests just yet, so you can safely ignore it for now. We'll come back to it in ClojureScript Testing, on page 339.

Shadow-cljs uses NPM to manage Node.js modules, and so we need to create a package.json file and declare NPM dependencies there:

guestbook-shadow/package.json
```
{
  "devDependencies": {
    "shadow-cljs": "^2.11.14"
  },
  "dependencies": {
    "react": "17.0.1",
    "react-dom": "17.0.1",
    "xregexp": "^4.4.1"
  }
}
```

We've added the xregexp module because it's required by the Struct validation library, while the React modules are used by Reagent. Note that if you forget to include these dependencies, shadow-cljs will usually tell you exactly what you need to install.

At this point we no longer need the cljsbuild configuration in project.clj since we'll be using shadow-cljs to build ClojureScript from this point on. We can now remove the following items from project.clj:

1. The plugin lein-cljsbuild.
2. :cljsbuild key along with its configuration.
3. :clean-targets key along with the cljsbuild targets.

Next, we need to add shadow-cljs and Closure compiler dependencies for shadow-cljs to work. Also, we need to add "src/cljs" to our top-level :source-paths, since cljsbuild is no longer configuring this for us.

While we're updating our project.clj, we'll also add cljs-devtools,[10] a library that enhances compatibility with Chrome DevTools.

```
;; Add these dependencies
[com.google.javascript/closure-compiler-unshaded "v20200830"
 :scope "provided"]
[org.clojure/google-closure-library "0.0-20191016-6ae1f72f"
 :scope "provided"]
[thheller/shadow-cljs "2.11.14" :scope "provided"]

;; Update source paths
:source-paths ["src/clj" "src/cljs" "src/cljc"]

;; Add devtools dependency to dev profile
:project/dev { ;; ...
              :dependencies [ ;; ...
                             [binaryage/devtools "1.0.2"]]}
```

The first thing we have to do is separate our initialization logic from our rendering logic. If we call (rf/dispatch [:app/initialize]) from the home component, then our app-db will be reset whenever we try to remount our components. We'll also need to annotate our mount-components function with :dev/after-load so that it's called whenever our code is reloaded. Let's write our initialization like so:

guestbook-shadow/src/cljs/guestbook/core.cljs
```
(defn home []
  (let [messages (rf/subscribe [:messages/list])]
    (fn []
      [:div.content>div.columns.is-centered>div.column.is-two-thirds
       (if @(rf/subscribe [:messages/loading?])
         [:h3 "Loading Messages..."]
         [:div
          [:div.columns>div.column
           [:h3 "Messages"]
           [message-list messages]]
          [:div.columns>div.column
           [message-form]]])])))

(defn ^:dev/after-load mount-components []
  (rf/clear-subscription-cache!)
  (.log js/console "Mounting Components...")
  (dom/render [#'home] (.getElementById js/document "content"))
  (.log js/console "Components Mounted!"))

(defn init! []
  (.log js/console "Initializing App...")
  (rf/dispatch [:app/initialize])
  (get-messages)
  (mount-components))
```

---

10. https://github.com/binaryage/cljs-devtools

We also need to make sure our init! function is called somewhere, and we may want to do some development-specific initialization. We can accomplish this by using environment-specific source paths just like we did in Running Code Selectively, on page 56. Let's create a file at env/dev/cljs/guestbook/app.cljs with our development initialization logic:

guestbook-shadow/env/dev/cljs/guestbook/app.cljs

```
(ns ^:dev/once guestbook.app
  (:require
   [devtools.core :as devtools]
   [guestbook.core :as core]))
```

```
(enable-console-print!)
```

```
(println "loading env/dev/cljs/guestbook/app.cljs...")
```

```
(devtools/install!)
```

```
(core/init!)
```

Then we update our :project/dev Leiningen profile in project.clj to include env/dev/cljc and env/dev/cljs in :source-paths:

```
:project/dev {...
              :source-paths ["env/dev/clj" "env/dev/cljc" "env/dev/cljs"]}
```

Since NPM modules are managed using NPM, we need to install them by running the following command:

```
$ npm install
```

Now let's restart our server and start shadow-cljs in the terminal:

```
$ npx shadow-cljs watch app
shadow-cljs - config: guestbook/shadow-cljs.edn  cli version:...  node:...
shadow-cljs - running: lein run -m shadow.cljs.devtools.cli --npm watch app
... Logging Provider: org.jboss.logging.Slf4jLoggerProvider
... starting undertow server io.undertow.Undertow@3a7d5e1a
... XNIO version X.X.X.Final
... JBoss Threads version X.X.X.Final
... Configuring listener with protocol HTTP for ... and port 9630
shadow-cljs - server version: X.X.X running at http://localhost:9630
shadow-cljs - nREPL server started on port 7002
shadow-cljs - watching build :app
[:app] Configuring build.
[:app] Compiling ...
[:app] Build completed. (XXX files, XXX compiled, 0 warnings, XX.XXs)
```

Shadow-cljs has started and is waiting for us to open our application. Let's open our app in the browser to confirm that everything is compiling correctly. Once we open our app, it connects via WebSocket and we see a confirmation message in the browser console.

```
shadow-cljs: WebSocket connected!
shadow-cljs: REPL session start successful
```

Our ClojureScript is compiling, and our web app is working as intended. Now, let's get a REPL connected to the browser.

Connect your editor to the shadow-cljs nREPL on port 7002 (See Appendix 2, Editor Configuration, on page 387, for details). If you need to connect from the terminal instead of your editor, you can do so by running the following command:

```
$ npx shadow-cljs cljs-repl app
shadow-cljs - config: .../shadow-cljs.edn  cli version: X.X.X  node: vX.X.X
shadow-cljs - connected to server
cljs.user=>
```

Let's run a command from the REPL to confirm that we're connected:

```
cljs.user=> (js/alert "Hello from shadow-cljs")
```

In the browser, we should see an alert like this:

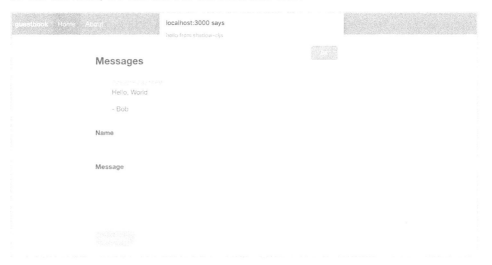

The alert blocked the REPL process, but once we handle it in the browser by clicking OK, it returns. Once the alert is dismissed, we see nil printed in the REPL, which is the result of running the js/alert function, followed by the REPL prompt.

```
cljs.user=> (js/alert "Hello from shadow-cljs")
nil
cljs.user=>
```

Now we have a REPL connected to the browser, which is pretty great, but let's not forget about live code reloading. We have some logging in our mount-components function to make sure it's being called on reload. We also have some logging in our init! function and in the top level of guestbook.app to confirm that they aren't being rerun. Let's add a log statement to the top level of guestbook.core temporarily so we can see when the file is being evaluated.

```
guestbook-shadow-demo/src/cljs/guestbook/core.cljs
(defn ^:dev/after-load mount-components []
  (rf/clear-subscription-cache!)
  (.log js/console "Mounting Components...")
  (dom/render [#'home] (.getElementById js/document "content"))
  (.log js/console "Components Mounted!"))

(defn init! []
  (.log js/console "Initializing App...")
  (rf/dispatch [:app/initialize])
  (get-messages)
  (mount-components))

(.log js/console "guestbook.core evaluated!")
```

When we save the file, we should see a compilation notificaton in our shadow-cljs watch app terminal, and we should see our top-level and mount-components log statements, but not our init! or our guestbook.app log statements.

```
[:app] Compiling ...
[:app] Build completed. (324 files, 2 compiled, 0 warnings, X.XXs)

shadow-cljs: reloading code but no :after-load hooks are configured! ...
browser.cljs:25 shadow-cljs: load JS guestbook/core.cljs
re-frame: overwriting :event handler for:
...
core.cljs:129 guestbook.core evaluated!
```

Let's call init! from the REPL to make sure our changes were loaded:

```
cljs.user=> (guestbook.core/init!)
nil
cljs.user=>
```

We should see the following in the browser console:

```
Initializing App...
Mounting Components...
Components Mounted!
```

Now we've confirmed that changes to functions are showing up live in the browser without refreshing the page and that our mount-components function is called whenever shadow-cljs reloads code. Let's try building up some state and see how shadow-cljs handles it. For the sake of demonstration, let's mark any comments posted in this client by adding [CLIENT] to the username.

guestbook-shadow-demo/src/cljs/guestbook/core.cljs
```clojure
(defn send-message! [fields errors]
  (if-let [validation-errors (validate-message @fields)]
    (reset! errors validation-errors)
    (POST "/api/message"
        {:format :json
         :headers
         {"Accept" "application/transit+json"
          "x-csrf-token" (.-value (.getElementById js/document "token"))}
         :params @fields
         :handler (fn [_]
                     (rf/dispatch
                      [:message/add (-> @fields
                                        (assoc :timestamp (js/Date.))
                                        (update :name str " [CLIENT]"))])
                     (reset! fields nil)
                     (reset! errors nil))
         :error-handler (fn [e]
                          (.log js/console (str e))
                          (reset! errors (-> e :response :errors)))}))))
```

Without refreshing the browser, let's post a comment and see if the change is reflected.

It's updated. Now, if we refresh the browser, the [CLIENT] annotations disappear as shown in the figure on page 126.

This is because the success callback in send-message! modifies the message after it's sent to the server. The message is saved *without* the annotation, but the client annotates it before adding it to the app-db.

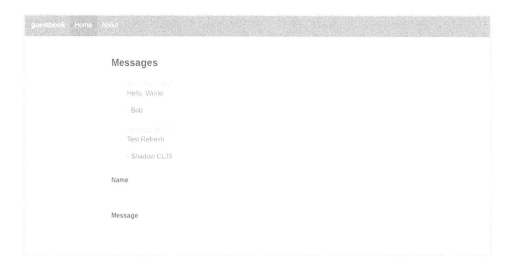

However, if we update our message-list component, we'll change the way *all* messages are displayed. Let's add an @ before the author's name to see this in action. While we're at it, let's also see how our form state behaves with shadow-cljs. First, let's make a message that has the [CLIENT] annotation. Then we'll write a message with no name filled in and try sending it so we have a validation error in our errors atom and a message draft in our fields atom. Now, without refreshing, let's add our @ to our message-list component:

guestbook-shadow-demo/src/cljs/guestbook/core.cljs
```
(defn message-list [messages]
  [:ul.messages
   (for [{:keys [timestamp message name]} @messages]
     ^{:key timestamp}
     [:li
      [:time (.toLocaleString timestamp)]
      [:p message]
      [:p "@" name]])])
```

Your messages should look like the figure on page 127.

Our message-list has updated to reflect our changes, and it even kept our [CLIENT] annotations, but our message-form input and errors have been cleared! Why could this be? It's because our message-form state is stored in a *closure*.

When shadow-cljs reloads, we remount our root component home and this destroys and re-creates all child components. That means a brand-new message-form component with brand-new fields and errors atoms. The message-list preserves the [CLIENT] annotations because they're stored in re-frame's app-db, and the app-db isn't touched when shadow-cljs reloads code.

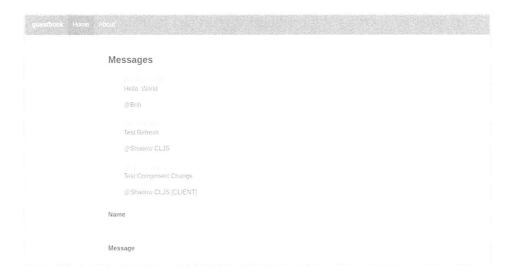

Now that we have a feel for how state behaves with Reagent, re-frame, and shadow-cljs, we can make informed decisions on whether to use closures or the app-db. Generally, using closures to store state locally is preferred in libraries and general purpose components, and global state like re-frame's app-db is preferred for application-specific components.

Since our form is specific to our application, we'll refactor it to use re-frame. But first, we should tidy up a bit, install re-frame-10x, and test our production build. Let's remove our top-level log and our [CLIENT] annotation, and change our @ back into to a dash. Then, let's also configure our :uberjar profile before we forget.

Remember, since our [CLIENT] annotations are stored in our app-db, they won't be cleared by hotloading. To get rid of them, we could refresh the page, but we can also clear them manually by calling get-messages from the REPL:

```
cljs.user=> (guestbook.core/get-messages)
#object[Object [object Object]]
cljs.user=>
```

Now that we've tidied up, let's check out our next tool, re-frame-10x.

Re-Frame-10x

Our next development task is to refactor our app to make better use of re-frame. In fact, as our app grows, most of our client's complexity will be in re-frame events and subscriptions. To manage this, we'll use a re-frame aware debugging and inspection tool.

Two popular tools are used for debugging re-frame: re-frisk[11] and re-frame-10x.[12] re-frame-10x is the more full-featured tool, but it can get slow in large applications. We'll use re-frame-10x here since it will be useful for learning about re-frame. It shouldn't slow us down much, since our application is fairly small. Check out re-frisk's documentation for instructions if you'd like to try it out.

Re-frame-10x is a helpful and feature-rich re-frame dashboard that allows us to inspect our db, see our event history, check subscriptions, profile performance, and more. Let's get it set up and see what it can do.

Since it's a development tool, we'll install it inside our :project/dev profile. Add this entry to your :dependencies:

guestbook-10x/project.clj
```
[day8.re-frame/re-frame-10x "0.7.0"]
```

Then update the :app build's :dev and :devtools in shadow-cljs.edn, like so:

guestbook-10x/shadow-cljs.edn
```
{:target :browser
 :output-dir "target/cljsbuild/public/js"
 :asset-path "/js"
 :modules {:app {:entries [guestbook.app]}}
 :dev {:closure-defines {"re_frame.trace.trace_enabled_QMARK_" true}}
 :devtools {:preloads [day8.re-frame-10x.preload]
            :watch-dir "resources/public"}}
```

And re-frame-10x is installed. Let's start up our application and shadow-cljs servers, and see re-frame-10x in action. Open the app in the browser and press Ctrl-H to toggle the dashoard as shown in the figure on page 129.

A lot's going on here, so let's break it down. At the top, a textbox shows the most recent event. To its left is the previous epoch button, which reverts the state to before the displayed event. To its right is the next epoch button, which moves the state forward by one event and then skips to latest epoch button, which sets the app state to after the latest event.

Let's try out the time travel function. Write and submit a message in our message-form. We can see that re-frame-10x has picked up the change, and a new event is displayed. Click the previous epoch button. We've undone the event, and our app is as it was before the event happened. Remember that this is only in the browser, so our message is still on the server.

---

11. https://github.com/flexsurfer/re-frisk
12. https://github.com/Day8/re-frame-10x

Below that, we have the main panel of the dashboard, which has six tabs and a replay button.

The replay button sets the app state to immediately before the selected event and re-dispatches it. This is very useful for debugging event handlers. We can edit and reload our event handler with shadow-cljs, then we can replay it. It will be dispatched from the exact state where we discovered the bug, but it'll be handled by our new handler. We don't have to reproduce our buggy state for every edit; we can just click replay.

The features above the tabs are all actions, but the six tabs of our dashboard allow us to inspect different aspects of our current state. We'll cover some of these tabs in greater detail as we refactor and extend our client. For now, here's a brief description of each tab.

Event
> Shows how your handler computes its effect map. It's nifty, but it requires extra setup and is experimental. We'll ignore it for now.

Fx
> Shows us the Effects, Co-Effects, and Interceptors of this event. This tab is useful, but advanced. We'll come back to it.

App-db
> Allows us to inspect paths of our app-db. This tab is especially useful.

Subs

Shows us which subscriptions were created, run, destroyed, or not run due to this event's occurrence. Very useful for understanding an app's behavior.

Trace

Similar to the Subs tab, but more low level. Tells us what occurred due to this event, and the time each action took. Allows us to look at Reagent events, such as component re-rendering, as well.

Timing

Shows us the time it takes for the event to be handled and the UI to be updated. Gives us a high-level look at our performance so we can dig deeper with the Trace tab if necessary.

If you'd like to see re-frame-10x in action, the project's README[13] has a great interactive demo.

The Importance of a Tight Feedback Loop

Now that we've spent a good amount of time on setup, let's reflect on why.

As we mentioned earlier when we introduced the Clojure REPL, one of the biggest advantages of using Clojure is the excellent development tooling. It's imperative to have as little friction as possible, and as much insight into your application as possible, during development. If you're able to quickly experiment with your application and see first-hand what the results are, you're able to learn naturally and build a deep understanding of the problems you're solving. This is a much better circumstance for building proficiency and insight than relying solely on documentation and reference implementations.

If it's a burden to tinker with a problem, developers are much more likely to accept something as "good enough" and move on. From our experience, being unable to easily explore leads to quicker accumulation of technical debt and reliance on "cargo-culting." So if you encounter pain points during development, we strongly advise that you research solutions thoroughly and implement your own if they don't exist. You'll be a happier, more productive developer, and your co-workers and community will thank you for it.

Production Build Profile

Finally, let's configure and test our production build so we can get back to actually building our application. Since we've changed the way we compile

---

13. https://github.com/Day8/re-frame-10x/blob/master/README.md

ClojureScript, we need to update our production build profile accordingly. We need to update our :source-paths to include env/prod/cljs, and we need to add the shadow-cljs release task to our :prep-tasks.

Let's update our :uberjar profile, like so:

```
guestbook-10x/project.clj
:source-paths    ["env/prod/clj" "env/prod/cljc" "env/prod/cljs"]
:prep-tasks ["compile"
             ["run" "-m" "shadow.cljs.devtools.cli" "release" "app"]]
```

The change we made to :source-paths is straightforward, but :prep-tasks are new. By default, Leiningen runs the compile task for us. But if we specify our own :prep-tasks, we need to tell Leiningen when to call compile explicitly. After "compile", we have a vector that starts with "run". This tells Leiningen to invoke the run task, passing the rest of the vector as arguments. By calling run with the -m shadow.cljs.devtools.cli flag, we're calling shadow-cljs release through Leiningen.[14] This task will compile our ClojureScript with advanced optimization to improve performance and reduce bundle size.

Note that

```
$ lein run -m shadow.cljs.devtools.cli release app'
```

and

```
$ npx shadow-cljs release app
```

are equivalent, but the former can be invoked from Leiningen. This is what allows us to use shadow-cljs from :prep-tasks. While it's possible to do this with any shadow-cljs task, we recommend using shadow-cljs directly in most cases.

Now that our project.clj is updated, let's write our production guestbook.app. Since we won't be using any development tools, it's straightforward. We just make *print-fn* do nothing so that any debugging won't be printed, and we call (guestbook.core/init!).

```
guestbook-10x/env/prod/cljs/guestbook/app.cljs
(ns guestbook.app
  (:require
   [guestbook.core :as core]))

;;ignore println statements in prod
(set! *print-fn* (fn [& _]))

(core/init!)
```

---

14. https://shadow-cljs.github.io/docs/UsersGuide.html#_running_tasks_directly_from_leiningen

Let's make sure that everything works as intended by creating an UberJAR and running it (we'll use our dev-config.edn instead of writing our prod-config.edn right now). First, let's stop our application and shadow-cljs servers, and clean any stale files. Then let's build and run our UberJAR:

```
$ lein clean
$ lein uberjar
Compiling guestbook.env
Compiling guestbook.core
...
[:app] Compiling ...
...
[:app] Build completed. (XXX files, XXX compiled, 0 warnings, XX.XXs)
Created ...guestbook/target/uberjar/guestbook-0.1.0-SNAPSHOT.jar
Created ...guestbook/target/uberjar/guestbook.jar
$ java -jar -Dconf=dev-config.edn target/uberjar/guestbook.jar
```

Now that our UberJAR is running, let's open our app in the browser. In the web console, we see our log statements from init! and mount-components, but since we are using env/prod/cljs, we do not see our guestbook.app log statement. We have confirmed that our app builds correctly for production, so let's refactor our form.

Embracing Re-Frame

In Managing State with Re-Frame, on page 94, we introduced re-frame at a glance, but we didn't really go into detail. Now that we have our environment set up, let's take a closer look at re-frame and why we chose it.

At its core, re-frame only does two things. It defines our view using layers of pure functions (that is, subscriptions), and it defines state transitions as data (events) to be handled using pure functions (event handlers). Re-frame provides plenty of useful features on top of these two things, but fundamentally re-frame just queries and updates state.

Let's take a look at how re-frame handles views first, then we'll look at state transitions afterward. We'll have to move some of our logic into re-frame events, but we won't worry too much about correctness until later.

Views in Re-Frame

Every application has to get from its state to a rendered view in some manner. In fact, this is often the most complicated and volatile part of web applications. Reagent provides the foundation by conceiving of views as *pure* computations on pieces of data, but re-frame goes a step further. Re-frame models view computation as four layers in a signal graph: the app-db at the root, then direct subscriptions, then derived subscriptions, and finally view components (that is, Reagent components) at the leaves. When a node's input signals change, it recomputes its value from the new inputs. If its value has changed, it sends its new value as an input to downstream nodes. These cascade until a layer has no changes or until a leaf node is changed. If a leaf changes, it triggers a component repaint via Reagent and our user sees the change.

Layer 1 - The app-db

Re-frame insists on a single data store at the root of our app. Having a single source of truth greatly simplifies view computation and ensures data consistency.

Layer 2 - Direct Subscriptions

Direct subscriptions pull data out of our app-db's structure; they are pure functions of app-db. This layer loosens the coupling of complex logic (in layer 3) to the structure of our app-db. It also provides some performance benefits by reducing how often derived subscriptions are recomputed.

Layer 3 - Derived Subscriptions

Derived subscriptions don't depend on our app-db directly but instead are pure functions of one or more subscriptions (direct or derived). This is where complex application logic belongs. Since they listen to layer 2 and not the app-db, they're only recomputed when necessary. This layer is optional in small apps but can be significant in larger apps.

Layer 4 - View Components

View components connect our subscriptions to Reagent. These are just Reagent components that use subscriptions. To get the most leverage out of re-frame, we try to make these view components as straightforward as possible. They should just be adapters between re-frame and the DOM. All interaction with app state should be via subscriptions and events.

By separating our view logic into layers, we can make sure it isn't duplicated across our application. This makes computation more efficient and prevents us from accidentally missing components when we update our code.

Let's refactor our view to use re-frame. We'll move all of our state into the app-db and access it via subscriptions. While we're at it, we'll also replace our function calls with event dispatches. We haven't talked about state transitions in re-frame yet, so we'll keep our handlers basic for now. We'll come back and clean them up when we discuss state transitions in Events and Effects in Re-Frame, on page 153.

Updating Our View

Our home and message-list components can stay the same, but our message-form has local state and calls send-message!. Let's update message-form to use re-frame.

First, let's add a :fields map to our app-db and write two subscriptions for accessing it: :form/fields and form/field. Now write two events for modifying it: :form/set-field and :form/clear-fields.

guestbook-re-frame-1/src/cljs/guestbook/core.cljs
```
(rf/reg-event-db
 :form/set-field
 [(rf/path :form/fields)]
 (fn [fields [_ id value]]
   (assoc fields id value)))

(rf/reg-event-db
 :form/clear-fields
 [(rf/path :form/fields)]
 (fn [_ _]
   {}))

(rf/reg-sub
 :form/fields
 (fn [db _]
   (:form/fields db)))

(rf/reg-sub
 :form/field
 :<- [:form/fields]
 (fn [fields [_ id]]
   (get fields id)))
```

Take a look at our reg-sub for :form/field. This is an example of a derived subscription with one input, [:form/fields]. It looks the same as the subscriptions we've written before, except for the :<- line, which declares the subscription we're deriving from.

Also, look at how we registered our :form/set-field event handler. A vector between the event-id and the handler function is our interceptor vector, and it contains one interceptor, path. Interceptors are similar to Ring's middleware. They allow us to transform the inputs and outputs of our event handlers. For example, the path interceptor makes it seem like the value at our path, in this case [:form/fields], is the entire db. We'll cover interceptors in more detail in Events and Effects in Re-Frame, on page 153.

Next, let's rethink errors a bit. We have two types of errors so far: validation errors which we compute on the client and server errors we get in our Ajax response. When using re-frame, we should look for opportunities to refactor imperative state changes into values derived from data. Validation is a simple computation on our fields map, so validation errors are a perfect candidate for a derived subscription. But validation errors aren't the whole picture. We also have server errors that must be imperative, since our server doesn't support our reactive style.

Let's register our error events and subscriptions with this in mind:

guestbook-re-frame-1/src/cljs/guestbook/core.cljs
```
(rf/reg-event-db
 :form/set-server-errors
 [(rf/path :form/server-errors)]
 (fn [_ [_ errors]]
   errors))

(rf/reg-sub
 :form/server-errors
 (fn [db _]
   (:form/server-errors db)))

;;Validation errors are reactively computed
(rf/reg-sub
 :form/validation-errors
 :<- [:form/fields]
 (fn [fields _]
   (validate-message fields)))

(rf/reg-sub
 :form/validation-errors?
 :<- [:form/validation-errors]
 (fn [errors _]
   (not (empty? errors))))
```

```
(rf/reg-sub
 :form/errors
 :<- [:form/validation-errors]
 :<- [:form/server-errors]
 (fn [[validation server] _]
   (merge validation server)))

(rf/reg-sub
 :form/error
 :<- [:form/errors]
 (fn [errors [_ id]]
   (get errors id)))
```

We have two data sources for errors: :form/server-errors and :form/validation-errors. One is managed by the :form/set-server-errors event, and the other is derived from our :form/fields subscription. The :form/errors subscription is a derived subscription that combines all types of errors and presents them as a single map. This means the message-form component doesn't have to worry about our different types of errors. We can change how we gather our errors as we please without needing to touch our UI. We've also added a Boolean subscription :form/validation-errors? that checks if there are any validation errors—we'll see how this helps us soon.

Now, let's change our send-message! function into an event. As we said earlier, we're just doing this to get our data into re-frame. A few things are wrong with this version, but we'll come back and fix them later.

guestbook-re-frame-1/src/cljs/guestbook/core.cljs
```
(rf/reg-event-fx
 :message/send!
 (fn [{:keys [db]} [_ fields]]
   (POST "/api/message"
         {:format :json
          :headers
          {"Accept" "application/transit+json"
           "x-csrf-token" (.-value (.getElementById js/document "token"))}
          :params fields
          :handler #(rf/dispatch
                      [:message/add
                       (-> fields
                           (assoc :timestamp (js/Date.)))])
          :error-handler #(rf/dispatch
                            [:form/set-server-errors
                             (get-in % [:response :errors])])})
   {:db (dissoc db :form/server-errors)}))
```

Our event handler isn't all that different from our initial function, but at least it shows up in re-frame-10x. Note that we're passing the fields in as a parameter rather than looking it up from the database, since it's more flexible. This could allow us to post messages different ways in the future.

Finally, let's hook up our events and subscriptions to our form component.

```
guestbook-re-frame-1/src/cljs/guestbook/core.cljs
(defn errors-component [id]
  (when-let [error @(rf/subscribe [:form/error id])]
    [:div.notification.is-danger (string/join error)]))

(defn message-form []
  [:div
   [errors-component :server-error]
   [:div.field
    [:label.label {:for :name} "Name"]
    [errors-component :name]
    [:input.input
     {:type :text
      :name :name
      :on-change #(rf/dispatch
                    [:form/set-field
                     :name
                     (.. % -target -value)])
      :value @(rf/subscribe [:form/field :name])}]]
   [:div.field
    [:label.label {:for :message} "Message"]
    [errors-component :message]
    [:textarea.textarea
     {:name :message
      :value @(rf/subscribe [:form/field :message])
      :on-change #(rf/dispatch
                    [:form/set-field
                     :message
                     (.. % -target -value)])}]]
   [:input.button.is-primary
    {:type :submit
     :disabled @(rf/subscribe [:form/validation-errors?])
     :on-click #(rf/dispatch [:message/send!
                               @(rf/subscribe [:form/fields])])
     :value "comment"}]])
```

Now that all of our state is external, this component is much simpler. We don't have to worry about shuffling around local atoms, and we could easily update this component to take actions and subscriptions as parameters to make it more reusable. Our actions are labeled semantically, and all of our querying logic is computed ahead of time and attached to a meaningful label. All our component has to do is render those premade pieces in a meaningful way.

Initializing our Re-Frame Application

Now that we have our form logic in re-frame, let's take a quick look at our init! function.

It has to take care of bootstrapping our application, but we should make sure that actions involving data are handled inside the :app/initialize event rather than the init! function. We're currently calling get-messages directly, so let's convert it into an event, :messages/load, and use the :dispatch effect to trigger it from :app/initialize.

guestbook-re-frame-1/src/cljs/guestbook/core.cljs

```
(rf/reg-event-fx
 :app/initialize
 (fn [_ _]
   {:db {:messages/loading? true}
    :dispatch [:messages/load]}))

(rf/reg-event-fx
 :messages/load
 (fn [{:keys [db]} _]
   (GET "/api/messages"
        {:headers {"Accept" "application/transit+json"}
         :handler #(rf/dispatch [:messages/set (:messages %)])})
   {:db (assoc db :messages/loading? true)}))
```

Let's see what's changed. In the browser, refresh the app and take a look at the re-frame-10x dashboard to see the events that occur on start.

It starts with [:app/initialize]. We can see in the Effects section that it's setting our db and is dispatching [:messages/load].

If we look at [:message/load], we see that it's setting our db, but we can't see what else it's doing. Then, from the function called in our handler, some time later [:messages/set ...] is called as shown in the figure on page 139.

Reloading Messages

Our event handlers may not be pure yet, but the reactive model already gives us a lot of power. Now that we have an independent :messages/load event, it

should be easy enough to add a reload button. We'll add a button that dispatches :messages/load when clicked, and we'll disable it and change the text if :messages/loading? is true.

guestbook-websockets/src/cljs/guestbook/core.cljs
```
(defn reload-messages-button []
  (let [loading? (rf/subscribe [:messages/loading?])]
    [:button.button.is-info.is-fullwidth
     {:on-click #(rf/dispatch [:messages/load])
      :disabled @loading?}
     (if @loading?
       "Loading Messages"
       "Refresh Messages")]))

(defn home []
  (let [messages (rf/subscribe [:messages/list])]
    (fn []
      [:div.content>div.columns.is-centered>div.column.is-two-thirds
       [:div.columns>div.column
        [:h3 "Messages"]
        [message-list messages]]
       [:div.columns>div.column
        [reload-messages-button]]
       [:div.columns>div.column
        [message-form]]]))))
```

Let's take a look in the browser to see what's changed.

It's not terribly interesting with just one session since we get our own messages immediately.

Let's open a second browser window and post a message as shown in the figure on page 140.

As you can see, only the user that posted the message can see it in the list. Now let's try out our reload button in the other window:

Aha! Now we have the message being shared between users. We're reusing part of our application initialization logic to refresh only some parts of our app. This is better than refreshing the page, but not by much. Unfortunately, there's no way for our users to know *when* they need to refresh, and they still need to trigger the refresh themselves.

Let's take a look at fixing this.

Multi-User with WebSockets

Instead of just having a refresh messages button, let's add a push notification for new messages using WebSockets.

We'll take a look at using WebSockets for client-server communication. In the traditional Ajax approach, the client first sends a message to the server and then handles the reply using an asynchronous callback. WebSockets allow the web server to initiate the message exchange with the client.

Currently, our guestbook application doesn't provide a way to display messages generated by other users without reloading the page. If we wanted to solve this problem using Ajax, our only option would be to poll the server and check if any new messages are available since the last poll. This is inefficient since the clients end up continuously polling the server regardless of whether any new messages are actually available.

Instead, we'll have the clients open a WebSocket connection when the page loads, and then the server will notify all the active clients anytime a new message is created. This way the clients are notified in real time and the messages are only sent as needed.

Configuring the Server

WebSockets require support on both the server and the client side. While the browser API is standard, each server provides its own way of handling Web-Socket connections. In this section we'll take a look at using the API for the HTTP Kit web server that Luminus defaults to.

Let's start by updating the server-side code in the project to provide a Web-Socket connection. Once the server is updated, we'll look at the updates required for the client.

First we add a new namespace for our WebSocket connection handler. Let's call it guestbook.routes.websockets and add the following requirements:

guestbook-websockets/src/clj/guestbook/routes/websockets.clj
```clojure
(ns guestbook.routes.websockets
  (:require [clojure.tools.logging :as log]
            [org.httpkit.server :as http-kit]
            [clojure.edn :as edn]
            [guestbook.messages :as msg]))
```

We'll need org.httpkit.server for managing our WebSocket connections.

While we figure out the basics of WebSockets, we'll just use pr-str and edn/read-string to serialize and de-serialize our data.

If we want to communicate to clients, the first thing we need to do is keep track of our connections. Let's create an atom containing our open connections and write connect! and disconnect! functions to manage it.

guestbook-websockets/src/clj/guestbook/routes/websockets.clj
```clojure
(defonce channels (atom #{}))

(defn connect! [channel]
  (log/info "Channel opened")
  (swap! channels conj channel))

(defn disconnect! [channel status]
  (log/info "Channel closed: " status)
  (swap! channels disj channel))
```

To keep it simple, let's assume our WebSocket will only receive save-message! messages. Let's copy our logic from guestbook.routes.services but replace HTTP responses with maps and add serialization and de-serialization where necessary.

guestbook-websockets/src/clj/guestbook/routes/websockets.clj
```clojure
(defn handle-message! [channel ws-message]
  (let [message (edn/read-string ws-message)
        response (try
                   (msg/save-message! message)
                   (assoc message :timestamp (java.util.Date.))
                   (catch Exception e
                     (let [{id     :guestbook/error-id
                            errors :errors} (ex-data e)]
                       (case id
                         :validation
                         {:errors errors}
                         ;;else
                         {:errors
                          {:server-error ["Failed to save message!"]}})))))]
    (if (:errors response)
      (http-kit/send! channel (pr-str response))
      (doseq [channel @channels]
        (http-kit/send! channel (pr-str response))))))
```

Finally, we need to write a connection handler:

guestbook-websockets/src/clj/guestbook/routes/websockets.clj
```clojure
(defn handler [request]
  (http-kit/with-channel request channel
    (connect! channel)
    (http-kit/on-close channel (partial disconnect! channel))
    (http-kit/on-receive channel (partial handle-message! channel))))

(defn websocket-routes []
  ["/ws"
   {:get handler}])
```

We reference it from guestbook.handler, exposing a route in our app for accepting connections:

```clojure
(ns guestbook.handler
  (:require
   ;;...
   [guestbook.routes.websockets :refer [websocket-routes]]
   ;;...
   ))

(mount/defstate app
  :start
  (middleware/wrap-base
    (ring/ring-handler
```

```
(ring/router
  [;;...
   (websocket-routes)])
;;...
)))
```

Now, let's connect from the client.

Connecting from ClojureScript

To connect on the client side, we use js/WebSocket to create a WebSocket connection object, which we use to communicate.

guestbook-websockets/src/cljs/guestbook/websockets.cljs
```
(ns guestbook.websockets
  (:require [cljs.reader :as edn]))

(defonce channel (atom nil))

(defn connect! [url receive-handler]
  (if-let [chan (js/WebSocket. url)]
    (do
      (.log js/console "Connected!")
      (set! (.-onmessage chan) #(->> %
                                     .-data
                                     edn/read-string
                                     receive-handler))
      (reset! channel chan))
    (throw (ex-info "Websocket Connection Failed!"
                    {:url url}))))

(defn send-message! [msg]
  (if-let [chan @channel]
    (.send chan (pr-str msg))
    (throw (ex-info "Couldn't send message, channel isn't open!"
                    {:message msg}))))
```

In our core namespace, everything stays mostly the same. The only things we need to do are: update our :message/send event to use our WebSocket, add a handle-response! function that will deal with responses, and call ws/connect! from our init! function.

guestbook-websockets/src/cljs/guestbook/core.cljs
```
(rf/reg-event-fx
 :message/send!
 (fn [{:keys [db]} [_ fields]]
   (ws/send-message! fields)
   {:db (dissoc db :form/server-errors)}))

(defn handle-response! [response]
  (if-let [errors (:errors response)]
    (rf/dispatch [:form/set-server-errors errors])
```

```
    (do
      (rf/dispatch [:message/add response])
      (rf/dispatch [:form/clear-fields response]))))
(defn init! []
  (.log js/console "Initializing App...")
  (rf/dispatch [:app/initialize])
  (ws/connect! (str "ws://" (.-host js/location) "/ws")
               handle-response!)
  (mount-components))
```

Let's try it out in the browser. Let's respond to our earlier message via Web-Sockets.

It automatically loads! Since re-frame is event driven, using WebSockets is actually a lot simpler! We just dispatch our events from our WebSocket message handler instead of from our Reagent components. If we look at re-frame-10x's history in the left browser, we can see that [:message/add ...] was indeed triggered even though we didn't submit anything.

From here, we could do a lot to improve our re-frame app, but let's swap out our from-scratch WebSocket implementation for a much richer one—Sente.

Upgrading to Sente

Now that we've done a scratch implementation of WebSockets, let's look at a popular Clojure(Script) WebSockets library: Sente.[15]

---

15. https://github.com/ptaoussanis/sente

Sente is a little more complicated than our toy implementation, but it brings a lot of great features in exchange.

Ajax Fallback Support
    Sente automatically switches to Ajax polling if WebSockets aren't available.

Keep-Alives
    Sends messages periodically to prevent connections from dropping and to kill stale connections.

Message Buffering
    Leverages core.async to buffer messages for us.

Encoding
    Serializes and de-serializes data for us.

Security
    Supports Ring anti-forgery middleware.

Let's add the dependency to our project.clj and get started:

guestbook-sente-setup/project.clj
```
[com.taoensso/sente "1.16.0"]
```

Upgrading the Server

We can now update the guestbook.routes.websockets namespace to use Sente to manage the server-side WebSocket connection. Let's update the dependencies to add taoensso.sente and taoensso.sente.server-adapters.http-kit references. Also, since Sente manages the serialization of data and the management of our connections, let's remove clojure.edn and org.httpkit.server.

guestbook-sente-setup/src/clj/guestbook/routes/websockets.clj
```
(ns guestbook.routes.websockets
  (:require
    [clojure.tools.logging :as log]
    [guestbook.messages :as msg]
    [guestbook.middleware :as middleware]
    [mount.core :refer [defstate]]
    [taoensso.sente :as sente]
    [taoensso.sente.server-adapters.http-kit :refer [get-sch-adapter]]))
```

We initialize Sente by calling the sente/make-channel-socket! function. This function accepts the server adapter and a map of initialization options. We pass in the HTTP Kit server adapter, since that's the server we're using, and we set the :user-id-fn option to use the :client-id key in the request parameters. The reason we have to specify our :user-id-fn is that Sente defaults to using the :uid key from the session. Since we aren't creating Ring sessions for our clients, we'll need to use something else. The :client-id is a UUID that's automatically generated for each Sente client, so it's a perfect fit for us.

guestbook-sente-setup/src/clj/guestbook/routes/websockets.clj
```
(defstate socket
  :start (sente/make-channel-socket!
           (get-sch-adapter)
           {:user-id-fn (fn [ring-req]
                          (get-in ring-req [:params :client-id]))}))

(defn send! [uid message]
  (println "Sending message: " message)
  ((:send-fn socket) uid message))
```

The sente/make-channel-socket! function returns a map that contains a number of variables that were initialized.

:ajax-post-fn

    The function that handles Ajax POST requests.

:ajax-get-or-ws-handshake-fn

    The function that negotiates the initial connection.

:ch-recv

    The receive channel for the socket.

:send-fn

    The function that's used to send push notifications to the client.

:connected-uids

    An atom containing the IDs of the connected clients.

We'll usually access the keys on our socket map using helper functions such as send!.

In our first implementation, we sent our guestbook message as a map of fields with no metadata. This restricted us to only one type of message. We should change this so that we can accept multiple message types. We also *must* change this because Sente will call our handler function whenever an event occurs, passing it a map with a bunch of metadata describing the event.

Let's do this with a *multimethod*:

guestbook-sente-setup/src/clj/guestbook/routes/websockets.clj
```
(defmulti handle-message (fn [{:keys [id]}]
                           id))

(defmethod handle-message :default
  [{:keys [id]}]
  (log/debug "Received unrecognized websocket event type: " id))
```

```
(defmethod handle-message :message/create!
  [{:keys [?data uid] :as message}]
  (let [response (try
                   (msg/save-message! ?data)
                   (assoc ?data :timestamp (java.util.Date.))
                   (catch Exception e
                     (let [{id      :guestbook/error-id
                            errors :errors} (ex-data e)]
                       (case id
                         :validation
                         {:errors errors}
                         ;;else
                         {:errors
                          {:server-error ["Failed to save message!"]}}))))]
    (if (:errors response)
      (send! uid [:message/creation-errors response])
      (doseq [uid (:any @(:connected-uids socket))]
        (send! uid [:message/add response])))))
(defn receive-message! [{:keys [id] :as message}]
  (log/debug "Got message with id: " id)
  (handle-message message))
```

We've replaced our old handle-message! function with a receive-message! function and a handle-message multimethod. We place any logic that applies to *all* events in our receive-message! wrapper function. It will call handle-message, which will dispatch to different methods based on the :id of the message.

Sente's event-message maps have some useful keys on them besides just :id.

event
> The full event vector.

id
> The ID keyword (first event).

?data
> The data sent in the event (second event).

send-fn
> A function to send a message via the socket this message was received from.

?reply-fn (Server Only)
> Sends an arbitrary response body to the callback function specified client-side (only exists if the client specified a callback function).

uid (Server Only)

A user-id (that is, may correspond to one or many connections. Is managed based on :user-id-fn; compare :client-id).

ring-req (Server Only)

The Ring request received in an Ajax post or the initial WebSocket hand-shake.

client-id (Server Only)

A client-id that is specific to a single connection.

Since send! only communicates with a single user, we must use a doseq if we want to broadcast messages. Now that we've got the meat of it set up, let's update how it connects to the rest of our application.

```clojure
guestbook-sente-setup/src/clj/guestbook/routes/websockets.clj
(defstate channel-router
  :start (sente/start-chsk-router!
          (:ch-recv socket)
          #'receive-message!)
  :stop (when-let [stop-fn channel-router]
          (stop-fn)))

(defn websocket-routes []
  ["/ws"
   {:middleware [middleware/wrap-csrf
                 middleware/wrap-formats]
    :get (:ajax-get-or-ws-handshake-fn socket)
    :post (:ajax-post-fn socket)}])
```

In addition to managing our socket, Sente provides a helper for creating a message router that passes incoming messages to our handler function. Since our router depends on the initialization of our socket, we have to define it as a defstate so that Mount knows to start our socket first before starting our router. Once we have our router initialized, the last step is to connect the socket to our web server. Unlike our from-scratch implementation Sente works well with Ring middlewares, so we use wrap-csrf and wrap-formats. It also has both :get and :post handler functions so that the client can use Ajax if it doesn't support WebSockets.

Upgrading the Client

Now that we've changed our server to use Sente, we need to update the client as well. Our client WebSocket connection will look similar to our server, with a few key differences. We'll use Mount on the client, as well, so we won't have to manually connect in our init! function. We'll have two defstate definitions: our socket and our router. We'll have a receive-message! function wrapping a handle-message multimethod. And we'll have a send! function for sending messages over our socket.

Let's start by updating our namespace declaration and creating our socket and send! function:

guestbook-sente-setup/src/cljs/guestbook/websockets.cljs
```
(ns guestbook.websockets
  (:require-macros [mount.core :refer [defstate]])
  (:require [re-frame.core :as rf]
            [taoensso.sente :as sente]
            mount.core))

(defstate socket
  :start (sente/make-channel-socket!
          "/ws"
          (.-value (.getElementById js/document "token"))
          {:type :auto
           :wrap-recv-evs? false}))

(defn send! [message]
  (if-let [send-fn (:send-fn @socket)]
    (send-fn message)
    (throw (ex-info "Couldn't send message, channel isn't open!"
                    {:message message}))))
```

Our call to make-channel-socket! looks a bit different. As the first argument, the web server adapter is replaced by a URL. The second argument, our CSRF token, is new. Since we're in the browser now, we need to send our CSRF token to ensure that our connection is secure. The last argument is an options map like we had on the server, but it has a different set of options available. The only ones we're passing for now are :type and wrap-recv-evs?. The :type option determines whether we use WebSockets or Ajax as the underlying connection method. Choose :auto to let Sente use whichever method it prefers. The wrap-recv-evs? option specifies whether we want to receive all application messages wrapped in an outer :chsk/recv event. Turn this off by passing false so that our client events are structured like our server events.

Our send! function looks similar to the server, but not quite the same. We're dereferencing our socket before using its :send-fn. This is a minor detail of how Mount works when targeting JavaScript rather than Java. This isn't for any interesting reason, so we'll just have to remember that we need to dereference any Mount states before using them in cljs.

Now that we have our socket set up, let's write our handle-message and receive-message! functions and connect them to a channel-router.

guestbook-sente-setup/src/cljs/guestbook/websockets.cljs

```clojure
(defmulti handle-message
  (fn [{:keys [id]} _]
    id))

(defmethod handle-message :message/add
  [_ msg-add-event]
  (rf/dispatch msg-add-event))

(defmethod handle-message :message/creation-errors
  [_ [_ response]]
  (rf/dispatch
   [:form/set-server-errors (:errors response)]))

;; -------------------------------------------------------------------
;; Default Handlers

(defmethod handle-message :chsk/handshake
  [{:keys [event]} _]
  (.log js/console "Connection Established: " (pr-str event)))

(defmethod handle-message :chsk/state
  [{:keys [event]} _]
  (.log js/console "State Changed: " (pr-str event)))

(defmethod handle-message :default
  [{:keys [event]} _]
  (.warn js/console "Unknown websocket message: " (pr-str event)))

;; -------------------------------------------------------------------
;; Router

(defn receive-message!
  [{:keys [id event] :as ws-message}]
  (do
    (.log js/console "Event Received: " (pr-str event))
    (handle-message ws-message event)))

(defstate channel-router
  :start (sente/start-chsk-router!
          (:ch-recv @socket)
          #'receive-message!)
  :stop (when-let [stop-fn @channel-router]
          (stop-fn)))
```

Our handle-message function is structured similarly to the one on our server, but instead of interacting with the database, it dispatches re-frame events based on the message received.

We also have to handle a couple Sente-specific events. The :chsk/handshake and :chsk/state events are related to the status of our connection. While they're important for notifying users about lost or spotty connections, we'll just log them in the console for now.

Now that we've sorted out our guestbook.websockets namespace, let's update guestbook.core to use it correctly so that we can get back to coding interactively.

```
guestbook-sente-setup/src/cljs/guestbook/core.cljs
(ns guestbook.core
  (:require
   ;;...
   [mount.core :as mount]))
;;...
(rf/reg-event-fx
 :message/send!
 (fn [{:keys [db]} [_ fields]]
   (ws/send! [:message/create! fields])
   {:db (dissoc db :form/server-errors)}))
;;...
(defn init! []
  (.log js/console "Initializing App...")
  (mount/start)
  (rf/dispatch [:app/initialize])
  (mount-components))
```

We required mount.core, called mount/start from our init! function and changed the value we sent from ws/send! in our :message/send! event. We finally have our app functionally migrated from our from-scratch WebSockets implementation over to Sente. Since we required a new library, we need to restart our app to load the new dependency. Once that's done, let's try it out. You might've noticed that our fields don't clear when we submit our form. That was intentionally left out because it's well suited to the callback feature of Sente.

Leveraging Sente Callbacks

Sente is primarily a WebSockets library, but it allows you to get the best of both the Ajax and WebSocket workflows. Generally speaking, having the server *push* the results of an action to all concerned parties is incredibly powerful, as it separates the concerns of keeping state synchronized from the logistics of client-server communication. But this starts to break down when we want information *about* our actions. In this case, the request/response model of Ajax is a better fit. Sente allows you to mix the two by specifying a callback function when you send a message from a client.

We have two behaviors that are related to the state of our actions: clearing fields after a message is successfully sent and displaying server errors after a message is rejected.

Let's update our code to use a reply function to accomplish these tasks.

First, we need to allow our client-side send! function to take multiple arguments:

guestbook-sente-cb/src/cljs/guestbook/websockets.cljs
```
(defn send! [& args]
  (if-let [send-fn (:send-fn @socket)]
    (apply send-fn args)
    (throw (ex-info "Couldn't send message, channel isn't open!"
                    {:message (first args)}))))
```

Next, we need to require [guestbook.websockets :as ws] and pass our timeout and our callback function from :message/send!:

guestbook-sente-cb/src/cljs/guestbook/core.cljs
```
(rf/reg-event-fx
 :message/send!
 (fn [{:keys [db]} [_ fields]]
   (ws/send!
    [:message/create! fields]
    10000
    (fn [{:keys [success errors] :as response}]
      (.log js/console "Called Back: " (pr-str response))
      (if success
        (rf/dispatch [:form/clear-fields])
        (rf/dispatch [:form/set-server-errors errors]))))
   {:db (dissoc db :form/server-errors)}))
```

Finally, we need to update our server to invoke the :?reply-fn on the message:

guestbook-sente-cb/src/clj/guestbook/routes/websockets.clj
```
(defmulti handle-message (fn [{:keys [id]}]
                           id))

(defmethod handle-message :default
  [{:keys [id]}]
  (log/debug "Received unrecognized websocket event type: " id)
  {:error (str "Unrecognized websocket event type: " (pr-str id))
   :id    id})

(defmethod handle-message :message/create!
  [{:keys [?data uid] :as message}]
  (let [response (try
                   (msg/save-message! ?data)
                   (assoc ?data :timestamp (java.util.Date.))
                   (catch Exception e
                     (let [{id      :guestbook/error-id
                            errors :errors} (ex-data e)]
                       (case id
                         :validation
                         {:errors errors}
                         ;;else
                         {:errors
                          {:server-error ["Failed to save message!"]}}))))]
```

```
    (if (:errors response)
      (do
        (log/debug "Failed to save message: " ?data)
        response)
      (do
        (doseq [uid (:any @(:connected-uids socket))]
          (send! uid [:message/add response]))
        {:success true})))))
(defn receive-message! [{:keys [id ?reply-fn]
                         :as   message}]
  (log/debug "Got message with id: " id)
  (let [reply-fn (or ?reply-fn (fn [_]))]
    (when-some [response (handle-message message)]
      (reply-fn response))))
```

There we go, that's much better. Our handle-message multimethod now returns a map that gets passed to the connection's reply-fn by receive-message! if it exists. Not only does this change handle the clearing of our fields, but it handles a bug we might've encountered later. We were sending the message errors to the :uid of the sender, which is correct as long as a :uid is exactly one connected client. This is currently the case, but when we add user accounts it won't be. A connection's :uid corresponds to *all* connections belonging to that user. This means that if a user were to submit a message from their desktop, errors would display in every one of their active connections (for example, their phone, their five other browser tabs,...). It would be even worse if we'd implemented clearing fields on success in the same way—users could lose long drafted messages in other windows on other devices! Luckily, using :?reply-fn is an easy and elegant way to handle *client*-specific concerns.

Events and Effects in Re-Frame

Now that we have our WebSockets layer all set up, let's get the rest of our re-frame stuff in order. Earlier, we accomplished the goal of making our application's view a computation of our app-db. Now, we want to go a step further and make sure that we properly separate *events* from *effects*.

Until now, we've been writing event handlers by using re-frame's built-in effects (for example, :db, :dispatch, and so on) and calling effectful functions where built-in effects fall short. We've gotten pretty far with this approach, but we need to improve this sooner or later. As we discussed earlier, re-frame's distinction between events and effects is crucial.

The Value of Isolating Effects

Our ultimate goal in using re-frame is to express any necessary complexity as pure functions and to make any necessary impurity as simple as possible. With our view, we separated the impure and fiddly rendering behavior from any and all application logic. We connected the two minimally; they only interact via dispatch and subscribe.

Actions are a bit trickier, but the goal is the same. We want to separate any impure and fiddly *effects*, such as Ajax, from our pure application logic (that is, our events). This allows us to inspect, wrap, and test our logic easily, since it'll just be a translation from a dispatched event vector to an event map. All our events should do is transform data.

Since we still need to do impure things (that is, *actually* send Ajax requests), we should make sure to keep the implementation as straightforward as possible. Just like our UI components, we want our effect handlers to be easy to read and understand despite their impurity.

Effect Handlers

To purify our events, we'll have to write some *effect handlers*. Let's start with an effect called :ws/send! that sends a WebSocket message and handles the callback for us.

Let's add the following to our guestbook.websockets namespace:

guestbook-re-frame-2/src/cljs/guestbook/websockets.cljs
```
(defn send! [& args]
  (if-let [send-fn (:send-fn @socket)]
    (apply send-fn args)
    (throw (ex-info "Couldn't send message, channel isn't open!"
                    {:message (first args)}))))

(rf/reg-fx
 :ws/send!
 (fn [{:keys [message timeout callback-event]
       :or {timeout 30000}}]
   (if callback-event
     (send! message timeout #(rf/dispatch (conj callback-event %)))
     (send! message))))
```

Then let's update our event handlers in guestbook.core:

guestbook-re-frame-2/src/cljs/guestbook/core.cljs
```
(rf/reg-event-fx
 :message/send!-called-back
 (fn [_ [_ {:keys [success errors]}]]
   (if success
```

```
      {:dispatch [:form/clear-fields]}
      {:dispatch [:form/set-server-errors errors]})))
(rf/reg-event-fx
 :message/send!
 (fn [{:keys [db]} [_ fields]]
   {:db (dissoc db :form/server-errors)
    :ws/send! {:message [:message/create! fields]
               :timeout 10000
               :callback-event [:message/send!-called-back]}}))
```

Now, instead of calling a function inside of our event handler, we simply add the :ws/send! key to our returned map. Let's try it out in the browser.

Great! We can now see our effect in the fx tab. This is nice, but we get much more than this. Since our effect is data, we can transform it with interceptors. Also, since effect handling is registered from event handling, we can change the way effects are handled across all of our events.

We've also changed our API a bit. The :ws/send! effect takes a callback event instead of a callback function. This restricts what can be done on reply, but it means that we can see exactly what will be dispatched.

Now that we've got our :message/send! purified, let's move on to :messages/load. We need to write a separate effect to handle HTTP requests. Some implementations are available as libraries, such as re-frame-http-fx,[16] but let's write a spartan GET effect on our own:

guestbook-re-frame-2/src/cljs/guestbook/core.cljs
```
(rf/reg-fx
 :ajax/get
 (fn [{:keys [url success-event error-event success-path]}]
   (GET url
        (cond-> {:headers {"Accept" "application/transit+json"}}
          success-event (assoc :handler
                               #(rf/dispatch
                                  (conj success-event
                                        (if success-path
                                          (get-in % success-path)
                                          %))))))
```

---

16. https://github.com/Day8/re-frame-http-fx

```
        error-event   (assoc :error-handler
                          #(rf/dispatch
                             (conj error-event %)))))))

(rf/reg-event-fx
 :messages/load
 (fn [{:keys [db]} _]
   {:db (assoc db :messages/loading? true)
    :ajax/get {:url "/api/messages"
               :success-path [:messages]
               :success-event [:messages/set]}}))
```

This is fairly similar to our :ws/send! effect. We have a URL instead of a message, and we have two types of callback event: :success-event and :error-event. We've also added a small convenience in :success-path. It allows us to specify a path in the response we'd like to pass to our :success-event rather than just passing the whole thing. This means we can keep using :messages/set as our event instead of adding an intermediate event to process our response.

The separation we've introduced is nice, but we won't feel the benefits too much at this scale. This approach to managing actions will really start to pay off once our application grows, and adopting it this early is much easier than switching over later.

Using Reagent Atoms to Reduce Event Noise

Now that our events are pure, let's come back to our earlier :on-change dispatch. As we've been using re-frame-10x, you've probably noticed that as soon as we start typing, our event history gets blown up unnecessarily. This is because our input is *directly* connected to our re-frame db. This is okay with components like checkboxes or dropdowns since :on-change happens once per user change. But text inputs call :on-change every time a character is entered.

We can mitigate this by using a local atom and a Reagent track. A Reagent track is pretty much like a re-frame derived subscription, but it works with any dereffables, not just subscriptions. Let's start with our text input.

guestbook-re-frame-2/src/cljs/guestbook/core.cljs
```
(defn text-input [{val    :value
                   attrs :attrs
                   :keys [on-save]}]
  (let [draft (r/atom nil)
        value (r/track #(or @draft @val ""))]
    (fn []
      [:input.input
       (merge attrs
              {:type :text
               :on-focus #(reset! draft (or @val ""))
```

```
                    :on-blur (fn []
                              (on-save (or @draft "")) 
                              (reset! draft nil))
                    :on-change #(reset! draft (.. % -target -value))
                    :value @value})])))
;;...

(defn message-form []
  [:div
    ;;...
    [text-input {:attrs {:name :name}
                  :value (rf/subscribe [:form/field :name])
                  :on-save #(rf/dispatch [:form/set-field :name %])}]
    ;;...
    ])
```

We have a draft atom that contains nil until we focus it. value is a track that's either the draft or value from our re-frame subscription. Finally, when we unfocus our component, the draft is "saved" by the on-save function. Let's see it in action.

As we edit the field, we can see no events have been dispatched in our re-frame-10x panel. But when we unfocus the field, we see a single [:form/set-field] event fire. Since we only save when we blur our input, it only happens once.

Next, let's create a textarea version:

```
guestbook-re-frame-2/src/cljs/guestbook/core.cljs
(defn textarea-input [{val    :value
                          attrs :attrs
                          :keys [on-save]}]
  (let [draft (r/atom nil)
         value (r/track #(or @draft @val ""))]
     (fn []
       [:textarea.textarea
        (merge attrs
               {:on-focus #(reset! draft (or @val ""))
                :on-blur (fn []
                              (on-save (or @draft ""))
                              (reset! draft nil))
                :on-change #(reset! draft (.. % -target -value))
                :value @value})])))
;;...

(defn message-form []
  [:div
   ;;...
    [textarea-input
     {:attrs {:name :message}
      :value (rf/subscribe [:form/field :message])
      :on-save #(rf/dispatch [:form/set-field :message %])}]
    ;;...
   ])
```

This is the same as the text input, but it has some parts changed.

What You've Learned

We've got our project set up nicely now, and it'll pay dividends. Having your service API and front end easily inspectable and testable will make you more efficient and improve your understanding. We also haven't sacrificed anything because we've been careful about keeping development tools separate from our production profile.

We've also learned quite a bit about separating our application into layers. By modeling our application as a series of layers with data flowing through them, we can reason about them independently and enhance them easily. We took advantage of this by swapping out some Ajax requests for live Web-Socket connections.

We now have all the tools we need to build a robust Clojure(Script) web application. In the next chapter, we'll draft a plan for upgrading our guestbook application into our very own microblogging application.

CHAPTER 6

Planning Our Application

We've got a good foundation for our application, now let's decide what our final application will be.

For the remainder of this book, we'll take our guestbook application and grow it into our very own microblogging platform. We'll add accounts, feeds, likes, tags, media, and all of the things you'd expect from a modern social media platform.

This is a lot to do, so we need to plan how to tackle this bit by bit. Let's start by brainstorming features that we might want, then we'll trim them down to core functionality so we have a place to start.

What's in Our MVP?

Since we're building a microblogging platform, we have some obvious requirements. We'll have multiple users, each having an account. These users will create content and engage with other users' content. Engagement could take multiple forms, such as liking, sharing, commenting on posts, or tagging users.

The core architecture of any social media platform is going to take the same shape. Before a user does anything, they have to have an account. Once registered, users create content that is consumed and shared by others across the network.

Regardless of the direction our application takes, we'll need to implement these core features.

Core Features

Let's break down the core of a social media platform into five categories.

Account Management
  Users should be able to register, log in, and perform permitted actions.

Content Creation
> Users should be able to compose posts and replies.

Passive Consumption
> Users should be able to view a global and a personal feed.

Sharing and Discovery
> Users should be able to share, tag, and search posts.

Personalization
> Users should be able to change their display name, profile picture, and other attributes.

Most features we add will belong to one or more of these categories. Let's make sure that we have a strong foundation for each so that we can safely build upon it.

Account Management

Until now, our application used a simplistic approach to account management. All we have are author names, supplied by users for each message. To provide the features we want, we need a more robust approach toward accounts. Moreover, this component is absolutely necessary before anyone can meaningfully engage with our app.

Accounts have several vital purposes, especially access control and ownership. Since these both apply to most aspects of our application, we need to be especially thoughtful as we implement this functionality.

Our first concern is security. We want to ensure that we safeguard sensitive data, such as personal information. We also want to restrict access in a standard and uniform way so that it's hard to mess up.

Our second concern is identity. Any data generated by a user has to be associated with their identity. This includes post authorship, account preferences, and so on.

Both of these are far reaching, and they'll see many changes as our application grows. We'll need to keep this in mind as we flesh out our other features.

First and foremost, we need to separate users from messages. We'll do this by creating a separate users table and replacing the author column with a reference to a user.

Next, we'll need to allow users to create and manage their accounts. This means adding login, registration, and profile pages.

Finally, we'll need to restrict page access to authenticated and authorized users. To accomplish this, we'll add middleware to manage access to restricted routes.

Content Creation

This is how applications become relevant. Without content, a social media platform is nothing.

Our current content creation options are very limited. Users can only post messages, and there isn't even a concept of a user account.

At a minimum, we need to associate each post with its author. This allows us to do many things. We can allow authors to edit or delete their posts. We can view posts by author. Authors can track engagement with their posts.

We also want posts to be more interesting to create. This could include media embedding and custom formatting. To do this, we'll switch from plain text posts to Markdown. We can gradually implement parts of Markdown's spec as we add new features.

The core purpose of social media is user interaction. All we have so far is a single shared timeline. To support rich user interactions, we'll add the ability to reply to posts.

Passive Consumption

Passive consumption starts on the home page. Users will see their feed here if authenticated or the global feed if not. It's the face of our application, and this is where most users will spend most of their time. It should be pleasant to use and serve as a gateway to the rest of our application.

To this end, we'll be spending a great deal of our front-end work on this section, so it better be flexible and easy to work with.

A large part of usability is giving users quick access to the content they want to see. Content curation is an interesting UX problem—we want to streamline the process without restricting users too much. One obvious way of grouping posts is by user, but as our app evolves we'll want to add new ways to categorize and consume content.

Sharing and Discovery

Once we have users on the platform, we want to enable them to grow and refine their network. We'll do so by allowing users to re-post content they like, thereby sharing it with their followers. We'll also have tags and shared timelines so that users can actively seek out content. Also, we want to ensure that we take full advantage of the rest of the blogosphere; it should be easy to share and embed posts from our platform elsewhere.

The possibilities are endless, but we'll start with re-posts because it's the simplest form of sharing.

Personalization

We also want to allow users to personalize their experience, which may include setting a profile picture, UI theme, and so on.

This could apply to many different parts of our application, so we should consider it up front. We'll start with a profile picture and display name, along with a profile settings page to change them. As we add personalization features, we'll enhance our profile settings page accordingly.

The Elephant in the Room

Upon reviewing our core features, some core concerns jump out.

We need a great deal of flexibility in many parts of our app, such as user profiles and posts. Additionally, we need a way of working with some complex relationships, such as posts written by or re-posted by users that are followed.

Our next objective is to design our application's data model, but first we should address these concerns. The key shortfall of our current implementation is H2. It has served us well so far, but it's missing some key features we want, the most notable being PostgreSQL's JSONB type.

Before we get started, you need a running PostgreSQL instance. Take a look at Appendix 4, Database Access, on page 395, first if you need to set one up.

Let's start by creating a role and a database for our guestbook. Connect to the psql shell, and do the following:

```
CREATE USER guestbook WITH PASSWORD 'password';
CREATE DATABASE guestbook WITH OWNER guestbook;
```

Then let's change our application config to contain our new database URL:

guestbook-postgres/dev-config.edn
```
{:dev true
 :port 3000
 :nrepl-port 7000

 :database-url
 "postgresql://localhost:5432/guestbook?user=guestbook&password=password"}
```

And add the PostgreSQL driver dependency to our project.clj:

guestbook-postgres/project.clj
```
[org.postgresql/postgresql "42.2.18"]
```

Next, we restart our app and rewrite our migrations for Postgres. Let's start up our application's REPL and generate some new migration files. Since we're going to have multiple tables, let's rename our guestbook table to posts.

```
user> (create-migration "create-posts-table")
nil
user>
```

Now let's write our migrations based on our old ones.

guestbook-postgres/resources/migrations/20190916013321-create-posts-table.up.sql
```
CREATE TABLE posts
(id SERIAL PRIMARY KEY,
 name text not null,
 message text not null,
 timestamp TIMESTAMP not null DEFAULT now());
```

guestbook-postgres/resources/migrations/20190916013321-create-posts-table.down.sql
```
DROP TABLE posts;
```

Looks pretty similar, but you'll notice a couple syntactic differences. We used the serial type for our primary key instead of integer ... AUTO_INCREMENT, and we used now() instead of CURRENT_TIMESTAMP. These mean the same thing but are just syntactic differences between H2 and Postgres. We also added some not null constraints to our columns because they're nice to have. We'll make some further adjustments as our data model becomes more concrete, but we'll stay as close as we can to our H2 version for now.

Then, make sure to delete the old migration files; they're redundant and won't work with Postgres.

Now we just have to change our table name in our queries.sql file:

guestbook-postgres/resources/sql/queries.sql
```
-- :name save-message! :! :n
-- :doc creates a new message using the name and message keys
INSERT INTO posts
(name, message)
VALUES (:name, :message)

-- :name get-messages :? :*
-- :doc selects all available messages
SELECT * from posts
```

That should be all. Let's start up our application from the REPL, run our migrations, reload our queries, and make sure they work:

```
user> (start)
{:started [...]}
user> (migrate)
...
nil
user> (in-ns 'guestbook.db.core)
#namespace[guestbook.db.core]
guestbook.db.core> (conman/bind-connection *db* "sql/queries.sql")
{...}
guestbook.db.core> (save-message! {:name "Postgres"
                                   :message "An elephant never forgets."})
1
guestbook.db.core> (get-messages)
({:id 1,
  :name "Postgres",
  :message "An elephant never forgets.",
  :timestamp #inst "..."})
guestbook.db.core>
```

Everything is working as expected. Congratulations! You successfully switched to Postgres.

As a final optional step, let's look at how we can get the data from our H2 instance into Postgres. Since we removed our H2 URL from our config and changed our queries, we have to manually use next.jdbc. We can specify a custom connection by calling next.jdbc/get-datasource and passing it a connection specification map. We call next.jdbc.sql/query with our H2 connection to get all of our messages, then we call next.jdbc.sql/insert-multi! with our Postgres connection to place them in the posts table.

```
guestbook.db.core> (require '[next.jdbc :as jdbc]
                            '[next.jdbc.sql :as sql]
                            '[next.jdbc.result-set :as rs])
nil
guestbook.db.core> (->>
                   (sql/query
                     (jdbc/with-options
                       (jdbc/get-datasource
                         {:jdbcUrl "jdbc:h2:./guestbook_dev.db"})
                       {:builder-fn rs/as-unqualified-lower-maps})
                     ["select name, message, timestamp from guestbook"])
                   (mapv (juxt :name :message :timestamp))
                   (sql/insert-multi! *db* :posts
                    [:name :message :timestamp]))
```

```
({:id 2,
  :name "Alice",
  :message "Hello, Bob!",
  :timestamp #inst "..."}
 {:id 3,
  :name "Bob",
  :message "Oh! Hi, Alice!",
  :timestamp #inst "..."})
guestbook.db.core>
```

Note that we didn't select the id column from guestbook, since that would conflict with the message we added earlier. We don't need the message IDs to stay the same, so we let Postgres generate new ones.

Now that we're completely done with H2 we can remove our H2 driver dependency:

guestbook-postgres/project.clj
```
[com.h2database/h2 "1.4.200"]
```

That's it! We're fully migrated to Postgres now. We haven't covered its features yet, but we'll discuss them as we need them. Now that we have a full-featured database, let's build out our data model.

Data Modeling

Now that we have a database that properly supports our desired features, let's create a data model that supports the commonalities and that can be extended to support all of them.

As we discussed in Account Management, on page 160, account management impacts many parts of our app and should be tackled first. We have a users table, which will be referenced by posts and by other users in multiple ways. Let's think about which columns are essential and which columns we might add later.

We definitely need login and password columns, and we want a created_at column for auditing and metadata.

In the future, we'll probably want to add a bunch of user data, such as username, avatar, last login, and so on, but we'll address those later.

Let's create a migration for our users table with login, password, and created_at.

```
guestbook.db.core> (in-ns 'user)
#namespace[user]
user> (create-migration "add-users-table")
nil
user>
```

guestbook-postgres-2/resources/migrations/20190919232336-add-users-table.up.sql
```
CREATE TABLE users
(login text PRIMARY KEY,
 password text not null,
 created_at TIMESTAMP not null DEFAULT now());
```

guestbook-postgres-2/resources/migrations/20190919232336-add-users-table.down.sql
```
DROP TABLE users;
```

That's all the migrations we'll write for now, but let's take a moment to think through how our data model will evolve as we grow our application.

First, let's take a look at posts. We'll eventually replace the name column with a reference to a user in the users table, add an optional parent post to facilitate replies, and update message to use richer encoding to support additional features, such as embedded media.

Then let's think through users. We'll want to add a username or display-name, we'll want to add an avatar, we'll want a user profile, and we'll want to store preferences.

Finally, we'll have a number of rich relationships between our entities. We'll want relationships between users such as follows and blocks. And we'll want relationships beteen users and posts such as stars and boosts.

Adding User Management

Before we can move forward, we need to address the user management aspect of our application. We'll start by implementing the service endpoints for user registration and authentication. From there, we'll build the corresponding UI components.

Service Endpoints

Let's start by running the migration we wrote in Data Modeling, on page 165, if you haven't done so already:

```
user> (migrate)
... INFO  migratus.core - Starting migrations
...
... INFO  migratus.core - Ending migrations
nil
user>
```

Now let's update our queries.sql to create and look up users. Note, we need to hash and salt our password *before* we pass it to our insert statement, so we add an asterisk to the end of the name to denote that we shouldn't call it directly.

```
guestbook-postgres-2/resources/sql/queries.sql
-- :name create-user!* :! :n
-- :doc creates a new user with the provided login and hashed password
INSERT INTO users
(login, password)
VALUES (:login, :password)

-- :name get-user-for-auth* :? :1
-- :doc selects a user for authentication
SELECT * FROM users
WHERE login = :login
```

Next, let's create a new namespace for managing accounts, authentication, and authorization called guestbook.auth. We need to include a new dependency for managing our cryptography first.

```
guestbook-postgres-2/project.clj
[buddy "2.0.0"]
```

The encryption library we'll be using, Buddy,[1] has many useful features for working with passwords and authentication/authorization. Its buddy.hashers/derive and buddy.hashers/check functions allow us to work with passwords easily and securely. The derive function generates a salt, hashes the salted password, and joins the chosen algorithm, salt, and hashed password into a single string. The check function compares the supplied password against the hashed one, managing the details for us

Since we've added a new dependency, we have to restart our app. Once we've done so, let's create our guestbook.auth namespace and write create-user! and authenticate-user functions using our new queries.

```
guestbook-postgres-2/src/clj/guestbook/auth.clj
(ns guestbook.auth
  (:require
   [buddy.hashers :as hashers]
   [next.jdbc :as jdbc]
   [guestbook.db.core :as db]))

(defn create-user! [login password]
  (jdbc/with-transaction [t-conn db/*db*]
    (if-not (empty? (db/get-user-for-auth* t-conn {:login login}))
      (throw (ex-info "User already exists!"
                      {:guestbook/error-id ::duplicate-user
                       :error "User already exists!"}))
      (db/create-user!* t-conn
                        {:login    login
                         :password (hashers/derive password)}))))
```

---

1. https://github.com/funcool/buddy

```
(defn authenticate-user [login password]
  (let [{hashed :password :as user} (db/get-user-for-auth* {:login login})]
    (when (hashers/check password hashed)
      (dissoc user :password))))
```

Note that we're using a db transaction in create-user! to ensure that our queries are performed atomically. We're checking if a user exists explicitly so that we can throw a more informative error than the default.

Now that we have our auth functions written, let's try them out from the REPL:

```
user> (in-ns 'guestbook.auth)
#namespace[guestbook.auth]
guestbook.auth> (create-user! "testuser" "testpass")
1
guestbook.auth> (authenticate-user "testuser" "testpass")
{:login "testuser", :created_at #inst "2019-09-20T02:22:53.217-00:00"}
guestbook.auth> (authenticate-user "testuser" "wrongpass")
nil
guestbook.auth>
```

Good! We're able to create a user, and we authenticate only when our password is correct.

Next, let's add a simple login route to our API. We start by requiring our guestbook.auth namespace from guestbook.routes.services:

guestbook-postgres-2/src/clj/guestbook/routes/services.clj
```
[guestbook.auth :as auth]
```

Then let's add the "/api/login" route to our API (inside service-routes):

guestbook-postgres-2/src/clj/guestbook/routes/services.clj
```
["/login"
 {:post {:parameters
         {:body
          {:login string?
           :password string?}}
         :responses
         {200
          {:body
           {:identity
            {:login string?
             :created_at inst?}}}
          401
          {:body
           {:message string?}}}
         :handler
         (fn [{{{:keys [login password]} :body} :parameters
               session                           :session}]
```

```
(if-some [user (auth/authenticate-user login password)]
  (->
   (response/ok
    {:identity user})
   (assoc :session (assoc session
                          :identity
                          user)))
  (response/unauthorized
   {:message "Incorrect login or password."})))}}]
```

We've written our handler that wraps our guestbook.auth/authenticate-user function and provides informative HTTP status codes and error messages. Let's try it out in Swagger UI:

First, try the credentials we created earlier:

Response Content Type application/edn   ▽

Parameters

Parameter	Value	Description	Parameter Type	Data Type

body	{:login "testuser"
	:password "testpass"}
			body	Model
				
				inline_model {
				  login (string),
				  password (string)
				}

	Parameter content type: application/edn ▽			

Response Messages

HTTP Status Code	Reason	Response Model	Headers
401		Example Value {	

[Try it out!]

Curl

```
curl -X POST --header 'Content-Type: application/edn' --header 'Accept: application/edn' -d '{:login "testuser" \
 :password "testpass"}' 'http://localhost:3000/api/login'
```

Request URL

```
http://localhost:3000/api/login
```

Response Body

```
{:identity {:login "testuser", :created at #inst "2021-02-27T23:36:06.242-00:00"}}
```

We get a 200 OK response with our account info.

Now let's try an incorrect password as shown in the figure on page 170.

We get a 401 Unauthorized response with a helpful error message.

Now, let's add a user registration route:

guestbook-postgres-2/src/clj/guestbook/routes/services.clj

```clojure
["/register"
 {:post {:parameters
         {:body
          {:login string?
           :password string?
           :confirm string?}}
         :responses
         {200
          {:body
           {:message string?}}
          400
          {:body
           {:message string?}}
          409
          {:body
           {:message string?}}}
         :handler
         (fn [{{{:keys [login password confirm]} :body} :parameters}]
           (if-not (= password confirm)
             (response/bad-request
```

```
            {:message
             "Password and Confirm do not match."})
          (try
            (auth/create-user! login password)
            (response/ok
             {:message
              "User registration successful. Please log in."})
            (catch clojure.lang.ExceptionInfo e
              (if (= (:guestbook/error-id (ex-data e))
                     ::auth/duplicate-user)
                (response/conflict
                 {:message
                  "Registration failed! User with login already exists!"})
                (throw e))))))}}]
```

We've wrapped guestbook.auth/create-user! with logic that checks if our password and confirm are equal, attempts to create a new user, and catches our custom error. Let's try it out in Swagger UI:

First, try creating a new account:

We get a 200 OK response with our success message.

Now let's try creating a user that already exists:

We get a 409 Conflict response with our error message.

Finally, let's see what happens when we provide an incorrect :confirm value as shown in the first figure on page 173.

We get a 400 Bad Request response with a helpful error message.

Finally, let's add a simple logout route:

guestbook-postgres-2/src/clj/guestbook/routes/services.clj

```
["/logout"
 {:post {:handler
         (fn [_]
           (->
            (response/ok)
            (assoc :session nil)))}}]
```

Everything is working as expected, as shown in the second figure on page 173. Now we can move on to building UI components that work with these endpoints.

Response Content Type [application/edn   ▼]

Parameters

Parameter	Value	Description	Parameter Type	Data Type

body	{:login "testuser3"
	:password "testpass"
	:confirm "wrongpass"}
	
	Parameter content type:
	[application/edn ▼]
			body	Model Example Value
				
				inline_model_2 {
				    login (string),
				    password (string),
				    confirm (string)
				}

Response Messages

HTTP Status Code	Reason	Response Model	Headers
400		Example Value	
409		Example Value	

[Try it out!]

Curl

```
curl -X POST --header 'Content-Type: application/edn' --header 'Accept: application/edn' -d '{:login    "testuser3" \
    :password "testpass" \
    :confirm  "wrongpass"}' 'http://localhost:3000/api/register'
```

Request URL

```
http://localhost:3000/api/register
```

Response Body

```
{:message "Password and Confirm do not match."}
```

Response Code

```
400
```

[POST] /api/logout

Response Messages

HTTP Status Code	Reason	Response Model	Headers
default			

[Try it out!]

Curl

```
curl -X POST --header 'Content-Type: application/json' --header 'Accept: application/octet-stream' 'http://localhost:38
```

Request URL

```
http://localhost:3000/api/logout
```

Response Body

```
no content
```

Response Code

```
200
```

Client

Now that we have our login and registration endpoints fully functional, let's add login and registration to our SPA. We start by adding the login and register buttons to the right side of our navbar. Clicking these buttons displays the relevant modal.

Currently our app renders our navbar on the server. The simplest way to modify the navbar using ClojureScript is to remove all server-side rendering and move any layout from HTML into our Reagent component. We aren't using the placeholder about page, so let's delete about.html and then move our navbar and and container components into ClojureScript.

Let's update our base.html as follows:

```
guestbook-postgres-2/resources/html/base.html
<!DOCTYPE html>
<html>
  <head>
    <meta charset="UTF-8"/>
    <meta name="viewport" content="width=device-width, initial-scale=1">
    <title>Welcome to guestbook</title>

    <!-- styles -->
    {% style "/assets/bulma/css/bulma.min.css" %}
    {% style "/assets/material-icons/css/material-icons.min.css" %}

    {% style "/css/screen.css" %}
  </head>
  <body>

      {% block content %}
      {% endblock %}

    <!-- scripts -->
    {% block page-scripts %}
    {% endblock %}
  </body>
</html>
```

Then we create two Reagent components, navbar and app. The navbar component will be the exact same navbar for now, and the app component will contain navbar and wrap home in a section and a container:

```
guestbook-postgres-2/src/cljs/guestbook/core.cljs
(defn navbar []
  (let [burger-active (r/atom false)]
    (fn []
      [:nav.navbar.is-info
       [:div.container
        [:div.navbar-brand
```

```
      [:a.navbar-item
       {:href "/"
        :style {:font-weight "bold"}}
       "guestbook"]
      [:span.navbar-burger.burger
       {:data-target "nav-menu"
        :on-click #(swap! burger-active not)
        :class (when @burger-active "is-active")}
       [:span]
       [:span]
       [:span]]]
     [:div#nav-menu.navbar-menu
      {:class (when @burger-active "is-active")}
      [:div.navbar-start
       [:a.navbar-item
        {:href "/"}
        "Home"]]]]])))

(defn app []
  [:div.app
   [navbar]
   [:section.section
    [:div.container
     [home]]]])
```

And finally, let's update our call to reagent.core/render to use our app component instead of home:

guestbook-postgres-2/src/cljs/guestbook/core.cljs
```
(defn ^:dev/after-load mount-components []
  (rf/clear-subscription-cache!)
  (.log js/console "Mounting Components...")
  (dom/render [#'app] (.getElementById js/document "content"))
  (.log js/console "Components Mounted!"))
```

Adding Login

Now that our navbar is rendering on the client, let's add our login modal. The first thing we need to do is create a modal component that wraps Bulma modals:

guestbook-login/src/cljs/guestbook/core.cljs
```
(rf/reg-event-db
 :app/show-modal
 (fn [db [_ modal-id]]
   (assoc-in db [:app/active-modals modal-id] true)))

(rf/reg-event-db
 :app/hide-modal
 (fn [db [_ modal-id]]
   (update db :app/active-modals dissoc modal-id)))

(rf/reg-sub
 :app/active-modals
```

```
  (fn [db _]
    (:app/active-modals db {}))))
(rf/reg-sub
 :app/modal-showing?
 :<- [:app/active-modals]
 (fn [modals [_ modal-id]]
   (get modals modal-id false)))
(defn modal-card [id title body footer]
  [:div.modal
   {:class (when @(rf/subscribe [:app/modal-showing? id]) "is-active")}
   [:div.modal-background
    {:on-click #(rf/dispatch [:app/hide-modal id])}]
   [:div.modal-card
    [:header.modal-card-head
     [:p.modal-card-title title]
     [:button.delete
      {:on-click #(rf/dispatch [:app/hide-modal id])}]]
    [:section.modal-card-body
     body]
    [:footer.modal-card-foot
     footer]]])
(defn modal-button [id title body footer]
  [:div
   [:button.button.is-primary
    {:on-click #(rf/dispatch [:app/show-modal id])}
    title]
   [modal-card id title body footer]])
```

We have two modal events, show and hide. These events add and remove entries in a map that tracks all active modals. We're only adding true as a value for now, but theoretically we could place arguments to our modal rendering function instead. We then have two subscriptions, one that gets our active modals map and one that gets a specific modal if it's active.

Our simplest modal component, modal-card, takes an id along with some contents and displays if the modal is active. Then, since our login and registration modals will be spawned by clicking a button, we have a wrapper called modal-button. This component creates a button that triggers :app/show-modal and a modal-card component.

Note that the way we're managing modals is specific to Bulma CSS. Larger apps or apps that use different CSS frameworks may require having a multi-method as a registry of modal types along with a subscription used by a single global modal component to specify the modal type and contents to be displayed.

Now that we have a modal component, let's create our login modal-button, along with a user nameplate, a logout button, and any required re-frame events or subscriptions:

guestbook-login/src/cljs/guestbook/core.cljs

```clojure
(rf/reg-event-db
 :auth/handle-login
 (fn [db [_ {:keys [identity]}]]
   (assoc db :auth/user identity)))

(rf/reg-event-db
 :auth/handle-logout
 (fn [db _]
   (dissoc db :auth/user)))

(rf/reg-sub
 :auth/user
 (fn [db _]
   (:auth/user db)))

(defn login-button []
  (r/with-let
    [fields (r/atom {})
     error  (r/atom nil)

     do-login
     (fn [_]
       (reset! error nil)
       (POST "/api/login"
             {:headers {"Accept" "application/transit+json"}
              :params @fields
              :handler (fn [response]
                         (reset! fields {})
                         (rf/dispatch [:auth/handle-login response])
                         (rf/dispatch [:app/hide-modal :user/login]))
              :error-handler (fn [error-response]
                               (reset! error
                                       (or
                                        (:message (:response error-response))
                                        (:status-text error-response)
                                        "Unknown Error")))}))]
    [modal-button :user/login
     ;; Title
     "Log In"
     ;; Body
     [:div
      (when-not (string/blank? @error)
        [:div.notification.is-danger
         @error])
      [:div.field
       [:div.label "Login"]
       [:div.control
```

```clojure
      [:input.input
       {:type "text"
        :value (:login @fields)
        :on-change #(swap! fields assoc :login (.. % -target -value))}]]]
     [:div.field
      [:div.label "Password"]
      [:div.control
       [:input.input
        {:type "password"
         :value (:password @fields)
         :on-change #(swap! fields assoc :password (.. % -target -value))
         ;; Submit login form when `Enter` key is pressed
         :on-key-down #(when (= (.-keyCode %) 13)
                          (do-login))}]]]]
    ;; Footer
    [:button.button.is-primary.is-fullwidth
     {:on-click do-login
      :disabled (or (string/blank? (:login @fields))
                    (string/blank? (:password @fields)))}
     "Log In"]]))

(defn logout-button []
  [:button.button
   {:on-click #(POST "/api/logout"
                     {:handler (fn [_]
                                  (rf/dispatch [:auth/handle-logout]))})}
   "Log Out"])

(defn nameplate [{:keys [login]}]
  [:button.button.is-primary
   login])
```

We've added :auth/user to our re-frame db, the :auth/handle-login and :auth/handle-logout events to modify it, and the :auth/user subscription to access it. Our markup is straightforward, but we have some bundled logic and state. We've written our Ajax logic inside of our login and logout components. This is generally discouraged, but since login and logout are necessarily isolated, it makes sense to keep it contained. Although we chose plain Reagent to keep it simple, it would be just as valid to handle this workflow using re-frame.

Now let's add our buttons to the navbar so we can see what they look like:

```clojure
guestbook-login/src/cljs/guestbook/core.cljs
(defn navbar []
  (let [burger-active (r/atom false)]
    (fn []
      [:nav.navbar.is-info
       [:div.container
        [:div.navbar-brand
         [:a.navbar-item
          {:href "/"
```

```
           :style {:font-weight "bold"}}
          "guestbook"]
        [:span.navbar-burger.burger
         {:data-target "nav-menu"
          :on-click #(swap! burger-active not)
          :class (when @burger-active "is-active")}
         [:span]
         [:span]
         [:span]]]
       [:div#nav-menu.navbar-menu
        {:class (when @burger-active "is-active")}
        [:div.navbar-start
         [:a.navbar-item
          {:href "/"}
          "Home"]]
        [:div.navbar-end
         [:div.navbar-item
          (if-some [user @(rf/subscribe [:auth/user])]
            [:div.buttons
             [nameplate user]
             [logout-button]]
            [:div.buttons
             [login-button]])]]]]]])))
```

Now that we've done the login modal, registration should be straightforward:

guestbook-register/src/cljs/guestbook/core.cljs
```
(defn register-button []
  (r/with-let
    [fields (r/atom {})
     error  (r/atom nil)

     do-register
     (fn [_]
       (reset! error nil)
       (POST "/api/register"
             {:headers {"Accept" "application/transit+json"}
              :params @fields
              :handler (fn [response]
                         (reset! fields {})
                         (rf/dispatch [:app/hide-modal :user/register])
                         (rf/dispatch [:app/show-modal :user/login]))
              :error-handler (fn [error-response]
                               (reset! error
                                       (or
                                        (:message (:response error-response))
                                        (:status-text error-response)
                                        "Unknown Error")))}))]
    [modal-button :user/register
     ;; Title
     "Create Account"
```

```
    ;; Body
    [:div
     (when-not (string/blank? @error)
       [:div.notification.is-danger
        @error])
     [:div.field
      [:div.label "Login"]
      [:div.control
       [:input.input
        {:type "text"
         :value (:login @fields)
         :on-change #(swap! fields assoc :login (.. % -target -value))}]]]
     [:div.field
      [:div.label "Password"]
      [:div.control
       [:input.input
        {:type "password"
         :value (:password @fields)
         :on-change #(swap! fields assoc :password (.. % -target -value))}]]]
     [:div.field
      [:div.label "Confirm Password"]
      [:div.control
       [:input.input
        {:type "password"
         :value (:confirm @fields)
         :on-change #(swap! fields assoc :confirm (.. % -target -value))
         ;; Submit login form when `Enter` key is pressed
         :on-key-down #(when (= (.-keyCode %) 13)
                         (do-register))}]]]]
    ;; Footer
    [:button.button.is-primary.is-fullwidth
     {:on-click do-register
      :disabled (or (string/blank? (:login @fields))
                    (string/blank? (:password @fields))
                    (string/blank? (:confirm @fields)))}
     "Create Account"]]))
```

Next, let's add our registration button to our navbar, like so:

guestbook-register/src/cljs/guestbook/core.cljs

```
(defn navbar []
  (let [burger-active (r/atom false)]
    (fn []
      [:nav.navbar.is-info
       [:div.container
        [:div.navbar-brand
         [:a.navbar-item
          {:href "/"
           :style {:font-weight "bold"}}
          "guestbook"]
         [:span.navbar-burger.burger
```

```
      {:data-target "nav-menu"
       :on-click #(swap! burger-active not)
       :class (when @burger-active "is-active")}
      [:span]
      [:span]
      [:span]]]
    [:div#nav-menu.navbar-menu
     {:class (when @burger-active "is-active")}
     [:div.navbar-start
      [:a.navbar-item
       {:href "/"}
       "Home"]]
     [:div.navbar-end
      [:div.navbar-item
       (if-some [user @(rf/subscribe [:auth/user])]
         [:div.buttons
          [nameplate user]
          [logout-button]]
         [:div.buttons
          [login-button]
          [register-button]])]]]]]))))
```

Our registration modal is almost identical to our login modal; we've just added the :confirm field, changed the URL, and tweaked the success handler.

Finally, you might've noticed that we no longer display the logged in user if we refresh the page.

Let's fix that by loading our user from the session if we have one.

We start by requiring spec-tools.data-spec in our guestbook.routes.services namespace. We'll see how it comes in handy in a moment.

guestbook-session/src/clj/guestbook/routes/services.clj
```
[spec-tools.data-spec :as ds]
```

Then add an endpoint under /api/session to fetch our current session if it exists:

guestbook-session/src/clj/guestbook/routes/services.clj
```
["/session"
 {:get
  {:responses
   {200
    {:body
     {:session
      {:identity
       (ds/maybe
         {:login string?
          :created_at inst?})}}}}}
   :handler
   (fn [{{:keys [identity]} :session}]
```

```
(response/ok {:session
               {:identity
                (not-empty
                 (select-keys identity [:login :created_at]))}})))}}]
```

We need to be careful about what we return to the client. We should explicitly specify what is sent so that we're sure we're not leaking any sensitive data. We used spec-tools.data-spec/maybe in our response spec to indicate that we might not have an identity available.

Now let's load this information when we load our page:

guestbook-session/src/cljs/guestbook/core.cljs
```
(rf/reg-event-fx
 :app/initialize
 (fn [_ _]
   {:db {:messages/loading? true
         :session/loading? true}
    :dispatch-n [[:session/load] [:messages/load]]}))
;;...
(rf/reg-event-fx
 :session/load
 (fn [{:keys [db]} _]
   {:db (assoc db :session/loading? true)
    :ajax/get {:url "/api/session"
               :success-path [:session]
               :success-event [:session/set]}}))
;;...
(rf/reg-event-db
 :session/set
 (fn [db [_ {:keys [identity]}]]
   (assoc db
          :auth/user identity
          :session/loading? false)))

(rf/reg-sub
 :session/loading?
 (fn [db _]
   (:session/loading? db)))
```

Finally, let's update our navbar to depend on whether our session is loading or not:

guestbook-session/src/cljs/guestbook/core.cljs
```
(rf/reg-sub
 :auth/user-state
 :<-[:auth/user]
 :<-[:session/loading?]
 (fn [[user loading?]]
   (cond
     (true? loading?) :loading
```

```
        user            :authenticated
        :else           :anonymous)))
(defn navbar []
  (let [burger-active (r/atom false)]
    (fn []
      [:nav.navbar.is-info
       [:div.container
        [:div.navbar-brand
         [:a.navbar-item
          {:href "/"
           :style {:font-weight "bold"}}
          "guestbook"]
         [:span.navbar-burger.burger
          {:data-target "nav-menu"
           :on-click #(swap! burger-active not)
           :class (when @burger-active "is-active")}
          [:span]
          [:span]
          [:span]]]
        [:div#nav-menu.navbar-menu
         {:class (when @burger-active "is-active")}
         [:div.navbar-start
          [:a.navbar-item
           {:href "/"}
           "Home"]]
         [:div.navbar-end
          [:div.navbar-item
           (case @(rf/subscribe [:auth/user-state])
             :loading
             [:div {:style {:width "5em"}}
              [:progress.progress.is-dark.is-small {:max 100} "30%"]]

             :authenticated
             [:div.buttons
              [nameplate @(rf/subscribe [:auth/user])]
              [logout-button]]

             :anonymous
             [:div.buttons
              [login-button]
              [register-button]])]]]]])))
```

There we go, all better.

What You've Learned

We've learned how to identify the core components of our application without restricting future enhancements. We covered the standard approach for account management in Clojure, including cryptographic best practices.

In the next chapter, we'll build upon the foundation we laid down. We'll deliver the core features we described in our MVP. We'll leverage our users table by adding authors to posts and requiring users to be authenticated in order to compose posts. Once we do that, we'll have all the scaffolding necessary to add interesting features on demand. Then we'll incrementally grow our pet project into a full-fledged social media application.

CHAPTER 7

Account Management

At this point, we have users set up, but we aren't doing much with them. In this chapter, we'll associate posts with their authors, enrich the user model (for example, avatar and display name), and add an account management page. Our goal is to implement user accounts and leverage user profiles across the application. This includes creating an author page that includes a bio and a banner image and an account management page for adding and modifying a user profile.

Authorship

Currently, posts have an author name associated with them, but there's no association with an account. Let's add that relationship so that we can enhance posts to include elements from the author's profile.

Associate Messages with Accounts

Let's think about what the author relationship will look like. Is an author *always* present? Not necessarily. What if an account is deleted? What if we want to allow anonymous posts? All these concerns can be addressed by creating an optional foreign key and handling posts without it.

Also, since we're constructing the expected message rather than getting it back from the save-message! function, we need to update this behavior in two different places: Ajax and WebSockets. We can do better than this, especially now that we have PostgreSQL. Let's add a RETURNING clause to our SQL so that we get all of our data exactly as it is in the database. Then we'll be able to return the full message from our save-message! function, and any generation will be in one place.

Let's start by creating a migration that will add the relevant column to our posts table:

guestbook-author/resources/migrations/20200126004141-alter-posts-add-author-column.up.sql
```
ALTER TABLE posts
  ADD COLUMN author TEXT
    REFERENCES users(login)
    ON DELETE SET NULL
    ON UPDATE CASCADE;
```

Don't forget the down migration:

guestbook-author/resources/migrations/20200126004141-alter-posts-add-author-column.down.sql
```
ALTER TABLE posts
  DROP COLUMN author;
```

Then let's update our save-message! SQL to accept an identity and add our RETURNING clause:

guestbook-author/resources/sql/queries.sql
```
-- :name save-message! :<! :1
-- :doc creates a new message using the name and message keys
INSERT INTO posts
(author, name, message)
VALUES (:author, :name, :message)
RETURNING *;
```

Now update guestbook.messages/save-message! to accept an identity:

guestbook-author/src/clj/guestbook/messages.clj
```
(defn save-message! [{:keys [login]} message]
  (if-let [errors (validate-message message)]
    (throw (ex-info "Message is invalid"
                    {:guestbook/error-id :validation
                     :errors errors}))
    (db/save-message! (assoc message :author login))))
```

Then we update routes/services.clj to pass in the identity from the session and return our newly authored :post:

guestbook-author/src/clj/guestbook/routes/services.clj
```
(fn [{{params :body} :parameters
      {:keys [identity]} :session}]
  (try
    (->> (msg/save-message! identity params)
         (assoc {:status :ok} :post)
         (response/ok))
    (catch Exception e
      (let [{id      :guestbook/error-id
             errors :errors} (ex-data e)]
        (case id
          :validation
```

```
(response/bad-request {:errors errors})
;;else
(response/internal-server-error
 {:errors
 {:server-error ["Failed to save message!"]}})))))))
```

Lastly, we need to update routes/websockets.clj to pass the identity to save-message!—but we have a problem: the only session map we have is from when we first opened our connection! We need a way to access our session from our handle-message methods, but this is impossible with the default session middleware configuration. Luckily, it's easy to provide our own session store so it can be accessed where necessary.

guestbook-author/src/clj/guestbook/session.clj
```
(ns guestbook.session
  (:require
   [ring-ttl-session.core :refer [ttl-memory-store]]))

(defonce store (ttl-memory-store (* 60 30)))

(defn ring-req->session-key [req]
  (get-in req [:cookies "ring-session" :value]))

(defn read-session [req]
  (.read-session store (ring-req->session-key req)))

(defn write-session [req v]
  (.write-session store (ring-req->session-key req) v))
```

Now that we have an accessible session store, we need to pass it to wrap-defaults instead of the default ring-ttl-session generated by Luminus:

guestbook-author/src/clj/guestbook/middleware.clj
```
(ns guestbook.middleware
  (:require
   ;;...
   [guestbook.session :as session]))
;;...
(defn wrap-base [handler]
  (-> ((:middleware defaults) handler)
      (wrap-defaults
        (-> site-defaults
            (assoc-in [:security :anti-forgery] false)
            (assoc-in [:session :store] session/store)))
      wrap-internal-error))
```

Next, let's update our guestbook.routes.websockets/receive-message! function to read the session directly from the session store and associate it onto the message map that's passed to handle-message:

guestbook-author/src/clj/guestbook/routes/websockets.clj
```
(defn receive-message! [{:keys [id ?reply-fn ring-req]
                         :as   message}]
  (log/debug "Got message with id: " id)
  (let [reply-fn (or ?reply-fn (fn [_]))
        session (session/read-session ring-req)
        response (-> message
                     (assoc :session session)
                     handle-message)]
    (when response
      (reply-fn response)))))
```

Finally, update the :message/create! method of handle-message to pass the identity from the session to msg/save-message!:

guestbook-author/src/clj/guestbook/routes/websockets.clj
```
(defmethod handle-message :message/create!
  [{:keys [?data uid session] :as message}]
  (let [response (try
                   (msg/save-message! (:identity session) ?data)
                   ;;...
```

There we go. We have accounts associated on the server side.

Next, let's update our client to show the author's handle next to the name.

guestbook-author/src/cljs/guestbook/core.cljs
```
(defn message-list [messages]
  [:ul.messages
   (for [{:keys [timestamp message name author]} @messages]
     ^{:key timestamp}
     [:li
      [:time (.toLocaleString timestamp)]
      [:p message]
      [:p " - " name]
      ;; Add the author (e.g. <@username>)
      " <"
      (if author
        (str "@" author)
        [:span.is-italic "account not found"])
      ">"]])])
```

All done! Our posts should now look like the figure on page 189.

Next, we'll prevent anonymous users from posting.

Restrict Posting to Authenticated Users

Currently, we're able to pass a null author. We decided this may be allowed later, but let's disable it for now.

If we were just using Ajax through our Ring handler, we'd use default middle-ware provided by Buddy,[1] but we have to make sure that WebSocket messages are properly restricted as well. We can deal with this by writing our own authorization functions.

Let's start by adding some authorization functions to our guestbook.auth namespace, keeping as much logic as possible protocol agnostic.

guestbook-authorization/src/clj/guestbook/auth.clj
```clojure
(defn identity->roles [identity]
  (cond-> #{:any}
    (some? identity) (conj :authenticated)))

(def roles
  {:message/create! #{:authenticated}
   :auth/login #{:any}
   :auth/logout #{:any}
   :account/register #{:any}
   :session/get #{:any}
   :messages/list #{:any}
   :swagger/swagger #{:any}})
```

We need two things to decide if authorization checks out: the roles that belong to the user performing the request and the roles authorized to perform the request. Our identity->roles function takes a user's identity and returns a set of roles to which that user belongs. Our roles map defines the roles that can perform each action.

Next, let's create two new namespaces: guestbook.auth.ring for Ring-specific authorization and guestbook.auth.ws for WebSocket-specific authorization.

First, guestbook.auth.ring:

---

1.   https://github.com/funcool/buddy

guestbook-authorization/src/clj/guestbook/auth/ring.clj

```
(ns guestbook.auth.ring
  (:require
    [clojure.tools.logging :as log]
    [guestbook.auth :as auth]
    [reitit.ring :as ring]))

(defn authorized? [roles req]
  (if (seq roles)
    (->> req
         :session
         :identity
         auth/identity->roles
         (some roles)
         boolean)
    (do
      (log/error "roles: " roles " is empty for route: " (:uri req))
      false)))

(defn get-roles-from-match [req]
  (-> req
      (ring/get-match)
      (get-in [:data ::auth/roles] #{})))

(defn wrap-authorized [handler unauthorized-handler]
  (fn [req]
    (if (authorized? (get-roles-from-match req) req)
      (handler req)
      (unauthorized-handler req))))
```

Then guestbook.auth.ws:

guestbook-authorization/src/clj/guestbook/auth/ws.clj

```
(ns guestbook.auth.ws
  (:require
    [guestbook.auth :as auth]))

(defn authorized? [roles-by-id msg]
  (boolean
    (some (roles-by-id (:id msg) #{})
          (-> msg
              :session
              :identity
              (auth/identity->roles)))))
```

We start by applying our authorization logic to our WebSocket message handler. First, we need to require guestbook.auth and guestbook.auth.ws:

guestbook-authorization/src/clj/guestbook/routes/websockets.clj

```
[guestbook.auth :as auth]
[guestbook.auth.ws :refer [authorized?]]
```

Then we update our receive-message! function to apply our authorization logic to all messages *except* system ones:

```
guestbook-authorization/src/clj/guestbook/routes/websockets.clj
(defn receive-message! [{:keys [id ?reply-fn ring-req]
                         :as   message}]
  (case id
    :chsk/bad-package   (log/debug "Bad Package:\n" message)
    :chsk/bad-event     (log/debug "Bad Event: \n" message)
    :chsk/uidport-open  (log/trace (:event message))
    :chsk/uidport-close (log/trace (:event message))
    :chsk/ws-ping       nil
    ;; ELSE
    (let [reply-fn (or ?reply-fn (fn [_]))
          session (session/read-session ring-req)
          message (-> message
                      (assoc :session session))]
      (log/debug "Got message with id: " id)
      (if (authorized? auth/roles message)
        (when-some [response (handle-message message)]
          (reply-fn response))
        (do
          (log/info "Unauthorized message: " id)
          (reply-fn {:message "You are not authorized to perform this action!"
                     :errors {:unauthorized true}}))))))
```

We have a case statement which handles our system messages, and any other messages get checked with authorized? and handled accordingly. This means that we have to explicitly allow any new message types, which makes it difficult to accidentally break our authorization rules. Since our unauthorized error is handled outside handle-message, we can't provide a specific error message like we do with :message/create!. Let's just return :unauthorized true and let the client set the message text.

Finally, we can remove our handle-message method for :chsk/ws-ping, since we're handling it directly from receive-message! now.

Now let's add authorization to our API routes.

First, we require the necessary namespaces:

```
guestbook-authorization/src/clj/guestbook/routes/services.clj
[guestbook.auth.ring :refer [wrap-authorized get-roles-from-match]]
[clojure.tools.logging :as log]
```

Then let's add our middleware function with an unauthorized handler provided:

guestbook-authorization/src/clj/guestbook/routes/services.clj
```
(defn service-routes []
  ["/api"
   {:middleware [;;...
                 (fn [handler]
                   (wrap-authorized
                    handler
                    (fn handle-unauthorized [req]
                      (let [route-roles (get-roles-from-match req)]
                        (log/debug
                         "Roles for route: "
                         (:uri req)
                         route-roles)
                        (log/debug "User is unauthorized!"
                                   (-> req
                                       :session
                                       :identity
                                       :roles))
                      (response/forbidden
                       {:message
                        (str "User must have one of the following roles: "
                             route-roles)})))))))]
    :muuntaja formats/instance
    :coercion spec-coercion/coercion
    :swagger {:id ::api}}
   ;; API routes ...
   ])
```

Finally, we use our roles map to set :guestbook.auth/roles on each endpoint:

guestbook-authorization/src/clj/guestbook/routes/services.clj
```
["" {:no-doc true
     ::auth/roles (auth/roles :swagger/swagger)}
 ["/swagger.json"
  {:get (swagger/create-swagger-handler)}]
 ["/swagger-ui*"
  {:get (swagger-ui/create-swagger-ui-handler
         {:url "/api/swagger.json"})}]]
;;...
["/login"
 {::auth/roles (auth/roles :auth/login)
  ;;...}]
  ;;...
["/logout"
 {::auth/roles (auth/roles :auth/logout)
  ;;...}]
  ;;...
["/register"
 {::auth/roles (auth/roles :account/register)
  ;;...}]
  ;;...
```

```
["/session"
 {::auth/roles (auth/roles :session/get)
  ;;...}]
  ;;...
["/messages"
 {::auth/roles (auth/roles :messages/list)
  ;;...}]
  ;;...
["/message"
 {::auth/roles (auth/roles :message/create!)
  ;;...}]
  ;;...
```

Now, like we did in WebSockets, we're checking authorization on each API call and returning an unauthorized response if it fails. Also, we're returning unauthorized if there are no roles provided on :guestbook.auth/roles. Again, this is to prevent accidentally breaking authorization rules by requiring that they be specified in order for the endpoint to be usable.

Now that we have our authorization set up, let's make sure our client shows any errors to the user.

Let's add an :unauthorized errors component, and let's update errors-component to take an optional second parameter, message, which allows us to set a message explicitly.

guestbook-authorization/src/cljs/guestbook/core.cljs
```
(defn errors-component [id & [message]]
  (when-let [error @(rf/subscribe [:form/error id])]
    [:div.notification.is-danger (if message
                                   message
                                   (string/join error))]]))
;;...

(defn message-form []
  [:div
   [errors-component :server-error]
   [errors-component :unauthorized "Please log in before posting."]
   ;;...])
```

Now we have a generic error for message posting authorization, but ideally we shouldn't even let users try if they aren't logged in. Let's wrap our message-form in a case statement that only displays it if a user is logged in; it displays a prompt to login or register otherwise. We used this pattern in our navbar component, and we'll use it again in home.

guestbook-authorization/src/cljs/guestbook/core.cljs
```
(defn home []
  (let [messages (rf/subscribe [:messages/list])]
    (fn []
```

```
[:div.content>div.columns.is-centered>div.column.is-two-thirds
 [:div.columns>div.column
  [:h3 "Messages"]
  [message-list messages]]
 [:div.columns>div.column
  [reload-messages-button]]
 [:div.columns>div.column
  (case @(rf/subscribe [:auth/user-state])
    :loading
    [:div {:style {:width "5em"}}
     [:progress.progress.is-dark.is-small {:max 100} "30%"]]

    :authenticated
    [message-form]

    :anonymous
    [:div.notification.is-clearfix
     [:span "Log in or create an account to post a message!"]
     [:div.buttons.is-pulled-right
      [login-button]
      [register-button]]])]])))
```

There we go. Let's check the browser to see how that looks:

Now users can't post messages until they log in, and even if authorization becomes more complicated, a message will still show up.

Add API Endpoint for Posts by Author

Any new message we receive now has an author associated with it. This is incredibly useful and is the cornerstone of nearly every successful social media platform. Let's build some API endpoints to make use of this new relationship.

We start by adding a SQL query to get messages by author:

guestbook-author-2/resources/sql/queries.sql
```
-- :name get-messages-by-author :? :*
-- :doc selects all messages posted by a user
SELECT * from posts
WHERE author = :author
```

Then we write a wrapper function in guestbook.messages:

guestbook-author-2/src/clj/guestbook/messages.clj
```
(defn messages-by-author [author]
  {:messages (vec (db/get-messages-by-author {:author author}))})
```

Next, we write an endpoint in guestbook.routes.services to fetch the messages:

guestbook-author-2/src/clj/guestbook/routes/services.clj
```
["/messages"
 {::auth/roles (auth/roles :messages/list)}
 ["" {:get
      {:responses
       {200
        {:body ;; Data Spec for response body
         {:messages
          [{:id pos-int?
            :name string?
            :message string?
            :timestamp inst?}]}}}
       :handler
       (fn [_]
         (response/ok (msg/message-list)))}}]
 ["/by/:author"
  {:get
   {:parameters {:path {:author string?}}
    :responses
    {200
     {:body ;; Data Spec for response body
      {:messages
       [{:id pos-int?
         :name string?
         :message string?
         :timestamp inst?}]}}}
    :handler
    (fn [{{{:keys [author]} :path} :parameters}]
      (response/ok (msg/messages-by-author author)))}}]]
```

Notice that we've updated the /api/messages route to have two children which share the same authorization. This means that as we add additional ways to search messages, we can place them all under the same parent route so that they can share configuration. Also notice that we haven't updated our spec to include our :author key. It will still work because clojure.spec is open, meaning that additional keys are ignored.

Let's try it out with Swagger to make sure it works as shown in the figure on page 196.

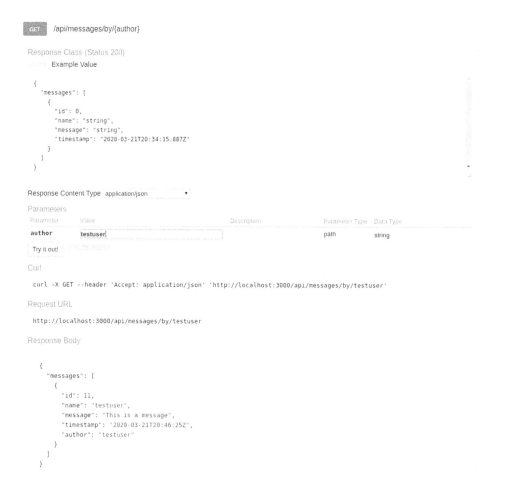

Looks good.

Now that we have that sorted, let's add an author page that displays all posts by a given author.

Add Author's Posts Page

Now that we have posts associated with authors, it'd be nice to have a page for each author. Let's add a new page to our client that shows all posts for a specific user. To accomplish this, we need to change the code that's run based on the URL we load. Our task includes two parts. First, we need to ensure that all of our front-end URLs return the same HTML, so that our ClojureScript can control what happens. Second, we need some conditional logic to change behavior based on the URL. Additionally, although it isn't strictly necessary, we'd like to prevent our page from fully reloading anytime we navigate. We'll do this by leveraging the HTML5 history API to change what happens on page navigation.

To do this, we'll be using the front-end module of Reitit,[2] the routing library we've been using on the server.

Setting Up Front-End Routing

The first thing we need to do is get a trivial routing setup that simply wraps our main page. Let's start by requiring the namespaces we'll be using:

guestbook-author-2/src/cljs/guestbook/core.cljs
```
(ns guestbook.core
  (:require
   ;;...
   [reitit.coercion.spec :as reitit-spec]
   [reitit.frontend :as rtf]
   [reitit.frontend.easy :as rtfe]
   ;;...))
```

Then let's create our routes and our router:

guestbook-author-2/src/cljs/guestbook/core.cljs
```
(def routes
  ["/"
   ["" {:name ::home
        :view home}]])

(def router
  (rtf/router
   routes
   {:data {:coercion reitit-spec/coercion}}))
```

Now we need a way to connect our router to our browser URL and to re-frame. Let's write a :router/navigated event to be fired after browser navigation, write a :router/current-route subscription to access our current route, and then connect our event and our router to the HTML5 history API by using reitit.frontend.easy/start!:

guestbook-author-2/src/cljs/guestbook/core.cljs
```
(rf/reg-event-db
 :router/navigated
 (fn [db [_ new-match]]
   (assoc db :router/current-route new-match)))

(rf/reg-sub
 :router/current-route
 (fn [db]
   (:router/current-route db)))

(defn init-routes! []
```

---

2. https://metosin.github.io/reitit/frontend/basics.html

```
  (rtfe/start!
   router
   (fn [new-match]
     (when new-match
       (rf/dispatch [:router/navigated new-match])))
   {:use-fragment false}))
;;...
(defn ^:dev/after-load mount-components []
  (rf/clear-subscription-cache!)
  (.log js/console "Mounting Components...")
  (init-routes!)
  (dom/render [#'app] (.getElementById js/document "content"))
  (.log js/console "Components Mounted!"))
```

Finally, we need to modify our app component to reflect the state of the current route:

```
guestbook-author-2/src/cljs/guestbook/core.cljs
(defn page [{{:keys [view name]} :data
             path                 :path}]
  [:section.section>div.container
   (if view
     [view]
     [:div "No view specified for route: " name " (" path ")"])])

(defn app []
  (let [current-route @(rf/subscribe [:router/current-route])]
    [:div.app
     [navbar]
     [page current-route]]))
```

Great! We now have our router initializing, and we're responding to the changes to the current route from our main Reagent component via the re-frame db. As we add individual pages to routes, they'll work seamlessly.

We haven't changed our app's behavior in any noticable way. Let's add a dummy page to stand in for our author page so we can see what's going on.

```
guestbook-author-3/src/cljs/guestbook/core.cljs
(defn author []
  [:div
   [:p "This page hasn't been implemented yet!"]
   [:a {:href "/"} "Return home"]])

(def routes
  ["/"
   [""
    {:name ::home
     :view home}]
   ["user/:user"
    {:name ::author
     :view author}]])
```

Then add a link to this new page from our message-list component:

```
guestbook-author-3/src/cljs/guestbook/core.cljs
(defn message-list [messages]
  [:ul.messages
   (for [{:keys [timestamp message name author]} @messages]
     ^{:key timestamp}
     [:li
      [:time (.toLocaleString timestamp)]
      [:p message]
      [:p " - " name
       ;; Add the author (e.g. <@username>)
       " <"
       (if author
         [:a {:href (str "/user/" author)} (str "@" author)]
         [:span.is-italic "account not found"])
       ">"]])])
```

Now if we click one of these URLs, we should see a page like this:

Looks like everything is working, but we missed something. If you try refreshing this page, you'll get a 404 response! We forgot to update our server to respond to all of our valid front-end routes with our app page.

We can accomplish this in multiple ways. The most thorough way is to define your front-end routes in a cljc file and have each match respond with our app. Alternatively, you could have a top-level path (for example, /app/) which always responds with our app and prefixes all front-end routes with it. Or you could have a default route that responds with our app if no other match is found.

Before we get too far ahead of ourselves, we're gonna take a moment to move our front-end routes to a cljc file. While we're at it, we should organize our front-end code so that it doesn't get out of hand as it grows.

Sharing Routes Across Client and Server

We're about to refactor our ClojureScript pretty substantially, so let's map out what we want to put where. First, we move our routes declaration into src/cljc/guestbook/routes/app.cljc so that it can be referenced from the server in addition to the client. Inside our routes, we also define a top-level :get handler for the Clojure version based on the home-page we defined in guestbook.routes.home.

guestbook-cljc-routing/src/cljc/guestbook/routes/app.cljc
```clojure
(ns guestbook.routes.app
  (:require
   #?@(:clj [[guestbook.layout :as layout]
             [guestbook.middleware :as middleware]]
       :cljs [[guestbook.views.home :as home]
              [guestbook.views.author :as author]])))

#?(:clj
   (defn home-page [request]
     (layout/render
      request
      "home.html")))

(defn app-routes []
  [""
   #?(:clj {:middleware [middleware/wrap-csrf]
            :get home-page})
   ["/"
    (merge
     {:name ::home}
     #?(:cljs
        {:view #'home/home}))]
   ["/user/:user"
    (merge
     {:name ::author}
     #?(:cljs {:view #'author/author}))]])
```

If you're unfamiliar with #? and #?@ reader conditionals, see Reader Conditionals, on page 384, for more details. Additionally, we've used #' in front of our views. This denotes a resolved var, so that if our view declarations change, these changes will be reloaded properly. Otherwise, routes will keep the stale definition of the views even if our code is reloaded.

Next, we update guestbook.handler to reference guestbook.routes.app/app-routes instead of guestbook.routes.home/home-routes:

guestbook-cljc-routing/src/clj/guestbook/handler.clj
```clojure
(ns guestbook.handler
  (:require
   ;;...
   [guestbook.routes.app :refer [app-routes]]
   ;;...))
;;...
```

```
(mount/defstate routes
  :start
  (ring/ring-handler
    (ring/router
     [(app-routes)
      ;;...])
     ;;...))
;;...

(defn app []
  (middleware/wrap-base #'routes))
```

Notice that we had to rename our app-routes state since it conflicts with the app-routes we just added. This isn't a problem, since it's not referenced from outside this namespace. We'll just have to remember to restart our app once we're finished refactoring.

Now we can delete guestbook.routes.home, since it's been replaced.

That's it for the server and the cljc, now let's refactor our ClojureScript. We structure our ClojureScript files like so:

```
src/cljs/guestbook/
├── ajax.cljs
├── auth.cljs
├── core.cljs
├── messages.cljs
├── modals.cljs
├── views
│   ├── author.cljs
│   └── home.cljs
└── websockets.cljs
```

Let's start with the guestbook.views.* namespaces, since they're referenced from our cljc. The views/ directory will have a file corresponding to each page we have in our application—just author and home for now. Each file will contain the top-level component for the page, in addition to any components and logic that are tightly coupled to that page.

This is what guestbook.views.home should look like:

guestbook-cljc-routing/src/cljs/guestbook/views/home.cljs
```
(ns guestbook.views.home
  (:require
   [re-frame.core :as rf]
   [guestbook.messages :as messages]
   [guestbook.auth :as auth]))
```

```clojure
(defn home [_]
  (let [messages (rf/subscribe [:messages/list])]
    (fn []
      [:div.content>div.columns.is-centered>div.column.is-two-thirds
       [:div.columns>div.column
        [:h3 "Messages"]
        [messages/message-list messages]]
       [:div.columns>div.column
        [messages/reload-messages-button]]
       [:div.columns>div.column
        (case @(rf/subscribe [:auth/user-state])
          :loading
          [:div {:style {:width "5em"}}
           [:progress.progress.is-dark.is-small {:max 100} "30%"]]

          :authenticated
          [messages/message-form]

          :anonymous
          [:div.notification.is-clearfix
           [:span "Log in or create an account to post a message!"]
           [:div.buttons.is-pulled-right
            [auth/login-button]
            [auth/register-button]]])]])))
```

And this is what guestbook.views.author should look like:

guestbook-cljc-routing/src/cljs/guestbook/views/author.cljs

```clojure
(ns guestbook.views.author)

(defn author [match]
  [:div
   [:p "This page hasn't been implemented yet!"]
   [:a {:href "/"} "Return home"]])
```

Now let's look at the namespaces referenced by our home view, starting with guestbook.messages:

guestbook-cljc-routing/src/cljs/guestbook/messages.cljs

```clojure
(ns guestbook.messages
  (:require
   [clojure.string :as string]
   [reagent.core :as r]
   [re-frame.core :as rf]
   [guestbook.validation :refer [validate-message]]))

;; All code is copied in from guestbook.core

(rf/reg-event-fx
 :messages/load
 (fn [{:keys [db]} _]
   {:db (assoc db :messages/loading? true)
    :ajax/get {:url "/api/messages"
```

```
                        :success-path [:messages]
                        :success-event [:messages/set]}}}))
(rf/reg-event-db
 :messages/set
 (fn [db [_ messages]]
   (-> db
       (assoc :messages/loading? false
              :messages/list messages))))
(rf/reg-sub
 :messages/loading?
 (fn [db _]
   (:messages/loading? db)))
(rf/reg-sub
 :messages/list
 (fn [db _]
   (:messages/list db [])))
(defn reload-messages-button []
  ;; Copied from guestbook.core...
  )
(defn message-list [messages]
  ;; Copied from guestbook.core...
  )
(rf/reg-event-db
 :message/add
 (fn [db [_ message]]
   (update db :messages/list conj message)))
(rf/reg-event-db
 :form/set-field
 [(rf/path :form/fields)]
 (fn [fields [_ id value]]
   (assoc fields id value)))
(rf/reg-event-db
 :form/clear-fields
 [(rf/path :form/fields)]
 (fn [_ _]
   {}))
(rf/reg-sub
 :form/fields
 (fn [db _]
   (:form/fields db)))
(rf/reg-sub
 :form/field
 :<- [:form/fields]
 (fn [fields [_ id]]
   (get fields id)))
```

```clojure
(rf/reg-event-db
 :form/set-server-errors
 [(rf/path :form/server-errors)]
 (fn [_ [_ errors]]
   errors))

(rf/reg-sub
 :form/server-errors
 (fn [db _]
   (:form/server-errors db)))

(rf/reg-sub
 :form/validation-errors
 :<- [:form/fields]
 (fn [fields _]
   (validate-message fields)))

(rf/reg-sub
 :form/validation-errors?
 :<- [:form/validation-errors]
 (fn [errors _]
   (not (empty? errors))))

(rf/reg-sub
 :form/errors
 :<- [:form/validation-errors]
 :<- [:form/server-errors]
 (fn [[validation server] _]
   (merge validation server)))

(rf/reg-sub
 :form/error
 :<- [:form/errors]
 (fn [errors [_ id]]
   (get errors id)))

(rf/reg-event-fx
 :message/send!-called-back
 (fn [_ [_ {:keys [success errors]}]]
   (if success
     {:dispatch [:form/clear-fields]}
     {:dispatch [:form/set-server-errors errors]})))

(rf/reg-event-fx
 :message/send!
 (fn [{:keys [db]} [_ fields]]
   {:db (dissoc db :form/server-errors)
    :ws/send! {:message [:message/create! fields]
               :timeout 10000
               :callback-event [:message/send!-called-back]}}))
```

```clojure
(defn errors-component [id & [message]]
  (when-let [error @(rf/subscribe [:form/error id])]
    [:div.notification.is-danger (if message
                                   message
                                   (string/join error))]))

(defn text-input [{val   :value
                   attrs :attrs
                   :keys [on-save]}]
  ;; Copied from guestbook.core...
  )

(defn textarea-input [{val   :value
                       attrs :attrs
                       :keys [on-save]}]
  ;; Copied from guestbook.core...
  )

(defn message-form []
  ;; Copied from guestbook.core...
  )
```

This namespace contains everything pertaining to our messages. It has the re-frame events for fetching and setting our message-list and for managing and submitting our message-form. It also has the subscriptions and components for viewing our messages.

Next we have guestbook.auth:

guestbook-cljc-routing/src/cljs/guestbook/auth.cljs
```clojure
(ns guestbook.auth
  (:require
   [clojure.string :as string]
   [reagent.core :as r]
   [re-frame.core :as rf]
   [guestbook.modals :as m]
   [ajax.core :refer [POST]]))

(rf/reg-event-fx
 :session/load
 (fn [{:keys [db]} _]
   {:db (assoc db :session/loading? true)
    :ajax/get {:url "/api/session"
               :success-path [:session]
               :success-event [:session/set]}}))

(rf/reg-event-db
 :session/set
 (fn [db [_ {:keys [identity]}]]
   (assoc db
          :auth/user identity
          :session/loading? false)))
```

```
(rf/reg-sub
 :session/loading?
 (fn [db _]
   (:session/loading? db)))

(rf/reg-event-db
 :auth/handle-login
 (fn [db [_ {:keys [identity]}]]
   (assoc db :auth/user identity)))

(rf/reg-event-db
 :auth/handle-logout
 (fn [db _]
   (dissoc db :auth/user)))

(rf/reg-sub
 :auth/user
 (fn [db _]
   (:auth/user db)))

(rf/reg-sub
 :auth/user-state
 :<- [:auth/user]
 :<- [:session/loading?]
 (fn [[user loading?]]
   (cond
     (true? loading?) :loading
     user             :authenticated
     :else            :anonymous)))

(defn login-button []
  ;; Copied from guestbook.core...
  )

(defn logout-button []
  [:button.button
   {:on-click #(POST "/api/logout"
                {:handler (fn [_] (rf/dispatch [:auth/handle-logout]))})}
   "Log Out"])

(defn nameplate [{:keys [login]}]
  [:button.button.is-primary
   login])

(defn register-button []
  ;; Copied from guestbook.core...
  )
```

This namespace references our modal implementation in guestbook.modals and contains all logic and components related to the user and the session.

Here's what guestbook.modals looks like:

guestbook-cljc-routing/src/cljs/guestbook/modals.cljs

```clojure
(ns guestbook.modals
  (:require
   [re-frame.core :as rf]))

(rf/reg-event-db
 :app/show-modal
 (fn [db [_ modal-id]]
   (assoc-in db [:app/active-modals modal-id] true)))

(rf/reg-event-db
 :app/hide-modal
 (fn [db [_ modal-id]]
   (update db :app/active-modals dissoc modal-id)))

(rf/reg-sub
 :app/active-modals
 (fn [db _]
   (:app/active-modals db {})))

(rf/reg-sub
 :app/modal-showing?
 :<- [:app/active-modals]
 (fn [modals [_ modal-id]]
   (get modals modal-id false)))

(defn modal-card [id title body footer]
  ;; Copied from guestbook.core...
  )

(defn modal-button [id title body footer]
  [:div
   [:button.button.is-primary
    {:on-click #(rf/dispatch [:app/show-modal id])}
    title]
   [modal-card id title body footer]])
```

It's just our modal implementation moved to its own namespace.

Likewise, we move our :ajax/get effect to its own namespace, guestbook.ajax:

guestbook-cljc-routing/src/cljs/guestbook/ajax.cljs

```clojure
(ns guestbook.ajax
  (:require
   [ajax.core :refer [GET]]
   [re-frame.core :as rf]))
```

```
(rf/reg-fx
 :ajax/get
 (fn [{:keys [url success-event error-event success-path]}]
   (GET url
     (cond-> {:headers {"Accept" "application/transit+json"}}
       success-event (assoc :handler
                             #(rf/dispatch
                               (conj success-event
                                     (if success-path
                                       (get-in % success-path)
                                       %))))
       error-event   (assoc :error-handler
                             #(rf/dispatch
                               (conj error-event %)))))))
```

And finally, we clean up our guestbook.core namespace, where it all comes together:

guestbook-cljc-routing/src/cljs/guestbook/core.cljs
```
(ns guestbook.core
  (:require
   [reagent.core :as r]
   [reagent.dom :as dom]
   [re-frame.core :as rf]
   [reitit.coercion.spec :as reitit-spec]
   [reitit.frontend :as rtf]
   [reitit.frontend.easy :as rtfe]
   [clojure.string :as string]

   [guestbook.routes.app :refer [app-routes]]
   [guestbook.websockets :as ws]
   [guestbook.auth :as auth]
   [guestbook.messages :as messages]
   [guestbook.ajax :as ajax]
   [mount.core :as mount]))

(rf/reg-event-fx
 :app/initialize
 (fn [_ _]
   {:db {:messages/loading? true
         :session/loading? true}
    :dispatch-n [[:session/load] [:messages/load]]}))

(def router
  (rtf/router
   (app-routes)
   {:data {:coercion reitit-spec/coercion}}))

(rf/reg-event-db
 :router/navigated
 (fn [db [_ new-match]]
   (assoc db :router/current-route new-match)))
```

```clojure
(rf/reg-sub
 :router/current-route
 (fn [db]
   (:router/current-route db)))

(defn init-routes! []
  (rtfe/start!
   router
   (fn [new-match]
     (when new-match
       (rf/dispatch [:router/navigated new-match])))
   {:use-fragment false}))

(defn navbar []
  ;; Same as before, but with references to moved code (e.g. `auth/nameplate`)
  )

(defn page [{{:keys [view name]} :data
             path                 :path
             :as                  match}]
  [:section.section>div.container
   (if view
     [view match]
     [:div "No view specified for route: " name " (" path ")"])])

(defn app []
  (let [current-route @(rf/subscribe [:router/current-route])]
    [:div.app
     [navbar]
     [page current-route]]))

(defn ^:dev/after-load mount-components []
  (rf/clear-subscription-cache!)
  (.log js/console "Mounting Components...")
  (init-routes!)
  (dom/render [#'app] (.getElementById js/document "content"))
  (.log js/console "Components Mounted!"))

(defn init! []
  (.log js/console "Initializing App...")
  (mount/start)
  (rf/dispatch [:app/initialize])
  (mount-components))
```

All that guestbook.core does now is initialize our re-frame db, initialize our router, connect our router to our re-frame db, and define our navbar and page components. Also notice that to keep our server consistent, we changed routes to app-routes and we made it a function. We had to change that on the front end to match.

After all that refactoring, our code looks much nicer. Note that we haven't really written any new code; we've just rearranged existing code into sensible namespaces. But this is meaningless unless it still works as intended. Restart the application and make sure everything still works, and then we're ready to move on.

Reitit has some additional front-end features we may eventually use, such as controllers and history manipulation, but we'll discuss them as they come up. Let's build out our client-side pages, starting with our author page.

Implementing the Client Page

The first thing we do is add an event to load our messages for a specific author and set :messages/list from there.

guestbook-author-4/src/cljs/guestbook/messages.cljs
```
(rf/reg-event-fx
 :messages/load-by-author
 (fn [{:keys [db]} [_ author]]
   {:db (assoc db :messages/loading? true)
    :ajax/get {:url (str "/api/messages/by/" author)
               :success-path [:messages]
               :success-event [:messages/set]}}))
```

Then let's update our author page to dispatch our :messages/load-by-author event when it mounts and have it display the messages list, like so:

guestbook-author-4/src/cljs/guestbook/views/author.cljs
```
(ns guestbook.views.author
  (:require
   [re-frame.core :as rf]
   [guestbook.messages :as messages]))


(defn author [{{{:keys [user]} :path} :parameters}]
  (rf/dispatch [:messages/load-by-author user])
  (let [messages (rf/subscribe [:messages/list])]
    (fn [{{{:keys [user]} :path} :parameters}]
      [:div.content>div.columns.is-centered>div.column.is-two-thirds
       [:div.columns>div.column
        [:h3 "Messages By " user]
        [messages/message-list messages]]])))
```

Now if we go to the author page, everything looks correct. We have our list of messages posted by the author, and we have their name in the header. However, we've made a few oversights we should address.

First, if we navigate back to our home page, we only see the messages by our author! This is because we're only triggering :messages/load once—from :app/initialize. If you click the Refresh Messages button to reload them manually, you see the correct list of messages. So we need to update our code to trigger

:messages/load anytime we navigate to our home page, not just when we first open our app.

Second, if you refresh the browser from the author page a few times, you might see the full message list instead of the author's messages. This is because we've introduced a race condition. In fact, we've introduced two!

Third, we forgot about our WebSocket's :message/add event broadcast. If we're on an author's page and someone submits a new post, it's added to the page regardless of who the author is. Since the core functionality of our app is to display differently filtered lists of messages, this is a critical issue.

The first problem we've introduced relates to the way re-frame handles events. When dispatched, re-frame events are added to the back of an event queue. Asynchronously, events are taken from this queue and handled, which resolves their effects. In the case of :app/initialize we have a :dispatch-n effect, which dispatches the specified events, adding them to the back of the event queue. This can introduce a race condition if there are other related events that may be dispatched shortly after. In our case, we are dispatching :messages/load-by-author almost immediately after :app/initialize. Consider what happens if :messages/load-by-author is dispatched before :app/initialize is handled. Once :app/initialize is handled, it adds :messages/load to the back of the event queue, *behind* :messages/load-by-author. This means that our Ajax request to fetch the author's messages is sent before our Ajax request for the full list of messages, and so our author's messages will likely come back first. If that happens, then for a brief moment :messages/list will be our author's messages, but it will quickly be overwritten by the result of our second request, and so it ends up being the full list of messages.

This alludes to our second race condition, but let's solve this one first. We change our init! function to use dispatch-sync instead of dispatch.

guestbook-author-4/src/cljs/guestbook/core.cljs
```
(defn init! []
  (.log js/console "Initializing App...")
  (mount/start)
  (rf/dispatch-sync [:app/initialize])
  (mount-components))
```

This tells re-frame to handle the event immediately—don't queue it, don't do it asynchronously, handle it now. Usually, this should be avoided for many reasons. However, initialization is one of the few cases where it's often used. If we use dispatch-sync to initialize, we can guarantee that is handled before any components are rendered. This prevents a ton of headaches and possible race conditions.

Now, let's try our author page test a second time. It should work *most* of the time, but we still get a flash of the full messages list before we render the author's messages. Also, even though it's rare, we still have the *second* race condition we alluded to. To see this more clearly, let's make our /api/messages handler a bit slower. Temporarily update the handler in guestbook.routes.services, like so:

```
["/messages"
  {::auth/roles (auth/roles :messages/list)}
  ["" {:get
       {:responses
        ;;...
        :handler
        (fn [_]
          (Thread/sleep 500)
          (response/ok (msg/message-list)))}}]]
```

If this handler slows down a bit, our author page almost always breaks! This is no good. Even if it did work, we'd still be doing an entirely useless HTTP call. We'll fix this by using controllers, but let's resolve our critical WebSocket issue first.

Add an add-message? predicate, which takes a filter declaration from our db and the message to be added and decides whether or not to add the message to our :messages/list.

guestbook-author-5/src/cljs/guestbook/messages.cljs
```
(defn add-message? [filter-map msg]
  (every?
    (fn [[k matcher]]
      (let [v (get msg k)]
        (cond
          (set? matcher)
          (matcher v)
          (fn? matcher)
          (matcher v)
          :else
          (= matcher v))))
    filter-map))

(rf/reg-event-db
 :message/add
 (fn [db [_ message]]
   (if (add-message? (:messages/filter db) message)
     (update db :messages/list conj message)
     db)))
```

Then let's set our filter when we fetch a new message list, like so:

guestbook-author-5/src/cljs/guestbook/messages.cljs
```
(rf/reg-event-fx
 :messages/load
 (fn [{:keys [db]} _]
   {:db (assoc db
               :messages/loading? true
               :messages/filter nil)
    :ajax/get {:url "/api/messages"
               :success-path [:messages]
               :success-event [:messages/set]}}))

(rf/reg-event-fx
 :messages/load-by-author
 (fn [{:keys [db]} [_ author]]
   {:db (-> db
            (assoc :messages/loading? true
                   :messages/filter {:author author}))
    :ajax/get {:url (str "/api/messages/by/" author)
               :success-path [:messages]
               :success-event [:messages/set]}}))
```

Let's test that in the UI to make sure we don't render any messages that aren't supposed to appear.

Great! Now that that's taken care of, let's return to our intermittent page initialization bug.

Using Reitit Controllers

Right now, we have a single initialize event that's dispatched when our application loads. But we also have some setup and teardown we need to perform for each individual page. Controllers[3] provide a way to run start and stop functions based on our Reitit route.

The simplest controller is something like this:

```
["/foo/:bar"
 {:controllers [{:start (fn [_] (println "Starting..."))
                 :stop  (fn [_] (println "Stopping..."))}]}]
```

This runs the :start function when we navigate to any URL that matches /foo/:bar, and runs the :stop function when we navigate away from any route that matches /foo/:bar. Since we haven't specified anything to pass in, the argument will be nil. Also, if we navigate between two matches—for example, /foo/one and /foo/two—we won't run :start a second time.

---

3.   https://metosin.github.io/reitit/frontend/controllers.html

If we want to "restart" a controller, we have to specify an identity. We can do this in two ways, either by specifying an :identity function which computes our identity from our Reitit Match or by specifying a :parameters declaration to compute our identity based on our Match's parameters.

For example, we can do something like this:

```
["/foo/:bar"
 {:controllers
  [{:parameters {:path [:bar]}
    :start (fn [{{:keys [bar]} :path}] (println "Starting... " bar))
    :stop  (fn [{{:keys [bar]} :path}] (println "Stopping... " bar))}]}]
```

This controller calls :start and :stop similarly to the previous one, but it also calls both of them if the :bar parameter is changed.

So if we go to /foo/one, we see the following:

```
Starting... one
```

Then if we go to /foo/two, we see this:

```
Stopping... one
Starting... two
```

And we see this if we go to a route that doesn't match:

```
Stopping... two
```

Note that it *won't* restart if we go from /foo/two?a=1 to /foo/two?a=2, because we haven't specified query parameters in our :parameters declaration.

Before we can start using controllers, we have to do a little bit of setup to call reitit.frontend.controllers/apply-controllers when we navigate. So let's update our call to reitit.frontend.easy/start! in guestbook.core/init-routes! to do just that:

guestbook-controllers/src/cljs/guestbook/core.cljs
```
(ns guestbook.core
  (:require
   ;;...
   [reitit.frontend.controllers :as rtfc]
   ;;...))

;;...

(defn init-routes! []
  (rtfe/start!
   router
   (fn [new-match]
     (when new-match
       (let [{controllers :controllers}
             @(rf/subscribe [:router/current-route])
```

```
      new-match-with-controllers
      (assoc new-match
             :controllers
             (rtfc/apply-controllers controllers new-match))]
    (rf/dispatch [:router/navigated new-match-with-controllers]))))
{:use-fragment false}))
```

There. Now we're ready to write controllers for our home and author pages and fix our race condition.

We start by writing a controller to load our full list of messages for the home page.

guestbook-controllers/src/cljs/guestbook/views/home.cljs
```
(def home-controllers
  [{:start (fn [_] (rf/dispatch [:messages/load]))}])
```

Then let's write our author page controller and remove the dispatch from inside the author component.

guestbook-controllers/src/cljs/guestbook/views/author.cljs
```
(def author-controllers
  [{:parameters {:path [:user]}
    :start (fn [{{:keys [user]} :path}]
             (rf/dispatch [:messages/load-by-author user]))}])
```

```
;; Don't forget to remove (rf/dispatch [:messages/load-by-author user])
;; from the author view!
```

Next, we need to add the controllers to our router.

guestbook-controllers/src/cljc/guestbook/routes/app.cljc
```
(defn app-routes []
  [""
   #?(:clj {:middleware [middleware/wrap-csrf]
            :get home-page})
   ["/"
    (merge
     {:name ::home}
     #?(:cljs
        {:controllers home/home-controllers
         :view #'home/home}))]
   ["/user/:user"
    (merge
     {:name ::author}
     #?(:cljs {:controllers author/author-controllers
               :view #'author/author}))]])
```

And finally, we need to remove our call to :messages/load from :app/initialize, and we can also remove the unnecessary :messages/loading? from its :db effect.

guestbook-controllers/src/cljs/guestbook/core.cljs

```
(rf/reg-event-fx
 :app/initialize
 (fn [_ _]
   {:db {:session/loading? true}
    :dispatch [:session/load]}))
```

Final Touches

Everything is working properly now, but we still have some leftover data for a split second, and even if we didn't, we have some unpleasant jumping on the home page. To solve this, let's make sure that we clear :messages/list before we send an Ajax request to fetch an updated version.

guestbook-controllers/src/cljs/guestbook/messages.cljs

```
(rf/reg-event-fx
 :messages/load
 (fn [{:keys [db]} _]
   {:db (assoc db
               :messages/loading? true
               :messages/list nil
               :messages/filter nil)
    :ajax/get {:url "/api/messages"
               :success-path [:messages]
               :success-event [:messages/set]}}))

(rf/reg-event-fx
 :messages/load-by-author
 (fn [{:keys [db]} [_ author]]
   {:db (assoc db
               :messages/loading? true
               :messages/filter {:author author}
               :messages/list nil)
    :ajax/get {:url (str "/api/messages/by/" author)
               :success-path [:messages]
               :success-event [:messages/set]}}))
```

Also, let's write a placeholder for the message-list component to render instead if :messages/loading? is true.

guestbook-controllers/src/cljs/guestbook/messages.cljs

```
(defn message-list-placeholder []
  [:ul.messages
   [:li
    [:p "Loading Messages..."]
    [:div {:style {:width "10em"}}
     [:progress.progress.is-dark {:max 100} "30%"]]]])
```

Then we replace our uses of message-list in guestbook.views.home and guest-book.views.author with the following:

```
(if @(rf/subscribe [:messages/loading?])
  [messages/message-list-placeholder]
  [messages/message-list messages])
```

There we go!

Finally, let's add a link to our own posts in the navbar if we're logged in. Since we have Reitit front end set up, we can use reitit.frontend.easy/href to do reverse routing.

guestbook-controllers/src/cljs/guestbook/core.cljs
```
(defn navbar []
  ;; Same as before, but with references to moved code (e.g. `auth/nameplate`)
  (let [burger-active (r/atom false)]
    (fn []
      [:nav.navbar.is-info
       [:div.container
        ;;...
        [:div#nav-menu.navbar-menu
         {:class (when @burger-active "is-active")}
         [:div.navbar-start
          [:a.navbar-item
           {:href "/"}
           "Home"]
          (when (= @(rf/subscribe [:auth/user-state]) :authenticated)
            [:a.navbar-item
             {:href (rtfe/href :guestbook.routes.app/author
                               {:user (:login @(rf/subscribe [:auth/user]))})}
             "My Posts"])]]
        ;;...
        ]]])))
```

We have the basics of our author page done, and we've laid the groundwork for adding future pages. Next, let's add the ability for users to write a profile and customize their author page.

Account Customization

Now that we have a page for each author, it'd be nice for authors to be able to personalize it. Let's add a user bio at the top of the page, along with a display name, birth date, display picture, and a banner picture.

Let's start by adding a profile column to the users table.

Create a new migration file from the REPL, like so:

```
user=> (create-migration "alter-users-add-profile")
nil
```

Then we write the database migration to add our profile column.

guestbook-profile/resources/migrations/20200415001222-alter-users-add-profile.up.sql
```
ALTER TABLE users
  ADD COLUMN profile JSONB DEFAULT '{}'::JSONB;
```

And we add the rollback migration.

guestbook-profile/resources/migrations/20200415001222-alter-users-add-profile.down.sql
```
ALTER TABLE users
  DROP COLUMN profile;
```

Now, let's run our migration from the REPL.

```
user=> (migrate)
... INFO  migratus.core - Starting migrations
... DEBUG migratus.migrations - Looking for migrations in ...
... INFO  migratus.core - Running up for [20200415001222]
... INFO  migratus.core - Up 20200415001222-alter-users-add-profile
... DEBUG migratus.migration.sql - found 1 up migrations
... DEBUG migratus.database - marking 20200415001222 complete
... INFO  migratus.core - Ending migrations
nil
user=>
```

We made our profile a JSONB column so that it's convenient to add features gradually and edit all at once. However, we need to add extensions to the IResultSetReadColumn and ISQLValue protocols to support reading and writing Clojure data structures as JSONB. Let's add those to guestbook.db.core before we forget.

guestbook-profile/src/clj/guestbook/db/core.clj
```
(ns guestbook.db.core
  (:require
   ;;...
   [next.jdbc.prepare]
   [jsonista.core :as json])
  (:import org.postgresql.util.PGobject
           clojure.lang.IPersistentMap
           clojure.lang.IPersistentVector))
;;...
(defn read-pg-object [^PGobject obj]
  (cond-> (.getValue obj)
    (#{"json" "jsonb"} (.getType obj))
    (json/read-value json/keyword-keys-object-mapper)))
```

```clojure
(defn write-pg-object [v]
  (doto (PGobject.)
    (.setType "jsonb")
    (.setValue (json/write-value-as-string v))))

(extend-protocol next.jdbc.prepare/SettableParameter
  IPersistentMap
  (set-parameter [m ^java.sql.PreparedStatement s i]
    (.setObject s i (write-pg-object m)))
  IPersistentVector
  (set-parameter [v ^java.sql.PreparedStatement s i]
    (.setObject s i (write-pg-object v))))

(extend-protocol next.jdbc.result-set/ReadableColumn
  ;;...
  PGobject
  (read-column-by-label [^PGobject v _]
    (read-pg-object v))
  (read-column-by-index [^PGobject v _2 _3]
    (read-pg-object v)))
```

We've required cheshire.core's generate-string and parse-string functions for working with converting between JSON and EDN, and we've imported the classes for which we'll need to implement the IResultSetReadColumn and ISQLValue protocols.

We've implemented IResultSetReadColumn for Array, returning a Clojure vector, and for PGObjects of type JSON and JSONB, returning a Clojure map.

Then, we've written a helper function to-pg-json to convert maps and vectors to PGObjects. We use this function in our implementations of ISQLValue for IPersistentMap and IPersistentVector to convert them into JSONB for use in queries.

With that, we're all ready to work with our new JSONB column.

Let's add two SQL statements: one to edit our new profile column and one to be used for selecting a user's publicly available information.

guestbook-profile/resources/sql/queries.sql
```sql
-- :name set-profile-for-user*  :<! :1
-- :doc sets a profile map for the specified user
UPDATE users
SET profile = :profile
where :login = login
RETURNING *;

-- :name get-user* :? :1
-- :doc gets a user's publicly available information
SELECT login, created_at, profile from users
WHERE login = :login
```

Great! Let's try using these new queries from the REPL:

```
user=> (in-ns 'guestbook.db.core)
#object[clojure.lang.Namespace ... "guestbook.db.core"]
guestbook.db.core=> (conman/bind-connection *db* "sql/queries.sql")
{:snips {}, :fns {...}}
guestbook.db.core=> (get-user* {:login "testuser"})
{:login "testuser", :created_at #inst "...", :profile {}}
guestbook.db.core=> (set-profile-for-user* {:login "testuser"
                                            :profile {:bio "A test user"}})
{:login "testuser",
 :password "...",
 :created_at #inst "...",
 :profile {:bio "A test user"}}
guestbook.db.core=>
```

Success! We're able to set and read the user's profile. Next, let's add a namespace for dealing with author accounts and add a couple endpoints for reading and writing profiles.

guestbook-profile/src/clj/guestbook/author.clj
```
(ns guestbook.author
  (:require [guestbook.db.core :as db]))

(defn get-author [login]
  (db/get-user* {:login login}))

(defn set-author-profile [login profile]
  (db/set-profile-for-user* {:login login
                             :profile profile}))
```

Now we add two endpoints for getting an author and setting the currently logged in author's profile. Also, when we set the currently logged in author's profile, we need to remember to update the author on the session.

guestbook-profile/src/clj/guestbook/routes/services.clj
```
["/author/:login"
 {::auth/roles (auth/roles :author/get)
  :get {:parameters
        {:path {:login string?}}

        :responses
        {200
         {:body map?}
         500
         {:errors map?}}

        :handler
        (fn [{{{:keys [login]} :path} :parameters}]
          (response/ok (author/get-author login)))}}]
```

```
["/my-account"
 ["/set-profile"
  {::auth/roles (auth/roles :account/set-profile!)
   :post {:parameters
          {:body
           {:profile map?}}

          :responses
          {200
           {:body map?}
           500
           {:errors map?}}

          :handler
          (fn [{{{:keys [profile]} :body}      :parameters
               {:keys [identity] :as session} :session}]
            (try
              (let [identity
                    (author/set-author-profile (:login identity) profile)]
                (update (response/ok {:success true})
                        :session
                        assoc :identity identity))
              (catch Exception e
                (log/error e)
                (response/internal-server-error
                 {:errors {:server-error
                           ["Failed to set profile!"]}}))))}}]]
```

We also need to add two entries to our roles map in guestbook.auth for these endpoints, or else they'll always respond with 403 Forbidden.

guestbook-profile/src/clj/guestbook/auth.clj
```
(def roles
  {:message/create! #{:authenticated}
   :author/get #{:any}
   :account/set-profile! #{:authenticated}
   ;;...})
```

Alright, now let's try our endpoints out from Swagger UI as shown in the figures on page 222 and on page 223.

Everything's working as expected on the server side. Let's put our new feature to use!

Creating a My Profile Page

The first thing we need to do is allow users to create and edit their profiles. Let's create a new page in our app to do just that.

We create stubs for our profile page and controllers so that we can get our router set up correctly first.

guestbook-profile/src/cljs/guestbook/views/profile.cljs
```clojure
(ns guestbook.views.profile
  (:require
  [reagent.core :as r]
  [re-frame.core :as rf]))

   (def profile-controllers
     [{:start (fn [_] (println "Entering Profile Page"))
       :stop  (fn [_] (println "Leaving Profile Page"))}])

  (defn profile [_]
    [:div>h1 "My Profile"])
```

Next, let's add them to a new route in guestbook.routes.app/app-routes:

guestbook-profile/src/cljc/guestbook/routes/app.cljc

```clojure
(ns guestbook.routes.app
  (:require
   #?@(:clj [[guestbook.layout :as layout]
             [guestbook.middleware :as middleware]]
       :cljs [[guestbook.views.home :as home]
              [guestbook.views.author :as author]
              [guestbook.views.profile :as profile]])))
;;...

;;(defn app-routes []
;;[""
;; ...
   ["/my-account/edit-profile"
    (merge
     {:name ::profile}
     #?(:cljs
        {:controllers profile/profile-controllers
         :view #'profile/profile}))]
   ;;...])
```

Then we update our guestbook.auth/nameplate component to link to our new profile page.

guestbook-profile/src/cljs/guestbook/auth.cljs
```
(defn nameplate [{:keys [login]}]
  [:a.button.is-primary
   {:href (rtfe/href :guestbook.routes.app/profile)}
   login])
```

Now if we log in and click the nameplate button, we should see our profile page:

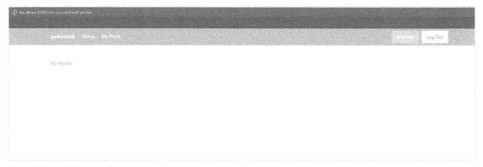

Great! We're all ready to build our edit profile page. The first thing we need to do is load our user's profile from the server. We're already fetching our session, but we're restricting the keys on the identity.

Let's update our /api/session endpoint to include the user's profile.

guestbook-profile/src/clj/guestbook/routes/services.clj
```
["/session"
 {::auth/roles (auth/roles :session/get)
  :get
  {:responses
   {200
    {:body
     {:session
      {:identity
       (ds/maybe
        {:login string?
         :created_at inst?
         :profile map?})}}}}
   :handler
   (fn [{{:keys [identity]} :session}]
     (response/ok
      {:session
       {:identity
        (not-empty
         (select-keys identity [:login :created_at :profile]))}}))}}]
```

Now that we have our :profile on our session, we can read it from [:auth/user].

Let's update our profile page to allow us to edit our profile.

We start by creating a textarea for our bio. Remember, we already wrote some general text and textarea inputs for our message form, so let's use those.

For the sake of cleanliness, let's also move these two components into a general guestbook.components namespace.

guestbook-profile/src/cljs/guestbook/components.cljs
```clojure
(ns guestbook.components
 (:require
  [reagent.core :as r]))

(defn text-input [{val    :value
                   attrs :attrs
                   :keys [on-save]}]
  (let [draft (r/atom nil)
        value (r/track #(or @draft @val ""))]
    (fn []
      [:input.input
       (merge attrs
              {:type :text
               :on-focus #(reset! draft (or @val ""))
               :on-blur (fn []
                          (on-save (or @draft ""))
                          (reset! draft nil))
               :on-change #(reset! draft (.. % -target -value))
               :value @value})])))

(defn textarea-input [{val    :value
                       attrs :attrs
                       :keys [on-save]}]
  (let [draft (r/atom nil)
        value (r/track #(or @draft @val ""))]
    (fn []
      [:textarea.textarea
       (merge attrs
              {:on-focus #(reset! draft (or @val ""))
               :on-blur (fn []
                          (on-save (or @draft ""))
                          (reset! draft nil))
               :on-change #(reset! draft (.. % -target -value))
               :value @value})])))
```

And don't forget to update the guestbook.messages namespace declaration to require the components we moved.

guestbook-profile/src/cljs/guestbook/messages.cljs
```clojure
(ns guestbook.messages
  (:require
    [clojure.string :as string]
    [reagent.core :as r]
    [re-frame.core :as rf]
    [guestbook.validation :refer [validate-message]]
    [guestbook.components :refer [text-input textarea-input]]))
```

Now we'll be able to use our standard components from our profile page.

Let's start by creating some re-frame subscriptions for the edited state of our profile:

guestbook-profile/src/cljs/guestbook/views/profile.cljs
```clojure
(rf/reg-sub
 :profile/changes
 (fn [db _]
   (get db :profile/changes)))
(rf/reg-sub
 :profile/changed?
 :<- [:profile/changes]
 (fn [changes _]
   (not (empty? changes))))

(rf/reg-sub
 :profile/field-changed?
 :<- [:profile/changes]
 (fn [changes [_ k]]
   (contains? changes k)))

(rf/reg-sub
 :profile/field
 :<- [:profile/changes]
 :<- [:auth/user]
 (fn [[changes {:keys [profile]}] [_ k default]]
   (or (get changes k) (get profile k) default)))

(rf/reg-sub
 :profile/profile
 :<- [:profile/changes]
 :<- [:auth/user]
 (fn [[changes {:keys [profile]}] _]
   (merge profile changes)))

(rf/reg-event-db
 :profile/save-change
 (fn [db [_ k v]]
   (update db :profile/changes
           (if (nil? v)
             #(dissoc % k)
             #(assoc % k v)))))
```

We have a map, :profile/changes, which contains the updated values of the :profile keys we've changed and some helper subscriptions for accessing individual fields.

Next, we need to add some events to change our profile, but first we need to create a new effect to perform POST requests so that we can target our /api/my-account/set-profile endpoint.

guestbook-profile/src/cljs/guestbook/ajax.cljs

```
(rf/reg-fx
 :ajax/post
 (fn [{:keys [url success-event error-event success-path params]}]
   (POST url
     (cond-> {:headers {"Accept" "application/transit+json"}}
       params        (assoc :params params)
       success-event (assoc :handler
                            #(rf/dispatch
                               (conj success-event
                                     (if success-path
                                       (get-in % success-path)
                                       %))))
       error-event   (assoc :error-handler
                            #(rf/dispatch
                               (conj error-event %)))))))
```

Now let's write an event to POST our updated profile and another to handle the response.

guestbook-profile/src/cljs/guestbook/views/profile.cljs

```
(rf/reg-event-fx
 :profile/set-profile
 (fn [_ [_ profile]]
   {:ajax/post {:url "/api/my-account/set-profile"
                :params {:profile profile}
                :success-event [:profile/handle-set-profile profile]}}))

(rf/reg-event-db
 :profile/handle-set-profile
 (fn [db [_ profile]]
   (-> db
       (assoc-in [:auth/user :profile] profile)
       (dissoc :profile/changes))))
```

Finally, let's create some simple components for editing our display name and bio, and update our profile page view:

guestbook-profile/src/cljs/guestbook/views/profile.cljs

```
(ns guestbook.views.profile
  (:require
   ;; require components
   [guestbook.components :refer [text-input textarea-input]]
```

```clojure
    [reagent.core :as r]
    [re-frame.core :as rf]))

;; ...

(defn display-name []
  (r/with-let [k :display-name
               value (rf/subscribe [:profile/field k ""])]
    [:div.field
     [:label.label {:for k} "Display Name"
      (when @(rf/subscribe [:profile/field-changed? k])
        " (Changed)")]
     [:div.field.has-addons
      [:div.control.is-expanded
       [text-input {:value value
                    :on-save #(rf/dispatch [:profile/save-change k %])}]]
      [:div.control>button.button.is-danger
       {:disabled (not @(rf/subscribe [:profile/field-changed? k]))
        :on-click #(rf/dispatch [:profile/save-change k nil])} "Reset"]]]))

(defn bio []
  (r/with-let [k :bio
               value (rf/subscribe [:profile/field k ""])]
    [:div.field
     [:label.label {:for k} "Bio"
      (when @(rf/subscribe [:profile/field-changed? k])
        " (Changed)")]
     [:div.control {:style {:margin-bottom "0.5em"}}
      [textarea-input {:value value
                       :on-save #(rf/dispatch [:profile/save-change k %])}]]
     [:div.control>button.button.is-danger
      {:disabled (not @(rf/subscribe [:profile/field-changed? k]))
       :on-click #(rf/dispatch [:profile/save-change k nil])} "Reset"]]))

(defn profile [_]
  (if-let [{:keys [login created_at profile]} @(rf/subscribe [:auth/user])]
    [:div.content
     [:h1 "My Account"
      (str "  <@" login ">")]
     [:p (str "Joined: " (.toString created_at))]
     [display-name]
     [bio]
     [:button.button.is-primary
      {:on-click
       #(rf/dispatch [:profile/set-profile
                      @(rf/subscribe [:profile/profile])])
       :disabled (not @(rf/subscribe [:profile/changed?]))}
      "Update Profile"]]
    [:div.content
     [:div {:style {:width "100%"}}
      [:progress.progress.is-dark {:max 100} "30%"]]]))
```

We've written two components, display-name and bio, which allow us to change the value of our display name and bio locally, along with a reset button. We use them from our profile page, which also includes an updated header and an Update Profile button to send our changes to the server.

Next, we'll need to support media uploading to select an avatar and a banner image.

Managing Media

The first step to managing media uploading is having a place to store it. In our case, we'll store it in the database as a BLOB for simplicity, but you could just as easily store it on the filesystem or a CDN. Let's write another migration to create a media table.

First write the up migration:

guestbook-profile-2/resources/migrations/20200507221422-create-media-table.up.sql
```
CREATE TABLE media
(name text PRIMARY KEY,
 owner text references users(login) ON DELETE set null ON UPDATE CASCADE,
 type text NOT NULL,
 data bytea NOT NULL);
```

Then write the down migration:

guestbook-profile-2/resources/migrations/20200507221422-create-media-table.down.sql
```
DROP TABLE media;
```

And then run the migration:

```
user=> (migrate)
... INFO  migratus.core - Starting migrations
... DEBUG migratus.migrations - Looking for migrations in ...
... INFO  migratus.core - Running up for [20200507221422]
... INFO  migratus.core - Up 20200507221422-create-media-table
... DEBUG migratus.migration.sql - found 1 up migrations
... DEBUG migratus.database - marking 20200507221422 complete
... INFO  migratus.core - Ending migrations
nil
user=>
```

Now we need a query to insert our files and a query to get our files:

guestbook-profile-2/resources/sql/queries.sql
```
-- :name save-file! :! :n
-- saves a file to the database
INSERT INTO media
(name, type, owner, data)
VALUES (:name, :type, :owner, :data)
ON CONFLICT (name) DO UPDATE
```

```
SET type = :type,
    data = :data
WHERE media.owner = :owner

-- :name get-file :? :1
-- Gets a file from the database
select * from media
where name = :name
```

Note the ON CONFLICT (name) logic: this is to ensure that files don't get overwritten by other users.

Let's reload our queries and test them out:

```
user=> (in-ns 'guestbook.db.core)
#object[clojure.lang.Namespace ... "guestbook.db.core"]
guestbook.db.core=> (require '[clojure.java.io :as io])
nil
guestbook.db.core=> (conman/bind-connection *db* "sql/queries.sql")
{:snips {}, :fns {...}}
guestbook.db.core=> (with-open [in (io/input-stream
                                       (io/resource
                                          "public/img/warning_clojure.png"))
                                out (java.io.ByteArrayOutputStream.)]
                        (io/copy in out)
                        (.toByteArray out))
#object["[B" 0x1d42779f "[B@1d42779f"]
guestbook.db.core=> (save-file! {:name "test.png"
                                 :data *1
                                 :owner "testuser"
                                 :type "image/png"})
1
guestbook.db.core=> (save-file! {:name "test.png"
                                 :data *2
                                 :owner "foo"
                                 :type "image/png"})
0
guestbook.db.core=> (get-file {:name "test.png"})
{:name "test.png",
 :owner "testuser",
 :type "image/png",
 :data #object["[B" 0x5586f180 "[B@5586f180"]}
guestbook.db.core=>
```

Our queries are working as intended, so let's get started on our upload and fetch endpoints.

Let's start by adding some auth rules for media:

guestbook-profile-2/src/clj/guestbook/auth.clj

```
:media/get #{:any}
:media/upload #{:authenticated}
```

Since we've just added a test image to our database, let's create an endpoint
and see if we can view it in the browser.

guestbook-profile-2/src/clj/guestbook/routes/services.clj

```
;; require these namespaces
[clojure.java.io :as io]
[guestbook.db.core :as db]
;; ...
["/media/:name"
 {::auth/roles (auth/roles :media/get)
  :get {:parameters
        {:path {:name string?}}
        :handler (fn [{{{:keys [name]} :path} :parameters}]
                   (if-let [{:keys [data type]} (db/get-file {:name name})]
                     (-> (io/input-stream data)
                         (response/ok)
                         (response/content-type type))
                     (response/not-found)))}}]
```

This endpoint is simply returning the data as a stream along with an appropriate content-type header. With this, we should be able to see our test image
at localhost:3000/api/media/test.png.

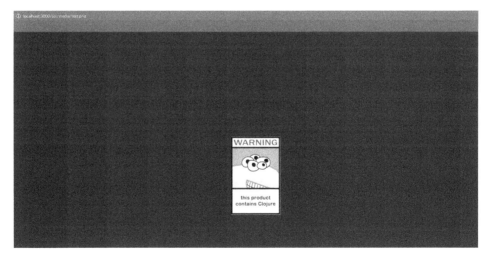

Now we need to be able to upload images. We do this by using a POST with a content type of multipart/form-data. We can instruct Reitit to coerce this type of parameter with a :parameters spec that looks like this:

```
(ns guestbook.routes.services
  (:require
    ...
    [reitit.ring.middleware.multipart :as multipart]))

;;...

{:multipart {:foo multipart/temp-file-part
             :bar multipart/temp-file-part}}
```

This tells the multipart-middleware to coerce our :foo and :bar form fields into maps containing their respective tempfiles. The result is a :parameters map on the request that looks like this:

```
{:multipart {:foo {:filename     "some-tempname.png"
                   :content-type "image/png"
                   :tempfile     <instance of java.io.File>
                   :size         778330}
             :bar {:filename     "bar-tempname.jpg"
                   :content-type "image/jpg"
                   :tempfile     <instance of java.io.File>
                   :size         1663227}}}
```

Let's start by creating a new namespace called guestbook.media and writing a helper function that takes a single temp-file-part map and options, saves the file to the database, and returns its filename.

```
(ns guestbook.media
  (:require
    [guestbook.db.core :as db]
    [clojure.java.io :as io]
    [clojure.tools.logging :as log])
  (:import
    [java.io ByteArrayOutputStream]))

(defn insert-image-returning-name [{:keys [tempfile filename content-type]}
                                   {:keys [owner]}]
  (with-open [in (io/input-stream tempfile)
              out (ByteArrayOutputStream.)]
    (io/copy in out)
    (if (= 0
           (db/save-file! {:name filename
                           :data (.toByteArray out)
                           :owner owner
                           :type content-type}))
```

```
(do
  (log/error "Attempted to overwrite an image that you don't own!")
  (throw (ex-info "Attempted to overwrite an image that you don't own!"
                  {:name filename})))
  filename)))
```

Then we write an endpoint that accepts multipart params and returns a map of names to URLs where the uploaded files can be found.

```
(ns guestbook.routes.services
  (:require
    ;;...
    [guestbook.media :as media]))

;;...

(defn service-routes []
  ["/api"
   ;;...
   ["/my-account"
    ["/set-profile"
     ;;...
     ]
    ["/media/upload"
     {::auth/roles (auth/roles :media/upload)
      :post {:parameters {:multipart {:avatar multipart/temp-file-part
                                      :banner multipart/temp-file-part}}
             :handler
             (fn [{{{:keys [avatar banner] :as mp} :multipart} :parameters
                   {:keys [identity] :as session} :session
                   :as req}]
               (response/ok
                 {:avatar (str "/api/media/"
                               (media/insert-image-returning-name
                                 (assoc avatar
                                        :filename
                                        (str (:login identity)
                                             "_avatar"))
                                 {:owner (:login identity)}))
                  :banner (str "/api/media/"
                               (media/insert-image-returning-name
                                 (assoc banner
                                        :filename
                                        (str (:login identity)
                                             "_banner"))
                                 {:owner (:login identity)}))}))}}]]])
```

Now let's try this out from Swagger as shown in the figure on page 234.

It worked! Now we can access our avatar and banner, like so:

We've got the basics set up, but we're trusting the user to upload a sensible image, and we're retaining the original size and format. Let's update our insert-image-returning-name function to take more options, such as width, height, max-width, and max-height, and use them to scale our image and convert it to a standard format, image/png.

guestbook-profile-2/src/clj/guestbook/media.clj
```clojure
(ns guestbook.media
  (:require
   [guestbook.db.core :as db]
   [clojure.tools.logging :as log])
  (:import [java.awt.image AffineTransformOp BufferedImage]
           [java.io ByteArrayOutputStream]
           java.awt.geom.AffineTransform
           javax.imageio.ImageIO))

(defn insert-image-returning-name [{:keys [tempfile filename]}
                                   {:keys [width height
                                           max-width max-height
                                           owner]}]
  (let [baos (ByteArrayOutputStream.)
        img (ImageIO/read tempfile)
        img-width (.getWidth img)
        img-height (.getHeight img)
        ratio (cond
                (and (some? height) (some? width))
                (min (/ width img-width) (/ height img-height))

                (some? height)
                (/ height img-height)

                (some? width)
                (/ width img-width)

                (and (some? max-height) (some? max-width))
                (min 1 (/ img-width max-width) (/ img-height max-height))

                (some? max-height)
                (min 1 (/ img-height max-height))

                (some? max-width)
                (min 1 (/ img-width max-width))

                :else
                1)
        img-scaled (if (= 1 ratio)
                     img
                     (let [scale
                           (AffineTransform/getScaleInstance
                            (double ratio) (double ratio))

                           transform-op
                           (AffineTransformOp.
                            scale  AffineTransformOp/TYPE_BILINEAR)]
```

```clojure
                              (.filter transform-op
                                  img
                                  (BufferedImage. (* ratio img-width)
                                                  (* ratio img-height)
                                                  (.getType img)))))))]
      (ImageIO/write img-scaled "png" baos)
      (if (= 0
             (db/save-file! {:name filename
                             :data (.toByteArray baos)
                             :owner owner
                             :type "image/png"}))
        (do
          (log/error "Attempted to overwrite an image that you don't own!")
          (throw (ex-info "Attempted to overwrite an image that you don't own!"
                          {:name filename})))
        filename)))
```

The preceding code is using java.awt.geom.AffineTransform class provided by the Java standard library to create a scale operation, and we use java.awt.image. AffineTransformOp to do the transformation. The filter method on the transform-op uses the original image to produce the scaled image we require.

Now let's update our endpoint. Let's allow for as many files as neccessary to be uploaded in parallel, but let's ensure that each one is under 5 MiB and is indeed an image file. Additionally, let's keep the behavior where we generate a name for :avatar and :banner images.

guestbook-profile-2/src/clj/guestbook/routes/services.clj
```clojure
;;require these namespaces
[guestbook.media :as media]
[clojure.spec.alpha :as s]
[clojure.string :as string]
;; ...
 ["/media/upload"
  {::auth/roles (auth/roles :media/upload)
   :post
   {:parameters {:multipart {:multipart (s/map-of keyword? multipart/temp-file-part)}
    :handler
    (fn [{{mp :multipart}    :parameters
          {:keys [identity]} :session}]
      (response/ok
       (reduce-kv
        (fn [acc name {:keys [size content-type] :as file-part}]
          (cond
            (> size (* 5 1024 1024))
            (do
              (log/error "File " name
                         " exceeded max size of 5 MB. (size: " size ")")
              (update acc :failed-uploads (fnil conj []) name))
```

```clojure
(re-matches #"image/.*" content-type)
(-> acc
    (update :files-uploaded conj name)
    (assoc name
           (str "/api/media/"
                (cond
                  (= name :avatar)
                  (media/insert-image-returning-name
                   (assoc file-part
                          :filename
                          (str (:login identity) "_avatar.png"))
                   {:width 128
                    :height 128
                    :owner (:login identity)})

                  (= name :banner)
                  (media/insert-image-returning-name
                   (assoc file-part
                          :filename
                          (str (:login identity) "_banner.png"))
                   {:width 1200
                    :height 400
                    :owner (:login identity)})

                  :else
                  (media/insert-image-returning-name
                   (update
                    file-part
                    :filename
                    string/replace #"\.[^\.]+$" ".png")
                   {:max-width 800
                    :max-height 2000
                    :owner (:login identity)})))))
    :else
    (do
      (log/error "Unsupported file type" content-type "for file" name)
      (update acc :failed-uploads (fnil conj []) name))))
{:files-uploaded []}
mp)))}}]
```

Our new handler has a few noteworthy changes.

First, by using (s/map-of keyword? multipart/temp-file-part), we allow any number of files to be posted to this endpoint. Unfortunately, this doesn't play well with Swagger, but we'll be able to test it from our application shortly.

Second, instead of explicitly handling :avatar and :banner, we're using reduce-kv to perform our image saving logic for each file in our multipart parameter map.

Third, we've added a `cond` statement with several checks in place. We reject files which are larger than 5 MiB or which have a Content-Type that doesn't start with image/. It's possible to add additional clauses to handle other media, such as video or audio, but we'll leave that for now.

We're keeping our avatar- and banner-specific behavior, and we're specifying a specific size for each.

Now, let's update our profile page to support uploading avatar and banner images.

Uploading Images from the Browser

The first thing we need to do is add a new type of effect to handle media uploads. We can't reuse our :ajax/post request, because we have to send a FormData object in order to use multipart parameters.

guestbook-profile-2/src/cljs/guestbook/ajax.cljs
```
(rf/reg-fx
 :ajax/upload-media!
 (fn [{:keys [url success-event files handler]}]
   (let [form-data (js/FormData.)]
     (doseq [[k v] files]
       (when (some? v)
         (.append form-data (name k) v)))
     (POST url {:body form-data
                :handler handler}))))
```

Since we are not using an actual form submission, we have to construct a FormData object to send. We'll have a map, files, which will contain the files in our file re-frame components keyed by name. We'll then append each of these to our FormData and then finally POST it to our endpoint.

Now, let's update our re-frame events and subscriptions.

Add a new top-level subscription called :profile/media to track any files to be uploaded and have :profile/changed?, :profile/field-changed?, and :profile/field handle entries in :profile/media in addition to their current behavior. We also add an event to change the :profile/media map.

guestbook-profile-2/src/cljs/guestbook/views/profile.cljs
```
(rf/reg-sub
 :profile/media
 (fn [db _]
   (get db :profile/media)))

(rf/reg-sub
 :profile/changed?
 :<- [:profile/changes]
 :<- [:profile/media]
```

```
 (fn [[changes media] _]
   (not
    (and
     (empty? changes)
     (empty? media)))))
(rf/reg-sub
 :profile/field-changed?
 :<- [:profile/changes]
 :<- [:profile/media]
 (fn [[changes media] [_ k]]
   (or
    (contains? changes k)
    (contains? media k))))
(rf/reg-sub
 :profile/field
 :<- [:profile/changes]
 :<- [:auth/user]
 :<- [:profile/media]
 (fn [[changes {:keys [profile]} media] [_ k default]]
   (or
    (when-let [file (get media k)] (js/URL.createObjectURL file))
    (get changes k)
    (get profile k)
    default)))
(rf/reg-event-db
 :profile/save-media
 (fn [db [_ k v]]
   (update db
           :profile/media
           (if (nil? v)
             #(dissoc % k)
             #(assoc % k v)))))
```

Note that in :profile/field we're creating a temporary URL based on the file on the client side. Since we plan on storing :avatar and :banner as image URLs inside profile, this allows us to treat pending changes and existing values interchangeably.

Next, we update :profile/set-profile event to optionally take a second argument with files to be uploaded, and have it upload any files specified before sending the POST request to /api/my-account/set-profile. We'll keep the existing behavior if no files need to be uploaded.

guestbook-profile-2/src/cljs/guestbook/views/profile.cljs
```
(rf/reg-event-fx
 :profile/set-profile
 (fn [_ [_ profile files]]
   (if (some some? (vals files))
```

```
 {:ajax/upload-media!
  {:url "/api/my-account/media/upload"
   :files files
   :handler
   (fn [response]
     (rf/dispatch
       [:profile/set-profile
        (merge profile
               (select-keys response (:files-uploaded response)))])))}}
  {:ajax/post
   {:url "/api/my-account/set-profile"
    :params {:profile profile}
    :success-event [:profile/handle-set-profile profile]}})))

(rf/reg-event-db
 :profile/handle-set-profile
 (fn [db [_ profile]]
   (-> db
       (assoc-in [:auth/user :profile] profile)
       (dissoc
        :profile/media
        :profile/changes))))
```

Note that we're adding the new permanent URLs returned in our Ajax response
to our profile before we re-dispatch :profile/set-profile.

Now that we have re-frame set up, let's create some general components for
working with images.

guestbook-profile-2/src/cljs/guestbook/components.cljs

```
(defn image [url width height]
  [:div {:style {:width width
                 :height height
                 :display :flex
                 :justify-content :center
                 :align-items :center
                 :background-color "#F5F5F5"
                 :margin-bottom "0.5em"}}
   [:img {:src url :style {:max-width width
                           :max-height height}}]])

(defn image-uploader [save-fn label-text]
  [:div.file>label.file-label
   [:input.file-input {:type :file
                       :on-change #(save-fn
                                    (-> %
                                        .-target
                                        .-files
                                        (aget 0)))}]
   [:span.file-cta
    [:span.file-label label-text]]])
```

Then let's refer to them from our guestbook.views.profile namespace:

```
(ns guestbook.views.profile
  (:require
   [guestbook.components :refer [text-input textarea-input
                                 image image-uploader]]
   ;;...
   ))
```

And create avatar and banner components following the same pattern we used for display-name and bio.

guestbook-profile-2/src/cljs/guestbook/views/profile.cljs
```
(defn avatar []
  (r/with-let [k :avatar
               url  (rf/subscribe [:profile/field k ""])]
    [:<>
     [:h3 "Avatar"
      (when @(rf/subscribe [:profile/field-changed? k])
        " (Changed)")]
     [image @url 128 128]
     [:div.field.is-grouped
      [:div.control
       [image-uploader
        #(rf/dispatch [:profile/save-media k %])
        "Choose an Avatar..."]]
      [:div.control>button.button.is-danger
       {:disabled (not @(rf/subscribe [:profile/field-changed? k]))
        :on-click #(rf/dispatch [:profile/save-media k nil])}
       "Reset Avatar"]]]]))

(defn banner []
  (r/with-let [k :banner
               url  (rf/subscribe [:profile/field k ""])]
    [:<>
     [:h3 "Banner"
      (when @(rf/subscribe [:profile/field-changed? k])
        " (Changed)")]
     [image @url 1200 400]
     [:div.field.is-grouped
      [:div.control
       [image-uploader
        #(rf/dispatch [:profile/save-media k %])
        "Choose a Banner..."]]
      [:div.control>button.button.is-danger
       {:disabled (not @(rf/subscribe [:profile/field-changed? k]))
        :on-click #(rf/dispatch [:profile/save-media k nil])}
       "Reset Banner"]]]]))
```

Finally, let's add them to our profile page:

guestbook-profile-2/src/cljs/guestbook/views/profile.cljs
```clojure
(defn profile [_]
  (if-let [{:keys [login created_at profile]} @(rf/subscribe [:auth/user])]
    [:div.content
     [:h1 "My Account"
      (str "  <@" login ">")]
     [:p (str "Joined: " (.toString created_at))]
     [display-name]
     [bio]
     [avatar]
     [banner]
     (let [disabled? (not @(rf/subscribe [:profile/changed?]))]
       [:button.button.is-primary.is-large
        {:style {:width "100%"
                 :position :sticky
                 :bottom 10
                 :visibility (if disabled?
                               :hidden
                               :visible)}
         :on-click
         #(rf/dispatch [:profile/set-profile
                        @(rf/subscribe [:profile/profile])
                        @(rf/subscribe [:profile/media])])
         :disabled disabled?}
        "Update Profile"])]
    [:div.content
     [:div {:style {:width "100%"}}
      [:progress.progress.is-dark {:max 100} "30%"]]]))
```

We've included avatar and banner, and we've also made some changes to our "Update Profile" button. First, we've updated the :on-click function to pass our :profile/media map to our :profile/set-profile event. Also, since our page is quite a bit longer, we've added some CSS to ensure that it's onscreen, large, and prominent if there are any pending changes. This should prevent users from forgetting to save their profile changes.

Now our profile page should look something like the figure on page 243.

We're able to edit our Display Name, Bio, Avatar, and Banner with ease.

But we've missed a subtle bug with regards to our image-uploader components that we need to address before we move on. To illustrate this, try the following:

- Select an image to upload by clicking Choose an Avatar....
- Click Reset Avatar to clear it.
- Select the *same* image to upload a second time.
- The image no longer shows up in our preview!

This bug appears because our [:input {:type "file"}] component can't be controlled in the same way as display-name or bio (that is, it's impossible to set :value). As a result, the value from before Reset stays on our input, and thus selecting the same file doesn't trigger our :on-change function, so the preview remains unchanged.

To fix this, we need to do some extra work to ensure that our input stays in sync with our re-frame state. We can do this a couple ways. You could have the :on-click function of the "Reset" buttons use JavaScript interop to set the value of the corresponding file inputs to "", or you could have the component remount when the value is cleared in various ways. We're going to use a simple trick with React keys to force our component to remount when our value is reset.

Adding a key to an element gives React an explicitly defined identifier for a component. It's usually used with lists of items which may be rearranged so that React can manage changes more efficiently. However, we can use it to tell React when a component should be considered a brand-new instance and thus should be remounted from scratch. We can do this like so:

```
[:div.control
 ^{:key @(rf/subscribe [:profile/field-changed? k])}
 [image-uploader
  #(rf/dispatch [:profile/save-media k %])
  "Choose a..."]]
```

Now if our field goes into an unchanged state, it will remount, and thus have an empty value. We still have some inconsistent behavior if the user selects the same image twice *without* resetting. But all this results in is our save-fn being called a second time in this case.

We can do even better with a small trade-off. Since we're managing our file reference externally, we only need the value of our file input when save-fn is called. This means we don't actually need to keep it synchronized and can just clear it after *every* change instead. Now we don't have to change the way our image-uploader component is used across our app; we can just update its on-change function like so:

```
(defn image-uploader [save-fn label-text]
  [:div.file>label.file-label
   [:input.file-input {:type :file
                       :on-change (fn [e]
                                    (save-fn
                                     (-> e
                                         .-target
                                         .-files
                                         (aget 0)))
                                    (-> e
                                        .-target
                                        .-value
                                        (set! "")))}]
   [:span.file-cta
    [:span.file-label label-text]]]])
```

This may result in some slight performance reduction due to repeated calls to save-fn, but in practice we don't expect our users to repeatedly select the same image for uploading. Additionally, our first solution isn't without its drawbacks. Re-rendering our component is also a cost, and it's more likely to occur with regular use.

Now we can go back and remove our :key from avatar and banner, and we can use image-uploader in a straightforward way in the future.

Next, let's update our app to make use of the author profile.

Integrating the Profile into the App

Now that we have a profile for our authors, let's update a few things. Let's update our posts to display an avatar image, use the current display name for new posts, and add the banner and bio to the top of the author page.

Adding Avatar to Posts

Let's start by displaying our avatar on posts. The first thing we need to do is update our posts query and our posts by author query to do a SQL JOIN with the authors table so that we can get the avatar of the author:

guestbook-profile-2/resources/sql/queries.sql
```
-- :name get-messages :? :*
-- :doc selects all available messages
SELECT
  p.id              as id,
  p.timestamp       as timestamp,
  p.message         as message,
  p.name            as name,
  p.author          as author,
  a.profile->>'avatar' as avatar
from posts as p join users as a
on a.login = p.author
```

guestbook-profile-2/resources/sql/queries.sql
```
-- :name get-messages-by-author :? :*
-- :doc selects all messages posted by a user
SELECT
  p.id              as id,
  p.timestamp       as timestamp,
  p.message         as message,
  p.name            as name,
  p.author          as author,
  a.profile->>'avatar' as avatar
from posts as p join users as a
on a.login = p.author
WHERE author = :author
```

Then we need to update our :responses spec on /api/messages and /api/messages/by/:author to account for avatar.

```
{200
 {:body
  {:messages
   [{:id pos-int?
     :name string?
     :message string?
     :timestamp inst?
     :author (ds/maybe string?)
     :avatar (ds/maybe string?)}]}}}
```

Now we need to update our message-list. Let's create a separate message component and use Bulma's media component to render our post with an avatar.

guestbook-profile-2/src/cljs/guestbook/messages.cljs

```clojure
(defn message [{:keys [timestamp message name author avatar] :as m}]
  [:article.media
   [:figure.media-left
    [image (or avatar "/img/avatar-default.png") 128 128]]
   [:div.media-content>div.content
    [:time (.toLocaleString timestamp)]
    [:p message]
    [:p " - " name
     " <"
     (if author
       [:a {:href (str "/user/" author)} (str "@" author)]
       [:span.is-italic "account not found"])
     ">"]]]])

(defn message-list [messages]
  ;; Copied from guestbook.core...
  [:ul.messages
   (for [m @messages]
     ^{:key (:timestamp m)}
     [:li
      [message m]])])
```

Since we may not always have an avatar set by the author, we'll fall back on "/img/avatar-default.png".

Let's add this image (or one of your choosing) to our project under resources/public/img/avatar-default.png so that our message component uses it by default.

Now our posts on the home page and /user/:author should look like this:

Using Display Name for New Posts

Next, let's use our author's display name when posting messages. We could follow the same approach we took with avatars, but instead, let's keep the display name from when the post is written.

First, let's update our guestbook.messages/save-message! function like so:

```
guestbook-profile-2/src/clj/guestbook/messages.clj
(defn save-message! [{{:keys [display-name]} :profile
                       :keys [login]}
                      message]
  (if-let [errors (validate-message message)]
    (throw (ex-info "Message is invalid"
                    {:guestbook/error-id :validation
                     :errors errors}))
    (db/save-message! (assoc message
                             :author login
                             :name (or display-name login)))))
```

Then let's update the spec for /api/message to only accept a :message, since we're going to get the display name from the current user:

```
["/message"
 ;;...
 :post
 {:parameters
  {:body
   {:message string?}}
 ;;...
 }]
```

Then we update our message-schema to no longer require :name:

```
guestbook-profile-2/src/cljc/guestbook/validation.cljc
(ns guestbook.validation
  (:require
   [struct.core :as st]))

(def message-schema
  [[:message
    st/required
    st/string
    {:message "message must contain at least 10 characters"
     :validate (fn [msg] (>= (count msg) 10))}]])

(defn validate-message [params]
  (first (st/validate params message-schema)))
```

Finally, let's update our message-form component to display the current display name instead of prompting the user for one:

guestbook-profile-2/src/cljs/guestbook/messages.cljs

```clojure
(defn message-form []
  ;; Copied from guestbook.core...
  [:div
   [errors-component :server-error]
   [errors-component :unauthorized "Please log in before posting."]
   [:div.field
    [:label.label {:for :name} "Name"]
    (let [{:keys [login profile]} @(rf/subscribe [:auth/user])]
      (:display-name profile login))]
   [:div.field
    [:label.label {:for :message} "Message"]
    [errors-component :message]
    [textarea-input
     {:attrs {:name :message}
      :value (rf/subscribe [:form/field :message])
      :on-save #(rf/dispatch [:form/set-field :message %])}]]
   [:input.button.is-primary
    {:type :submit
     :disabled @(rf/subscribe [:form/validation-errors?])
     :on-click #(rf/dispatch [:message/send!
                              @(rf/subscribe [:form/fields])])
     :value "comment"}]])
```

Now we should be able to post messages with our current display name seamlessly. Our home page and /user/:author pages' message forms should look like this:

Enhancing the Author Page

First, we need to fetch the author when we navigate to their page.

Let's add some re-frame events and subscriptions and update our controllers
to load our author:

guestbook-profile-2/src/cljs/guestbook/views/author.cljs

```clojure
(rf/reg-event-fx
 ::fetch-author
 (fn [{:keys [db]} [_ login]]
   {:db (assoc db
               ::author nil
               ::loading? true)
    :ajax/get {:url (str "/api/author/" login)
               :success-event [::set-author]}}))

(rf/reg-event-db
 ::set-author
 (fn [db [_ author]]
   (if author
     (assoc db
            ::author author
            ::loading? false)
     (dissoc db ::author))))

(rf/reg-sub
 ::author
 (fn [db _]
   (get db ::author)))

(rf/reg-sub
 ::is-current-author?
 :<- [:auth/user]
 :<- [::author]
 (fn [[user author] _]
   (= (:login user) (:login author))))

(rf/reg-sub
 ::loading?
 (fn [db _]
   (::loading? db)))

(def author-controllers
  [{:parameters {:path [:user]}
    :start (fn [{{:keys [user]} :path}]
             (rf/dispatch [:messages/load-by-author user]))}
   {:parameters {:path [:user]}
    :start (fn [{{:keys [user]} :path}]
             (rf/dispatch [::fetch-author user]))
    :stop  (fn [_] (rf/dispatch [::set-author nil]))}])
```

Then we update the author page, like so:

guestbook-profile-2/src/cljs/guestbook/views/author.cljs

```
(defn banner-component [url]
  [:figure.image {:style {:width "100%"
                          :height "10vw"
                          :overflow "hidden"
                          :margin-left 0
                          :margin-right 0}}
   [:img {:src url}]])

(defn title []
  (if @(rf/subscribe [::is-current-author?])
    [:div.level
     [:h2.level-left "My Author Page"]
     [:a.level-right {:href (rtfe/href :guestbook.routes.app/profile)}
      "Edit Page"]]
    (let [{:keys [display-name login]} @(rf/subscribe [::author])]
      [:h2 display-name " <@" login ">'s Page"])))

(defn author [{{{:keys [user]} :path} :parameters}]
  (let [messages (rf/subscribe [:messages/list])
        author (rf/subscribe [::author])]
    (fn [{{{:keys [user]} :path} :parameters}]
      (if @(rf/subscribe [::loading?])
        [:div.content
         [:div {:style {:width "100%"}}
          [:progress.progress.is-dark {:max 100} "30%"]]]
        (let [{{:keys [display-name banner bio]} :profile} @author]
          [:div.content
           [banner-component (or banner "/img/banner-default.png")]
           [title]
           (when bio
             [:p bio])
           [:div.columns.is-centered>div.column.is-two-thirds
            [:div.columns>div.column
             [:h3 "Posts by " display-name " <@" user ">"]
             (if @(rf/subscribe [:messages/loading?])
               [messages/message-list-placeholder]
               [messages/message-list messages])]
            (when @(rf/subscribe [::is-current-author?])
              [:div.columns>div.column
               [:h4 "New Post"]
               [messages/message-form]])]])))))
```

We've created banner-component to render our banner as a wide image at the top of our page, and title to render a title bar. Then we've updated our author page in a few ways. Since we depend on ::author being loaded, we've added a loading bar if ::loading? is true. Then we've added our banner-component, title, and a :p tag with our author bio if it exists. Finally, we've added a message-form to the bottom if the author is the logged in user.

Our author page should now look like this:

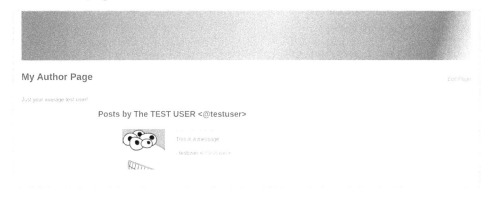

Great! We've got profiles leveraged across our app, so now users can customize their identity on our site.

Account Settings

Now that we've learned how to modify the profile, we should add some features for managing accounts. Let's enable users to change their passwords and delete their accounts.

Change Password

The first thing we need to do is write a SQL query to change the password, along with a function to call it.

```
guestbook-account/resources/sql/queries.sql
-- :name set-password-for-user!* :! :n
UPDATE users
SET password = :password
where login = :login
```

```
guestbook-account/src/clj/guestbook/auth.clj
(defn change-password! [login old-password new-password]
  (jdbc/with-transaction [t-conn db/*db*]
    (let [{hashed :password} (db/get-user-for-auth* t-conn {:login login})]
      (if (hashers/check old-password hashed)
        (db/set-password-for-user!*
          t-conn
          {:login login
           :password (hashers/derive new-password)})
        (throw (ex-info "Old password must match!"
                        {:guestbook/error-id ::authentication-failure
                         :error "Passwords do not match!"}))))))
```

Our change-password! function opens a database transaction, authenticates the old password, then hashes and sets the new password. It throws an error if the password check fails.

Then we need to create a service endpoint that calls our function. We'll reuse our :account/set-profile! role for now.

```
guestbook-account/src/clj/guestbook/routes/services.clj
["/change-password"
 {::auth/roles (auth/roles :account/set-profile!)
  :post {:parameters
         {:body
          {:old-password     string?
           :new-password     string?
           :confirm-password string?}}
         :handler
         (fn [{{{:keys [old-password
                        new-password
                        confirm-password]} :body} :parameters
               {:keys [identity]}                 :session}]
           (if
             (not= new-password confirm-password)
             (response/bad-request
              {:error :mismatch
               :message "Password and Confirm fields must match!"})
             (try
               (auth/change-password! (:login identity)
                                      old-password
                                      new-password)
               (response/ok {:success true})
               (catch clojure.lang.ExceptionInfo e
                 (if (= (:guestbook/error-id (ex-data e))
                        ::auth/authentication-failure)
                   (response/unauthorized
                    {:error :incorrect-password
                     :message "Old Password is incorrect, please try again."})
                   (throw e))))))}}]
 ;;...
 ]
```

This endpoint checks that the new password and confirmation match, then calls change-password!. If there's a mismatch or an authentication error, it replies with a helpful 4XX response.

Now we move to the client and write a component for our profile page to allow users to change their passwords. Since we're dealing with sensitive information, we keep everything in a local atom to prevent stale data or accidental leaking. This causes our component to be large, so we use letfn to keep it readable.

Here's the general structure of the component:

guestbook-account/src/cljs/guestbook/views/profile.cljs
```
;; require [ajax.core :as ajax]
;; ...

(defn change-password []
  (let [fields (r/atom {})
        errors (r/atom {})
        success (r/atom {})]
    (letfn [(password-field [id label]
              ;;helper component
              )
            (change-password! []
              ;;helper function
              )]
      (fn []
        [:<>
         [:h3 "Change Password"]
         [password-field :old-password "Current Password"]
         [password-field :new-password "New Password"]
         [password-field :confirm-password "New Password (confirm)"]
         [:div.field
          (when-let [message (:server @errors)]
            [:p.message.is-danger message])
          (when-let [message (:message @success)]
            [:p.message.is-success message])
          [:button.button
           {:on-click
            (fn [_]
              (change-password!))}
           "Change Password"]]]))))
```

Now we have to fill in our password-field component and our change-password!
function.

First, let's write our password-field:

guestbook-account/src/cljs/guestbook/views/profile.cljs
```
(password-field [id label]
  (r/with-let [v (r/cursor fields [id])
               e (r/cursor errors [id])]
    [:div.field
     [:label.label {:for id} label]
     [:input.input {:id id
                    :type :password
                    :value @v
                    :on-change #(reset! v (.. % -target -value))}]
     (when-let [message @e]
       [:p.help.is-danger message])]))
```

It's fairly straightforward. It's just a label, a password input which is bound to a key on our fields atom, and an error message from the same key on our errors atom.

Next, let's write our change-password! function:

guestbook-account/src/cljs/guestbook/views/profile.cljs
```
(change-password! []
  (let [{:keys [new-password
                confirm-password]
         :as params} @fields]
    (if (not= new-password confirm-password)
      (reset! errors
              {:new-password     "New Password and Confirm must match!"
               :confirm-password "New Password and Confirm must match!"})
      (ajax/POST "/api/my-account/change-password"
        {:params params
         :handler
         (fn [_]
             ;; Display success message for 5 seconds
           (swap! success
                  (fn [{:keys
                        [timeout]}]
                    (when timeout
                      (js/clearTimeout timeout))
                    {:message "Password change successful!"
                     :timeout (js/setTimeout
                                (fn []
                                  (reset! success {}))
                                5000)}))
           (reset! fields {})
           (reset! errors {}))
         :error-handler
         (fn [{r :response}]
           (println r)
           (reset!
            errors
            (case (:error r)
              :incorrect-password
              {:old-password (:message r)}

              :mismatch
              {:new-password     (:message r)
               :confirm-password (:message r)}

                ;; ELSE
              {:server
               "Unknown Server Error. Please try again!"})))}))))
```

The change-password! function is a bit longer, but it's fairly straightforward. It validates our fields atom, sends a POST request, and processes the response. If there's an issue, it sets the errors atom accordingly. If the password is changed successfully, it clears our fields and errors and sets our success message for five seconds.

Now we just have to add an account settings section to our profile page and include our change-password component:

guestbook-account/src/cljs/guestbook/views/profile.cljs
```clojure
(defn account-settings []
  [:<>
   [:h2 "Account Settings"]
   [change-password]])

(defn profile [_]
  (if-let [{:keys [login created_at]} @(rf/subscribe [:auth/user])]
    [:div.content
     [:h1 "My Account"
      (str " <@" login ">")]
     [:p (str "Joined: " (.toString created_at))]
     [:h2 "My Profile"]
     [display-name]
     [bio]
     [avatar]
     [banner]
     (let [disabled? (not @(rf/subscribe [:profile/changed?]))]
       [:button.button.is-primary.is-large
        {:style {:width "100%"
                 :position :sticky
                 :bottom 10
                 :visibility (if disabled?
                               :hidden
                               :visible)}
         :on-click
         #(rf/dispatch [:profile/set-profile
                        @(rf/subscribe [:profile/profile])
                        @(rf/subscribe [:profile/media])])
         :disabled disabled?}
        "Update Profile"])
     [account-settings]]
    [:div.content
     [:div {:style {:width "100%"}}
      [:progress.progress.is-dark {:max 100} "30%"]]]))
```

Our profile page should now look like the figure on page 256.

Next, let's add the option to delete the account.

Delete Account

Just like with changing passwords, we start with a query:

guestbook-account/resources/sql/queries.sql
```
-- :name delete-user!* :! :n
DELETE FROM users
where login = :login
```

And write a wrapper function to handle authentication:

guestbook-account/src/clj/guestbook/auth.clj
```
(defn delete-account! [login password]
  (jdbc/with-transaction [t-conn db/*db*]
    (let [{hashed :password} (db/get-user-for-auth* t-conn {:login login})]
      (if (hashers/check password hashed)
        (db/delete-user!* t-conn {:login login})
        (throw (ex-info "Password is incorrect!"
                        {:guestbook/error-id ::authentication-failure
                         :error "Password is incorrect!"}))))))
```

Then we write a service endpoint to call this function from the client:

guestbook-account/src/clj/guestbook/routes/services.clj
```
["/my-account"
 ["/delete-account"
  {::auth/roles (auth/roles :account/set-profile!)
   :post
   {:parameters
    {:body {:login string?
            :password string?}}
    :handler
```

```
(fn [{{{:keys [login password]} :body} :parameters
      {{user :login} :identity} :session
      :as req}]
  (if (not= login user)
    (response/bad-request
     {:message "Login must match the current user!"})
    (try
      (auth/delete-account! user password)
      (-> (response/ok)
          (assoc :session
                 (select-keys
                  (:session req)
                  [:ring.middleware.anti-forgery/anti-forgery-token])))
      (catch clojure.lang.ExceptionInfo e
        (if (= (:guestbook/error-id (ex-data e))
               ::auth/authentication-failure)
          (response/unauthorized
           {:error :incorrect-password
            :message "Password is incorrect, please try again!"})
          (throw e)))))))}}]
  ;;...
  ]
```

Now we're ready to start writing our client-side code.

Let's use a modal to handle account deletion. We can reuse our modal-button component, but let's refactor it first to allow us to change the button styling.

Let's update our modal-button to accept an opts map so that we can add the is-danger class to our button for account deletion:

guestbook-account/src/cljs/guestbook/modals.cljs
```
(defn modal-button
  ([id title body footer]
   [modal-button id {:button {:class ["is-primary"]}} title body footer])
  ([id opts title body footer]
   [:div
    [:button.button
     (merge (:button opts)
            {:on-click #(rf/dispatch [:app/show-modal id])})
     title]
    [modal-card id title body footer]]))
```

We've kept the original 4-arity form so that our existing code still works, but we've added a 5-arity version that handles the optional opts map. The only key on our opts map that's used is :button, but we can easily add additional keys to this map in the future.

Now let's write our delete account component using our updated modal-button.

guestbook-account/src/cljs/guestbook/views/profile.cljs

```clojure
;; require [reitit.frontend.easy :as rtfe]
;;         [guestbook.modals :as m]
;; ...
(defn delete-account [username]
  (r/with-let [fields (r/atom {})
               login (r/cursor fields [:login])
               password (r/cursor fields [:password])
               status (r/atom {})]
    [:<>
     [:h3 "Delete Account"]
     [m/modal-button
      ::delete-account
      {:button {:class ["is-danger"]}}
      "Delete Account"
      ;; Modal Body
      [:section
       [:div.message.is-danger
        [:div.message-header (str "Deleting Account " username)]
        [:div.message-body "Are you sure you wish to delete your account?"]]
       (when-let [message (:error @status)]
         [:div.message.is-danger>div.message-body message])
       [:div.field.is-horizontal
        [:div.field-label.is-normal>label.label {:for :login} "Login"]
        [:div.field-body>input.input
         {:id :login
          :autocomplete false
          :value @login
          :on-change #(reset! login (.. % -target -value))
          :disabled (:loading @status)
          :type :text}]]
       [:div.field.is-horizontal
        [:div.field-label.is-normal>label.label {:for :password} "Password"]
        [:div.field-body>input.input
         {:id :password
          :value @password
          :disabled (:loading @status)
          :on-change #(reset! password (.. % -target -value))
          :type :password
          :autocomplete false}]]]
      ;; Modal Footer
      [:div.field.is-grouped
       [:p.control>button.button.is-light
        {:disabled (:loading @status)
         :on-click (fn [_]
                     (reset! fields {})
                     (reset! status {})
                     (rf/dispatch [:app/hide-modal ::delete-account]))}
        "Cancel"]
```

```
    [:p.control>button.button.is-danger
     {:disabled (or (:loading @status) (empty? @login) (empty? @password))
      :on-click
      (fn [_]
        (if (not= @login username)
          (reset! status
                  {:error
                   (str "Login must match current user: " username)})
          (do
            (reset! status {:loading true})
            (ajax/POST "/api/my-account/delete-account"
              {:params @fields
               :handler
               (fn [_]
                 (reset! status {})
                 (reset! fields {})
                 (rf/dispatch [:app/hide-modal ::delete-account])
                 (rf/dispatch [:auth/handle-logout])
                 (rtfe/push-state :guestbook.routes.app/home))
               :error-handler
               (fn [{r :response}]
                 (if (= (:error r) :incorrect-password)
                   (reset! status {:error
                                    "Incorrect password, please try again."})
                   (reset! status {:error
                                    "Unknown Error Occured."})))}))))}
     "Delete Account"]]]]))
```

Our delete-account component is long but is a straightforward instance of our
modal-button component. Our modal body has an error message at the top and
then our login and password fields bound to our fields atom. Our modal footer
has a "Cancel" button, and a "Delete Account" button. The majority of our logic is
inside the :on-click function of our "Delete Account" button. We start by ensuring
that our login field is correct, then we set our :loading flag in our status atom
and send our POST request. If we successfully delete the account, we clear
everything, close the modal, and redirect to the home page. If we encounter
an error, we clear our :loading flag and set our :error message.

Finally, let's add our delete-account component to our account-settings and see how
it looks:

guestbook-account/src/cljs/guestbook/views/profile.cljs
```
(defn account-settings []
  [:<>
   [:h2 "Account Settings"]
   [change-password]
   [delete-account (:login @(rf/subscribe [:auth/user]))]])
```

Now our page should look like this:

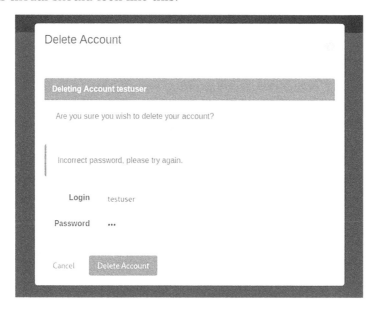

And our modal should look like this:

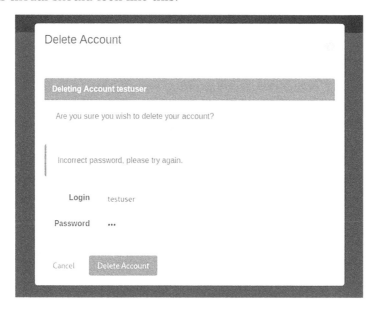

Our users are now able to effectively manage their accounts and preferences. In the future, we could add many things to our account profiles, such as location, birth date, theming preferences, account visibilty, privacy, and so on. It would follow the same pattern we've used here, and it would just be a matter of updating the app to respond to these options.

What You've Learned

The primary goal of this chapter was to introduce all aspects of creating an SPA. We created multiple independent pages that share a common foundation and established a pattern for adding more as needed. This includes creating shared routing between client and server, front-end page management, and protocol-agnostic authorization.

Meanwhile, we've covered media management tasks such as image manipulation with Java interop, file uploads, and file storage as BLOBs. Additionally, we leveraged Postgres's JSONB data type to create an easily extensible author profile. This allows us to iterate rapidly without having to repeatedly modify our database tables. It also maps well onto the Clojure philosophy of additive enhancement via associative data structures.

Now that we have some real experience with the ins and outs of working with a Clojure(Script) SPA, we're ready to add some more-sophisticated features. In the next chapter, we'll add some richer pages, including a user feed, and we'll add some features to posts.

CHAPTER 8

Social Interaction

Currently we have an app where users are able to generate content, but they don't have any meaningful ways to engage with each other. In this chapter, we'll enhance posts to allow for richer content such as images. We'll add tags and mentions to enrich post metadata. We'll add the ability to boost posts and reply to posts. Finally, we'll add the ability to follow users and subscribe to tags with a personalized feed.

Improving Posts

At this point our posts are pretty spartan, even though they are the reason people will use our app. Let's add richer interactions and features to posts. To start, let's create a new page for viewing an individual post. Once we have a dedicated page, we'll be able to build on it. Also, we can start by adding features to the post page and then adapt it to the smaller form factor of the post list.

First, we need a query.

guestbook-post-page/resources/sql/queries.sql
```
-- :name get-message :? :1
-- :doc selects a message
SELECT
  p.id                 as id,
  p.timestamp          as timestamp,
  p.message            as message,
  p.name               as name,
  p.author             as author,
  a.profile->>'avatar' as avatar
from posts as p join users as a
on a.login = p.author
where p.id = :id
```

Then we need a wrapper to handle params.

guestbook-post-page/src/clj/guestbook/messages.clj
```clojure
(defn get-message [post-id]
  (db/get-message {:id post-id}))
```

Then, before we can write a service endpoint, we need to add a new entry to guestbook.auth/roles.

```clojure
(def roles
 {;; ...
  :message/get #{:any}})
```

Now we can write an endpoint to get our single messsage. Since we have a handler under POST "/api/message" already, we'll have to move things around.

guestbook-post-page/src/clj/guestbook/routes/services.clj
```clojure
["/message"
 ["/:post-id"
  {::auth/roles (auth/roles :message/get)
   :get {:parameters
         {:path
          {:post-id pos-int?}}

         :responses
         {200 {:message map?}

          ;; e.g. author has blocked you or has private account
          403 {:message string?}

          404 {:message string?}

          500 {:message string?}}

         :handler
         (fn [{{{:keys [post-id]} :path} :parameters}]
           (if-some [post (msg/get-message post-id)]
             (response/ok
              {:message post})
             (response/not-found
              {:message "Post Not Found"})))}}]
 [""
  {::auth/roles (auth/roles :message/create!)
   :post { ;; Move save-message! handler here
   }}]]
```

Notice that we've moved the map that was under ["/message"] into another vector like so:

```clojure
["/message"
 ["" {}]]
```

This way, we can add additional matchers under "/api/message" without affecting our initial POST "/api/message" handler.

Let's try our new endpoint out in Swagger UI:

`GET` /api/message/{post-id}

Parameters

Parameter	Value	Description	Parameter Type	Data Type
post-id	5		path	long

Response Messages

HTTP Status Code	Reason	Response Model	Headers
200			
403			
404			
500			

Try it out!

Curl

```
curl -X GET --header 'Accept: application/json' 'http://localhost:3000/api/message/5'
```

Request URL

```
http://localhost:3000/api/message/5
```

Response Body

```
{
  "message": {
    "name": "Test User",
    "author": "testuser",
    "id": 5,
    "avatar": null,
    "timestamp": "2020-08-29T21:05:04Z",
    "message": "This is a Message"
  }
}
```

Response Code

```
200
```

Looks good. Now let's write our post page.

guestbook-post-page/src/cljs/guestbook/views/post.cljs
```clojure
(ns guestbook.views.post
  (:require
   [re-frame.core :as rf]
   [reagent.core :as r]
   [cljs.pprint :refer [pprint]]
   [guestbook.messages :as msg]))

(defn clear-post-keys [db]
  (dissoc db ::error ::post))

(rf/reg-event-fx
 ::fetch-post
 (fn [{:keys [db]} [_ post-id]]
   {:db (clear-post-keys db)
    :ajax/get {:url (str "/api/message/" post-id)
               :success-path [:message]
               :success-event [::set-post]
               :error-event [::set-post-error]}}))
```

```
(rf/reg-event-db
 ::set-post
 (fn [db [_ post]]
   (assoc db ::post post)))

(rf/reg-event-db
 ::set-post-error
 (fn [db [_ response]]
   (assoc db ::error response)))

(rf/reg-event-db
 ::clear-post
 (fn [db _]
   (clear-post-keys db)))

(rf/reg-sub
 ::post
 (fn [db _]
   (::post db nil)))

(rf/reg-sub
 ::error
 (fn [db _]
   (::error db)))

(rf/reg-sub
 ::loading?
 :<- [::post]
 :<- [::error]
 (fn [[post error] _]
   (and (empty? post) (empty? error))))

(def post-controllers
  [{:parameters {:path [:post]}
    :start (fn [{{:keys [post]} :path}]
            (rf/dispatch [::fetch-post post]))
    :stop (fn [_]
            (rf/dispatch [::clear-post]))}])

(defn loading-bar []
  [:progress.progress.is-dark {:max 100} "30%"])

(defn post [{:keys [name author message timestamp avatar] :as post-content}]
  [:div.content
   [:h3.title.is-3 "Post by " name
    "<" [:a {:href (str "/user/" author)} (str "@" author)] ">"]
   [:h4.subtitle.is-4 "Posted at " (.toLocaleString timestamp)]
   [msg/message post-content]])

(defn post-page [_]
  (let [post-content @(rf/subscribe [::post])
        {status :status
         {:keys [message]} :response
         :as error} @(rf/subscribe [::error])]
```

```
(cond
  @(rf/subscribe [::loading?])
  [:div.content
   [:p "Loading Message..."]
   [loading-bar]]

  (seq error)
  (case status
    404
    [:div.content
     [:p (or message "Post not found.")]
     [:pre (with-out-str (pprint error))]]

    403
    [:div.content
     [:p (or message "You are not allowed to view this post.")]
     [:pre (with-out-str (pprint @error))]]

    [:div
     [:p (or message "Unknown Error")]
     [:pre (with-out-str (pprint @error))]])

  (seq post-content)
  [post post-content])))
```

We have some standard re-frame events and subscriptions for our post. Then we have our post component that renders the happy case; for now this is just a wrapper around guestbook.messages/message. Finally, we have our post-page at the top level handling errors and loading.

Now, let's add our post page to our app routes.

guestbook-post-page/src/cljc/guestbook/routes/app.cljc
```
;; require [guestbook.views.post :as post]
;; inside #?&(:cljs [...])

["/post/:post"
 (merge
  {:name ::post}
  #?(:cljs {:parameters {:path {:post pos-int?}}
            :controllers post/post-controllers
            :view #'post/post-page}))]
```

Now we can visit a post by ID if we type it into the URL manually as shown in the figure on page 268.

Looks good.

Next, let's update the messages in the message-list component to link to this page, along with a way to return to our place in the timeline.

Let's add a link to our message component:

```
(defn message [{:keys [id timestamp message name author avatar] :as m}]
  [:article.media
   ;;...
   [:p>a {:href (str "/post/" id)}]
   ;;...
   ])
```

And add a back button to our post page:

```
(defn post [{:keys [timestamp message name author avatar] :as m}]
  [:div.content
   [:button.button.is-info.is-outlined.is-fullwidth
    {:on-click #(.back js/window.history)}
    "Back to Feed"]
   ;;...
   ])
```

This works for now, but it could be very frustrating for users when there are a lot of posts, since they'll lose their place. Let's add some functionality to ensure that we go back to the post we expanded if we go back in history.

The first thing we need to do is add a way for any page that renders a message-list to scroll to a specific post:

```
guestbook-post-page/src/cljs/guestbook/messages.cljs
(defn msg-li [m message-id]
  (r/create-class
   {:component-did-mount
    (fn [this]
      (when (= message-id (:id m))
        (.scrollIntoView (dom/dom-node this))))
    :reagent-render
    (fn [_]
      [:li
       [message m]])}))

(defn message-list
  ([messages]
   [message-list messages nil])
```

```
  ([messages message-id]
   [:ul.messages
    (for [m @messages]
      ^{:key (:timestamp m)}
      [msg-li m message-id])]))
```

Now if we pass a message-id to message-list, any message that matches the ID is scrolled into vision. Let's update our author and home pages to pass this ID in from their query parameters.

First we add the query parameter to our app-routes declaration:

guestbook-post-page/src/cljc/guestbook/routes/app.cljc
```
;; require [spec-tools.data-spec :as ds]

["/"
 (merge
  {:name ::home}
  #?(:cljs
     {:parameters {:query {(ds/opt :post) pos-int?}}
      :controllers home/home-controllers
      :view #'home/home}))]
;;...
["/user/:user"
 (merge
  {:name ::author}
  #?(:cljs {:parameters {:query {(ds/opt :post) pos-int?}
                         :path {:user string?}}
            :controllers author/author-controllers
            :view #'author/author}))]
```

Then we pass it into message-list from their respective view components:

guestbook-post-page/src/cljs/guestbook/views/home.cljs
```
(defn home [{{{post :post} :query} :parameters}]
  ;;...
          [messages/message-list messages post]
          ;;...)
```

guestbook-post-page/src/cljs/guestbook/views/author.cljs
```
(defn author [{{{:keys [user]} :path
                {:keys [post]} :query} :parameters}]
  ;;...
              [messages/message-list messages post]
              ;;...)
```

Now we can trigger this behavior manually by adding a query parameter to the URL, like the figure on page 270.

We still have a problem, though. We don't have that ID in our browser history, and there's no easy way for the post page to know which page linked to it. Let's

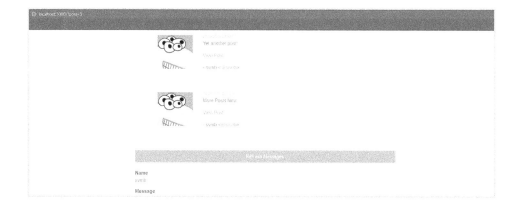

solve this by adding some logic to our view post link that modifies our browser history to include the :post query parameter in the URL.

guestbook-post-page/src/cljs/guestbook/messages.cljs
```
;; require [reitit.frontend.easy :as rtfe]
[:p>a {:on-click (fn [_]
                  (let [{{:keys [name]} :data
                         {:keys [path query]} :parameters}
                        @(rf/subscribe [:router/current-route])]
                    (rtfe/replace-state name path (assoc query :post id)))
                  (rtfe/push-state :guestbook.routes.app/post {:post id}))}
 "View Post"]
```

Instead of using an :href on our anchor tag, we're using an :on-click that uses the history API functions provided by reitit.frontend.easy. This changes our current URL in the history to include the post-id in the query parameters. So if we click the back button, we'll scroll to the post we clicked on! We don't even need to change our button on the post page, since the URL in history is all we need.

Now that we have the basic structure for working with posts in place, let's add some features.

Post Types

Right now, we can only post text. This is fine, but it'd be nice if we were able to post different types of media, such as images, videos, audio, links, or articles. Let's update our posts table to allow for multiple types of posts, and let's implement three of them: text, articles (Markdown), and images.

All of these can be special cases of Markdown, so let's do that first.

We'll use the markdown-clj library[1] to parse Markdown posts. Let's start by ensuring it's included in project.clj before we get started.

```
[markdown-clj "1.10.5"]
```

An important consideration here is that this library will return raw HTML, so we'll have to ensure that we properly sanitize user input. Also, we'll have to use :dangerouslySetInnerHTML for these posts. This should be avoided in most cases, but it's an important escape hatch for cases where you need to render predefined markup.

Let's start by writing a general purpose component for rendering Markdown strings safely in guestbook.components:

```
guestbook-post-md/src/cljs/guestbook/components.cljs
(defn escape-html
  "Change special characters into HTML character entities."
  [text state]
  (if (or (:code state) (:codeblock state))
    [text state] ;; Don't escape code blocks!
    [(string/escape text {\& "&amp;"
                          \< "&lt;"
                          \> "&gt;"
                          \" "&quot;"
                          \' "&#39;"})
     state]))
(def transformers
  (into [escape-html] transformer-vector))

(defn parse-message [message]
  (md->html message :replacement-transformers transformers))

(defn md
  ([content]
   [md :p {} content])
  ([tag content]
   [md tag {} content])
  ([tag attrs content]
   [tag (-> attrs
            (assoc :dangerouslySetInnerHTML
                   {:__html (parse-message content)})
            (update :class (fnil conj []) "markdown"))]))
```

Here, we're adding an escape-html transformer to the front of our :replacement-transformers so that before markdown-clj does any parsing, we've sanitized any user provided HTML.

---

1.   https://github.com/yogthos/markdown-clj

Next, let's update our message component to use our md component instead of just a :p tag:

```
guestbook-post-md/src/cljs/guestbook/messages.cljs
;; Update `:require` to include:
;; [guestbook.components :refer [text-input textarea-input image md]]
(defn message
  ([m] [message m {}])
  ([{:keys [id timestamp message name author avatar] :as m}
    {:keys [include-link?]
     :or {include-link? true}}]
   [:article.media
    [:figure.media-left
     [image (or avatar "/img/avatar-default.png") 128 128]]
    [:div.media-content>div.content
     [:time (.toLocaleString timestamp)]
     [md message]
     (when include-link?
       [:p>a {:on-click
              (fn [_]
                (let [{{:keys [name]} :data
                       {:keys [path query]} :parameters}
                      @(rf/subscribe [:router/current-route])]
                  (rtfe/replace-state name path (assoc query :post id)))
                (rtfe/push-state :guestbook.routes.app/post {:post id}))}
        "View Post"])
     [:p " - " name
      " <"
      (if author
        [:a {:href (str "/user/" author)} (str "@" author)]
        [:span.is-italic "account not found"])
      ">"]]]]))
```

Let's try writing a simple Markdown post:

Now users can write arbitrary Markdown in their posts and it will render properly. They can even include images, links, and blockquotes.

Before we move on, let's add transformers for mentions and tags as well. We'll leave the server-side processing for later, but we can insert the links while we're here.

guestbook-post-md/src/cljs/guestbook/components.cljs
```clojure
(defn linkify-tags
  "Change tags into links"
  [text state]
  (if (or (:code state) (:codeblock state))
    [text state]
    [(string/replace
      text
      #_#"(?<=\s|^)#([-\w]+)(?=\s|$)"
      #"(\s|^)#([-\w]+)(?=\s|$)"
      "$1<a href=\"/tag/$2\"
          title=\"View posts tagged #$2\"
          target=\"_blank\">
        #$2
      </a>")
     state]))

(defn linkify-mentions
  "Change mentions into links"
  [text state]
  (if (or (:code state) (:codeblock state))
    [text state]
    [(string/replace
      text
      #_#"@([-\w]+)(?=\s|$)"
      #"(\s|^)@([-\w]+)(?=\s|$)"
      "$1<a href=\"/user/$2\"
          title=\"Homepage of @$2\"
          target=\"_blank\">
        @$2
      </a>")
     state]))

(def transformers
  (into [escape-html linkify-tags linkify-mentions] transformer-vector))
```

These transformers are doing very similar things. They're both looking for strings starting with a special character with whitespace on either side and replacing them with HTML anchors based on their capture group. Following common conventions, our tags begin with # and our mentions begin with @. Notice that we're inserting them *after* the escape-html transformer so that our returned HTML isn't getting escaped.

Great, now we're able to have links to user pages, as well as not-yet-implemented tag pages.

Next, let's improve our message-form component so that users can leverage these new features.

Post Composition

Markdown can represent pretty much every type of post, but we need to enhance how users compose this Markdown to ensure that they are able to easily create rich posts leveraging Markdown's full feature set.

Post Preview

With most Markdown editors online, users expect a preview before they submit a post, so let's add that. Let's create a post-preview component and add it to our message form:

```
guestbook-post-md/src/cljs/guestbook/messages.cljs
(defn message-preview [m]
  (r/with-let [expanded (r/atom false)]
    [:<>
     [:button.button.is-secondary.is-fullwidth
      {:on-click #(swap! expanded not)}
      (if @expanded
        "Hide Preview"
        "Show Preview")]
     (when @expanded
       [:ul.messages
        {:style
         {:margin-left 0}}
        [:li
         [message m
          {:include-link? false}]]])]))

(defn message-form []
  [:div.card
   [:div.card-header>p.card-header-title
    "Post Something!"]
   (let [{:keys [login profile]} @(rf/subscribe [:auth/user])
         display-name (:display-name profile login)]
     [:div.card-content
      [message-preview {:message @(rf/subscribe [:form/field :message])
                        :id -1
                        :timestamp (js/Date.)
                        :name display-name
                        :author login
                        :avatar (:avatar profile)}]
      [errors-component :server-error]
      [errors-component :unauthorized "Please log in before posting."]
      [:div.field
       [:label.label {:for :name} "Name"]
       display-name]
      [:div.field
       [:label.label {:for :message} "Message"]
       [errors-component :message]
```

```
[textarea-input
 {:attrs {:name :message}
  :value (rf/subscribe [:form/field :message])
  :on-save #(rf/dispatch [:form/set-field :message %])}]]
[:input.button.is-primary.is-fullwidth
 {:type :submit
  :disabled @(rf/subscribe [:form/validation-errors?])
  :on-click #(rf/dispatch [:message/send!
                            @(rf/subscribe [:form/fields])])
  :value "comment"}]])])
```

Now let's try it out.

It's showing up, but only when we blur the field (for example, when we first click the Show Preview button). Ideally, we should have the preview update as we type if we have it expanded. To do this, we'll add a call to on-save inside of our :on-change event handler. But we don't want to overload our re-frame event queue. Even though our current app could handle rapid-fire save events, it's unneccessary and could cause performance issues as our app gets larger. To mitigate this, we'll debounce this call to on-save. Also, since different uses of our textarea-input may require more or less frequent saves, we'll allow the timeout to be parameterized.

First, let's update our textarea-input component like so:

```
guestbook-post-md/src/cljs/guestbook/components.cljs
;; require [goog.functions :as gf]
(defn textarea-input [{val    :value
                       attrs :attrs
                       ms     :save-timeout
                       :keys [on-save]}]
  (let [draft (r/atom nil)
        value (r/track #(or @draft @val ""))
        save-on-change (if ms
                         (gf/debounce on-save ms)
                         (fn [& _]))]
    (fn []
      [:textarea.textarea
       (merge attrs
              {:on-focus #(reset! draft (or @val ""))
               :on-blur (fn []
                          (on-save (or @draft ""))
                          (reset! draft nil))
               :on-change (fn [e]
                            (let [v (.. e -target -value)]
                              (reset! draft v)
                              (save-on-change v)))
               :value @value})])))
```

Then we update our message-form's textarea-input to provide a :save-timeout to use this new feature:

```
guestbook-post-md/src/cljs/guestbook/messages.cljs
[textarea-input
 {:attrs {:name :message}
  ;; Add save-timeout to refresh preview after 1s without edits
  :save-timeout 1000
  :value (rf/subscribe [:form/field :message])
  :on-save #(rf/dispatch [:form/set-field :message %])}]]
```

That should do it. Let's test it out in the browser.

Great! If we're actively typing, it doesn't try to save, but if we pause for a second, it renders the preview for us while we contemplate what to write next.

Multimedia Uploads

At this point, users can manually type in image URLs and they'll show up in their Markdown posts. But we'd like to allow users to upload media as they're composing a post.

Let's add a button to insert an image in our post's Markdown.

First, let's add some events for inserting the image Markdown at the end of the post's message and keeping track of our files and URLs.

guestbook-post-media/src/cljs/guestbook/messages.cljs

```clojure
(rf/reg-event-db
 :message/save-media
 (fn [db [_ img]]
   (let [url (js/URL.createObjectURL img)
         name (keyword (str "msg-" (random-uuid)))]
     (-> db
         (update-in [:form/fields :message] str "![](" url ")")
         (update :message/media (fnil assoc {}) name img)
         (update :message/urls (fnil assoc {}) url name)))))

(rf/reg-event-db
 :message/clear-media
 (fn [db _]
   (dissoc db :message/media :message/urls)))

(rf/reg-sub
 :message/media
 (fn [db [_]]
   (:message/media db)))
```

Then let's add a form control to our message-form to dispatch our event:

guestbook-post-media/src/cljs/guestbook/messages.cljs

```clojure
;;...
[:div.field
 [:div.control
  [image-uploader
   #(rf/dispatch [:message/save-media %])
   "Insert an Image"]]]
;;...
```

Finally, let's update :message/send! to upload our images before sending our message over the WebSocket.

guestbook-post-media/src/cljs/guestbook/messages.cljs

```clojure
(rf/reg-event-fx
 :message/send!-called-back
 (fn [_ [_ {:keys [success errors]}]]
   (if success
     {:dispatch-n [[:form/clear-fields] [:message/clear-media]]}
     {:dispatch [:form/set-server-errors errors]})))

(rf/reg-event-fx
 :message/send!
 (fn [{:keys [db]} [_ fields media]]
   (if (not-empty media)
     {:db (dissoc db :form/server-errors)
      :ajax/upload-media!
```

```
    {:url "/api/my-account/media/upload"
     :files media
     :handler
     (fn [response]
       (rf/dispatch
        [:message/send!
         (update fields :message
                 string/replace
                 #"\!\[(.*)\]\((.+)\)"
                 (fn [[old alt url]]
                   (str "![" alt "]("
                        (if-some [name ((:message/urls db) url)]
                          (get response name)
                          url) ")")))])])}}
    {:db (dissoc db :form/server-errors)
     :ws/send! {:message [:message/create! fields]
                :timeout 10000
                :callback-event [:message/send!-called-back]}}})))
(defn message-form []
  [:div.card
   [:div.card-header>p.card-header-title
    "Post Something!"]
   (let [{:keys [login profile]} @(rf/subscribe [:auth/user])
         display-name (:display-name profile login)]
     [:div.card-content
      [:input.button.is-primary.is-fullwidth
       {:type :submit
        :disabled @(rf/subscribe [:form/validation-errors?])
        :on-click #(rf/dispatch [:message/send!
                                 @(rf/subscribe [:form/fields])
                                 @(rf/subscribe [:message/media])])
        :value "comment"}]])])
```

Let's give it a try in the browser. Try uploading a few images, as well as manually including a link to an exernal image as shown in the figure on page 279.

Great! It works as expected. Now users can post media, and they can arrange their posts however they see fit with standard Markdown.

Now that we have rich posts, let's improve our post interaction and aggregation features.

Boosting Posts

Let's add the most basic form of interaction—a boost. This is equivalent to a re-post. It should push the post to the top of the global timeline, and it should add the post to the re-poster's author page.

We'll need to do a few things to accomplish this.

First, we need a table for boosts. Then we need to update our posts queries to use this boosts table. Then we need to add a way for users to boost posts from the UI. Let's start by adding a boosts table:

```
user=> (create-migration "add-boosts-table")
```

And add the follwing up migration:

guestbook-boosts/resources/migrations/20200822195958-add-boosts-table.up.sql

```
CREATE TABLE boosts
(user_id text not null references users(login) ON DELETE cascade
                                               ON UPDATE cascade,
 post_id integer not null references posts(id) ON DELETE cascade
                                               ON UPDATE cascade,
 poster   text references users(login)         ON DELETE set null
                                               ON UPDATE cascade,
 timestamp TIMESTAMP not null DEFAULT now(),
 PRIMARY KEY(user_id, post_id));
```

Don't forget the down migration as well:

guestbook-boosts/resources/migrations/20200822195958-add-boosts-table.down.sql
```
DROP TABLE IF EXISTS boosts;
```

In our boosts table, we have four columns: user_id, post_id, poster, and timestamp. The primary key, (user_id, post_id), means that a user can only boost a post once. The poster column is the person who the user got the post from (that is, the nearest booster), not to be confused with the author. This column allows us to treat boosts as linked lists in one direction and trees in the other. We can see the way in which a post was disseminated through a network by tracing the poster through the boosts back to the original post.

Now that we have this table, let's write some SQL for interacting with it. Let's start with inserting a boost and selecting all boosts for a post:

guestbook-boosts/resources/sql/queries.sql
```
-- :name boost-post! :! :n
-- Boosts a post, or moves a boost to the top of the user's timeline
INSERT INTO boosts
(user_id, post_id, poster)
VALUES (:user, :post, nullif(:poster, :user))
ON CONFLICT (user_id, post_id) DO UPDATE
SET timestamp = now()
WHERE boosts.user_id = :user
AND   boosts.post_id = :post

-- :name boosters-of-post :? :*
-- Get all boosters of a post
SELECT user_id as user from boosts
where post_id = :post
```

For our INSERT statement, we have an ON CONFLICT clause that refreshes the boost if it already exists. This allows users to signal boost content at a later date without flooding the timeline with duplicates. It also ensures that poster never equals user. Our select is fairly straightforward, but we'll likely use more sophisticated queries in most cases.

Next, let's use the poster column in recursive queries to get our trees and linked lists described previously:

guestbook-boosts/resources/sql/queries.sql
```
-- :name get-reboosts :? :*
-- Gets all boosts descended from a given boost
WITH RECURSIVE reboosts AS
(WITH post_boosts AS
 (SELECT user_id, poster
  FROM boosts
  WHERE post_id = :post)
```

```
 SELECT user_id, poster
 FROM post_boosts
 where user_id = :user
 UNION
 SELECT b.user_id, b.poster
 FROM post_boosts b INNER JOIN reboosts r ON r.user_id = b.poster)
select user_id as user, poster as source from reboosts

-- :name get-boost-chain :? :*
-- Gets all boosts above the original boost
WITH RECURSIVE reboosts AS
(WITH post_boosts AS
 (SELECT user_id, poster
  FROM boosts
  WHERE post_id = :post)
 SELECT user_id, poster
 FROM post_boosts
 where user_id = :user
 UNION
 SELECT b.user_id, b.poster
 FROM post_boosts b INNER JOIN reboosts r ON r.poster = b.user_id)
select user_id as user, poster as source from reboosts
```

Our first query, get-reboosts, gets the subtree with root of (:user, :post). We first select the boost with (:user, :post), then we recursively select boosts where booster is in the set of user_ids from our current selection until there are no additional boosts to select.

Our second query, get-boost-chain, does the inverse. It recursively walks up the tree, returning the path from (:user, :boost) up to the original post.

Now we have a boost table, but we haven't connected it to any of our post queries. Since the usual pattern will be to select a bunch of data with the same structure, but filtered in various ways, let's create a view to avoid unneccessary duplication of SQL and complex nesting of SELECT statements.

We write another migration to do so:

user=> (**create-migration** "*add-posts-with-meta-view*")

And add the following up migration:

guestbook-boosts/resources/migrations/20200822203854-add-posts-with-meta-view.up.sql
```
CREATE OR REPLACE VIEW posts_with_meta AS
SELECT
p.id                as id,
p.timestamp         as timestamp,
p.message           as message,
p.name              as name,
p.author            as author,
```

```
a.profile->>'avatar' as avatar,
count(b.user_id)      as boosts
from      posts as p
left join users  as a on a.login = p.author
left join boosts as b on p.id = b.post_id
group by p.id, a.login
--;;
CREATE OR REPLACE VIEW posts_and_boosts AS
select
p.id                                 as id,
p.timestamp                          as timestamp,
p.message                            as message,
p.name                               as name,
p.author                             as author,
p.avatar                             as avatar,
p.boosts                             as boosts,
b.post_id is not null                as is_boost,
coalesce(b.timestamp, p.timestamp)   as posted_at,
coalesce(b.user_id, p.author)        as poster,
coalesce(u.profile->>'avatar', p.avatar) as poster_avatar,
coalesce(b.poster, p.author)         as source,
coalesce(s.profile->>'avatar', p.avatar) as source_avatar
from posts_with_meta as p
left join boosts as b on b.post_id = p.id
left join users  as u on b.user_id = u.login
left join users  as s on b.poster = s.login
```

Don't forget the down migration as well:

guestbook-boosts/resources/migrations/20200822203854-add-posts-with-meta-view.down.sql

```
DROP VIEW IF EXISTS posts_and_boosts
--;;
DROP VIEW IF EXISTS posts_with_meta
```

Note that we have *two* SQL statements in our migration, so we've added --;; to tell migratus to run them separately.

Our first view, posts_with_meta, is essentially the SELECT statement we were using from our get-messages, get-message, and get-mesasges-by-author queries with an additional column boosts added. This additional column simply counts the number of times the post has been boosted.

Our second view, posts_and_boosts, contains each post and also each boost with its post's data joined on. This allows us to get a timeline of posts and boosts.

Let's update our existing queries to use posts_with_meta, and then let's add some new timeline queries:

guestbook-boosts/resources/sql/queries.sql

```
-- :name get-messages :? :*
-- :doc selects all available messages
SELECT * from posts_with_meta

-- :name get-message :? :1
-- :doc selects a message
SELECT * from posts_with_meta
where id = :id

-- :name get-messages-by-author :? :*
-- :doc selects all messages posted by a user
SELECT * from posts_with_meta
WHERE author = :author
```

That cut out a bunch of duplication. It's much nicer now.

Now let's write our timeline queries:

guestbook-boosts/resources/sql/queries.sql

```
-- :name get-timeline :? :*
-- Gets the latest post or boost for each post
select * from
(select distinct on (p.id) * from posts_and_boosts as p
 order by p.id, p.posted_at desc) as t
order by t.posted_at asc


-- :name get-timeline-for-poster :? :*
-- Gets the latest post or boost for each post
select * from
(select distinct on (p.id) * from posts_and_boosts as p
 where p.poster = :poster
 order by p.id, p.posted_at desc) as t
order by t.posted_at asc

-- :name get-timeline-post :? :1
-- Gets the boosted post for updating timelines
select * from posts_and_boosts
where is_boost = :is_boost
and poster = :user
and id = :post
order by posted_at asc
limit 1
```

Our first query, get-timeline, is the most basic form for the timeline version of the queries above. Since we have posts *and* boosts in our view, we have to use select distinct to remove posts with duplicate IDs. Using order by p.id, p.posted_at in our select distinct means we'll get the latest boost for each post.

Finally, our outer select returns the posts in descending chronological order based on the date of their latest boost.

Our second query, get-timeline-for-poster, does the same thing, but it filters our select distinct by :poster. This means that it'll get the latest boost by our :poster even if it isn't the most recent.

Our third query, get-boosted-post, gets an individual boosted post so that a user's feed can broadcast changes.

Now that we have our neccessary tables and queries, let's make them available from our API.

First, let's wrap them from our guestbook.messages namespace:

guestbook-boosts/src/clj/guestbook/messages.clj
```clojure
(defn boost-message [{{:keys [display-name]} :profile
                      :keys [login]} post-id poster]
  (conman/with-transaction [db/*db*]
    (db/boost-post! db/*db* {:post post-id
                             :poster poster
                             :user login})
    (db/get-timeline-post db/*db* {:post post-id
                                   :user login
                                   :is_boost true})))
```

guestbook-boosts/src/clj/guestbook/messages.clj
```clojure
(defn timeline []
  {:messages (vec (db/get-timeline))})

(defn timeline-for-poster [poster]
  {:messages (vec (db/get-timeline-for-poster {:poster poster}))})
```

Then, let's start by adding boost-message to our WebSocket.

First, we have to add an event-id to our auth map:

```clojure
(ns guestbook.auth)

;;...

(def roles
  {:message/boost! #{:authenticated}
   ;;...
   })
```

Then we need to add an event handler to our WebSocket.

guestbook-boosts/src/clj/guestbook/routes/websockets.clj

```
(defmethod handle-message :message/boost!
  [{:keys [?data uid session] :as message}]
  (let [response (try
                   (msg/boost-message (:identity session)
                                      (:id ?data)
                                      (:poster ?data))
                   (catch Exception e
                     {:errors
                      {:server-error ["Failed to boost message!"]}}))]
    (if (:errors response)
      (do
        (log/debug "Failed to boost message: " ?data)
        response)
      (do
        (doseq [uid (:any @(:connected-uids socket))]
          (send! uid [:message/add response]))
        {:success true}))))
```

Finally, for the sake of testing, let's add an endpoint for boosting via Ajax
as well.

guestbook-boosts/src/clj/guestbook/routes/services.clj

```
["/message"
 ["/:post-id"
  {:parameters
   {:path
    {:post-id pos-int?}}}
  [""
   ;;...
   ]
  ["/boost"
   {::auth/roles (auth/roles :message/boost!)
    :post {:parameters {:body {:poster (ds/maybe string?)}}
           :responses
           {200 {:body map?}
            400 {:message string?}}
           :handler
           (fn [{{{:keys [post-id]} :path
                  {:keys [poster]} :body} :parameters
                 {:keys [identity]} :session}]
             (try
               (let [post (msg/boost-message identity post-id poster)]
                 (response/ok {:status :ok
                               :post post}))
               (catch Exception e
                 (response/bad-request
                  {:message
                   (str "Could not boost message: " post-id
                        " as " (:login identity))}))))}}]]
```

Note that we've pulled out our :parameters spec map from our get-message end-point (for example, GET "/api/message/11") so that it can be shared by boost (for example, POST "/api/message/11/boost") as well.

Next, let's update our "/api/messages" and "/api/messages/by/:author" to use our timeline queries but also accept a query parameter in case we wish to only list original posts.

guestbook-boosts/src/clj/guestbook/routes/services.clj

```clojure
["/messages"
 {::auth/roles (auth/roles :messages/list)
  :parameters {:query {(ds/opt :boosts) boolean?}}}
 ["" {:get
      {:responses
       {200
        {:body ;; Data Spec for response body
         {:messages
          [{:id pos-int?
            :name string?
            :message string?
            :timestamp inst?
            :author (ds/maybe string?)
            :avatar (ds/maybe string?)}]}}}
       :handler
       (fn [{{{:keys [boosts]
               :or {boosts true}} :query} :parameters}]
         (response/ok (if boosts
                        (msg/timeline)
                        (msg/message-list))))}}]
 ["/by/:author"
  {:get
   {:parameters {:path {:author string?}}
    :responses
    {200
     {:body ;; Data Spec for response body
      {:messages
       [{:id pos-int?
         :name string?
         :message string?
         :timestamp inst?
         :author (ds/maybe string?)
         :avatar (ds/maybe string?)}]}}}
    :handler
    (fn [{{{:keys [author]} :path
           {:keys [boosts]
            :or {boosts true}} :query} :parameters}]
```

```
(response/ok
 (if boosts
   (msg/timeline-for-poster author)
   (msg/messages-by-author author)))))}}]]
```

Now that we have that all hooked up, let's test it out in Swagger. See the following figure and the two figures on page 288.

Great! We're able to boost a post and have it moved to the top of the shared timeline and add other users' posts to our own timeline.

Let's hook this up to the client.

Since we're defaulting to including boosts, the timeline itself should be properly reflected. However, we need to update our :messages/filter (introduced on page 212) to use :poster instead of :author.

`GET` /api/messages

Response Class (Status 200)

Example Value

Response Content Type | application/json ▾ |

Parameters

Parameter	Value	Description	Parameter Type	Data Type
boosts	true ▾		query	boolean

[Try it out!]

Curl

```
curl -X GET --header 'Accept: application/json' 'http://localhost:3000/api/messages?boosts=true'
```

Request URL

```
http://localhost:3000/api/messages?boosts=true
```

Response Body

```
      "timestamp": "2020-10-25T04:08:20Z",
      "message": "# This is a markdown post\n** Look at in its glory! **"
    },
    {
      "boosts": 1,
      "poster avatar": null,
      "name": "svmb",
      "is boost": true,
      "source avatar": null,
      "source": "svmb",
      "posted at": "2020-10-25T04:31:35Z",
      "author": "svmb",
      "poster": "svmb",
      "id": 1,
      "avatar": null,
      "timestamp": "2020-10-25T03:42:22Z",
```

`GET` /api/messages/by/{author}

Response Class (Status 200)

Example Value

Response Content Type | application/json ▾ |

Parameters

Parameter	Value	Description	Parameter Type	Data Type
boosts	▾		query	boolean
author	svmb		path	string

[Try it out!]

Curl

```
curl -X GET --header 'Accept: application/json' 'http://localhost:3000/api/messages/by/svmb'
```

Request URL

```
http://localhost:3000/api/messages/by/svmb
```

Response Body

```
      "timestamp": "2020-10-25T04:08:20Z",
      "message": "# This is a markdown post\n** Look at in its glory! **"
    },
    {
      "boosts": 1,
      "poster avatar": null,
      "name": "svmb",
      "is boost": true,
      "source avatar": null,
      "source": "svmb",
      "posted at": "2020-10-25T04:31:35Z",
      "author": "svmb",
      "poster": "svmb",
```

guestbook-boosts/src/cljs/guestbook/messages.cljs

```
(rf/reg-event-fx
 :messages/load-by-author
 (fn [{:keys [db]} [_ author]]
   {:db (assoc db
               :messages/loading? true
               :messages/filter {:poster author}
               :messages/list nil)
    :ajax/get {:url (str "/api/messages/by/" author)
               :success-path [:messages]
               :success-event [:messages/set]}}))
```

Now, we may end up with duplicates in the timeline if a user boosts a message over and over, but this is easy enough to resolve from our subscription. Since the feed is intended to be scrolled through, we ignore any duplicate messages, only rendering the first occurrence of each one.

guestbook-boosts/src/cljs/guestbook/messages.cljs

```
(rf/reg-sub
 :messages/list
 (fn [db _]
   (:list
    (reduce
     (fn [{:keys [ids list] :as acc} {:keys [id] :as msg}]
       (if (contains? ids id)
         acc
         {:list (conj list msg)
          :ids (conj ids id)}))
     {:list []
      :ids #{}}
     (:messages/list db [])))))
```

Let's update our message component to include some of our new metadata along with a reblog button.

guestbook-boosts/src/cljs/guestbook/messages.cljs

```
(defn message
  ([m] [message m {}])
  ([{:keys [id timestamp message name author avatar boosts is_boost]
     :or {boosts 0}
     :as m}
    {:keys [include-link?]
     :or {include-link? true}}]
   (let [{:keys [posted_at poster poster_avatar
                 source source_avatar] :as m}
         (if is_boost
           m
           (assoc m
                  :poster author
```

```clojure
                        :poster_avatar avatar
                        :posted_at timestamp))]
    [:article.media
     [:figure.media-left
      [image (or avatar "/img/avatar-default.png") 128 128]]
     [:div.media-content
      [:div.content
       (when is_boost
         [:div.columns.is-vcentered.is-1.mb-0
          [:div.column.is-narrow.pb-0
           [image (or poster_avatar "/img/avatar-default.png") 24 24]]
          [:div.column.is-narrow.pb-0
           [:a {:href (str "/user/" poster "?post=" id)} poster]]
          [:div.column.is-narrow.pb-0 "⟲"]
          [:div.column.is-narrow.pb-0
           [image (or source_avatar "/img/avatar-default.png") 24 24]]
          [:div.column.pb-0 #_{:style {:text-align "left"}}
           [:div.column.is-narrow.pb-0
            [:a {:href (str "/user/" source "?post=" id)} source]]]])
       [:div.mb-4>time
        (.toLocaleString posted_at)]
       [md message]
       [:p " - " name
        " <"
        (if author
          [:a {:href (str "/user/" author)} (str "@" author)]
          [:span.is-italic "account not found"])
        ">"]]
      [:nav.level
       [:div.level-left
        (when include-link?
          [:button.button.level-item
           {:class ["is-rounded"
                    "is-small"
                    "is-secondary"
                    "is-outlined"]
            :on-click
            (fn [_]
              (let [{{:keys [name]} :data
                     {:keys [path query]} :parameters}
                    @(rf/subscribe [:router/current-route])]
                (rtfe/replace-state name path (assoc query :post id)))
                (rtfe/push-state :guestbook.routes.app/post {:post id}))}
           [:i.material-icons
            "open_in_new"]])
        [:button.button.is-rounded.is-small.is-info.is-outlined.level-item
         {:on-click
          #(rf/dispatch [:message/boost! m])
          :disabled (nil? @(rf/subscribe [:auth/user]))}
         "⟲ " boosts]]]]]))
```

We've added a bar on the top to display the poster (that is, the author or booster) and the source they got it from. We've also added a toolbar at the bottom with a boost button, and moved our View Post button here as well.

Great, now we have boosts. Posts are living things now instead of just ephemeral messages.

Replying to Posts

Boosts are nice, but they don't exactly allow for a dialogue.

Let's add the ability to reply to a post.

First, let's add a new column, parent, to our posts table to allow a post to be a reply.

Let's create a migration from the REPL:

```
user=> (create-migration "alter-posts-add-parent")
```

Add the following to the up migration:

guestbook-replies/resources/migrations/20200829234648-alter-posts-add-parent.up.sql
```
ALTER TABLE posts
  ADD COLUMN parent integer references posts(id);
```

And the down migration:

guestbook-replies/resources/migrations/20200829234648-alter-posts-add-parent.down.sql
```
ALTER TABLE posts
  DROP COLUMN parent;
```

Now let's update our save-message! query and function to allow a parent:

guestbook-replies/resources/sql/queries.sql
```
-- :name save-message! :<! :1
-- :doc creates a new message using the name and message keys
INSERT INTO posts
(author, name, message, parent)
VALUES (:author, :name, :message, :parent)
RETURNING *;
```

guestbook-replies/src/clj/guestbook/messages.clj
```
(defn save-message!
  [{{:keys [display-name]} :profile
    :keys [login]}
   message]
  (if-let [errors (validate-message message)]
    (throw (ex-info "Message is invalid"
                    {:guestbook/error-id :validation
                     :errors errors}))
```

```
    (let [tags (map second
                (re-seq #"(?<=\s|^)#([-\w]+)(?=\s|$)"
                        (:message message)))]
  (conman/with-transaction [db/*db*]
    (let [post-id (:id
                    (db/save-message! db/*db*
                                      (assoc message
                                             :author login
                                             :name (or display-name login)
                                             :parent (:parent message))))]
        (db/get-timeline-post db/*db* {:post post-id
                                       :user login
                                       :is_boost false}))))))
```

Then, let's update the parameters to our POST "/api/message" endpoint to option-ally accept a :parent, like so:

```
[""
 {::auth/roles (auth/roles :message/create!)
  :post
  {:parameters
   {:body ;; Data Spec for Request body parameters
    {:message string?
     (ds/opt :parent) (ds/maybe int?)}}
   ;;...
  }
  ;;...
 }]
```

Then let's run our migration:

```
user=> (migrate)
```

And then test it out in Swagger as shown in the figure on page 293.

Great, now we have the ability to create a message as a reply.

Next, let's update our views and queries to return our replies with their parent messages so that they can be rendered as a message chain.

```
user=> (create-migration "replace-post-and-boosts-view-add-replies")
```

Here's our up migration:

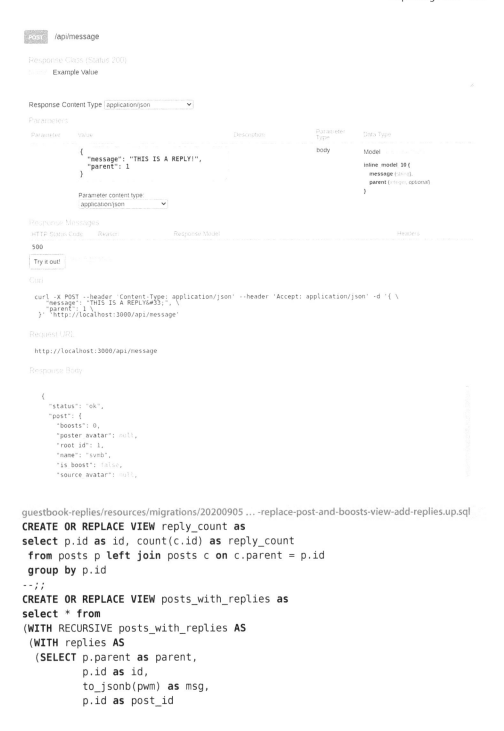

POST /api/message

Response Class (Status 200)

    Example Value

Response Content Type application/json

Parameters

Parameter	Value	Description	Parameter Type	Data Type

	`{`
	`  "message": "THIS IS A REPLY!",`
	`  "parent": 1`
	`}`
	
	Parameter content type:
	application/json
			body	Model
				
				inline model 10 {
				  message (string),
				  parent (integer, optional)
				}

Response Messages

HTTP Status Code	Reason	Response Model	Headers
500			

[Try it out!]

Curl

curl -X POST --header 'Content-Type: application/json' --header 'Accept: application/json' -d '{ \
   "message": "THIS IS A REPLY!", \
   "parent": 1 \
}' 'http://localhost:3000/api/message'

Request URL

http://localhost:3000/api/message

Response Body

{
  "status": "ok",
  "post": {
    "boosts": 0,
    "poster avatar": null,
    "root id": 1,
    "name": "svmb",
    "is boost": false,
    "source avatar": null,

guestbook-replies/resources/migrations/20200905 ... -replace-post-and-boosts-view-add-replies.up.sql

```sql
CREATE OR REPLACE VIEW reply_count as
select p.id as id, count(c.id) as reply_count
 from posts p left join posts c on c.parent = p.id
 group by p.id
--;;
CREATE OR REPLACE VIEW posts_with_replies as
select * from
(WITH RECURSIVE posts_with_replies AS
 (WITH replies AS
  (SELECT p.parent as parent,
          p.id as id,
          to_jsonb(pwm) as msg,
          p.id as post_id
```

```
   from posts p
   left join posts_with_meta pwm
   on p.id = pwm.id)
  SELECT parent, id, msg, post_id
  FROM replies
  UNION
  SELECT r.parent, r.id, r.msg, p.post_id
  FROM replies r
       INNER JOIN posts_with_replies p
       ON r.id = p.parent)
 SELECT post_id                    AS id,
        jsonb_agg(msg)             AS messages,
        (array_agg(id))[count(id)] AS root_id,
        count(id) <> 1             AS is_reply
 FROM posts_with_replies
 GROUP BY post_id) as pwr
--;;
ALTER VIEW posts_and_boosts RENAME TO posts_and_boosts_no_replies
--;;
CREATE OR REPLACE VIEW posts_and_boosts AS
select
*
from posts_with_replies
inner join reply_count using (id)
inner join posts_and_boosts_no_replies using (id)
```

And here's the corresponding down migration:

guestbook-replies/resources/migrations/20200905 … eplace-post-and-boosts-view-add-replies.down.sql

```
DROP VIEW IF EXISTS posts_and_boosts
--;;
ALTER VIEW posts_and_boosts_no_replies RENAME TO posts_and_boosts
--;;
DROP VIEW IF EXISTS posts_with_replies
--;;
DROP VIEW IF EXISTS reply_count
```

Before we run our migration, let's walk through what we're doing.

First, we're creating a reply_count view to display the number of direct replies to a post.

Then we're creating our posts_with_replies view. This is a recursive select that is aggregating all parents of a post into a jsonb vector of post maps. It has four columns: id, which is the post ID; messages, which is our vector of messages; root_id, which is the ID of the top-level post; and is_reply, which indicates whether this message is a reply.

Next, we're renaming our old posts_and_boosts view to posts_and_boosts_no_replies so that we can incrementally change our view instead of completely rewriting it.

Finally, we're updating our posts_and_boosts view by joining it with posts_and_replies and reply_count.

Our down migration is simply dropping our modified posts_and_boosts, replacing it with our old version, and then dropping posts_and_replies.

Now that we understand our migration, let's run it:

user=> (**migrate**)

Since our old columns are unmodified, everything should still work fine. Let's check quickly in the browser, then let's update our message component to make use of the columns we added.

We'll be adding some significant features, and we already have a great deal of complexity from our boost button.

Let's take a moment to refactor our message component first.

We start by rendering message content, including replies, in a dedicated component.

guestbook-replies/src/cljs/guestbook/messages.cljs
```
(defn message-content [{:keys [messages name author]
                        :as m}]
  [:<>
   (if (seq messages)
     (doall
      (for [{:keys [message id] :as msg} (reverse messages)]
        ^{:key id}
        [md :p.reply-chain-item message]))
     [md (:message m)])
   [:p " - " name
    " <"
    (if author
      [:a {:href (str "/user/" author)} (str "@" author)]
      [:span.is-italic "account not found"])
    ">"]])
```

Note that our messages column on posts_and_boosts is in order of newest to oldest, so we have to reverse it. Also, we've added an HTML class, reply-chain-item, to handle proper styling of our replies. We'll add the required CSS once our full refactor is complete.

Next, let's factor out the part at the top that shows the post metadata (boost data and timestamp) into its own component.

guestbook-replies/src/cljs/guestbook/messages.cljs
```
(defn post-meta [{:keys [id is_boost timestamp posted_at poster poster_avatar
                         source source_avatar] :as m}]
  (let [posted_at (or posted_at timestamp)]
        [:<> (when is_boost
               [:div.columns.is-vcentered.is-1.mb-0
                [:div.column.is-narrow.pb-0
                 [image (or poster_avatar "/img/avatar-default.png") 24 24]]
                [:div.column.is-narrow.pb-0
                 [:a {:href (str "/user/" poster "?post=" id)} poster]]
                [:div.column.is-narrow.pb-0 "⟳"]
                [:div.column.is-narrow.pb-0
                 [image (or source_avatar "/img/avatar-default.png") 24 24]]
                [:div.column.pb-0
                 [:div.column.is-narrow.pb-0
                  [:a {:href (str "/user/" source "?post=" id)} source]]]])
         [:div.mb-4>time
          (if posted_at
            (.toLocaleString posted_at)
            "NULL POSTED_AT")]]))
```

This is taken directly from our old message component. We've separated it so that we can omit it when we render our post page and our reply tree.

Next, let's pull out our buttons into expand-post-button and boost-button components:

guestbook-replies/src/cljs/guestbook/messages.cljs
```
(defn expand-post-button [{:keys [id root_id] :as m}]
  [:button.button.is-rounded.is-small.is-secondary.is-outlined.level-item
   {:on-click
    (fn [_]
      (let [{{:keys [name]} :data
             {:keys [path query]} :parameters}
            @(rf/subscribe [:router/current-route])]
        (rtfe/replace-state name path (assoc query :post id)))
      (rtfe/push-state :guestbook.routes.app/post {:post root_id}))}
   [:i.material-icons
    "open_in_new"]])

(defn boost-button [{:keys [boosts] :as m}]
  [:button.button.is-rounded.is-small.is-info.is-outlined.level-item
   {:on-click
    #(rf/dispatch [:message/boost! m])
    :disabled (nil? @(rf/subscribe [:auth/user]))}
   "⟳ " boosts])
```

We've updated our expand-post-button to account for replies. We'll be updating our post page to display all replies, so we'll always want to link to the root_id instead of the id. Once we update our Reitit route for the post page to accept query params, we'll make sure that this reply is focused on the root post's post page.

Now we have to add a reply-button component. We'll have to do some work with our message-form to get it fully working. Let's implement a placeholder for now so that we can get everything working and make sure we refactored our message component correctly.

guestbook-replies/src/cljs/guestbook/messages.cljs
```
(defn reply-button [{:keys [reply_count] :as m}]
  [:button.button.is-rounded.is-small.is-outlined.level-item
   {:on-click #(js/alert "TODO")}
   [:span.material-icons
    {:style {:font-size "inherit"}}
    "chat"]
   [:span.ml-1 reply_count]])
```

Finally, let's update our message component to use the components we've added (see figure on page 298):

guestbook-replies/src/cljs/guestbook/messages.cljs
```
(defn message
  ([m] [message m {}])
  ([{:keys [id timestamp messages name author
            avatar boosts is_boost reply_count]
     :or {boosts 0}
     :as m}
    {:keys [include-link? include-bar?]
     :or {include-link? true
          include-bar? true}}]
   [:article.media
    [:figure.media-left
     [image (or avatar "/img/avatar-default.png") 128 128]]
    [:div.media-content
     [:div.content
      [post-meta m]
      [message-content m]]
     (when include-bar?
       [:nav.level
        [:div.level-left
         (when include-link?
           [expand-post-button m])
         [boost-button m]
         [reply-button m]]])]]))
```

Now, let's go back and add some CSS for our replies:

guestbook-replies/resources/public/css/screen.css

```css
.reply-chain-item +.reply-chain-item {
    padding-top: 1em;
    border-top: 1px dashed #caa;
}
```

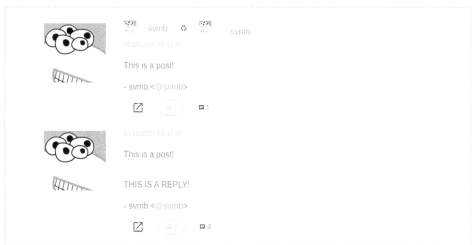

Great, looks good.

Next, we have to implement our reply functionality. We'd like to place our message form in a modal and pop it up when we click our reply-button. However, we don't have the pieces of our form separated enough to use from a modal. Let's break it up and add a reply-modal component.

First, let's take a look at our message-preview. Our change to message has actually broken it! Our message-form doesn't provide a :messages list, so it just renders an empty message. Let's add a wrapper component that takes a parent message and creates our :messages list so that it renders properly:

guestbook-replies/src/cljs/guestbook/messages.cljs

```
(defn message-form-preview [parent]
  (let [{:keys [login profile]} @(rf/subscribe [:auth/user])
        display-name (:display-name profile login)
        msg {:message @(rf/subscribe [:form/field :message])
             :id -1
             :timestamp (js/Date.)
             :name display-name
             :author login
             :avatar (:avatar profile)}]
    [message-preview
     (assoc msg :messages
            (cons msg (:messages parent)))]))
```

There, now we have a correctly constructed :messages list to render.

Next, let's add the content of the message form:

guestbook-replies/src/cljs/guestbook/messages.cljs

```
(defn message-form-content []
  (let [{:keys [login profile]} @(rf/subscribe [:auth/user])
        display-name (:display-name profile login)]
    [:<>
     [errors-component :server-error]
     [errors-component :unauthorized "Please log in before posting."]
     [:div.field
      [:label.label {:for :name} "Name"]
      display-name]
     [:div.field
      [:div.control
       [image-uploader
        #(rf/dispatch [:message/save-media %])
        "Insert an Image"]]]
     [:div.field
      [:label.label {:for :message} "Message"]
      [errors-component :message]
      [textarea-input
       {:attrs {:name :message}
        :save-timeout 1000
        :value (rf/subscribe [:form/field :message])
        :on-save #(rf/dispatch [:form/set-field :message %])}]]]))
```

Since this just modifies our fields, it doesn't yet require the parent to be passed.

Finally, let's update message-form and make sure everything still works:

guestbook-replies/src/cljs/guestbook/messages.cljs
```clojure
(defn message-form []
  [:div.card
   [:div.card-header>p.card-header-title
    "Post Something!"]
   [:div.card-content
    [message-form-preview {}]
    [message-form-content]
    [:input.button.is-primary.is-fullwidth
     {:type :submit
      :disabled @(rf/subscribe [:form/validation-errors?])
      :on-click #(rf/dispatch [:message/send!
                               @(rf/subscribe [:form/fields])
                               @(rf/subscribe [:message/media])])
      :value "comment"}]]])
```

Now, let's make sure everything looks correct.

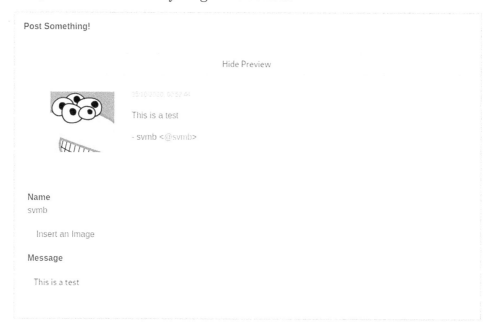

Great! Now that we have that updated, let's create a reply-modal component and update our reply-button to submit it.

guestbook-replies/src/cljs/guestbook/messages.cljs
```clojure
(defn reply-modal [parent]
  [modals/modal-card
   [:reply-modal (:id parent)]
   (str "Reply to post by user: " (:author parent))
```

```
[:<>
 [message-form-preview parent]
 [message-form-content]]
[:input.button.is-primary.is-fullwidth
 {:type :submit
  :disabled @(rf/subscribe [:form/validation-errors?])
  :on-click #(rf/dispatch [:message/send!
                           (assoc
                            @(rf/subscribe [:form/fields])
                            :parent (:id parent))
                           @(rf/subscribe [:message/media])])
  :value (str "Reply to " (:author parent))}]]])
```

Since we're going to be creating a more complex button, we're using modal-card directly instead of modal-button. We've used a different header than message-form, we're adding a :parent to the message args we pass to :message/send!, and we're using a different label for our submit button.

Now, let's update our reply-button to use this modal:

guestbook-replies/src/cljs/guestbook/messages.cljs
```
(declare reply-modal)

(defn reply-button [{:keys [reply_count] :as m}]
  [:<>
   [reply-modal m]
   [:button.button.is-rounded.is-small.is-outlined.level-item
    {:on-click #(rf/dispatch [:app/show-modal
                              [:reply-modal (:id m)]])
     :disabled (not= @(rf/subscribe [:auth/user-state]) :authenticated)}
    [:span.material-icons
     {:style {:font-size "inherit"}}
     "chat"]
    [:span.ml-1 reply_count]]])
```

Since reply-modal depends on reply-button via message-preview, we need to use declare to reference reply-modal from our reply-button component. The reply-button component itself is a fairly straightforward button based on the modal-button component.

Let's try it out! See the figure on page 302.

Our form is appearing correctly in the modal, but we have two issues.

First, our modal isn't closing after we successfully submit a reply.

Let's update our :message/send!-called-back event to hide our modals:

Reply to post by user: svmb

Hide Preview

25/10/2020, 09:54:41

This is a post!

THIS IS A REPLY!

This is another reply!

- svmb <@svmb>

Name
svmb

Insert an Image

Message
This is another reply!

Reply to svmb

guestbook-replies/src/cljs/guestbook/messages.cljs

```clojure
(rf/reg-event-db
 :app/hide-reply-modals
 (fn [db _]
   (update db :app/active-modals #(into
                                    {}
                                    (remove (fn [[k v]]
                                              (= :reply-modal (first k))))
                                    %)))))
```

```
(rf/reg-event-fx
 :message/send!-called-back
 (fn [_ [_ {:keys [success errors]}]]
   (if success
     {:dispatch-n [[:form/clear-fields]
                   [:message/clear-media]
                   [:app/hide-reply-modals]]}
     {:dispatch [:form/set-server-errors errors]})))
```

That should resolve that.

Second, all of our message forms share the same field state. If we wanted to preserve drafts, we could tweak how our :form/field subscriptions work. But we don't need to support this, so we'll take the simple approach of clearing our fields when needed.

Let's start by clearing whenever we open our reply modal:

guestbook-replies/src/cljs/guestbook/messages.cljs
```
(rf/reg-event-fx
 :form/clear
 (fn [_ _]
   {:dispatch-n [[:form/clear-fields]
                 [:message/clear-media]]}))

(defn reply-button [{:keys [reply_count] :as m}]
  [:<>
   [reply-modal m]
   [:button.button.is-rounded.is-small.is-outlined.level-item
    {:on-click (fn []
                 (rf/dispatch [:form/clear])
                 (rf/dispatch [:app/show-modal
                               [:reply-modal (:id m)]]))
     :disabled (not= @(rf/subscribe [:auth/user-state]) :authenticated)}
    [:span.material-icons
     {:style {:font-size "inherit"}}
     "chat"]
    [:span.ml-1 reply_count]]])
```

This covers most of it, but there's still the issue of canceling our reply when we close the modal. To account for this, we need to enrich our modal-card component to accept an on-close function.

Let's update our modal-card to optionally take an opts map containing an :id instead of just id as its first argument.

guestbook-replies/src/cljs/guestbook/modals.cljs
```
(defn modal-card [opts-or-id title body footer]
  (let [{:keys [id on-close] :as opts} (if (and
                                            (map? opts-or-id)
                                            (contains? opts-or-id :id))
```

```
                                          opts-or-id
                                          {:id opts-or-id})
        close-modal! (fn []
                        (when (fn? on-close)
                          (on-close id))
                        (rf/dispatch [:app/hide-modal id]))]
    [:div.modal
     {:class (when @(rf/subscribe [:app/modal-showing? id])
               "is-active")}
     [:div.modal-background
      {:on-click close-modal!}]
     [:div.modal-card
      [:header.modal-card-head
       [:p.modal-card-title title]
       [:button.delete
        {:on-click close-modal!}]]
      [:section.modal-card-body
       body]
      [:footer.modal-card-foot
       footer]]]]))
```

Now let's update our reply-modal to dispatch our new :form/clear event from :on-close:

guestbook-replies/src/cljs/guestbook/messages.cljs
```
(defn reply-modal [parent]
  [modals/modal-card
   {:on-close #(rf/dispatch [:form/clear])
    :id [:reply-modal (:id parent)]}
   (str "Reply to post by user: " (:author parent))
   [:<>
    [message-form-preview parent]
    [message-form-content]]
   [:input.button.is-primary.is-fullwidth
    {:type :submit
     :disabled @(rf/subscribe [:form/validation-errors?])
     :on-click #(rf/dispatch [:message/send!
                              (assoc
                               @(rf/subscribe [:form/fields])
                               :parent (:id parent))
                              @(rf/subscribe [:message/media])])
     :value (str "Reply to " (:author parent))}]])
```

Great! Our problems are resolved. If you open a reply with the message-form component still visible in the background, you'll still notice it updating. This isn't perfect, but it's acceptable.

Refactoring our message form re-frame events to allow separation by parent ID would be a good exercise for you to do on your own.

With that done, we have a fairly complete home page and global feed! Our next tasks will be updating the /post/:id page to render the replies as a tree.

Updating the Post Page

The first thing we need to do is change what we fetch when the page first loads so that we have all the replies neccessary to render, along with any neccessary metadata.

Let's start by updating our get-message query and adding a get-replies query:

guestbook-replies/resources/sql/queries.sql
```
-- :name get-message :? :1
-- :doc selects a message
SELECT * from posts_with_meta
            inner join (select id, parent from posts) as p using (id)
            inner join reply_count using (id)
where id = :id
-- :name get-replies :? :*
select * from posts_with_meta
            inner join (select id, parent from posts) as p using (id)
            inner join reply_count using (id)
  where id IN (select id from posts
                  where parent = :id)
```

We've updated our get-message query to include the parent and reply_count columns. This will be important for knowing if we need to render a reply tree and how many posts we need to render.

Our new query, get-replies, simply gets all the direct replies to a post. We'll use this to expand the reply tree.

Let's add a function to messages.clj to wrap our get-replies query:

guestbook-replies/src/clj/guestbook/messages.clj
```
(defn get-replies [id]
  (db/get-replies {:id id}))
```

And then let's add a service endpoint to fetch our replies:

guestbook-replies/src/clj/guestbook/routes/services.clj
```
;; Inside `/api/message/:post-id`
["/replies"
 {::auth/roles (auth/roles :message/get)
  :get {
        :handler (fn [{{{:keys [post-id]} :path} :parameters}]
                  (let [replies (msg/get-replies post-id)]
                    (response/ok
                      {:replies
                       replies})))}}]
```

Now, before we move forward, let's test out our updated get-message from our /api/message/:post-id endpoint and our new /api/message/:post-id/replies endpoint in Swagger UI:

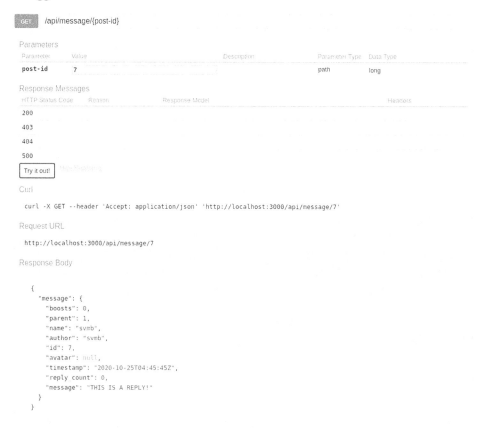

Great! Our server is all set up. Now let's update the front end.

The first thing we'll add is re-frame events for managing reply posts: ::fetch-replies, ::add-replies, ::set-replies-error, and ::clear-replies. Note, we'll be calling ::fetch-replies for *any* reply that has replies itself, not just the main post. This means that we need to track status by ID, since we may have more than one parallel request. Additionally, we have two separate views of our data that are relevant, the loaded reply IDs for the parent post and the post bodies of all of our loaded messages. For the sake of ease, we'll track status, reply-ids, and posts in three separate top-level maps.

guestbook-replies/src/cljs/guestbook/views/post.cljs
```
(rf/reg-event-fx
 ::fetch-replies
 (fn [{:keys [db]} [_ post-id]]
   {:db (assoc-in db [::replies-status post-id] :loading)
    :ajax/get {:url (str "/api/message/" post-id "/replies")
               :success-path [:replies]
               :success-event [::add-replies post-id]
               :error-event [::set-replies-error post-id]}}))

(rf/reg-event-db
 ::add-replies
 (fn [db [_ post-id replies]]
   (-> db
       (update ::posts (fnil into {}) (map (juxt :id identity)) replies)
       (assoc-in [::replies post-id] (map :id replies))
       (assoc-in [::replies-status post-id] :success))))

(rf/reg-event-db
 ::set-replies-error
 (fn [db [_ post-id response]]
   (-> db
       (assoc-in [::replies-status post-id] response))))

(rf/reg-event-db
 ::clear-replies
 (fn [db _]
   (dissoc db ::posts ::replies ::replies-status)))
```

Our ::fetch-replies, ::set-replies-error, and ::clear-replies events are fairly straightforward. Respectively, they send the Ajax request, store the error response, and clean up the re-frame db. The meat of our logic lies in ::add-replies. We're managing three maps with post-id as the keys. The ::posts map is for getting a post's content and metadata, the ::replies map is for getting the list of child post-ids, and the ::replies-status map is for getting the status of the post's ::fetch-replies Ajax request.

Let's write our subscriptions for working with these maps.

guestbook-replies/src/cljs/guestbook/views/post.cljs
```
(rf/reg-sub
 ::posts
 (fn [db _]
   (assoc
     (::posts db)
     (:id (::post db))
     (::post db))))

(rf/reg-sub
 ::reply
 :<- [::posts]
 (fn [posts [_ id]]
   (get posts id)))
```

```
(rf/reg-sub
 ::replies-map
 (fn [db _]
   (::replies db)))

(rf/reg-sub
 ::replies-for-post
 :<- [::replies-map]
 (fn [replies [_ id]]
   (get replies id)))

(rf/reg-sub
 ::replies-status-map
 (fn [db _]
   (::replies-status db)))

(rf/reg-sub
 ::replies-status
 :<- [::replies-status-map]
 (fn [statuses [_ id]]
   (get statuses id)))
```

We have three pairs of subscriptions. Each pair has a layer 2 subscription for the top-level maps, and a layer 3 subscription for getting the value for the specific post.

Now let's add our first call to ::fetch-replies to our post-controllers.

guestbook-replies/src/cljs/guestbook/views/post.cljs
```
(def post-controllers
  [{:parameters {:path [:post]}
    :start (fn [{{:keys [post]} :path}]
             (rf/dispatch [::fetch-post post])
             (rf/dispatch [::fetch-replies post]))
    :stop (fn [_]
            (rf/dispatch [::clear-post])
            (rf/dispatch [::clear-replies]))}])
```

We're finally ready to add some new UI components.

Let's add a reply-tree component to render all of the children of our root post and include it in our post component:

guestbook-replies/src/cljs/guestbook/views/post.cljs
```
(defn reply-tree [post-id]
  (let [reply-ids @(rf/subscribe [::replies-for-post post-id])
        status    @(rf/subscribe [::replies-status post-id])]
    (case status
      nil nil
      :success
      [:<>
       (doall
```

```
      (for [id reply-ids]
        (let [post @(rf/subscribe [::reply id])
              has-replies? (not= 0 (:reply_count post))]
          (if has-replies?
            ^{:key id}
            [:<>
             [msg/message post {:include-link? false}]
             [:button.button {:on-click #(rf/dispatch [::fetch-replies id])}
              "Load Replies"]
             [reply-tree id]]
            ^{:key id}
            [msg/message post {:include-link? false}])))))]
    :loading [loading-bar]
    ;; ELSE
    [:div
     [:h3 "Error"]
     [:pre (with-out-str (pprint status))]]])))

(defn post [{:keys [name author message timestamp avatar id]
             :as post-content}]
  [:div.content
   [:button.button.is-info.is-outlined.is-fullwidth
    {:on-click #(.back js/window.history)}
    "Back to Feed"]
   [:h3.title.is-3 "Post by " name
    "<" [:a {:href (str "/user/" author)} (str "@" author)] ">"]
   [:h4.subtitle.is-4 "Posted at " (.toLocaleString timestamp)]
   [msg/message post-content {:include-link? false}]
   [reply-tree id]])
```

We have a recursive component which renders all replies for a post, along with a button to load more replies and a nested reply-tree if a post has any replies.

Ideally, we'd like to separate the inner component so that we can refactor the rendering of individual posts independently of the tree structure. Also, we should add the ability to expand and collapse the sub-trees.

guestbook-replies/src/cljs/guestbook/views/post.cljs
```
(rf/reg-sub
 ::reply-count
 (fn [[_ id] _]
   (rf/subscribe [::reply id]))
 (fn [post _]
   (:reply_count post)))

(rf/reg-sub
 ::has-replies?
 (fn [[_ id] _]
   (rf/subscribe [::reply-count id]))
 (fn [c _]
   (not= c 0)))
```

```clojure
(rf/reg-sub
 ::replies-to-load
 (fn [[_ id] _]
   [(rf/subscribe [::reply-count id]) (rf/subscribe [::replies-for-post id])])
 (fn [[c replies] _]
   (- c (count replies))))

(rf/reg-event-db
 ::expand-post
 (fn [db [_ id]]
   (update db ::expanded-posts (fnil conj #{}) id)))

(rf/reg-event-db
 ::collapse-post
 (fn [db [_ id]]
   (update db ::expanded-posts (fnil disj #{}) id)))

(rf/reg-event-db
 ::collapse-all
 (fn [db [_ id]]
   (dissoc db ::expanded-posts)))

(rf/reg-sub
 ::post-expanded?
 (fn [db [_ id]]
   (contains? (::expanded-posts db) id)))

(def post-controllers
  [{:parameters {:path [:post]}
    :start (fn [{{:keys [post]} :path}]
             (rf/dispatch [::fetch-post post])
             (rf/dispatch [::fetch-replies post]))
    :stop (fn [_]
            (rf/dispatch [::collapse-all])
            (rf/dispatch [::clear-post])
            (rf/dispatch [::clear-replies]))}])
(defn reply [post-id]
  [msg/message @(rf/subscribe [::reply post-id]) {:include-link? false}])

(defn expand-control [post-id]
  (let [expanded? @(rf/subscribe [::post-expanded? post-id])
        reply-count @(rf/subscribe [::reply-count post-id])
        replies-to-load @(rf/subscribe [::replies-to-load post-id])
        loaded?        (= replies-to-load 0)
        status @(rf/subscribe [::replies-status post-id])]
    [:div.field.has-addons
     [:p.control>span.button.is-static  reply-count " replies"]
     [:p.control>button.button
      {:on-click (fn []
                   (if expanded?
                     (rf/dispatch [::collapse-post post-id])
```

```
                    (do
                      (when-not loaded?
                        (rf/dispatch [::fetch-replies post-id]))
                      (rf/dispatch [::expand-post post-id]))))
       :disabled (= status :loading)}
      (str (if expanded? "-" "+"))]
    (when expanded?
      [:p.control>button.button
       {:on-click #(rf/dispatch [::fetch-replies post-id])
        :disabled (= status :loading)}
       (if loaded?
         "↻"
         (str "Load " replies-to-load " New Replies"))])])]))

(defn reply-tree [post-id]
  (when @(rf/subscribe [::has-replies? post-id])
    (let [status @(rf/subscribe [::replies-status post-id])]
      [:<>
       [expand-control post-id]
       (case status
         nil nil
         :success
         (when @(rf/subscribe [::post-expanded? post-id])
           [:div
            {:style {:border-left "1px dotted blue"
                     :padding-left "10px"}}
            (doall
             (for [id @(rf/subscribe [::replies-for-post post-id])]
               ^{:key id}
               [:<>
                [reply id]
                [reply-tree id]]))])

         :loading [loading-bar]
         ;; ELSE
         [:div
          [:h3 "Error"]
          [:pre (with-out-str (pprint status))]])])))
```

We've added some helper subscriptions for our post, and we've added some events and a subscription for managing expand/collapse functionality, and we added cleanup for expanded-posts to our controller. We've also separated our reply-tree into three components, each responsible for a distinct part of the rendering logic. The reply-tree itself is responsible for the recursive rendering, expand-control is responsible for managing the loading and expanding/collapsing of replies, and reply is responsible for rendering the message itself. This structure allows us to modify each behavior independently without them impacting each other as shown in the figure on page 312.

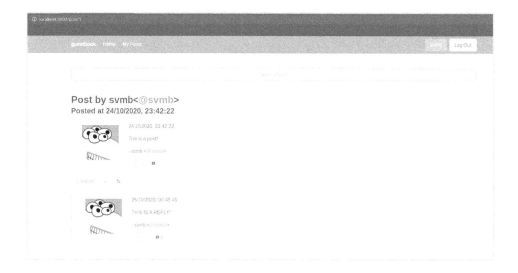

Now that we have our tree looking good, let's add some reloading functionality. We can't reuse our client-side logic for the home and author pages, because they have a different structure and they're currently tied directly into the :message/add event.

Let's tweak our WebSocket message handler so that we can override the event we wish to dispatch with new messages.

guestbook-replies-2/src/cljs/guestbook/websockets.cljs
```
(rf/reg-event-db
 :ws/set-message-add-handler
 (fn [db [_ ev]]
   (if ev
     (assoc db :ws/message-add-handler ev)
     (dissoc db :ws/message-add-handler))))

(rf/reg-sub
 :ws/message-add-handler
 (fn [db _]
   (:ws/message-add-handler db)))
(defmethod handle-message :message/add
  [_ [_ msg :as msg-add-event]]
  (if-some [ev @(rf/subscribe [:ws/message-add-handler])]
    (rf/dispatch (conj ev msg))
    (rf/dispatch msg-add-event)))
```

Now we can set the :ws/message-add-handler from our controller to be dispatched *instead* of :message/add when we receive a new message from the server.

Let's add a custom handler for our post page:

guestbook-replies-2/src/cljs/guestbook/views/post.cljs
```
(rf/reg-event-db
 ::add-message
 (fn [db [_ post-id {:keys [root_id messages]}]]
   (if (= post-id root_id)
     (let [parent-id (:id (second messages))]
       (if (= parent-id post-id)
         (update-in db [::post :reply_count] inc)
         (update db ::posts
                 #(if (contains? % parent-id)
                    (update-in % [parent-id :reply_count] inc)
                    %))))
     db)))

(def post-controllers
  [{:parameters {:path [:post]}
    :start (fn [{{:keys [post]} :path}]
             (rf/dispatch [:ws/set-message-add-handler [::add-message post]])
             (rf/dispatch [::fetch-post post])
             (rf/dispatch [::fetch-replies post]))
    :stop (fn [_]
            (rf/dispatch [:ws/set-message-add-handler nil])
            (rf/dispatch [::collapse-all])
            (rf/dispatch [::clear-post])
            (rf/dispatch [::clear-replies]))}
   ])
```

We don't want to shift content around, so we only update the reply_count field on the parent post if we have it loaded.

The last thing we'll add is the ability to focus a post in the tree. Let's add an endpoint for getting all of our focused message's parents, and then we'll scroll to it when they load.

Let's start by adding a query parameter declaration to our post page:

guestbook-replies-2/src/cljc/guestbook/routes/app.cljc
```
["/post/:post"
 (merge
  {:name ::post}
  #?(:cljs {:parameters {:query {(ds/opt :reply) pos-int?}
                         :path {:post pos-int?}}
            :controllers post/post-controllers
            :view #'post/post-page}))]
```

Then add a query, function, and API endpoint to get the parents of a reply:

guestbook-replies-2/resources/sql/queries.sql
```
-- :name get-parents
SELECT * from posts_with_meta
                inner join (select id, parent from posts) as p using (id)
                inner join reply_count using (id)
 where id in (with recursive parents as
                (select id, parent from posts
                  where id = :id
                 UNION
                 select p.id, p.parent from posts p
                                inner join parents pp
                                    on p.id = pp.parent)
                select id from parents)
```

This query gets the desired post, then iteratively includes parents of selected posts with a recursive union.

We need to wrap our query with a function:

guestbook-replies-2/src/clj/guestbook/messages.clj
```
(defn get-parents [id]
  (db/get-parents {:id id}))
```

And expose it as an endpoint:

guestbook-replies-2/src/clj/guestbook/routes/services.clj
```
;; Inside `/api/message/:post-id`
["/parents"
 {::auth/roles (auth/roles :message/get)
  :get {
        :handler (fn [{{{:keys [post-id]} :path} :parameters}]
                    (let [parents (msg/get-parents post-id)]
                      (response/ok
                        {:parents
                          parents})))}}]
```

Now let's add some events to fetch and set the parents of our post. We don't need to be as thorough as before, because the disruption to the user if it fails is minimal and it only gets called when our controller runs.

guestbook-replies-2/src/cljs/guestbook/views/post.cljs
```
(rf/reg-event-fx
 ::fetch-parents
 (fn [{:keys [db]} [_ post-id]]
   {:ajax/get {:url (str "/api/message/" post-id "/parents")
               :success-path [:parents]
               :success-event [::add-parents post-id]}}))

(defn add-post-to-db [db {:keys [id parent] :as post}]
  (-> db
```

```clojure
      (assoc-in [::posts id] post)
      (update-in [::replies parent]
                 #(if (some (partial = id) %)
                    %
                    (conj % id)))
      (assoc-in [::replies-status id] :success)
      (update ::expanded-posts (fnil conj #{}) id)))
(rf/reg-event-db
 ::add-parents
 (fn [db [_ post-id parents]]
   (reduce add-post-to-db db parents)))

(def post-controllers
  [{:parameters {:path [:post]}
    :start (fn [{{:keys [post]} :path}]
             (rf/dispatch [:ws/set-message-add-handler [::add-message post]])
             (rf/dispatch [::fetch-post post])
             (rf/dispatch [::fetch-replies post]))
    :stop (fn [_]
            (rf/dispatch [:ws/set-message-add-handler nil])
            (rf/dispatch [::collapse-all])
            (rf/dispatch [::clear-post])
            (rf/dispatch [::clear-replies]))}
   {:parameters {:query [:reply]}
    :start (fn [{{:keys [reply]} :query}]
             (when reply
               (rf/dispatch [::fetch-parents reply])))
    }
   ])
```

Since our parent posts aren't grouped as nicely, we add a helper function to add an individual post and then use reduce to add each of our parent posts to our db.

Next, let's update our expand-post-button to pass in the :reply ID as a query parameter, like so:

guestbook-replies-2/src/cljs/guestbook/messages.cljs
```clojure
(defn expand-post-button [{:keys [id root_id] :as m}]
  [:button.button.is-rounded.is-small.is-secondary.is-outlined.level-item
   {:on-click
    (fn [_]
      (let [{{:keys [name]} :data
             {:keys [path query]} :parameters}
            @(rf/subscribe [:router/current-route])]
        (rtfe/replace-state name path (assoc query :post id)))
        (rtfe/push-state :guestbook.routes.app/post {:post root_id}
                         (when (not= root_id id)
                           {:reply id})))}
   [:i.material-icons
    "open_in_new"]])
```

Now let's try it out.

Okay, we've got our parent posts loading and expanding, but we aren't focusing our chosen post. Let's try adding the same logic we had for our message-list by turning our reply component into a React class with a :component-did-mount function:

```
(defn reply [post-id]
  (r/create-class
    {:component-did-mount
     (fn [this]
       (let [message-id (-> @(rf/subscribe [:router/current-route])
                            :parameters
                            :query
                            :reply)]
         (when (= message-id post-id)
           (.scrollIntoView (dom/dom-node this)))))
     :reagent-render
     (fn [_]
       [msg/message
        @(rf/subscribe [::reply post-id])
        {:include-link? false}])}))
```

This seems to work, but try collapsing and expanding one of our post's parents. Oh no! We're scrolling to the post every time! Our msg-li component was never being remounted, so we never encountered this problem. Let's fix this by adding a flag to ensure that our :component-did-mount only ever gets called once.

```
(rf/reg-event-db
 ::set-scroll-to
 (fn [db [_ id]]
   (if (nil? id)
     (dissoc db ::scroll-to-post)
     (assoc db ::scroll-to-post id))))

(rf/reg-sub
 ::scroll?
 (fn [db [_ id]]
   (= id (::scroll-to-post db))))
   ;; In `post-controllers`
   {:parameters {:query [:reply]}
    :start (fn [{{:keys [reply]} :query}]
             (when reply
               (rf/dispatch [::set-scroll-to reply])
               (rf/dispatch [::fetch-parents reply])))
    :stop (fn [_]
            (rf/dispatch [::set-scroll-to nil]))
   }
(defn reply [post-id]
  (r/create-class
    {:component-did-mount
     (fn [this]
       (when @(rf/subscribe [::scroll? post-id])
         (rf/dispatch [::set-scroll-to nil])
         (.scrollIntoView (dom/dom-node this))))
     :reagent-render
     (fn [_]
       [msg/message
        @(rf/subscribe [::reply post-id])
        {:include-link? false}])}))
```

Instead of checking against the route directly, we're using our ::scroll? subscription to decide if we should scroll. We're also clearing the ::scroll-to value in the db once we do scroll, so that we don't scroll every time as shown in the figure on page 318.

Alright, our post page is looking pretty good! We have a way to look at the full discussion around a post. Next, let's build some richer feeds.

Curating Posts

Posts are looking pretty snazzy now, but we still don't have a way of easily finding posts a user might want to see. Discoverability of new content is integral to social media platforms, so we should really add this.

The first discoverability feature we'll address is tags. We implemented the Markdown for tags earlier—now let's add the queries and page to browse posts by tag.

Tags

We're going to use a PostgreSQL regex condition on our query, but we don't want to require knowledge of PostgreSQL specifics in our guestbook.messages namespace. So we'll use Clojure expressions in HugSQL to generate our regex inside our query.

First, let's create a namespace guestbook.db.util and write a helper function there:

```
guestbook-feeds/src/clj/guestbook/db/util.clj
(ns guestbook.db.util
  (:require [clojure.string :as string]))

(defn tag-regex [tag]
  (when-not (re-matches #"[-\w]+" tag)
    (throw (ex-info "Tag must only contain alphanumeric characters!"
                    {:tag tag})))
  (str "'.*(\\s|^)#"
       tag
       "(\\s|$).*'"))
```

Note that it's sanitizing our input. This is important when using Clojure expressions to inject generated strings because HugSQL has no way of knowing which parts of our returned SQL are meant to be escaped.

Now let's write a simple query using this helper function:

```
guestbook-feeds/resources/sql/queries.sql
-- :name get-feed-for-tag :? :*
-- :require [guestbook.db.util :refer [tag-regex]]
-- Given a tag, return its feed
select * from
(select distinct on (p.id) * from posts_and_boosts as p
  where
  /*~ (if (:tag params) */
    p.message ~*
    /*~*/
    false
    /*~ ) ~*/
    --~ (when (:tag params) (tag-regex (:tag params)))
  order by p.id, posted_at desc) as t
 order by t.posted_at asc
```

To use our helper function, we need to require the new guestbook.db.util namespace from guestbook.db.core.

```
(ns guestbook.db.core
  (:require
    ;;...
    [guestbook.db.util])
  ;;...
    )
```

Great, now let's try it out from the REPL:

```
guestbook.db.core> (conman/bind-connection *db* "sql/queries.sql")
;;...
guestbook.db.core> (get-feed-for-tag {:tag "bar"})
({:message "This is a tagged post #foo #bar #baz"
 ;;...
 }
 {:message "This is another tagged post #bar"
 ;;...
 })
guestbook.db.core>
```

Perfect, we're getting tagged posts correctly! Let's add a wrapper function and a service API endpoint to get our posts by tag:

```
guestbook-feeds/src/clj/guestbook/messages.clj
(defn get-feed-for-tag [tag]
  {:messages
    (db/get-feed-for-tag {:tag tag})})
```

```
guestbook-feeds/src/clj/guestbook/routes/services.clj
;; in "/api/messages"
["/tagged/:tag"
 {:get
  {:parameters {:path {:tag string?}}
```

```
:responses
{200
 {:body ;; Data Spec for response body
  {:messages
   [{:id pos-int?
     :name string?
     :message string?
     :timestamp inst?
     :author (ds/maybe string?)
     :avatar (ds/maybe string?)}]}}}
:handler
(fn [{{{:keys [tag]} :path
       {:keys [boosts]
        :or {boosts true}} :query} :parameters}]
  (if boosts
    (response/ok
     (msg/get-feed-for-tag tag))
    (response/not-implemented {:message "Tags only support boosts."})))}}]
```

Then let's test it out in Swagger:

Looks good. Now let's write our tag page based on our author page:

guestbook-feeds/src/cljs/guestbook/views/tag.cljs
```
(ns guestbook.views.tag
  (:require
   [re-frame.core :as rf]
   [guestbook.messages :as messages]))

(def tag-controllers
  [{:parameters {:path [:tag]}
    :start (fn [{{:keys [tag]} :path}]
             (rf/dispatch [:messages/load-by-tag tag]))}])

(defn tag [_]
  (let [messages (rf/subscribe [:messages/list])]
    (fn [{{{:keys [tag]} :path
           {:keys [post]} :query} :parameters}]
      [:div.content
       [:div.columns.is-centered>div.column.is-two-thirds
        [:div.columns>div.column
         [:h3 (str "Posts tagged #" tag)]
         (if @(rf/subscribe [:messages/loading?])
           [messages/message-list-placeholder]
           [messages/message-list messages post])]]]])))
```

We have the same core component as the author page but without the author-specific pieces. Let's write the supporting code for this page and then connect it to our routes.

guestbook-feeds/src/cljs/guestbook/messages.cljs
```
(rf/reg-event-fx
 :messages/load-by-tag
 (fn [{:keys [db]} [_ tag]]
   {:db (assoc db
               :messages/loading? true
               :messages/filter
               {:message #(re-find
                           (re-pattern (str "(?<=\\s|^)#" tag "(?=\\s|$)"))
                           %)}
               :messages/list nil)
    :ajax/get {:url (str "/api/messages/tagged/" tag)
               :success-path [:messages]
               :success-event [:messages/set]}}))
```

guestbook-feeds/src/cljc/guestbook/routes/app.cljc
```
;; require [guestbook.views.tag :as tag] in :cljs
["/tag/:tag"
 (merge
  {:name ::tag}
  #?(:cljs {:parameters {:query {(ds/opt :post) pos-int?}
                         :path {:tag string?}}
            :controllers tag/tag-controllers
            :view #'tag/tag}))]
```

Our :messages/load-by-tag is similar to our :messages/load-by-author; we've just changed two things. We've switched the :url in the :ajax/get effect to the one we just created, and we've changed the :messages/filter map to filter messages with a regular expression.

Let's try it out by clicking one of our tag links:

Great! Now we can view all posts with a specific tag.

We have the ability to view posts for a single tag and a single author. Next, let's add the ability for users to subscribe to authors or tags.

Personalized Feed

One of the core features of most social media is a personal curated feed, with posts relevant to them. Let's add the ability for users to subscribe/unsubscribe to users and/or tags and view a personalized feed based on their subscriptions.

First, let's write a query that takes a vector of users and a vector of tags and returns a feed.

```
guestbook-feeds-2/resources/sql/queries.sql
-- :name get-feed :? :*
-- :require [guestbook.db.util :refer [tags-regex]]
-- Given a vector of follows and a vector of tags, return a feed
select * from
(select distinct on (p.id) * from posts_and_boosts as p
  where
  /*~ (if (seq (:follows params)) */
    p.poster in (:v*:follows)
    /*~*/
    false
    /*~ ) ~*/
    or
    /*~ (if (seq (:tags params)) */
```

```
    p.message ~*
    /*~*/
    false
    /*~ ) ~*/
    --~ (when (seq (:tags params)) (tags-regex (:tags params)))
  order by p.id, posted_at desc) as t
order by t.posted_at asc
```

We need to write another helper function similar to tag-regex that takes a vector
of tags instead of just one.

guestbook-feeds-2/src/clj/guestbook/db/util.clj
```clojure
(defn tags-regex [tags-raw]
  (let [tags (filter #(re-matches #"[-\w]+" %) tags-raw)]
    (when (not-empty tags)
      (str "'.*(\\s|^)#("
           (string/join "|" tags)
           ")(\\s|$).*'"))))
```

Now we're able to get a feed based on a map of :follows and :tags, and we can
leave one or the other empty.

Next, we need to get this subscriptions map from somewhere. Let's add subscriptions to a user's :profile JSONB. We'll reuse our /api/my-account/set-profile
endpoint, so we just need to add some utilities for working with the :subscriptions
field on the :profile map.

Create a new ClojureScript namespace called guestbook.subscriptions and add a
subscribe-button component:

guestbook-feeds-2/src/cljs/guestbook/subscriptions.cljs
```clojure
(ns guestbook.subscriptions
  (:require [re-frame.core :as rf]))

(rf/reg-event-fx
 :subscription/set
 (fn [{:keys [db]} [_ subs-type sub subscribe?]]
   (let [profile (update-in
                   (get-in db [:auth/user :profile])
                   [:subscriptions subs-type]
                   (fnil
                    (if subscribe?
                      #(conj % sub)
                      (partial filterv (partial not= sub)))
                    []))]
     {:db (assoc db ::loading? true)
      :ajax/post
      {:url "/api/my-account/set-profile"
       :params {:profile profile}
       :success-event [:subscription/handle profile]}})))
```

```clojure
(rf/reg-event-db
 :subscription/handle
 (fn [db [_ profile]]
   (-> db
       (assoc-in [:auth/user :profile] profile)
       (dissoc
        ::loading?))))

(rf/reg-sub
 :subscription/subscribed?
 :<-[:auth/user]
 (fn [{:keys [profile]} [_ subs-type sub]]
   (boolean
    (some
     (partial = sub)
     (get-in profile [:subscriptions subs-type] [])))))

(rf/reg-sub
 :subscription/loading?
 (fn [db _]
   (::loading? db)))

(defn subscribe-button [subs-type sub]
  (let [subscribed? @(rf/subscribe [:subscription/subscribed? subs-type sub])
        loading? @(rf/subscribe [:subscription/loading?])]
    (case @(rf/subscribe [:auth/user-state])
      :authenticated
      [:button.button.is-primary.is-rounded
       {:class (when subscribed? "is-outlined")
        :on-click #(rf/dispatch
                    [:subscription/set subs-type sub (not subscribed?)])
        :disabled loading?}
       (if subscribed?
         "Unfollow "
         "Follow ")
       (str
        (case subs-type
          :follows "@"
          :tags    "#"
          "")
        sub)]
      ;;ELSE
      [:p "Log in to personalize your feed."])))
```

Our :subscription/set event is the core of our logic. Unlike our profile page where we have a bunch of local changes, we're doing a single change at a time. The subs-type parameter specifies whether we're working with a tag or a user, sub is the value itself, and subscribe? is whether we're adding or removing the subscription. Based on these parameters, we modify the profile we have and immediately send it to set-profile, and set a ::loading? flag to ensure that we don't send conflicting updates simultaneously. The rest of the namespace is fairly straightforward.

Now let's include the subscribe-button in our tag page and our author page:

guestbook-feeds-2/src/cljs/guestbook/views/tag.cljs
```
[:h3 (str "Posts tagged #" tag)]
[sub/subscribe-button :tags tag]
```

guestbook-feeds-2/src/cljs/guestbook/views/author.cljs
```
[:h3 "Posts by " display-name " <@" user ">"]
[sub/subscribe-button :follows user]
```

Great! We have the ability to manage subscriptions for our feed.

Now we just need to add a page to render it. Let's start with a new namespace called guestbook.views.feed:

guestbook-feeds-2/src/cljs/guestbook/views/feed.cljs
```
(ns guestbook.views.feed
  (:require
   [guestbook.auth :as auth]
   [guestbook.messages :as messages]
   [re-frame.core :as rf]))

(def feed-controllers
  [{:identity #(js/Date.)
    :start (fn [_]
             (rf/dispatch [:messages/load-feed]))}])

(defn feed [_]
  (let [messages (rf/subscribe [:messages/list])]
```

```clojure
(fn [{{{:keys [post]} :query} :parameters}]
  [:div.content
   [:div.columns.is-centered>div.column.is-two-thirds

    (case @(rf/subscribe [:auth/user-state])
      :loading
      [:div.columns>div.column {:style {:width "5em"}}
       [:progress.progress.is-dark.is-small {:max 100} "30%"]]

      :authenticated
      [:<>
       [:div.columns>div.column
        [:h3 (str "My Feed")]
        (if @(rf/subscribe [:messages/loading?])
          [messages/message-list-placeholder]
          [messages/message-list messages post])]
       [:div.columns>div.column
        [messages/message-form]]]

      :anonymous
      [:div.columns>div.column
       [:div.notification.is-clearfix
        [:span
         "Log in or create an account to curate a personalized feed!"]
        [:div.buttons.is-pulled-right
         [auth/login-button]
         [auth/register-button]]]])]]))
```

This is similar to our other message-list-based pages, but we have the added concern that the feed is dependent on the current user's session rather than parameters. To manage this, we've expanded the scope of our :auth/user-state case statement, and we've added an :identity function to our controller that changes with every reload. This ensures that we never get stuck with an old list of messages.

Before this page will work, we need to connect a service endpoint to the query we wrote earlier, and we need to write the :messages/load-feed event to call it.

Let's start with our endpoint:

guestbook-feeds-2/src/clj/guestbook/messages.clj
```clojure
(defn get-feed [feed-map]
  (when-not (every? #(re-matches #"[-\w]+" %) (:tags feed-map))
    (throw
     (ex-info
      "Tags must only contain alphanumeric characters, dashes, or underscores!"
      feed-map)))
  {:messages
   (db/get-feed (merge {:follows []
                        :tags []}
                       feed-map))})
```

guestbook-feeds-2/src/clj/guestbook/routes/services.clj
```
;; in "/api/messages"
["/feed"
 {::auth/roles (auth/roles :messages/feed)
  :get
  {:responses
   {200
    {:body ;; Data Spec for response body
     {:messages
      [{:id pos-int?
        :name string?
        :message string?
        :timestamp inst?
        :author (ds/maybe string?)
        :avatar (ds/maybe string?)}]}}}
   :handler
   (fn [{{{:keys [boosts]
          :or {boosts true}} :query} :parameters
         {{{:keys [subscriptions]} :profile} :identity} :session}]
     (if boosts
       (response/ok
        (msg/get-feed subscriptions))
       (response/not-implemented {:message "Feed only supports boosts."})))}}]
```

Note that we require an identity to be present on the request map, so we should add a new auth entry as well:

guestbook-feeds-2/src/clj/guestbook/auth.clj
```
;; Inside `roles`
:messages/feed #{:authenticated}
```

Now let's write our re-frame event:

guestbook-feeds-2/src/cljs/guestbook/messages.cljs
```
(rf/reg-event-fx
 :messages/load-feed
 (fn [{:keys [db]} _]
   (let [{:keys [follows tags]}
         (get-in db [:auth/user :profile :subscriptions])]
     {:db (assoc db
                 :messages/loading? true
                 :messages/list nil
                 :messages/filter
                 [{:message
                   #(some
                     (fn [tag]
                       (re-find
                        (re-pattern (str "(?<=\\s|^)#"` tag "(?=\\s|$)"))
                        %))
                     tags)}
```

```
                       {:poster
                        #(some
                            (partial = %)
                            follows)}])
        :ajax/get {:url "/api/messages/feed"
                   :success-path [:messages]
                   :success-event [:messages/set]}}))))
(defn add-message? [filter-map msg]
  (every?
    (fn [[k matcher]]
      (let [v (get msg k)]
        (cond
          (set? matcher)
          (matcher v)
          (fn? matcher)
          (matcher v)
          :else
          (= matcher v))))
    filter-map))

(rf/reg-event-db
 :message/add
 (fn [db [_ message]]
   (let [msg-filter (:messages/filter db)
         filters (if (map? msg-filter)
                   [msg-filter]
                   msg-filter)]
     (if (some #(add-message? % message) filters)
        (update db :messages/list conj message)
        db)))))
```

Notice that we have to update our :message/filter logic to account for multiple ways of matching. We've simply allowed for a vector of maps in place of a single map. This allows us to accomodate the feed filter without having to change our older, simpler filters.

Finally, let's add our feed page to our routes and our navbar:

guestbook-feeds-2/src/cljc/guestbook/routes/app.cljc
```
;; require [guestbook.views.feed :as feed] in :cljs
["/feed"
 (merge
  {:name ::feed}
  #?(:cljs {:parameters {:query {(ds/opt :post) pos-int?}}
            :controllers feed/feed-controllers
            :view #'feed/feed}))]
```

guestbook-feeds-2/src/cljs/guestbook/core.cljs
```
;; In navbar
(when (= @(rf/subscribe [:auth/user-state]) :authenticated)
  [:<>
   [:a.navbar-item
    {:href (rtfe/href :guestbook.routes.app/author
                      {:user (:login @(rf/subscribe [:auth/user]))})}
    "My Posts"]
   [:a.navbar-item
    {:href (rtfe/href :guestbook.routes.app/feed)}
    "My Feed"]])
```

Let's try it out.

Great! We have a personalized feed. Aside from enriching some features and tweaking style, we have a fully functional and feature-complete social media application! Congratulations!

What You've Learned

In this chapter we've added several different features that enhance our application in various ways. Note that we were able to do this without extensively modify our existing codebase. While we did enhance some functionality, we did so in an additive way. This is the desired flow: we incrementally built our data model and once it solidified we were able to rapidly build new features.

You might have noticed that a lot of the feed pages are variations on a theme. Some of the code we've written is a tad repetitive, especially our SQL. We won't cover refactoring our SQL in gritty detail, but it would be a good exercise to update the functions in guestbook.messages to reuse our general query rather than a bunch of individual ones. As long as the data we return is the same shape, we can optimize our SQL layer as much as we like. This has the added benefit of providing flexibility to enhance our current pages and add new ones.

CHAPTER 9

Deployment

In this chapter, we'll take a look at adding tests and packaging the application for deployment.

Unit Tests

Many schools of thought exist on how, what, and when to test, and it's a sensitive subject for many people. As such, we'll simply give an overview of the basic tools available for testing and leave it up to you to decide how and when to use them.

The Test API

Clojure provides built-in support for testing via the clojure.test namespace. When a new project is created, a test package is generated along with it.

Let's take a quick look at what the clojure.test API looks like and how to work with it. The simplest way to write tests is to create assertions using the is macro. The following are a few examples of how it works:

```
user> (require '[clojure.test :refer [is]])
nil
user> (is (= 4 (+ 2 2)))
true
user> (is (= 5 (+ 2 2)))

FAIL in () (form-init8422778450785897308.clj:50)
expected: 5
  actual: 4
    diff: - 5
          + 4
false
user> (is (even? 2))
true
user> (is (instance? String 123))
```

```
FAIL in () (form-init8422778450785897308.clj:60)
expected: (instance? String 123)
  actual: java.lang.Long
false
user> (is (instance? String 123) "Not a string!")

FAIL in () (form-init8422778450785897308.clj:66)
Not a string!
expected: (instance? String 123)
  actual: java.lang.Long
false
user>
```

As you can see, the is macro can take any expression as the first argument and a message string as an optional second argument. If the expression fails, the macro prints the expression along with the actual result and the message if provided and then returns false; otherwise it returns true.

We can also group our tests together by using the testing macro. This macro accepts a string name for the group of tests followed by the assertions.

```
user> (require '[clojure.test :refer [is testing]])
nil
user> (testing "Collections"
        (is (coll? {}))
        (is (coll? #{}))
        (is (coll? []))
        (is (coll? '()))))
true
user> (testing "Collections"
        (is (coll? {}))
        (is (coll? 123)))

FAIL in () (form-init8422778450785897308.clj:83)
Collections
expected: (coll? 123)
  actual: (not (coll? 123))
false
user>
```

Finally, we can define tests by using the deftest macro:

```
user> (require '[clojure.test :refer [is testing deftest run-tests]])
nil
user> (deftest collections-test
        (testing "Collections"
          (is (coll? {}))
          (is (coll? #{}))
          (is (coll? []))
          (is (coll? '())))))
#'user/collections-test
user> (collections-test)
```

```
nil
user> (deftest test-fails
        (is (true? false)))
#'user/test-fails
user> (test-fails)
FAIL in (test-fails) (form-init8422778450785897308.clj:112)
expected: (true? false)
  actual: (not (true? false))
nil
user> (clojure.test/run-tests)

Testing user

FAIL in (test-fails) (form-init8422778450785897308.clj:112)
expected: (true? false)
  actual: (not (true? false))

Ran 2 tests containing 5 assertions.
1 failures, 0 errors.
{:test 2, :pass 4, :fail 1, :error 0, :type :summary}
user>
```

The tests defined using deftest can be called like regular functions. You can also run all the tests in the read-evaluate-print loop by calling run-tests. All tests in the application's test folder can be run via Leiningen by calling lein test. The API contains a number of other helpers as well, but I hope that the preceding examples prove sufficient for you to get started.

You may also wish to explore Peridot[1] and Kaocha[2] libraries, which provide additional support for testing Ring-based web applications. These frameworks provide many features not found in the core testing API. If your testing needs go beyond the basics we explored here, these will make excellent tools in your Clojure toolbox.

Testing the Application

Our app has two types of routes. Some routes serve the user-interface (UI) portion of the application to be rendered by the browser, and others expose service endpoints accessed via Ajax by the client part of the application. We'll look at writing tests for both types of routes in our application.

Before we proceed, we need to make a couple of updates to our application. First thing we need to do is create a test database instance. Having a separate database for testing is always a good idea because it allows us to separate our test data from any development data we might have in flight. This allows

---

1.   https://github.com/xeqi/peridot
2.   https://github.com/lambdaisland/kaocha

us to ensure that we always have a clean database for testing and that the test data is consistent. Let's create a new database instance called gb_test with the same owner as our development database. Next, we need to add this database's URL to test-config.edn:

guestbook-tests/test-config.edn
```
{:port 3000
 :database-url
 "postgresql://localhost:5432/gb_test?user=guestbook&password=password"}
```

With that done, let's start on testing our routes. Luminus, by default, includes a library called ring-mock.[3] The library provides a number of helper functions for generating mock requests.

We already have a test harness defined for our application. You can find it under the test/clj/guestbook/test/ directory. The tests for our Ring handler are in handler.clj. If we open it up, we can see that it defines a test called test-app.

guestbook/test/clj/guestbook/handler_test.clj
```
(ns guestbook.handler-test
  (:require
    [clojure.test :refer :all]
    [ring.mock.request :refer :all]
    [guestbook.handler :refer :all]
    [guestbook.middleware.formats :as formats]
    [muuntaja.core :as m]
    [mount.core :as mount]))

(defn parse-json [body]
  (m/decode formats/instance "application/json" body))

(use-fixtures
  :once
  (fn [f]
    (mount/start #'guestbook.config/env
                 #'guestbook.handler/app-routes)
    (f)))

(deftest test-app
  (testing "main route"
    (let [response ((app) (request :get "/"))]
      (is (= 200 (:status response)))))

  (testing "not-found route"
    (let [response ((app) (request :get "/invalid"))]
      (is (= 404 (:status response))))))
```

---

3. https://github.com/ring-clojure/ring-mock

We have a glaring problem here, though. In Setting Up Front-End Routing, on page 197, we changed guestbook.handler/app-routes to guestbook.handler/routes but never updated it here. Let's address that and try it out.

```
$ lein test guestbook.test.handler

lein test guestbook.test.handler

lein test :only guestbook.test.handler/guestbook.test.handler

ERROR in (guestbook.test.handler) (core.cljc:80)
Uncaught exception in test fixture
expected: nil
  actual: java.lang.RuntimeException:
    could not start [#'guestbook.handler/routes] due to
 at ...
Caused by: clojure.lang.ExceptionInfo:
  path "/ws" doesn't have a :handler defined for :get
...

Ran 0 tests containing 1 assertions.
0 failures, 1 errors.
Tests failed.
$
```

We have an error in our fixture, specifically when we try to start our routes state. Let's investigate where "/ws" is defined to see why it's breaking here:

guestbook-tests/src/clj/guestbook/routes/websockets.clj
```
(defn websocket-routes []
  ["/ws"
   {:middleware [middleware/wrap-csrf
                 middleware/wrap-formats]
    :get (:ajax-get-or-ws-handshake-fn socket)
    :post (:ajax-post-fn socket)}])
```

It's subtle, but you might notice what our issue is. Our :get and :post handlers depend on our socket state, and we haven't started it in our use-fixtures!

Let's update our fixture like so:

guestbook-tests/test/clj/guestbook/handler_test.clj
```
(use-fixtures
  :once
  (fn [f]
    (mount/start #'guestbook.config/env
                 #'guestbook.routes.websockets/socket
                 #'guestbook.handler/routes)
    (f)))
```

With that fixed, let's take a closer look at our default test-app test.

```clojure
(deftest test-app
  (testing "main route"
    (let [response ((app) (request :get "/"))]
      (is (= 200 (:status response)))))

  (testing "not-found route"
    (let [response ((app) (request :get "/invalid"))]
      (is (= 404 (:status response))))))
```

The ring.mock.request/request function is used to generate the request. It accepts a keyword indicating the request method, followed by the target URI and an optional parameter map that isn't used in the example.

```clojure
(request <method> <url> <optional params>)
```

The request is then passed to the guestbook.handler/app function that is the main entry point for our application. The result of calling app with the mock request is a Ring-style response discussed in Chapter 2, Luminus Web Stack, on page 29.

The first test checks that the app responds with the status 200 when we request the / URI. The second test checks that status 404 is returned for a nonexistent URI.

Now let's see what's involved in creating a test for the login service operation. We'd like to call the /login URL and pass it the user ID and the password. However, the login credentials must be passed in as a JSON body.

Let's write a login-request function that generates the request and sets the body using the ring.mock.request/json-body function.

guestbook-tests/test/clj/guestbook/handler_test.clj
```clojure
(defn login-request [login pass]
  (-> (request :post "/api/login")
      (json-body {:login    login
                  :password pass})))
```

That leaves us with one last problem. The guestbook.auth/authenticate-user function calls guestbook.db.core/get-user-for-auth* to fetch user credentials from the database. But we wish to test the request handler in isolation, not the model. In some languages it's possible to use monkey patching to get around this problem. This approach allows you to simply redefine the offending function at runtime with your own version, but the downside is that the change is global and therefore might interact poorly with code that expects the original version. Clojure provides a with-redefs macro that redefines vars within the scope of its body. This approach gives us the ability to make runtime modifications in a safer fashion, where we know precisely the scope of the code that's affected. Let's look at how this works in action. First we define a mock function that returns a test user.

guestbook-tests/test/clj/guestbook/handler_test.clj
```
;; require [buddy.hashers :as hashers] in namespace declaration

(defn mock-user [{:keys [login]}]
  (when (= login "foo")
    {:login "foo"
     :password (hashers/encrypt "password")
     :created_at now
     :profile {}}))
```

We can now redefine the guestbook.db.core/get-user-for-auth* with the mock function
before running our test:

```
(with-redefs [guestbook.db.core/get-user-for-auth* mock-user]
  ((app) (login-request "foo" "bar")))
```

We can see that the response contains the status of 200. The response body
is an input stream, and we'll want to get data out of it. The Luminus template
helpfully includes a parse-json function for us.

guestbook-tests/test/clj/guestbook/handler_test.clj
```
(defn parse-json [body]
  (m/decode formats/instance "application/json" body))
```

We can now check that the response has reasonable data:

```
(with-redefs [guestbook.db.core/get-user-for-auth* mock-user]
  (-> (login-request "foo" "bar") ((app)) :body parse-json))
;;{:identity {...}}
```

If we provide incorrect credentials, we'll see a different response:

```
(with-redefs [guestbook.db.core/get-user-for-auth* mock-user]
  (-> (login-request "foo" "xxx") ((app)) :body parse-json))
;;{:message "Incorrect login or password."}
```

Now, let's wrap this up in an actual test that checks that our application
responds correctly in both scenarios:

guestbook-tests/test/clj/guestbook/handler_test.clj
```
;; require [clojure.instant :refer [read-instant-date]]
(deftest test-login
  (with-redefs [guestbook.db.core/get-user-for-auth* mock-user]
    (let [handler (app)]
      (testing "login success"
        (let [{:keys [body status] :as r} (handler
                                            (login-request "foo" "password"))
              json (parse-json body)]
          (println (assoc r :body json))
          (is (= 200 status))
          (is (= (->
                  (:identity json)
```

```
                    (update :created_at read-instant-date))
                  (-> {:login "foo"}
                      mock-user
                      (dissoc :password))))))
      (testing "password mismatch"
        (let [{:keys [status]} (handler (login-request "foo" "hacker"))]
          (is (= 401 status)))))))
```

We needed to add some additional parsing on top of parse-json because JSON doesn't have native support for dates. Our coercion middleware is handling this for us usually, but since we're parsing our response manually, we have to account for JSON's shortcomings ourselves.

The with-redefs macro proved useful here. It's handy that we didn't have to plan for testing or mocking when writing our application's business logic.

Database Testing

Now that we've seen some basics of testing, let's take a look at how we can test our app against a database. We have some default boilerplate in guestbook.test.db.core. Let's take a look:

guestbook/test/clj/guestbook/db/core_test.clj
```
(ns guestbook.db.core-test
  (:require
   [guestbook.db.core :refer [*db*] :as db]
   [java-time.pre-java8]
   [luminus-migrations.core :as migrations]
   [clojure.test :refer :all]
   [next.jdbc :as jdbc]
   [guestbook.config :refer [env]]
   [mount.core :as mount]))

(use-fixtures
  :once
  (fn [f]
    (mount/start
     #'guestbook.config/env
     #'guestbook.db.core/*db*)
    (migrations/migrate ["migrate"] (select-keys env [:database-url]))
    (f)))

(deftest test-messages
  (jdbc/with-transaction [t-conn *db* {:rollback-only true}]
    (is (= 1 (db/save-message!
              t-conn
              {:name "Bob"
               :message "Hello, World"}
              {:connection t-conn})))
    (is (= {:name "Bob"
            :message "Hello, World"}
```

```
        (-> (db/get-messages t-conn {})
            (first)
            (select-keys [:name :message]))))))))
```

The fixtures are used to initialize the database connection and run any out-standing migrations before the tests are run. The test-users test is out-of-date, so let's start from scratch:

guestbook-tests/test/clj/guestbook/db/core_test.clj
```
(deftest test-users
  (jdbc/with-transaction [t-conn *db* {:rollback-only true}]
    (is (= 1 (db/create-user!* t-conn
                                {:login "foo"
                                 :password "password"})))
    (is (= {:login "foo"
            :profile {}}
           (dissoc (db/get-user* t-conn
                      {:login "foo"}) :created_at)))))
```

We've covered the same functionality as the default test.

Using a test schema allows us to test our application end to end. I recommend-ed this approach for any integration and validation testing.

ClojureScript Testing

We've already added the boilerplate necessary to run ClojureScript tests back in Shadow-cljs, on page 119. Now, all we need to do is to add the actual tests and include the ClojureScript source path in our project.clj. First, let's create a new folder for the tests by running the following command in the root of the project:

```
$ mkdir -p test/cljs/guestbook/
```

Now that we've created an additional source path for the front-end tests, we also need to update our project.clj to reference this path in the test profile under the :test-paths key:

```
{ ;;...
  :test-paths ["test/clj" "test/cljs"]
  ;;...
}
```

Since our shadow-cljs.edn configuration contains the directive :lein true, it will infer the test paths from our project.clj file.

We can now create a file called core_test.cljs in the test/cljs/guestbook folder. This file contains the namespace that we'll be using for our tests. Let's add the following code in the namespace declaration:

guestbook-tests/test/cljs/guestbook/core_test.cljs
```clojure
(ns guestbook.core-test
  (:require [cljs.test :refer-macros [is are deftest testing use-fixtures]]
            [pjstadig.humane-test-output]
            [reagent.dom.server :as dom]
            [guestbook.components :as gc]))
```

The namespace requires some boilerplate for running the tests, along with a reference to reagent.dom.server and the guestbook.components namespace from our app. We can now try testing the components that we built for rendering the front end of our application. Let's add a test for the md function that renders Markdown to HTML and check that it produces the intended output:

guestbook-tests/test/cljs/guestbook/core_test.cljs
```clojure
(deftest test-md
  (is (= "<p class=\"markdown\" data-reactroot=\"\"><h3>Hello</h3></p>"
         (dom/render-to-string (gc/md "### Hello")))))
```

With the code in place, we can execute the following command to run the tests:

```
$ npx shadow-cljs compile test
shadow-cljs - config: .../shadow-cljs.edn
shadow-cljs - running: lein run -m shadow.cljs.devtools.cli --npm compile test
[:test] Compiling ...
========= Running Tests =======================

Testing guestbook.core-test

Ran 1 tests containing 1 assertions.
0 failures, 0 errors.
===============================================
[:test] Build completed. (81 files, 2 compiled, 0 warnings, 3.20s)
```

This is all that's needed for running tests with shadow-cljs using the Node.js runtime. For further documentation and examples on testing, please refer to the official shadow-cljs documentation.[4]

Package the Application

Our application is now ready to be packaged and deployed. Let's see how to accomplish this using Leiningen and go over some of the things to be aware of, depending on how you wish to run the application in production.

Up to this point, we've been running our application by calling lein run to start up the HTTP server in development mode. In this mode the server watches the files for changes and reloads them as needed, which obviously causes a significant performance hit. Since we should optimize our application for

---

4.   https://shadow-cljs.github.io/docs/UsersGuide.html#_testing

performance when we deploy in production, we need to package it differently. Let's look at what's involved in packaging and running a Clojure web applications in production.

Clojure applications are idiomatically packaged as stand-alone uberJars containing all the assets for a given application. An uberJar has no external dependencies, aside from having the Java Runtime Environment installed on the target system.

Any environment-specific configuration such as database connections, SSL configuration, and so on are typically managed using an EDN configuration file provided by the target environment.

Stand-alone Deployment

Here we'll take a closer look at what's involved in deployment as a stand-alone application.

Running as an UberJar

When we wish to package the application for stand-alone deployment, we simply run the following from the application's root:

```
$ lein uberjar
```

The resulting artifact is created in the target folder. The artifact can now be run using java command, but we do need to provide the production configuration. Luminus uses a library called cprop[5] for configuration management. The library provides a number of options for specifying the configuration settings.

The first option is to include the configuration directly in the JAR. The library looks for a config.edn file on the classpath and reads the configuration from there. Alternatively, we can specify the location of the EDN configuration file using an environment variable called conf. When multiple configurations are found, they're merged into a single configuration map when the application starts. The keys found in the external configuration overwrite the keys in the one packaged in the JAR. Finally, we can specify the configuration keys as environment variables.

We already have a dev-config.edn configuration file that we've been using during development, so let's use it to test that our app works stand-alone by passing it using the conf environment variable. Once the server starts, we should be able to confirm that the app is running by browsing to localhost:3000.

```
$ java -Dconf=dev-config.edn -jar target/uberjar/guestbook.jar
```

---

5. https://github.com/tolitius/cprop

To *actually* run the app in production, all you need to do is replace dev-config.edn with the appropriate filename. By convention, prod-config.edn is usually used.

Heroku Deployment

Heroku is a cloud service with a free hosting option. Before we start using Heroku, we need to make sure we have Git[6] and Heroku Toolbelt[7] installed.

Heroku uses the command specified in a file called Procfile to start up the application. This file must be placed in the project's root directory.

To run a Clojure application on Heroku, we need a Procfile that specifies the command that starts the application. Luminus generates this file for us by default:

```
web: java $JVM_OPTS -cp target/guestbook.jar \
    clojure.main -m guestbook.core
```

Next you need to initialize a Git repository for the application (if you haven't already) by running the following commands:

```
$ git init
$ git add .
$ git commit -m "init"
```

Once the repository is created, we can test the application by running foreman start in the project's root directory. If the application starts up fine, then we're ready to deploy it to the cloud by running the following command:

```
$ heroku create
```

To add PostgreSQL support for the application, run this command:

```
$ heroku addons:add heroku-postgresql
```

Now you can find the connection settings for the database on your Heroku dashboard. Heroku provides configuration via environment variables. It provides PORT and DATABASE_URL by default, and you can add any additional configuration to the environment via the Heroku dashboard. We're now ready to push our application to Heroku.

```
$ git push heroku master
```

Once the upload completes, Heroku attempts to build and deploy your application. If this process completes successfully, you should be able to browse to the application URL specified in your administration console.

---

6.   http://git-scm.com/
7.   https://toolbelt.heroku.com/

Docker

The final way you may want to deploy your application is by using a Docker container.[8] This an industry standard for cloud deployment and is supported by many cloud providers.

Your configuration strategy could vary dramatically based on your particular infrastructure, but the basic structure of a Dockerfile for a Clojure project is a straightforward starting point.

guestbook-tests/Dockerfile
```
FROM openjdk:11-buster

COPY target/uberjar/guestbook.jar /guestbook/app.jar

COPY prod-config.edn /guestbook/config.edn

EXPOSE 3000

CMD ["java", "-jar", "-Dconf=/guestbook/config.edn", "/guestbook/app.jar"]
```

This example bundles in a configuration file, but you could set environment variables or use whatever process you wish.

guestbook-tests/prod-config.edn
```
{:port 3000
 :database-url
 "postgresql://localhost:5432/guestbook?user=guestbook&password=password"}
```

Also, you should add a STDOUT appender to the env/prod/resources/logback.xml file so that logs are visible from docker logs.

guestbook-tests/env/prod/resources/logback.xml
```
<?xml version="1.0" encoding="UTF-8"?>
<configuration>
    <statusListener class="ch.qos.logback.core.status.NopStatusListener" />
    <appender name="STDOUT" class="ch.qos.logback.core.ConsoleAppender">
        <!-- encoders are assigned the type
             ch.qos.logback.classic.encoder.PatternLayoutEncoder
             by default -->
        <encoder>
            <charset>UTF-8</charset>
            <pattern>
            %date{ISO8601} [%thread] %-5level %logger{36} - %msg %n
            </pattern>
        </encoder>
    </appender>
```

---

8. https://docs.docker.com/

```xml
<appender name="FILE"
        class="ch.qos.logback.core.rolling.RollingFileAppender">
    <file>log/guestbook.log</file>
    <rollingPolicy
        class="ch.qos.logback.core.rolling.TimeBasedRollingPolicy">
        <fileNamePattern>
        log/guestbook.%d{yyyy-MM-dd}.%i.log
        </fileNamePattern>
        <timeBasedFileNamingAndTriggeringPolicy
        class="ch.qos.logback.core.rolling.SizeAndTimeBasedFNATP">
            <maxFileSize>100MB</maxFileSize>
        </timeBasedFileNamingAndTriggeringPolicy>
        <!-- keep 30 days of history -->
        <maxHistory>30</maxHistory>
    </rollingPolicy>
    <encoder>
        <charset>UTF-8</charset>
        <pattern>
        %date{ISO8601} [%thread] %-5level %logger{36} - %msg %n
        </pattern>
    </encoder>
</appender>
<appender name="STDOUT" class="ch.qos.logback.core.ConsoleAppender">
    <encoder>
        <pattern>%-5relative %-5level %logger{35} - %msg%n</pattern>
    </encoder>
</appender>
<logger name="org.apache.http" level="warn" />
<logger name="org.xnio.nio" level="warn" />
<logger name="com.zaxxer.hikari" level="warn" />
<root level="INFO">
    <appender-ref ref="FILE" />
    <appender-ref ref="STDOUT" />
</root>
</configuration>
```

Now all we have to do is test, compile our application, build our image, and run our container:

```
$ lein test

lein test guestbook.test.db.core
...

lein test guestbook.test.handler
...

Ran 3 tests containing 7 assertions.
0 failures, 0 errors.
```

Tests passed; let's compile:

```
$ lein uberjar
Compiling guestbook.auth
Compiling guestbook.auth.ring
Compiling guestbook.auth.ws
...
[:app] Compiling ...
...
[:app] Build completed. (458 files, 345 compiled, 0 warnings, 29.27s)
Created /.../guestbook/target/uberjar/guestbook-0.1.0-SNAPSHOT.jar
Created /.../guestbook/target/uberjar/guestbook.jar
```

Now build our image:

```
$ docker build -t guestbook:latest .
Sending build context to Docker daemon  209.8MB
Step 1/5 : FROM openjdk:11-buster
 ---> f2f9cd527eff
Step 2/5 : COPY target/uberjar/guestbook.jar /guestbook/app.jar
 ---> de20039db743
Step 3/5 : COPY prod-config.edn /guestbook/config.edn
 ---> 93f5738f47f8
Step 4/5 : EXPOSE 3000
 ---> Running in e6cca1c5d5a4
Removing intermediate container e6cca1c5d5a4
 ---> 9c2fe154a05f
Step 5/5 :
 CMD ["java", "-jar", "-Dconf=/guestbook/config.edn", "/guestbook/app.jar"]
 ---> Running in c5b66f03cf71
Removing intermediate container c5b66f03cf71
 ---> aa252f5824aa
Successfully built aa252f5824aa
Successfully tagged guestbook:latest
```

Finally, let's run our image as a local container:

```
$ docker run -i --net="host" guestbook:latest
... [main] INFO  guestbook.env -
-=[guestbook started successfully]=-
...
```

Voila! We have a Docker container running our app.

What You've Learned

This concludes the design, implementation, and deployment of our site. We covered many aspects of creating a real-world application during our journey, such as handling static resources, database access, Ajax, and WebSockets.

Although our site is functional, it clearly could use some improvements. We recommend that you experiment with adding new features or improving existing ones to build your confidence and expand your knowledge. We also include Chapter 10, Exercises, on page 347, to help you get started.

The skills you've learned by building applications throughout the book should allow you to create a wide variety of web applications using Clojure. It's our hope that you'll be able to apply these skills in building real-world applications going forward.

Exercises

Now that you have a complete Clojure web application under your belt, the next step is honing your ability to maintain and improve a Clojure codebase. One of the most important skills for any programmer is independent learning. New tools and libraries are constantly emerging, and users always want new and exciting features. By learning new libraries and building new features on your own, you'll validate what you've learned throughout this book and build your confidence and fluency with Clojure.

How to Read This Chapter

This chapter is a collection of tasks and exercises for you to do on your own. These challenges will validate and strengthen the skills you've learned throughout this book. Each is an enhancement or new feature to be added to the guestbook application we've built. In addition to the exercises included, we encourage you to implement features that you come up with on your own.

We've divided the exercises into two categories: Code Quality and Feature Enhancements.

The Code Quality section deals with improvements to the implementation of the application with little to no change in the functionality. The tasks will make the application more robust, more performant, and/or easier to work with.

The Feature Enhancements section is a collection of potential enhancements to the functionality of the application. Some are variations on features we covered throughout the book, and some are intended as an independent learning challenge. We'll point you toward sections of the book and/or external resources that may be useful in completing each task. While some of the features may be related, you should be able to do most exercises in any order you wish. Pick a feature that appeals to you and give it a go.

We placed the Code Quality section first because those exercises will likely make subsequent tasks easier to complete. But it's not neccessary to complete them first. It may be more intuitive to skim the section so that you're aware of what might be improved and then come back to them as you like.

Code Quality

This section will provide some tips on keeping the code in a good shape as you continue developing the application. We'll cover important aspects that ensure that the application will be maintainable and extensible going forward.

Flesh Out API Specification

One of the most important parts of maintaining a web application is ensuring that the API is stable and robust. A natural split occurs between the client and the server across the HTTP API boundary. The front end can be seen as a separate application that communicates with the server using this API. In fact, you may wish to add other clients, such as a mobile app, in the future.

Since the front end relies on the functionality provided via the API, it acts as a contract between the client and the server. Providing a detailed schema for each endpoint helps ensure that the API is stable, reducing the risk of breaking changes as new features are added.

Throughout the development process, we were very loose with our schemas because it allowed us to easily enhance and augment our application across the network boundary. We should still aim to retain this flexibility in areas we may change in the future, but fleshing out our schemas in areas we're confident won't change allows us to develop new features while knowing we won't break existing ones.

To improve the API specification, consider the following:

- Declare specs for post and user outside of guestbook.routes.services/service-routes to be shared across routes that use them.

- Make use of ds/opt to enforce structure for optional keys.

- Since data-specs are just plain maps, you can leverage dissoc, assoc, select-keys, rename-keys, and merge for cases where you need a variation on a standard specification.

Increase Test Coverage

Different types of applications have different testing requirements. Many different test strategies are out there, such as unit testing, property testing, integration testing, and regression testing, among others. You'll typically use a combination of these strategies based on the type of the application you're developing.

Regression testing is one of the more valuable testing strategies because it acts as a contract for the features of the application to ensure that the application is working as intended. Having a regression test suite makes sure that new features you're adding aren't negatively impacting the existing features of the application.

Expand the test harness to include all of the API endpoints. This will help ensure that you're not introducing regressions as you add new functionality to your application.

Front-End Testing

The client side of the application is the part that's visible to the users. Unfortunately, this is also the part that's difficult to test, since traditional testing of UI components is often brittle. But there's not much value in testing the visual aspect of the UI. What we're really interested in testing is the behavior of the components. Luckily for us, re-frame provides excellent separation between the presentation and behavior of the UI. As you've probably noticed, the behaviors present in UI components are generally restricted to observing subscriptions and dispatching events with all the business logic living behind the event API.

So client-side testing should be focused on ensuring that re-frame events and subscriptions conform to their intended behavior. This is similar to the situation we've discussed with the separation between the client and the server.

As part of the exercise, consider adding tests for each of the subscriptions and dispatches in the application. This will provide you with a reasonable guarantee that the front end continues working as intended as you continue to extend it.

Standardize Feed Queries

The guestbook app has a lot of SQL queries with similar functionality, and the feature exercises will add even more. While we tend to favor simple SQL over more advanced approaches, it can be worthwhile to restructure our database interaction layer as our model becomes more sophisticated. You can take two types of approaches to address this. You can leverage more advanced HugSQL features, such as snippets,[1] as well as expanding your use of Clojure expressions[2] to make your SQL more configurable and templated. Or you can use a declarative SQL DSL such as HoneySQL.[3]

Regardless of your choice, the objectives are the same:

- Currently, our guestbook makes use of views to reuse query logic. This is a decent solution, but it can be inconvenient to extend. We'd like to limit the use of views and move this generalization logic into sub-queries.

- One of the core features of our guestbook app is the feed. We'd like to optimize our query structure for configurable feeds and ensure that the returned ResultSet's structure is uniform. Think about the different predicates or attributes that might be used, and account for predicates you might not think of right now. You could even consider creating a small DSL for a feed that could be encoded as a JSON array or map. Check out Designing Data-Driven DSLs[4] by Rafal Dittwald and James Cash for some guidance on creating your own DSL.

- A major set of features involves universal control of who can see your posts and which authors you'd like to see (for example, blocking and muting). By generalizing our queries, we should be able to effectively apply rules like these to *all* of our queries for posts.

Lazy Loading and Pagination

During development we never had to worry about the size of our Ajax results, but as more posts are written, this could become a very important concern. We should update all of our feed queries to support pagination so that we can load only what we need. If you've already done the exercise in Standardize Feed Queries, on page 349, this should be a bit easier to accomplish.

Here are some steps you can use as a guide:

- Update SQL queries to accept LIMIT and OFFSET. Ensure that there's a sensible ORDER BY for each feed.

---

1. https://www.hugsql.org/#using-snippets
2. https://www.hugsql.org/#using-expressions
3. https://github.com/seancorfield/honeysql
4. https://www.youtube.com/watch?v=j382BLptxCc

- If you're feeling keen, consider what happens when there are new posts added before the user fetches the next set of posts. How might you ensure that you don't get any stale posts?

- Accept LIMIT and OFFSET parameters from API endpoints and include ORDER BY in each feed's configuration.

- Update re-frame events to pass appropriate LIMIT and OFFSET options, and trigger events from either navigation via a Next button or a scroll event.

Make sure to consider how the WebSocket connection factors into this. Consider updating the WebSocket functionality to align more closely with this use pattern.

Reduce WebSocket Noise

As we alluded to in the exercise Lazy Loading and Pagination, on page 350, our WebSocket's live loading of new posts is cumbersome. If we have a lot of activity, we could overload our clients with a lot of network traffic. We should be more conservative about what messages we send and to which users we send them. Tweaking a few different aspects could greatly reduce network load.

Send Messages to Users Based on Their Selected Feed

The first thing we can change to reduce noise is move our filtering logic to the server. We're unneccessarily sending new messages to *all* users and allowing them to selectively ignore them if they aren't relevant. We should capture which feed a user is viewing and store it along with their client ID so that we can filter messages *before* sending them.

Send Notifications Instead of Full Messages

Additionally, if users aren't on the first page, new messages aren't relevant at all. For these cases, we should just send a notification that a new message exists so that they can go back to the top of their feed if they wish.

Make Message Updates a Configurable Feature

Even if a user is on the first page, they may not want live loading of new messages. This is especially true for users on metered connections, such as cellular data. Consider adding a user setting for whether they want live messages, only notifications, or no messages at all. You could even add support for no WebSocket connection at all by providing the same functionality via Ajax.

Feature Enhancements

This section contains a selection of features you may wish to implement. The skills they'll build are varied, and most have several valid approaches. You can tackle them in any order, but some exercises build on work done in others.

We encourage you to be creative and independent in how you choose to do these exercises and to take our recommendations as a starting point.

Saved Posts

This feature allows users to keep a list of saved posts for quick access. It's a common feature on many social media platforms such as Twitter (likes) and Mastodon Social (stars). Once the feature is implemented, the users will see a button that toggles whether the post appears in the list of saved posts that's maintained for each user.

We've already added a more sophisticated feature of Boosting Posts, on page 278, and this feature will be similar in terms of implementation. The tasks to implement this feature are as follows:

- Create a table to track saved posts.

    - At the very minimum, the table needs to contain the user ID and the ID of the post that was liked.
    - Write SQL statements for insertion and deletion of posts from the saved posts table.

- Create a route for toggling post membership in the saved list.

    - This route should accept the ID of the post that's being saved, and the user ID should be read from the session on the server.

- Create the route for loading the list of saved posts.

    - The route will take no arguments and will return the currently saved posts for the user in the session.
    - Alternatively, you could consider adding pagination, where the client specifies the offset and the number of posts to be loaded.

- Create a button that toggles whether the post is saved.

    - This button will appear as part of the HTML element that renders the post, and it'll call the new route you've added to the API.
    - Reference guestbook.messages/boost-button for a similar example.

- Create a UI element that allows the users to navigate to the list.
  - This could be either a button or a link in the navbar. When the user clicks this element, they'll be navigated to the page displaying their saved posts.

- Leverage the existing component that renders the timeline to render the saved posts.
  - This feature can leverage the guestbook.messages/message-list component.

Blocking Users

Sometimes users may wish to limit their interactions with others. Blocking users is a common way to accomplish that. When a user decides to block another user on the platform, then neither user should be able to view or interact with each others posts in any way.

To do this, you need to consider each side of a block. You can easily filter out posts that a user has blocked based on the user ID associated with each post. On the reverse, you need to get a list of all of the users that have blocked the account and filter based on that. You should do this in the SQL query itself, as it may interfere with pagination and other features. Additionally, this is a security concern, so it's imperative that you filter on the server to ensure that blocked users never get access to posts they aren't allowed to see.

The following steps implement this feature:

- Create a table that contains two columns that are the user ID and the ID of the user they blocked.

- Write SQL queries to insert and delete blocked users.

- Update timeline queries to filter out any posts that contain IDs from the table of blocked users.

- Update timeline queries to filter out posts by users who blocked you.

- Update queries for replying, boosting, and saving to ensure that the user is not blocked by the post author.

- Create a route to list blocked users.

- Create a route to toggle membership of the user in the block list.

- Create a UI to list blocked users that allows the user to unblock users if they change their mind later.

You could also consider the option to simply mute a user or tag, in which case the content is simply filtered from the timeline of the user who decides to mute another user or a topic.

Private Accounts

If a user is blocking people, we should also allow them to restrict viewing their account/posts to authenticated users. In some cases, the user may not desire this (for example, if the block is simply for the purpose of preventing engagement).

The user will be able to toggle the status of their account as being set to private in their profile settings. Once the account is flagged as private, then only accounts that already follow the account or that the account follows will be able to interact with it.

This feature has similar functionality to the block feature we just implemented. The main difference is that it uses an inclusion instead of an exclusion list, where only the users on the list are able to interact with the content.

- Update the user profile table to add a private Boolean that indicates whether the account is marked as private.

- Modify SQL queries for loading and interacting with posts to filter posts based on whether the account associated with the post is marked as private and the user is either following it or is followed by it.

- Add a route that allows the user to toggle their account being public or private.

- Add a UI element on the user profile page to toggle the status of their account.

Batch Management of Follows/Blocks/Mutes

It's inconvenient for users to manage their follows from individual pages, so we should provide a management section to remove follows and/or block users. We've already discussed the need to manage blocked users, and it makes sense to expand this to a general user-management page. It will list all the users that the account interacts with and will allow unfollowing, blocking, or unblocking other users in one place.

- Create a new section in the account management page that contains three lists:

  - Users following the account.

– Users that the account follows.
– Users the account has blocked.

The user can easily toggle their relationship with other accounts using this feature.

Queued/Scheduled Posts

Allow users to write posts and schedule a specific time when they'll become visible to other users. A simple approach is to use an explicitly set created_at timestamp and update timeline queries to drop any posts where the timestamp is in the future.

- Update the insert statement that creates posts to accept an optional timestamp. When the timestamp is provided, it will override the default.

- Add a datepicker on the post creation UI that allows the user to select the time when the post will become visible.

- Update the Ajax call to contain the timestamp when provided by the user.

- Update the code that creates the post to account for the timestamp specifying the creation time.

Note that you also want to make sure you're handling time zones correctly. The easiest solution is to update the created_at column to be a timestamptz type, then to make sure that you're passing the timestamp along with the local time zone of the client.

Pinned Posts

Allow users to toggle pinned status of posts on their home page. Update query to always include them in the first page (by sorting or some other means).

- Create a table that tracks pinned posts for the user. The table will contain the user ID and the post ID columns.

- Write a statement to insert the post ID and the user ID in the pinned posts table.

- Create a route that accepts the ID of the post and selects the ID of the user from the session, then insert them in the table using the statement you defined.

- Update the author posts query to select the pinned posts and prepend them to the result.

- Add a UI element on the posts that allows marking them as pinned. This element should only be visible to the author of the post.

- Add an Ajax call to toggle the membership of the post in the pinned posts table.

DMs

Allow users to send direct messages to each other.

- Create a direct_messages table with author, recipient, message, and created_at.

- Create a statement to write a new DM.

- Create a query to get the message history for two users.

- Create an endpoint to write a DM and an endpoint to fetch DMs for a user pair and a timestamp window.

- Create either a page, a UI component, or a modal for rendering a DM conversation between two users.

- Ensure that authorization is respected throughout, including privacy and blocking. These are DMs, after all.

Moderation

Moderation is an important feature that's integral to any social media platform. It involves multiple intertwined features.

Before you get started, you'll need a roles field on the users table.

- Write a migration to add the roles field; it can be either JSONB or a text array field.

Mod Authorization/Role

The first thing you need to do is create a moderator auth level to restrict moderation actions to moderators. Also, you probably want at least one user to be a superuser with the power to promote/demote other moderators.

- Create a superuser manually (for example, run a SQL statement via the CLI, your favorite SQL client, or the REPL).

- Create a moderator management page accessible only to superusers.

    - Add an endpoint to promote/demote users to the moderator role.
    - Add a UI for viewing all current moderators and promoting/demoting them.

- Add a moderator action dropdown/button on posts, visible only to moderators.

- Add a moderator action dropdown/button on account pages, visible only to moderators.

- Allow moderators to circumvent being blocked for the purposes of moderation.

Deletion of Posts

To delete posts without ruining replies and boosts, we'll remove the content of the post with a standard "this post was deleted" body. Additionally, we'll remove the author reference by setting the author column to NULL. Since we permit NULL author references, this shouldn't cause any issues.

You can replace the message body a couple of ways. The simplest is to write a standard body into the message column. This has the downside of being easily mimicked by users, as well as being difficult to update. We could improve this by using a custom Markdown transformer and prohibiting the inclusion of it in any way other than deletion.

The more involved approach is to migrate our posts table to add a deleted? Boolean column, or a metadata JSONB column with a deleted? field. When deleting a post, the message column would still need to be cleared (for example, replaced with an empty string), but it wouldn't be responsible for the rendering logic itself.

Next, you have to write the post deletion SQL statement and expose it via an API endpoint. Ensure that posts can only be deleted by their authors or by moderators. If desired, you could render the deleted post's body differently, depending on why it was deleted.

Finally, if the current user is the author of a post or a moderator, it should render a delete button.

Deletion/Banning of Accounts

Similar to posts, we want to make sure that we scrub all content without breaking anything. First and foremost, we'll delete all of their posts, then we'll replace their account content with standard "deleted" content.

Note that the author column of the posts table has ON DELETE SET NULL. This could be a big problem if you have a GDPR request, since the deletion of a user will make it nearly impossible to track down their posts. You should update this constraint to ON DELETE CASCADE with a migration. This will ensure that all posts with a given author are deleted by default. If you wish to *deactivate* an account instead, you could do so by other means than deletion to preserve posts.

To build on this problem, consider implementing temporary bans, suspensions, or other disciplinary features as you see fit. You can do this by updating a JSONB column on the user row with the details and using authorization rules to prevent certain actions.

Reporting Process

Now, similar to DMs, we want a reporting process for users and/or posts. These should go to a shared inbox for moderators.

- Create a table for content_reports with a similar structure to DMs.

- It should likely contain the following:

    - Offending post
    - Reason
    - Comments
    - Reporting user

- These reports should be visible to the reporting user and all moderators (unless the offending post is authored by a moderator).

- It should implement a DM-like feature with a distinct conversation per incident.

Consider adding moderator management features, such as assigning reports to a specific moderator.

Verifying Accounts

While we haven't gone over email integration, several libraries are available for this purpose. Our preferred email library is postal.[5] Refer to the documentation for the various setup options.

Email can be finnicky, so try sending yourself an email from the REPL before getting bogged down with the particulars of integrating it into your app.

To associate an email with an account, you can send an email with a magic link to the address provided. The magic link should contain a generated UUID that's associated with the specific account and lasts for a limited duration. If the user navigates to this link and successfully authenticates, then we can be sure that they do indeed own the email address. Since these UUIDs are

---

5. https://github.com/drewr/postal

ephemeral, they can be stored in memory (for example, in an atom) for simplicity. Whenever doing something in memory, be aware of the trade-offs related to application scaling and the potential future need to move to a different implementation, such as creating a database table.

- Validate email setup.

- Generate a UUID and associate it with the account (for example, in a map of UUID to userid and expiry in an atom).

- Create a Magic Link route that will:
  - Check the UUID's associated user and expiry.
  - Authenticate the user.
  - Update the user row with the verified email if they match.
  - Clean out the UUID from the atom.

- Update the user account page with a field for setting and verifying an email address.

- Update the user account to display verified status.

- (Optional)—Set up a scheduled process to clean up expired UUIDs using Java Interop (see the example that follows).

```clojure
(ns guestbook.auth.verify
  (:require
    [clojure.tools.logging :as log]
    [mount.core :refer [defstate]])
  (:import [java.util.concurrent Executors TimeUnit ScheduledExecutorService]))

(def registrations (atom {}))

(defn cleanup-stale-registrations []
  ;; using a try/catch is important in order not to crash the whole scheduler
  ;; while this won't fail with an atom, you maybe end up with failures in
  ;; more complex cases that interact with IO, such as if you use a table
  ;; with a database connection
  (try
    (swap! registrations
           (fn [registrations]
             ;; your cleanup fn
             ))
    (catch Exception e
      (log/error e "error removing stale registrations")
      (throw e))))
```

```
(defn schedule-reminders [scheduler]
  (.scheduleWithFixedDelay scheduler
                           cleanup-stale-registrations
                           0
                           120
                           TimeUnit/SECONDS))
(defstate scheduler
  :start
  (when (site-config :notifications?)
    (let [scheduler
          ^ScheduledExecutorService (Executors/newScheduledThreadPool 1)]
      (schedule-reminders scheduler)
      scheduler))
  :stop
  (when scheduler (.shutdown scheduler)))
```

With email verification, you can reduce fake accounts and prevent people from easily circumventing moderator actions and/or blocks.

For even stronger protection, you can try SMS verification if you're feeling brave. The principle of using a code with an expiry is the same, but it's somewhat harder to send an SMS than it is to send an email. Several SMS providers with Java libraries are available. Select one you like and practice your Interop skills.

Trigger Warnings

As a special case of tags, we may want to add trigger warnings. If you did the preceding Deletion of Accounts exercise, you'll have a similar replacement of the UI but retain the content on the server side so that it can be displayed when a button is clicked. Think of different criteria a user may want to specify for placing posts behind a trigger warning. Additionally, allow authors to explicitly use the sensitive content UI component from their posts.

Consider adding a custom Markdown transformer for the Sensitive Content component.

Similar to blocking, allow users to specify a list of tags they wish to be placed behind Sensitive Content wrappers automatically.

Preventing Replies

Allow users to prevent replies either per-post or globally. Also consider applying auth granularity here if desired. Leverage functionality added in the exercises in Private Accounts, on page 354, and Verifying Accounts, on page 358.

You may wish to add several options to posts that change the way a post is rendered or used. Consider adding a JSONB column for post options, and update the various endpoints and UI components to respect these options.

Consider using the same JSONB column as the exercise in Deletion of Posts, on page 357, to keep all post visibility/authorization options in one place.

Custom Feeds

Build on the functionality implemented in the exercise Standardize Feed Queries, on page 349, by allowing users to create their own custom feeds. Allow feeds to be specified as JSON, and allow users to specify them with a GUI.

These are some example feeds you could test against:

- All posts tagged #cats or #dogs, but not #sad.

- All posts written by users @newsSite, @cableNews, and @satireVegetable, and posts and boosts from @influencer.

- All posts written by accounts I follow, but no boosts or replies, and any posts mentioning my account.

Render feeds as a list of tabs named by the user (for example, Cute Animals, News, About Me).

Allow users to share their feeds, and allow feeds to subscribe to other feeds.

When clicking follow on a user or tag, allow the user to specify which feeds to modify.

Search

Postgres supports full-text search.[6] You can either add this functionality, or use LIKE with a regex on post content. Add a front end for searches. At the very least allow users to be searched by account name/username.

Consider allowing specific searches for the following:

- Posts
- Users
- Posts by user
- Saved posts

---

6. https://www.postgresql.org/docs/12/functions-textsearch.html

Metrics

Write various metrics queries for different entities in the guestbook application and render them in an appealing way.

Consider the following metrics to query:

- Boosts/saves of a post over time.
- User activity (posts/boosts/replies per day).
- New followers over time.
- Posts in a tag over time.

Connect these metrics queries to UI elements and consider how public you wish to make them.

Trending Posts

Trending is similar to metrics but across all posts. Display the top performing posts and tags for the current day/week.

Similarly to the example in Verifying Accounts, on page 358, have a scheduled job that runs the trending query each interval (for example, hour, day, week) and updates the in-memory cached version to be returned to users.

Add a trending tab to the home page.

What You've Learned

Programming is a journey, and we hope that we've helped along the way by providing a solid foundation for real world projects. The ability to learn independently is the most important skill, and hopefully the exercises in this chapter helped you develop comfort using Clojure on your own. The best way to keep building your skills going forward is through continued practice. Perhaps the book has given you ideas for a project of your own. Alternatively you could consider contributing to an existing open source project or perhaps to even start writing Clojure professionally. Whatever path you choose, we hope that you'll continue using the language in the future.

Clojure Primer

Since numerous books for learning Clojure are already available, we'll keep this overview short. Even if you're not familiar with Clojure, we hope you'll find that most of the code in this book is easy to follow. Instead of looking at syntax in depth, we'd like to briefly go over the way Clojure programs are structured and some of the unique aspects of the language.

All the mainstream languages belong to the same family. Once you learn one of these languages, very little effort is involved in learning another. Generally, all you have to do is learn some syntax sugar and the useful functions in the standard library to become productive. You may find a new concept here and there, but most of your existing skills are easily transferable.

This isn't the case with Clojure. Being a Lisp dialect, it comes from a different family of languages and requires learning new concepts to use it effectively. However, we assure you that Clojure is not inherently more difficult to understand, and with a bit of practice you might even feel it's the opposite.

A Functional Perspective

Clojure is a functional language. This makes it extremely well positioned for writing modern applications. As the application grows, it's imperative to be able to reason about parts of the application in isolation. It's equally important to have code that is testable and reusable. Let's take a look at the aspects of functional programming that facilitate these qualities.

Managing State

Functional languages are ideal for writing large applications because they eschew global state and favor immutability as the default. When the data is predominantly immutable, we can safely reason about parts of the application in isolation.

"Immutable data structures" might sound like a strange idea at first. But many of the benefits associated with functional languages are directly facilitated by them. Let's look at what makes these data structures such a powerful tool.

In most languages, data can be passed around either by value or by reference. Passing data by value is safe since we know that any changes we make to the data won't have any effect outside the function. However, it's also prohibitively expensive in many cases, so any substantial amount of data is passed around by reference. This makes code more difficult to reason about, as you have to know all the places where a piece of data is referenced to update it safely.

Immutable data structures provide us with a third option. Every time a change is made to a data structure, a new revision is created. The price we pay when altering the data is proportional to the size of the change. When a piece of data is no longer referenced, it simply gets garbage-collected.

Instead of having to manually track every reference to a piece of data, we can offload this work to the language runtime. This allows us to effectively "copy" data anytime we make a change, without having to worry about where it comes from or what the scope of our change will be.

Having such data structures facilitates writing pure functions. A pure function is simply a function that has no side effects. Since such functions can be reasoned about in isolation, the applications written using them are composed of individual self-contained components. This type of code is referred to as being referentially transparent.

Achieving Code Reuse

Object-oriented languages tend to have strong coupling between the data and the functions that operate on it. In this scenario we can't easily reuse methods written in one class when we have a similar problem that we need to solve in another.

This problem doesn't exist in a functional language, because the logic and the data are kept separate. The language provides a small set of common data structures, such as lists, maps, and sets. All the functions operate on these data structures; and when we come to a new problem, we can easily reuse any function we write.

Each function represents a certain transformation that we wish to apply to our data. When we need to solve a problem, we simply have to understand the sequence of transformations and map those to the appropriate functions. This style of code is referred to as *declarative*.

Declarative code separates what is being done from how it is done. For example, when we wish to iterate over a collection, we use an iterator function. The logic that we want to execute on each step of the iteration is passed in as a parameter.

One important advantage of this style is that we benefit from having code reuse at the function level. An iterator function can be written once to handle the edge cases and boundary checks. We can now reuse this logic without having to worry about remembering to do these checks time and again.

Leveraging Multiprocessing

Functional code also makes it easier to tackle the difficult problems of parallelism and concurrency. While there's no silver bullet for addressing either problem, the language can certainly make it easier to reason about them.

Since pure functions depend solely on their arguments, they don't rely on any shared state and can be safely computed in parallel. This means we can easily parallelize many algorithms to take advantage of the extra cores. An example of this is mapping a function over the items in a collection. We can start by writing a version using the map function. Should we discover that each operation takes a significant amount of time, then we can simply switch to using pmap to run the operations in parallel.

Meanwhile, the immutable data structures provide an excellent tool for managing shared state. Clojure provides a software transactional memory (STM) API based on these data structures. With transactional memory, we no longer have to worry about manual locking when dealing with threads. Additionally, the data only needs to be locked for writing. Since the existing data is immutable, it can be read safely even while an update is happening.

Data Types

Clojure provides a number of data types, most of which are unsurprising:

- *Vars* provide mutable storage locations. These can be bound and rebound on a per-thread basis.

- *Booleans* can have a value of true or false; nil values are also treated as false.

- *Numbers* can be integers, doubles, floats, or fractions.

- *Symbols* are used as identifiers for variables.

- *Keywords* are symbols that reference themselves and are denoted by a colon; these are often used as keys in maps.

- *Strings* are denoted by double quotes and can span multiple lines.

- *Characters* are denoted by a preceding backslash.

- *Regular expressions* are strings prefixed with a hash symbol.

In addition to the data types, Clojure provides a rich set of standard collections. These include lists, vectors, maps, and sets.

- List: (1 2 3)
- Vector: [1 2 3]
- Map: {:foo "a" :bar "b"}
- Set: #{"a" "b" "c"}

Interestingly, Clojure logic is written using its data structures. Using the same syntax for both data and logic allows for powerful metaprogramming features. We can manipulate any piece of Clojure code just like we would any other data structure. This feature makes it trivial to template the code for recurring patterns in your problem domain. In Clojure, code is data and data is code.

Using Functions

Function calls in Clojure work the same as any mainstream languages, such as Python. The main difference is that the function name comes after the parenthesis in the Clojure version.

```
functionName(param1, param2)
```

```
(function-name param1 param2)
```

This difference can be explained very simply. The function call is just a list containing the function name and its parameters. In Clojure, a list is a special type of data structure reserved for creating callable expressions. To create a list data structure, we have to call the list function:

```
(list 1 2 3)
```

Anonymous Functions

As the name implies, anonymous functions are simply functions that aren't bound to a name. Let's take a look at the following function that accepts a single argument and prints it.

```
(fn [arg] (println arg))
```

The function is defined by using the fn form followed by the vector containing its argument and the body. We could call the preceding function by setting it as the first item in a list and its argument as the second.

```
((fn [arg] (println arg)) "hello")

=>"hello"
```

Clojure provides syntactic sugar for defining anonymous functions using the # notation. With it we can rewrite our function more concisely:

```
#(println %)
```

Here, the % symbol indicates an unnamed argument. If the function accepted multiple arguments, then each one would be followed by a number indicating its position. This can be seen in the next example:

```
#(println %1 %2 %3)
```

The preceding anonymous function accepts three arguments and prints them out in order. This type of function is useful when you need to perform a one-off operation that doesn't warrant defining a named function. These functions are often used in conjunction with the higher-order functions that we'll look at in a moment.

Named Functions

Named functions are simply anonymous functions bound to a symbol used as an identifier. Clojure provides a special form called def that's used for creating global variables. It accepts a name and the body to be assigned to it. We can create a named function by using def as follows:

```
(def square (fn ([x] (* x x))))
```

Since creating these variables is such a common operation, Clojure provides a special form called defn that does this for us:

```
(defn square [x]
  (* x x))
```

The first argument to defn is the name of the function being defined. It's followed by a vector containing the arguments and the body of the function. In the preceding code, we passed in a single item for the body, but we could pass as many items as we like.

```
(defn bmi [height weight]
  (println "height:" height)
  (println "weight:" weight)
  (/ weight (* height height)))
```

Here we define a function to calculate BMI using the height and weight parameters. The body consists of two print statements and a call to divide the weight by the square of the height. All the expressions are evaluated from the inside out. In the last statement, (* height height) is evaluated, then the weight is divided by the result and returned. In Clojure, mathematical operators (such as / and *) are regular functions, so we call them using the prefix notation as we would with any other function.

Note that only the result from the last expression is returned from the function; the results of all the other expressions are discarded. Therefore, any intermediate expressions should strictly be used for side effects, as is the case with the preceding println calls.

Clojure uses a single-pass compiler. For this reason, the functions must be declared before they're used. In the case where we need to refer to a function before it's been defined, we must use the declare macro to provide a forward declaration.

```
(declare down)

(defn up [n]
  (if (< n 10)
    (down (+ 2 n))
    n))

(defn down [n]
  (up (dec n)))
```

As you might have noticed, the code structure is a tree. This tree is called the *abstract syntax tree*, or AST for short. This is the same AST that the compiler sees when compiling the code. By being able to see the AST directly, we can visualize the relationships between pieces of logic.

Since we write our code in terms of data, we have fewer syntactic hints than in most languages. For example, we have no explicit return statements. Instead, the last expression of the function body is returned implicitly. This might take a little getting used to if you're accustomed to seeing a lot of annotations in your code. To aid readability, functions are often kept short (five lines or less is a good rule of thumb), while indentation and spacing are used for grouping code visually.

Clojure makes no distinction between functions and variables. You can assign a function to a label, pass it as a parameter, or return a function from another function. Functions that can be treated as data are referred to as being *first-class* because they don't have any additional restrictions attached to them.

Higher-Order Functions

Functions that take other functions as parameters are called higher-order functions. One example of such a function is map:

```
(map #(* % %) [1 2 3 4 5])
=>(1 4 9 16 25)
```

Here we pass in two parameters to the map function. The first parameter is an anonymous function that squares its argument and the second is a collection of numbers. The map function visits each item in the collection and squares it. One advantage of using higher-order functions is that we don't have to worry about boundary conditions, such as nil checks. The iterator function handles these for us.

Another example of a higher-order function is filter(). This function goes through a collection and keeps only the items matching the condition specified.

```
(filter even? [1 2 3 4 5])
=>(2 4)
```

You can, of course, chain these functions together to solve problems:

```
(filter even?
  (map #(* 3 %) [1 2 3 4 5]))
=>(6 12)
```

Here we multiply each item by 3, and then we use filter() to keep only the even items from the resulting sequence.

Thanks to higher-order functions, you should practically never have to write loops or explicit recursion. When you need to iterate over a collection, use a function such as map or filter instead. Since Clojure has a rich standard library, practically any data transformation can be achieved by a combination of several higher-order functions.

Instead of having to learn a lot of different language features and syntax, you simply have to learn the functions in the standard library. Once you learn to associate data transformations with specific functions, many problems can be solved by simply putting them together in the right order.

Here's a real-world example of this idea. The problem is to display a formatted address given the fields representing it. Commonly an address has a unit number, a street, a city, a postal code, and a country. We'll have to examine each of these pieces, remove the nil and empty ones, then insert a separator between them.

Let's say we have a table in our database that contains the following fields:

```
unit       | street          | city      | postal_code | country
""         | "1 Main Street" | Toronto   | nil         | Canada
```

Given the preceding data as strings, we'd like to output the following formatted string:

```
1 Main Street, Toronto, Canada
```

All we have to do is find the functions for the tasks of removing empty fields, interposing the separator, and concatenating the result into a string:

```
(defn concat-fields [& fields]
  (clojure.string/join ", " (remove empty? fields)))

(concat-fields "" "1 Main Street" "Toronto" nil "Canada")
=> "1 Main Street, Toronto, Canada"
```

The & notation in the preceding parameter definition states that the function accepts a variable number of arguments. The arguments are represented by a list inside the function body.

Notice that we didn't have to specify how to do any of the tasks when writing our code. Most of the time we simply say what we're doing by composing the functions representing the operations we wish to carry out. The resulting code also handles all the common edge cases:

```
(concat-fields) => ""
(concat-fields nil) => ""
(concat-fields "") => ""
```

Closures

We've now seen how we can declare functions, name them, and pass them as parameters to other functions. One last thing we can do is write functions that return other functions as their result. One use for this is to provide the functionality facilitated by constructors in object-oriented languages.

Let's say we wish to greet our guests warmly. We can write a function that accepts the greeting string as its parameter and returns a function that takes the name of the guest and prints a customized greeting for that guest:

```
(defn greeting [greeting-string]
  (fn [guest]
    (println greeting-string guest)))

(let [greet (greeting "Welcome to the wonderful world of Clojure")]
  (greet "Jane")
  (greet "John"))
```

The inner function in the greeting has access to the greeting-string value since the value is defined in its outer scope. The greeting function is called a *closure* because it closes over its parameters—in our case the greeting-string—and makes them available to the function that it returns.

You'll also notice that we're using a form called let to bind the greet symbol and make it available to any expressions inside it. The let form serves the same purpose as declaring variables in imperative languages.

Threading Expressions

By this point you've probably noticed that nested expressions can be difficult to read. Fortunately, Clojure provides a couple of helper forms to deal with this problem. Let's say we have a range of numbers, and we want to increment each number, interpose the number 5 between them, and then sum the result. We could write the following code to do that:

```
(reduce + (interpose 5 (map inc (range 10))))
```

It's a little difficult to tell what's happening in the preceding example at a glance. With a few more steps in the chain, we'd be really lost. On top of that, if we wanted to rearrange any of the steps, such as interposing 5 before incrementing, then we'd have to re-nest all our expressions. An alternative way to write this expression is to use the ->> form:

```
(->> (range 10) (map inc) (interpose 5) (reduce +))
```

Here, we use ->> to thread the operations from one to the next. This means that we implicitly pass the result of each expression as the last argument of the next one. To pass it as the first argument, we'd use the -> form instead.

Being Lazy

Many Clojure algorithms use lazy evaluation, where the operations aren't performed unless their result actually needs to be evaluated. Laziness is crucial for making many algorithms work efficiently. For example, you might think the preceding example is very inefficient since we have to iterate over the sequence each time to create the range, map across it, interpose the numbers, and reduce the result.

However, this isn't actually the case. The evaluation of each expression happens on demand. The first value in the range is generated and passed to the function, then the next, and so on, until the sequence is exhausted. This is similar to the approach that languages like Python take with their iterator mechanics.

Structuring the Code

One nontrivial difference between Clojure and imperative languages is the way the code is structured. In imperative style, it's a common pattern to declare a shared mutable variable and modify it by passing it different functions. Each time we access the memory location, we see the result of the code that previously worked with it. For example, if we have a list of integers and we wish to square each one and then print the even ones, the following Python code would be perfectly valid:

```python
l = list(range(1, 6))

for i, val in enumerate(l) :
  l[i] = val * val

for i in l :
  if i % 2 == 0 :
    print(i)
```

In Clojure this interaction has to be made explicit. Instead of creating a shared memory location and then having different functions access it sequentially, we chain functions together and pipe the input through them:

```clojure
(run! println
  (filter #(= (mod % 2) 0)
    (map #(* % %) (range 1 6))))
```

Or, as we've covered, we could use the ->> macro to flatten the operations:

```clojure
(->> (range 1 6)
     (map #(* % %))
     (filter #(= (mod % 2) 0))
     (run! println))
```

Each function returns a new value instead of modifying the existing data in place. You may think that this can get expensive, and it would be with a naïve implementation, where the entirety of the data is copied with every change.

In reality, Clojure is backed by persistent data structures that create in-memory revisions of the data.[1] Each time a change is made, a new revision is created proportional to the size of the change. With this approach we only pay the price of the difference between the old and the new data structures while ensuring that any changes are inherently localized.

---

1.   http://en.wikipedia.org/wiki/Persistent_data_structure

Destructuring Data

Clojure has a powerful mechanism called destructuring for declaratively accessing values in data structures. If you know the data structure's type, you can describe it using a literal notation in the binding. Let's look at some examples of what this means.

```clojure
(let [[small big] (split-with #(< % 5) (range 10))]
  (println small big))

=>(0 1 2 3 4) (5 6 7 8 9)
```

Here we use the split-with function to split a range of ten numbers into a sequence containing two elements: numbers less than 5 and numbers greater than or equal to 5. The split-with function returns a sequence containing two elements: the first is the sequence of items that are less than 5, and the other is the sequence that is greater than or equal to 5. Since we know the result's format, we can write it in a literal form as [small big] and then use these named elements within the let binding.

We can use this type of destructuring in function definitions as well. Let's say we have a function called print-user that accepts a vector with three items. It names the items name, address, and phone, respectively.

```clojure
(defn print-user [[name address phone]]
  (println name address phone))
(print-user ["Bob" "12 Jarvis street, Toronto" "416-987-3417"])
```

We can also specify variable arguments as a sequence in cases where a variable number of arguments can be supplied. This is done by using the ampersand followed by the name for the argument list.

```clojure
(defn foo [& args]
  (println args))

(foo "a" "b" "c")
=>(a b c)
```

Since the variable arguments are stored in a sequence, it can be destructured like any other.

```clojure
(defn foo [first-arg & [second-arg]]
  (println (if second-arg
             "two arguments were passed in"
             "one argument was passed in")))
(foo "bar")
=>"one argument was passed in"

(foo "bar" "baz")
=>"two arguments were passed in"
```

Destructuring can also be applied to maps. When destructuring a map, we create a new map where we supply the names for the local bindings pointing to the keys from the original map:

```clojure
(let [{foo :foo bar :bar} {:foo "foo" :bar "bar"}]
  (println foo bar)
```

It's possible to destructure a nested data structure as well. As long as you know the data's structure, you can simply write it out.

```clojure
(let [{[a b c] :items id :id} {:id "foo" :items [1 2 3]}]
  (println id " has the following items " a b c))
```

Finally, since extracting keys from maps is a common operation, Clojure provides syntactic sugar for this task.

```clojure
(defn login [{:keys [user pass]}]
 (and (= user "bob") (= pass "secret")))

(login {:user "bob" :pass "secret"})
```

Another useful destructuring option allows us to extract some keys while preserving the original map.

```clojure
(defn register [{:keys [id pass repeat-pass] :as user}]
  (cond
    (nil? id) "user id is required"
    (not= pass repeat-pass) "re-entered password doesn't match"
    :else user))
```

Namespaces

When writing real-world applications, we need tools to organize our code into separate components. Object-oriented languages provide classes for this purpose. The related methods are all defined in the same class. In Clojure, we group our functions into namespaces instead. Let's look at how a namespace is defined.

```clojure
(ns colors)

(defn hex->rgb [[_ & rgb]]
    (map #(->> % (apply str "0x") (Long/decode))
         (partition 2 rgb)))

(defn hex-str [n]
  (-> (format "%2s" (Integer/toString n 16))
      (clojure.string/replace " " "0")))

(defn rgb->hex [color]
  (apply str "#" (map hex-str color)))
```

Preceding, we have a namespace called colors containing three functions called hex->rgb, hex-str, and rgb->hex. The functions in the same namespace can call each other directly. But if we wanted to call these functions from a different namespace, we'd have to reference the colors namespace there first.

Clojure provides two ways to do this: we can use either the :use or the :require keyword.

The :use Keyword

When we reference a namespace with :use, all its vars become implicitly available, as if they were defined in the namespace that references it.

```
(ns myns
  (:use colors))

(hex->rgb "#33d24f")
```

This approach has two downsides. We don't know where the function was originally defined, making it difficult to navigate the code, and if we reference two namespaces that use the same name for a function, we'll get an error.

We can address the first problem by selecting the functions we wish to use explicitly using the :only keyword in our :use declaration.

```
(ns myns
  (:use [colors :only [rgb->hex]]))

(defn hex-str [c]
  (println "I don't do much yet"))
```

This way we document where rgb->hex comes from and we're able to declare our own hex-str function in the myns namespace without conflicts. Note that rgb->hex still uses the hex-str function defined in the colors namespace.

The :require Keyword

The approach of using the :require keyword to reference the namespace provides us with more flexible options. Let's look at each of these.

We can require a namespace without providing any further directives. In this case, any calls to vars inside it must be prefixed with the namespace declaration indicating their origin.

```
(ns myns
  (:require colors))

(colors/hex->rgb "#324a9b")
```

This approach is explicit about the origin of the vars being referenced and ensures that we won't have conflicts when referencing multiple namespaces. One problem is that when our namespace declaration is long, it gets tedious to have to type it out any time we wish to use a function declared inside it. To address this problem, the :require statement provides the :as directive, allowing us to create an alias for the namespace.

```
(ns myotherns
  (:require [colors :as c]))

(c/hex->rgb "#324a9b")
```

We can also require functions from a namespace by using the :refer keyword. This is synonymous with the :use notation we saw earlier. To require all the functions from another namespace, we can write the following:

```
(ns myns
  (:require [colors :refer :all]))
```

If we wish to select what functions to require by name, we can instead write this:

```
(ns myns
  (:require [colors :refer [rgb->hex]]))
```

As you can see, a number of options are available for referencing vars declared in other namespaces. If you're not sure what option to pick, then requiring the namespace by name or alias is the safest route.

Dynamic Variables

Clojure provides support for declaring dynamic variables that can have their value changed within a particular scope. Let's look at how this works.

```
(declare ^:dynamic *foo*)

(println *foo*)
=>#<Unbound Unbound: #'bar/*foo*>
```

Here we declare *foo* as a dynamic var and don't provide any value for it. When we try to print *foo*, we get an error indicating that this var hasn't been bound to any value. Let's look at how we can assign a value to *foo* using a binding.

```
(binding [*foo* "I exist!"]
  (println *foo*))
=>"I exist!"
```

We set *foo* to a string with value "I exist!" inside the binding. When the println function is called within the binding, we no longer get an error when trying to print its value.

This technique can be useful when dealing with resources such as file streams, database connections, or scoped variables. In general, the use of dynamic variables is discouraged since they make code more opaque and difficult to reason about. However, they have legitimate uses, and it's worth knowing how they work.

Polymorphism

One useful aspect of object orientation is polymorphism; while polymorphism happens to be associated with that style, it's in no way exclusive to object-oriented programming. Clojure provides two common ways to achieve runtime polymorphism. Let's look at each of these in turn.

Multimethods

Multimethods provide an extremely flexible dispatching mechanism using a selector function associated with one or more methods. The multimethod is defined using defmulti, and each method is defined using defmethod. For example, if we had different shapes and we wanted to write a multimethod to calculate the area, we could do the following:

```
(defmulti area :shape)

(defmethod area :circle [{:keys [r]}]
  (* Math/PI r r))

(defmethod area :rectangle [{:keys [l w]}]
  (* l w))

(defmethod area :default [shape]
  (throw (Exception. (str "unrecognized shape: " shape))))

(area {:shape :circle :r 10})
=> 314.1592653589793

(area {:shape :rectangle :l 5 :w 10})
=> 50
```

Preceding, the dispatch function uses a keyword to select the appropriate method to handle each type of map. This works because keywords act as functions and when passed a map return the value associated with them. The dispatch function can be as sophisticated as we like, however.

```
(defmulti encounter
  (fn [x y] [(:role x) (:role y)]))

(defmethod encounter [:manager :boss] [x y]
  :promise-unrealistic-deadlines)

(defmethod encounter [:manager :developer] [x y]
  :demand-overtime)
```

```
(defmethod encounter [:developer :developer] [x y]
  :complain-about-poor-management)

(encounter {:role :manager} {:role :boss})
=> :promise-unrealistic-deadlines
```

Protocols allow defining an abstract set of functions that can be implemented by a concrete type. Let's look at an example protocol:

```
(defprotocol Foo
  "Foo doc string"
  (bar [this b] "bar doc string")
  (baz [this] [this b] "baz doc string"))
```

As you can see, the Foo protocol specifies two methods, bar and baz. The first argument to the method is the object instance followed by its parameters. Note that the baz method has multiple arity. We can now create a type that implements the Foo protocol using the deftype macro:

```
(deftype Bar [data]
  Foo
  (bar [this param]
    (println data param))
  (baz [this]
    (println (class this)))
  (baz [this param]
    (println param)))
```

Here we create type Bar that implements protocol Foo. Each method prints out some of its parameters. Let's see what it looks like when we create an instance of Bar and call its methods:

```
(let [b (Bar. "some data")]
  (.bar b "param")
  (.baz b)
  (.baz b "baz with param"))

some data param
Bar
baz with param
```

The first method call prints out the data Bar was initialized with and the parameter that was passed in. The second method call prints out the object's class, while the last method call demonstrates the other arity of baz.

We can also use protocols to extend the functionality of existing types, including existing Java classes. For example, we can use extend-protocol to extend the java.lang.String class with the Foo protocol:

```
(extend-protocol Foo String
(bar [this param] (println this param)))

(bar "hello" "there")
=>"hello there"
```

The preceding examples illustrate the basic principles of how protocols can be used to write polymorphic code. However, protocols have many other uses as well, and we encourage you to discover these on your own.

What About Global State?

While predominantly immutable, Clojure provides support for shared mutable data, as well, via its STM library.[2] The STM ensures that all updates to mutable variables are done atomically. There are two major kinds of mutable types: the atom and the ref. The atom is used in cases where we need to do uncoordinated updates, and the ref is used when we might need to do multiple updates as a transaction.

Let's look at an example of defining an atom and using it.

```
(def global-val (atom nil))
```

We've defined an atom called global-val, and its current value is nil. We can now read its value by using the deref function, which returns the current value.

```
(println (deref global-val))
=>nil
```

Since this is a common operation, there's a shorthand for deref: the @ symbol. So writing (println @global-val) is equivalent to the preceding example.

Let's look at two ways of setting a new value for our atom. We can either use reset! and pass in the new value, or we can use swap! and pass in a function that accepts the current value and updates it.

```
(reset! global-val 10)
(println @global-val)
=>10
(swap! global-val inc)
(println @global-val)
=>11
```

Note that both swap! and reset! end in exclamation points (!); this convention indicates that these functions operate on mutable data.

---

2.   http://clojure.org/concurrent_programming

We define a ref the same way we define an atom, but the two are used different-ly. Let's take a quick look at a concrete example of how a ref is used.

```clojure
(def names (ref []))

(dosync
  (ref-set names ["John"])
  (alter names #(if (not-empty %)
                  (conj % "Jane") %)))
```

The preceding code defines a ref called names and then opens a transaction using a dosync statement. Inside the transaction, the names are set to a vector with the value "John". Next, the alter function is called to check if names is not empty and to add "Jane" to the vector of names when that's the case.

Note that since this is happening inside a transaction, the check for emptiness depends on the existing state along with any state built up within the same transaction. If we tried to add or remove a name in a different transaction, it would have no visible effect on ours. In case of a collision, one of the transactions would end up being retried.

Writing Code That Writes Code for You

Because Clojure is a dialect of Lisp, it provides a powerful macro system. Macros allow for templating of repetitive blocks of code and for deferring evaluation, among numerous other uses. A macro works by treating code as data instead of evaluating it. This allows us to manipulate the code tree just like any other data structure.

Macros execute before compile time, and the compiler sees the result of macro execution. Because of this level of indirection, macros can be difficult to reason about, and thus it's best not to use them when a function will do the job.

However, macros have legitimate uses, and it's worth understanding how they work. In this book we use very few macros, so we'll only touch on their syntax superficially.

Let's look at a concrete example of a macro and see how it differs from the regular code we saw previously. Imagine that we have a web application with a session atom that might contain a user. We might want to load certain content only if a user is present in the session and not otherwise.

```clojure
(def session (atom {:user "Bob"}))

(defn load-content []
  (if (:user @session)
    "Welcome back!"
    "please log in"))
```

This works, but it's tedious and error-prone to write our if statement every single time. Since our condition's logic stays the same, we can template this function as follows:

```
(defmacro defprivate [name args & body]
  `(defn ~(symbol name) ~args
     (if (:user @session)
       (do ~@body)
       "please log in")))
```

The macros are defined using the defmacro special form. The major difference between defn and defmacro is that the parameters passed to defmacro are not evaluated by default.

To evaluate the parameter, we use the tilde, as we're doing with ~(symbol name). Using the ~ notation indicates that we'd like to replace the name with the value it refers to. This is called *unquoting*.

The ~@ notation used in (do ~@body) is called *unquote splicing*. This notation is used when we're dealing with a sequence. The contents of the sequence are merged into the outer form during the splicing. In this case body consists of a list representing the function's body. The body must be wrapped in a do block because the if statement requires having no more than two arguments.

The backtick (`) sign means that we wish to treat the following list as data instead of executing it. This is the opposite of unquoting, and it's referred to as *syntax-quoting*.

As I mentioned earlier, the macros are executed before evaluation time. To see what the macro will be rewritten as when the evaluator sees it, we can call macroexpand-1.

```
(macroexpand-1 '(defprivate foo [greeting] (println greeting)))

(clojure.core/defn foo [greeting]
  (if (:user (clojure.core/deref session))
    (do (println greeting))
    "please log in"))
```

You can see that (defprivate foo (println "bar")) gets rewritten with a function definition that has the if statement inside. This resulting code is what the evaluator sees, and it's equivalent to what we would have to write by hand otherwise. Now we can simply define a private function using our macro, and it will check for us automatically.

```
(defprivate foo [message] (println message))

(foo "this message is private")
```

The preceding example might seem a little contrived, but it demonstrates the power of being able to easily template repetitions in code. This allows you to create a notation that expresses your problem domain using the language natural to it.

The Read-Evaluate-Print Loop

Another big aspect of working in Clojure is the read-evaluate-print loop (REPL). In many languages you write the code, and then you run the entire program to see what it does. In Clojure, most development is done interactively using the REPL. In this mode we can see each piece of code we write in action as soon as it's written.

In nontrivial applications, it's often necessary to build up a particular state before you can add more functionality. For example, a user has to log in and query some data from the database, and then you need to write functions to format and display this data. With a REPL you can get the application to the state where the data is loaded and then write the display logic interactively without having to reload the application and build up the state every time you make a change.

This method of development is particularly satisfying because you see immediate feedback when making changes. You can easily try things out and see what approach works best for the problem you're trying to solve. This encourages experimentation and refactoring of the code as you go, which in turn helps you to write better and cleaner code.

Calling Out to Java

One last thing that we'll cover is how Clojure embraces its host platform to benefit from the rich ecosystem of existing Java libraries. In some cases, we may wish to call a Java library to accomplish a particular task that doesn't have a native Clojure implementation. Calling Java classes is simple and follows the standard Clojure syntax fairly closely.

Importing Classes

When we wish to use a Clojure library, we employ :use and :require statements. However, when we wish to import a Java class, we have to use the :import statement.

```
(ns myns
  (:import java.io.File))
```

We can also group multiple classes from the same package in a single import, as follows:

```
(ns myns
 (:import [java.io File FileInputStream FileOutputStream]))
```

Instantiating Classes

To create an instance of a class, we can call new just as we would in Java.

```
(new File ".")
```

We could also use a common shorthand for creating new objects:

```
(File. ".")
```

Calling Methods

Once we have an instance of a class, we can call methods on it. The notation is similar to making a regular function call. When we call a method, we pass the object its first parameter, followed by any other parameters that the method accepts.

```
(let [f (File. ".")]
 (println (.getAbsolutePath f)))
```

Here we've created a new file object f and we've called .getAbsolutePath on it. Notice that methods have a period (.) in front of them to differentiate them from regular Clojure functions. If we wanted to call a static function or a variable in a class, we would use the / notation, as follows:

```
(str File/separator "foo" File/separator "bar")
```

```
(Math/sqrt 256)
```

We can also chain multiple method calls together using the double period (..) notation as our shorthand. Say we wanted to get the string indicating the file path and then get its bytes; we could write the code for that in two ways:

```
(.getBytes (.getAbsolutePath (File. ".")))
```

```
(.. (File. ".") getAbsolutePath getBytes)
```

The second notation looks more natural and is easier to read. Although there's other syntactic sugar for working with Java, the preceding is sufficient for following the material we cover in this book.

Reader Conditionals

Reader conditionals are the last feature of Clojure that we'll cover. Clojure has three official dialects, with Clojure JVM, ClojureScript, and Clojure CLR. While core Clojure functions work largely the same across these dialects, some platform-specific code can vary. Reader conditionals were introduced in Clojure 1.7 to allow mixing code that targets multiple platforms in the same source file.

The only rule is that source files using reader conditionals must use the *cljc* extension. Let's say we have a util.cljc file that contains some utility functions that use platform-specific interop. For example, let's write a function to return the current time in milliseconds that can be cross-compiled to Clojure and ClojureScript.

```clojure
(defn current-time []
  #?(:clj (.getTime (java.util.Date.))
     :cljs (.getTime (js/Date.))))
```

The current-time function uses #? syntax to declare a reader conditional and specifies the code that should be emitted for Clojure and ClojureScript using :clj and :cljs keywords, respectively. When the namespace is compiled, code using java.util.Date will be used for Clojure and code using js/Date will be used for ClojureScript.

```clojure
;; Clojure
(defn current-time []
  (.getTime (java.util.Date.)))

;; ClojureScript
(defn current-time []
  (.getTime (js/Date.)))
```

Another useful conditional flag is #?@, which allows splicing a collection into the outer form when compiling. For example, if we wanted to conditionally require specific namespaces based on whether we were compiling Clojure or ClojureScript, then we could do the following.

```clojure
(:require
 [clojure.string :as string]
 #?@(:clj  [[clojure.pprint :refer [pprint]]
            [clojure.java.io :as io]]
     :cljs [[cljs.pprint :refer [pprint]]
            [cljs.reader :as reader]]))
```

The code inside the vectors specified under the :clj and :cljs keys will be expanded into the outer :require form, resulting in the following code being compiled for each dialect.

```
;; Clojure
(:require
 [clojure.string :as string]
 [clojure.pprint :refer [pprint]]
 [clojure.java.io :as io])

;; ClojureScript
(:require
 [clojure.string :as string]
 [cljs.pprint :refer [pprint]]
 [cljs.reader :as reader]])
```

That's all there is to it. You may also wish to refer to the official documentation[3] regarding more advanced uses of reader conditionals.

Summary

This concludes our tour of Clojure basics. Altogether, we touched on only a small portion of the overall language. But if you understand the preceding examples, then you should have no trouble following any of the code in the rest of the book. Once you have your development environment up and running, don't hesitate to try out the examples shown here in the REPL and play around with them until you feel comfortable moving on.

3.　https://clojure.org/guides/reader_conditionals

Editor Configuration

In this appendix, we'll cover the most popular code editors for working with Clojure. We'll also discuss why you should configure editor integration and structural editing, along with some tips for best using them.

While you may see recommendations for a specific editor, such as Emacs, there are a number of excellent Clojure environments available. If you're already familiar with one of the editors listed here, we recommend sticking with it to avoid the distraction of switching editors while also learning Clojure. If you aren't familiar with any of these, it's possible that your favorite editor has some Clojure support. However, if you experience difficulty configuring your favorite editor, we recommend going with either VS Code or IntelliJ IDEA.

Why Is Editor Integration So Important?

In other (non-Lisp) languages, it's common to work with any text editor of choice or with a language-specific IDE. But with Clojure and most other Lisps, having an editor integrated REPL along with structural editing is invaluable.

The Clojure REPL

You may be familiar with the concept of a REPL if you've used languages such as Ruby or Python. But REPL environments in these languages function differently from the Clojure REPL. Typically, the REPL is used as a stand-alone toy as opposed to an integral part of the development process. The REPL in such languages doesn't connect to the runtime of the application you're developing or provide any meaningful integration with your editor.

By contrast, the REPL is a central tool for developing Clojure applications. The REPL is typically used by connecting your editor to the application runtime and sending code for evaluation directly from the editor. This approach allows developing applications interactively and creates a tight feedback loop where you can see the changes that you make in code immediately reflected in your application.

Structural Editing

Another Lisp trait that shines through in Clojure is the S-expression. Code written in S-expressions is relatively free of syntax and maps well onto units of computation. Rather than working with lines of code as text, we can manipulate programs more semantically. As a side benefit, since we're manipulating S-expressions themselves, our parentheses never become imbalanced through structural edits.

If you've never worked with a Lisp before, structural editing can take a bit of adjustment. Still, we promise it will be worth it many times over.

Following is a list of some commands you should be familiar with, in order of importance. You can find some pretty cool animations of them online.[1]

Structural Navigation and Selection
Move to sibling, parent, and child forms.

Shrink and expand selection for parenthesis-aware cutting and pasting.

Slurp and Barf
Unfortunate naming aside, slurp and barf are the most basic operations.

They'll add or remove a form to the current S-expression, respectively.

They can each be performed forward or backward.

Wrap and Unwrap
Adds/removes parentheses from the current S-expression.

Join and Split
They do exactly what their names imply, with the added feature of respecting types in Clojure.

Raise and Splice
Raise replaces the outer S-expression with the current one.

Splice merges the current S-expression into the outer one.

General Configuration Tips

Regardless of the editor you choose, you should ensure that you're able to do the following operations, and you should probably add a keybinding for each:

---

1. http://danmidwood.com/content/2014/11/21/animated-paredit.html

- Connect to a running application's nREPL.
- Evaluate expressions in the connected REPL from the editor.
- Load a file/namespace in the REPL.
- Do each of the structural editing commands in the preceding list.

VSCode + Calva

Calva[2] is a great choice for developers who user VS Code as their editor of choice. Calva provides many features that you'd expect to see in a full-featured IDE, and it's one of the easier editors to learn. If you don't currently have a preference, we suggest trying Calva as your first editor. Follow the instructions in the official documentation to get up and running.

IntelliJ IDEA + Cursive

Cursive[3] is a popular Clojure IDE based on the IntelliJ platform, and it's an excellent choice for anybody who's already using IntelliJ. It provides full structural editing, Leiningen dependency management, and REPL support via nREPL. The installation instructions are available on the official site.

Emacs + Cider

Emacs is one of the oldest IDEs still actively used today. Being a mature project, it has lots of features and plugins available, many of which don't have counterparts in other IDEs. However, it also means that Emacs doesn't follow any of the common patterns, since it predates them.

Emacs is available for all the major platforms and can be downloaded from the official site.[4] Additionally, Emacs comes in many different flavors, most notably Spacemacs,[5] Doom Emacs,[6] and Prelude.[7] For installation instructions, please see the respective documentation websites.

If you aren't already familiar with Emacs, be warned that it's significantly harder to learn than modern editors. We recommend only using Emacs if you are either a current Emacs user or are a Vim user unsatisfied with the Vim ecosystem's support of Clojure. If you do choose to use Emacs, be aware that a lot of power in configuration comes at the cost of some serious complexity.

---

2. https://calva.io/
3. https://cursive-ide.com
4. http://www.gnu.org/software/emacs/
5. https://www.spacemacs.org/
6. https://github.com/hlissner/doom-emacs
7. https://github.com/bbatsov/prelude

If you're coming from Vim, you should start with either Spacemacs or Doom Emacs. They both have great support for Vim emulation, or what is affectionately called *evil-mode* in the Emacs community. Additionally, they provide a decent amount of configuration out of the box, so it's far easier to get up and running.

Regardless of the flavor you choose, you need to configure the following packages: clojure-mode,[8] Cider,[9] and one of Smartparens[10] or Paredit.[11]

Vim

Vim users have a few options available. The two most popular plugins are vim-iced[12] and vim fireplace.[13]

8.   https://github.com/clojure-emacs/clojure-mode
9.   https://github.com/clojure-emacs/cider
10. https://github.com/Fuco1/smartparens
11. https://www.emacswiki.org/emacs/ParEdit
12. https://liquidz.github.io/vim-iced/
13. https://github.com/tpope/vim-fireplace

Working with EDN and Transit

Clojure has its own preferred data format, EDN.[1] It's also common to use a more performant format that has feature parity with EDN called Transit.[2] Transit leverages existing high-performance serializers for JSON[3] and MessagePack[4] while leaving the developer experience relatively unchanged.

This appendix provides a brief introduction to these two data formats, along with some common usage examples.

EDN

EDN, or extensible data notation, is a data format based on Clojure's data structure literal syntax. It includes keywords, symbols, strings, numbers, lists, sets, vectors, and maps as covered in Appendix 1, Clojure Primer, on page 363, along with tags.

Tags are the core differentiator for EDN and are why it's called *extensible* data notation.

Tagged Literals

EDN uses the # character as a dispatch, allowing the subsequent form to be parsed in a special way. For example, #_ is discard, which tells the parser to ignore the form that follows. Any # dispatch that has one or more alphabetic characters after it (for example, #uuid) is a tag. This tells the parser to transform the subsequent form based on the tag's implementation. The built-in #uuid

---

1.   https://github.com/edn-format/edn
2.   https://github.com/cognitect/transit-format
3.   https://www.json.org/json-en.html
4.   https://msgpack.org/index.html

tag converts a string representation of a UUID into the environment's underlying UUID implementation (for example, java.util.UUID). The #inst tag similarly parses string representations of instants in time.

In addition to the built-in tags, users can specify their own. Any consumers of EDN that contain these custom tags must have the implementation defined to parse correctly, but there's a default TaggedLiteral type that simply contains the tag name along with the form itself.

Adding Your Own Tags

To specify a custom EDN reader, you simply pass a map of tag symbols to reader functions like so:

```
(require '[clojure.edn :as edn])
(defn parse-my-ratio [{:keys [numerator denominator]}]
  (/ numerator denominator))

(edn/read-string
  {:readers {'my/ratio parse-my-ratio}}
  "{:foo \"bar\" :ratio #my/ratio {:numerator 1 :denominator 2}}")
;; => {:foo "bar" :ratio 1/2}
```

You can include as many custom readers as you like, but keep in mind that only namespaced tag symbols are officially supported.

Transit

Transit has feature parity with EDN but has some slight quirks because it's more optimized and it's more commonly used across different environments. Most notably, the default tags are different from EDN.

Here's an example of a reader/writer pair for a LocalDate type in Clojure taken from luminus-transit.[5]

```
;; In Clojure
(require '[cognitect.transit :as transit])
(import '[java.time LocalDate]
        '[java.io ByteArrayInputStream ByteArrayOutputStream]
        '[java.time.format DateTimeFormatter])

(def read-handlers {"LocalDate"
                     (transit/read-handler
                      #(java.time.LocalDate/parse %
                         (DateTimeFormatter/ofPattern "yyyy-MM-dd")))})
```

---

5.   https://github.com/luminus-framework/luminus-transit

```clojure
(def write-handlers
  {java.time.LocalDate
   (transit/write-handler
    (constantly "LocalDate")
    #(.format % (DateTimeFormatter/ofPattern "yyyy-MM-dd")))})

(def out (ByteArrayOutputStream. 4096))

(transit/write (transit/writer out :json {:handlers write-handlers})
               (LocalDate/of 2020 12 31))

(println (.toString out))
;; => ["~#LocalDate", "2020-12-31"]

(println
  (transit/read
    (transit/reader (ByteArrayInputStream. (.toByteArray out))
                    :json
                    {:handlers read-handlers})))
;; #object[java.time.LocalDate 0x56198302 2020-12-31]
```

By passing our read-handlers to transit/reader and our write-handlers to transit/writer, we can now read and write our custom LocalDate tag. We'd do the exact same thing in ClojureScript, only with implementations for goog.date.Date instead of java.time.LocalDate. By following this process with whatever types you need to support, you can easily serialize and transport them over the network and between environments. Check out luminus-transit's full implementation of transit readers and writers here.[6]

---

6. https://github.com/luminus-framework/luminus-transit/blob/master/src/luminus_transit/time.cljc

Database Access

In this appendix, we'll cover how to work with the PostgreSQL relational databases using the next.jdbc library. We'll then discuss how to write a simple application to generate a PDF report from database records that will teach you about serving binary content in your web application.

Work with Relational Databases

By virtue of running on the Java Virtual Machine, Clojure works with any database that can be accessed via Java Database Connectivity (JDBC).[1] With it, we can easily access a large number of RDBMS databases, such as MySQL, SQL Server, PostgreSQL, and Oracle. The core library for dealing with relational databases is next.jdbc. When using this library we have to write custom SQL for each type of database we intend to use.

Several libraries are available for working with next.jdbc. One such library that we'll cover in this chapter is called HugSQL.[2] This library takes the approach of keeping the SQL separate from the Clojure source files.

Another popular library is called Honey SQL.[3] This library represents SQL queries using Clojure data structures. The advantage of this approach is that we can manipulate and compose the queries directly in Clojure.

We'll start by seeing how to use the clojure.java.jdbc library since it provides all the functionality we need without any additional complexity. If you choose to use a different database engine, be aware that there might be slight syntactic differences in our SQL queries. Before we start working through the examples

---

1. http://en.wikipedia.org/wiki/Java_Database_Connectivity

2. http://www.hugsql.org/

3. https://github.com/seancorfield/honeysql

in this chapter, make sure you have an instance of the PostgreSQL database available in order to follow along.

Setting Up the PostgreSQL Database

Installing PostgreSQL is straightforward. If you're using OS X, then you can simply run Postgres.app.[4] On Linux, you can install PostgreSQL from your package manager. For example, if you're using Ubuntu, you can run sudo apt-get install postgresql. You may also need to modify the pg_hba.conf file to enable password-based authentication.[5]

Once PostgreSQL is installed, we set the password for the user postgres using the psql shell. The shell can be invoked by running the psql command from the console.

```
sudo -u postgres psql postgres
\password postgres
```

With the default user set up, let's create an admin user with the password set to admin.

```
CREATE USER admin WITH PASSWORD 'admin';
```

Then we can create a schema called REPORTING to store our reports by running the following command:

```
CREATE DATABASE REPORTING OWNER admin;
```

Note that we're using the admin user here to save time. You should always create a dedicated user and grant only the necessary privileges for any database you wish to run in production.

Accessing the Database

We'll start by creating a new project called *db-examples* by running Leiningen.

```
$ lein new db-examples
```

To access the database, we need to include the necessary libraries in our project.clj file. We need to reference the seancorfield/next.jdbc library as well as the driver for the database we're accessing. Because we're using PostgreSQL, we require the following dependencies:

---

4.   http://postgresapp.com/
5.   https://fedoraproject.org/wiki/PostgreSQL#pg_hba.conf

db-examples/project.clj
```
(defproject db-examples "0.1.0"
  :description "examples of using next.jdbc"
  :dependencies [[org.clojure/clojure "1.10.1"]
                 [seancorfield/next.jdbc "1.1.613"]
                 [org.postgresql/postgresql "42.2.8"]]])
```

With that in place, navigate to the db-examples.core namespace and reference the next.jdbc library the same way we did in the examples in Chapter 1, Getting Your Feet Wet, on page 1.

db-examples/src/db_examples/core.clj
```
(ns db-examples.core
  (:require
    [next.jdbc :as jdbc]
    [next.jdbc.sql :as sql]
    [next.jdbc.result-set :as rs]))
```

Next, we need to define our database connection. We can do this in several ways. Let's look at the pros and cons of the different options.

Defining a Parameter Map

The simplest way to define a connection is to provide a map of connection parameters.

db-examples/src/db_examples/core.clj
```
(def ds (jdbc/get-datasource
          {:subprotocol "postgresql"
           :subname "//localhost/reporting"
           :user "admin"
           :password "admin"}))
```

In the preceding example, we've defined a connection for an instance of the PostgreSQL database by specifying the database type using the :dbtype key and a name using the :dbname key.

This method is the most common approach for declaring the connection information. In a real-world application, the values should be read from a configuration file or from the environment instead of being hardcoded.

The map with the connection specification is passed to the next.jdbc/get-datasource function in order to create an instance of the JDBC datasource.

Specifying the Driver Directly

Another option is to provide a JDBC datasource and configure it manually. This option is useful if we wish to specify any driver-specific parameters not accessible through the idiomatic parameter map configuration.

```
(def db
  {:datasource
    (doto (PGPoolingDataSource.)
     (.setServerName    "localhost")
     (.setDatabaseName "my_website")
     (.setUser          "admin")
     (.setPassword      "admin")
     (.setMaxConnections 10))})
```

Creating Tables

We can create tables programmatically by calling the create-table-ddl function
and providing it the table name followed by the columns and their types. Let's
write a function to create a table to store user records, where each record has
an ID and a password.

db-examples/src/db_examples/core.clj
```
(defn create-users-table! [ds]
  (jdbc/execute! ds
    ["create table users (
       id varchar(32) primary key,
       pass varchar(100)
      )"]))
```

```
db-examples.core=> (create-users-table! ds)
[#:next.jdbc{:update-count 0}]
```

Here, the next.jdbc/execute! function is called to create a users table. The function
takes a datasource followed by a keyword specifying the table name, and a
vector with strings containing SQL statements.

Selecting Records

To select records from our database, we use the query function. It accepts the
connection and a vector containing the SQL string followed by its arguments,
and it returns a result as a lazy sequence. This function allows us to work with
the returned data without having to load the entire result set into memory.

db-examples/src/db_examples/core.clj
```
(defn get-user [ds id]
  (first (sql/query ds ["select * from users where id = ?" id])))
```

```
db-examples.core=> (get-user "foo")
nil
```

In the preceding code, we've created a function that accepts the user ID as
its argument and returns the first item from the result set. Note that we're
using a parameterized query by specifying a vector containing the prepared

statement string followed by its parameters. Always use this approach to prevent SQL injection attacks.

Inserting Records

A number of options are available for inserting records into the database. If we have a map whose keys match the names of the columns in the table, then we can simply use the insert! function.

db-examples/src/db_examples/core.clj
```
(defn add-user! [ds user]
  (sql/insert! ds :users user))

db-examples.core=> (add-user! ds {:id "foo" :pass "bar"})
nil
```

Now that we've created a user with :id foo, get-user will return it:

```
db-examples.core=> (get-user ds "foo")
#:USERS{:ID "foo", :PASS "bar"}
```

Notice that the result is a map qualified with the name of the table that the records were selected from and that the column names are uppercased. This can be toggled by wrapping the datasource with additional options. In case we didn't wish to qualify the result or uppercase the column names, we could provide a hint as follows:

```
db-examples.core=> (get-user
             #_=>   (jdbc/with-options ds
             #_=>      {:builder-fn rs/as-unqualified-lower-maps})
             #_=>   "foo")
{:id "foo", :pass "bar"}
```

If we wish to insert multiple records simultaneously, we can pass a vector of maps to the insert-multi! function instead. This function accepts a datasource, followed by the table name, a vector containing the column IDs that we wish to insert, and a vector of vectors representing the column values.

db-examples/src/db_examples/core.clj
```
(defn add-users! [ds users]
  (sql/insert-multi! ds :users [:id :pass] users))

db-examples.core=> (add-users! ds
             #_=>   [["bar" "secret"]
             #_=>    ["baz" "secret"]])
[]
```

Updating Existing Records

To update an existing record, use the update! function. The function expects to be passed the connection, followed by the table name, the map representing the updated rows, and the WHERE clause represented by a vector.

db-examples/src/db_examples/core.clj
```
(defn set-pass! [ds id pass]
  (sql/update!
    ds
    :users
    {:pass pass}
    ["id=?" id]))
```

```
db-examples.core=> (set-pass! ds "bar" "baz")
#:next.jdbc{:update-count 1}
```

```
db-examples.core=> (get-user ds "bar")
#:USERS{:ID "bar", :PASS "baz"}
```

Deleting Records

Records can be deleted from the database using the delete! function.

db-examples/src/db_examples/core.clj
```
(defn remove-user! [ds id]
  (sql/delete! ds :users ["id=?" id]))
```

```
db-examples.core=> (remove-user! ds "foo")
#:next.jdbc{:update-count 1}
```

```
db-examples.core=> (get-user ds "foo")
nil
```

Transactions

We use transactions when we want to run multiple statements and ensure that the statements are executed only if all of them can be run successfully. If any statement fails, then the transaction is rolled back to the state prior to running any of the statements.

```
db-examples.core=> (jdbc/with-transaction [t-conn ds]
        #_=>    (sql/update!
        #_=>        t-conn
        #_=>        :users
        #_=>        {:pass "foo"}
        #_=>        ["id=?" "bar"])
        #_=>
        #_=>      (sql/update!
        #_=>        t-conn
        #_=>        :users
```

```
        #_=>          {:pass "foo"}
        #_=>          ["id=?" "baz"]))
db-examples.core=> (get-user "bar")
#:USERS{:ID "bar", :PASS "fooz"}

db-examples.core=> (get-user "baz")
#:USERS{:ID "baz", :PASS "fooz"}

db-examples.core=> (jdbc/with-transaction [t-conn ds]
        #_=>    (sql/update!
        #_=>      t-conn
        #_=>      :users
        #_=>      {:pass "ROLLBACK"}
        #_=>      ["id=?" "bar"])
        #_=>
        #_=>    (sql/insert!
        #_=>      t-conn
        #_=>      :users
        #_=>      {:id "bar"}))
Execution error (JdbcSQLIntegrityConstraintViolationException) at ...
Unique index or primary key violation:
  "PUBLIC.PRIMARY_KEY_4 ON PUBLIC.USERS(ID) VALUES 2";
SQL statement:
INSERT INTO users (id) VALUES (?) [23505-199]

db-examples.core=> (get-user "bar")
#:USERS{:ID "bar", :PASS "fooz"}
```

As can be seen in the preceding code, we use the with-transaction macro to create a transactional connection that is used inside the transaction. The [t-conn db] part of the macro creates a binding the same way a let statement does. All the statements wrapped by with-transaction must use the t-conn connection to execute the queries. Should all the statements complete successfully, then the transaction is committed.

Use HugSQL

The major advantage of using HugSQL is that it allows us to write the SQL queries in separate files instead of having to embed strings in our code. This has a number of advantages, such as allowing us to use SQL tools to edit the queries.

Getting Things Done with HugSQL

HugSQL provides a flexible DSL for generating the functions for running SQL queries. We'll start by seeing how we can define a single query in a file and then create a function from it using the def-db-fns macro. Let's place the query in the resources/find_user.sql file in our project.

```
db-examples/resources/users.sql
-- :name add-user! :! :n
-- :doc   adds a new user
INSERT INTO users
(id, pass)
VALUES (:id, :pass)
```

HugSQL uses specially formatted SQL comments as metadata for defining functions that interact with the database. The name of the function that runs the query is defined using the -- :name comment.

The name of the function is followed by flags indicating the SQL command and the result. The preceding query uses the :! flag to indicate that the function modifies the data and uses the :n key to indicate that it returns the number of rows that were affected.

HugSQL supports the following command flags and defaults to :? when none is specified.

- :query or :?—indicates a query with a result set.
- :execute or :!—can be used for any statement.
- :returning-execute or :<!—is used to indicate an INSERT ... RETURNING query.
- :insert or :i!—attempts to return the generated keys.

The result flag is used to indicate the type of result that's returned by the query. The result defaults to :raw when none is specified.

- :one or :1—a result with a single row.
- :many or :*—a result with multiple rows.
- :affected or :n—the number of affected rows.
- :raw—the result generated by the underlying database adapter.

The only things to note about the SQL statement itself are the placeholder keys for the VALUES. HugSQL uses these keys to look up the parameters in the input map when the generated function is called.

Now that we've defined a query, let's create a new namespace called db-examples.hugsql with the following content:

```
db-examples/src/db_examples/hugsql.clj
(ns db-examples.hugsql
  (:require [db-examples.core :refer [db]]
            [next.jdbc :as jdbc]
            [hugsql.core :as hugsql]))

(hugsql/def-db-fns "users.sql")
```

We can now call add-user! just like any other function, and the comment identified by the -- :doc flag is available as its doc string.

```
db-examples.hugsql=> (add-user! db {:id "hug" :pass "sql"})
1
```

The function accepts the database connection as its first parameter, followed by the query map. Note that the keys in the map have the same names as those we defined earlier in the users.sql file. The connection we're using is the one that we defined earlier for our clojure.java.jdbc examples.

In case we want to return the fields from the record that was created, we can write the following query:

db-examples/resources/users.sql
```
-- :name add-user-returning! :i :1
-- :doc   adds a new user returning the id
INSERT INTO users
(id, pass)
VALUES (:id, :pass)
returning id
```

We have to rerun the def-db-fns macro to load the new query. Then we can run the generated function as follows:

```
db-examples.hugsql=> (add-user-returning! db {:id "hug2" :pass "return"})
{:id "hug2"}
```

Note that support for the returning queries is database-driver dependent: some drivers don't facilitate returning the result of the insert query.

You can use a tuple list to do a multirecord insert. Let's update the users.sql file by adding the following query there:

db-examples/resources/users.sql
```
-- :name add-users! :! :n
-- :doc add multiple users
INSERT INTO users
(id, pass)
VALUES :t*:users
```

The :t* flag indicates that the users key is a vector of records to insert. Each record is described by a vector where the value matches the position of the parameter in the INSERT statement. We can now insert multiple users using the function we defined, as follows:

```
db-examples.hugsql=> (add-users! db {:users
            #_=>                     [["bob" "Bob"]
            #_=>                      ["alice" "Alice"]]})
2
```

We can now query the users by adding the following query:

```
db-examples/resources/users.sql
-- :name find-user :? :1
-- find the user with a matching ID
SELECT *
FROM users
WHERE id = :id
```

When we call the function, it should return a single map that represents the record when it's found and a nil result when it's not.

```
db-examples.hugsql=> (find-user db {:id "bob"})
{:id "bob", :pass "Bob"}
db-examples.hugsql=> (find-user db {:id "nobody"})
nil
```

HugSQL supports in-list queries, where we can provide a vector of values as the parameter. The SQL query uses the :v* flag to indicate the value list parameter. Let's add a new file called resources/find_user.sql and place the following query there:

```
db-examples/resources/users.sql
-- :name find-users :? :*
-- find users with a matching ID
SELECT *
FROM users
WHERE id IN (:v*:ids)
```

The function parameters now consist of a map with the key :ids that points to a vector of IDs that we want to match.

```
db-examples.hugsql=> (find-users db {:ids ["alice" "bob" "nobody"]})
({:id "bob", :pass "Bob"} {:id "alice", :pass "Alice"})
```

It's also worth noting that we can easily mix it with clojure.java.jdbc. For example, if we wanted to run queries in a transaction, then we'd use the with-db-transaction macro to wrap the calls to HugSQL-generated functions, as seen here:

```
db-examples/src/db_examples/hugsql.clj
(defn add-user-transaction [user]
  (jdbc/with-transaction [t-conn db]
    (if-not (find-user t-conn {:id (:id user)})
      (add-user! t-conn user))))

db-examples.hugsql=> (add-user-transaction {:id "cheryl"
              #_=>                           :pass "Cheryl"})
1

db-examples.hugsql=> (add-user-transaction {:id "alice"
              #_=>                           :pass "I already exist"})
nil
```

As we've seen, HugSQL is a flexible library that allows us to define queries in a clean and intuitive way, without having to mix the SQL sources with our Clojure code. We've covered the core features of HugSQL, but it's worth noting that it provides many features that can facilitate for advanced use cases. Please do explore the official documentation to see what they are.

Generate Reports

In this section we'll cover how to generate reports from the data we collect in our database using the clj-pdf library.[6] Then we'll discuss how to serve the generated PDF to the browser using the appropriate response type.

Our application will have an employee table that will be populated with some sample data. We'll use this data to create a couple of different PDF reports, and we'll allow the users to select the type of report they wish to view. Let's create a new application called *reporting-example* using the Luminus template.

```
$ lein new luminus reporting-example +postgres
```

Now we open the project.clj file to add the clj-pdf dependency.

```
:dependencies [...
               [clj-pdf "2.5.5"]]
```

We also have to remember to update the database URL with the dev-config.edn file as follows:

reporting-example/dev-config.edn
```
{:dev true
 :port 3000
 ;; when :nrepl-port is set the application starts the nREPL server on load
 :nrepl-port 7000

 ; set your dev database connection URL here
 :database-url
 "jdbc:postgresql://localhost/reporting?user=admin&password=admin"}
```

Now let's update our migrations files, found in the resources/migrations folder. The "up" file creates the employee table, while the "down" file removes it.

```
CREATE TABLE employee
(name VARCHAR(50),
 occupation VARCHAR(50),
 place VARCHAR(50),
 country VARCHAR(50));

DROP TABLE employee;
```

---

6. https://github.com/yogthos/clj-pdf

With our migrations set up, run this command to initialize the database:

```
lein run migrate
```

Let's navigate to the namespace called reporting-example.db.core and see what we have there.

Luminus uses the conman library to handle external database connections. The library takes care of connection pooling and provides the connect! and disconnect! functions for managing the life cycle of the connection.[7]

When we generated our guestbook project, we used an embedded H2 database. In that case we created the datasource that was passed to the conman/connect! function explicitly. Now that we're using an external database, the datasource is specified declaratively using a map. The library knows how to create an instance of the PostgreSQL datasource given this map.

Serializing and Deserializing Data Based on Its Type

You'll note that the namespace comes with a couple of extend-protocol definitions. Extending the next.jdbc.result-set/ReadableColumn protocol allows us to deserialize the column types returned by the database, while extending the next.jdbc.prepare/SettableParameter protocol allows us to serialize custom column types.

```clojure
reporting-example/src/clj/reporting_example/db/core.clj
(defn pgobj->clj [^org.postgresql.util.PGobject pgobj]
  (let [type (.getType pgobj)
        value (.getValue pgobj)]
    (case type
      "json" (parse-string value true)
      "jsonb" (parse-string value true)
      "citext" (str value)
      value)))

(extend-protocol next.jdbc.result-set/ReadableColumn
  java.sql.Timestamp
  (read-column-by-label [^java.sql.Timestamp v _]
    (.toLocalDateTime v))
  (read-column-by-index [^java.sql.Timestamp v _2 _3]
    (.toLocalDateTime v))
  java.sql.Date
  (read-column-by-label [^java.sql.Date v _]
    (.toLocalDate v))
  (read-column-by-index [^java.sql.Date v _2 _3]
    (.toLocalDate v))
```

---

7. https://github.com/luminus-framework/conman

```
java.sql.Time
(read-column-by-label [^java.sql.Time v _]
  (.toLocalTime v))
(read-column-by-index [^java.sql.Time v _2 _3]
  (.toLocalTime v))
java.sql.Array
(read-column-by-label [^java.sql.Array v _]
  (vec (.getArray v)))
(read-column-by-index [^java.sql.Array v _2 _3]
  (vec (.getArray v)))
org.postgresql.util.PGobject
(read-column-by-label [^org.postgresql.util.PGobject pgobj _]
  (pgobj->clj pgobj))
(read-column-by-index [^org.postgresql.util.PGobject pgobj _2 _3]
  (pgobj->clj pgobj)))
```

The java.sql.Timestamp, java.sql.Date, and java.sql.Time types are converted to the java.time.LocalDateTime, java.time.LocalDate, and java.time.LocalTime types, respectively. The java.sql.Array is deserialized into a vector. And finally, org.postgresql.util.PGobject is deserialized as either JSON or text based on its type.

Conversely, the next.jdbc.prepare/SettableParameter protocol allows us to serialize Clojure maps and vectors into PostgreSQL JSON types.

reporting-example/src/clj/reporting_example/db/core.clj
```
(defn clj->jsonb-pgobj [value]
  (doto (PGobject.)
    (.setType "jsonb")
    (.setValue (generate-string value))))

(extend-protocol next.jdbc.prepare/SettableParameter
  clojure.lang.IPersistentMap
  (set-parameter [^clojure.lang.IPersistentMap v
                  ^java.sql.PreparedStatement stmt ^long idx]
    (.setObject stmt idx (clj->jsonb-pgobj v)))
  clojure.lang.IPersistentVector
  (set-parameter [^clojure.lang.IPersistentVector v
                  ^java.sql.PreparedStatement stmt
                  ^long idx]
    (let [conn      (.getConnection stmt)
          meta      (.getParameterMetaData stmt)
          type-name (.getParameterTypeName meta idx)]
      (if-let [elem-type (when (= (first type-name) \_)
                           (apply str (rest type-name)))]
        (.setObject stmt idx (.createArrayOf conn elem-type (to-array v)))
        (.setObject stmt idx (clj->jsonb-pgobj v))))))
```

This use of the IResultSetReadColumn and ISQLValue protocols allows us to keep all the type coercions in one place instead of having to remember to do them each time we need to store or retrieve a value.

Now that we've looked at all the database code that's been generated, let's start the REPL in this namespace and create the table that we'll be working with by running the following commands in it.

```
user=> (in-ns 'reporting-example.db.core)
#object[clojure.lang.Namespace 0x6233bca8 "reporting-example.db.core"]
reporting-example.db.core=> (mount.core/start #'env #'*db*)
{:started ["#'reporting-example.config/env"
           "#'reporting-example.db.core/*db*"]}
reporting-example.db.core=> (sql/insert-multi!
                   #_=>   *db*
                   #_=>   :employee
                   #_=>   [:name :occupation :place :country]
                   #_=>   [["Albert Einstein", "Engineer",
                   #_=>     "Ulm", "Germany"]
                   #_=>    ["Alfred Hitchcock", "Movie Director",
                   #_=>     "London", "UK"]
                   #_=>    ["Wernher von Braun", "Rocket Scientist",
                   #_=>     "Wyrzysk", "Poland"]
                   #_=>    ["Sigmund Freud", "Neurologist",
                   #_=>     "Pribor", "Czech Republic"]
                   #_=>    ["Mahatma Gandhi", "Lawyer",
                   #_=>     "Gujarat", "India"]
                   #_=>    ["Sachin Tendulkar", "Cricket Player",
                   #_=>     "Mumbai", "India"]
                   #_=>    ["Michael Schumacher", "F1 Racer",
                   #_=>     "Cologne", "Germany"]])
```

Note we're passing the *db* and env vars to mount.core/start in the example. This ensures that mount only starts the specified state.

Finally, we write the query to read the records from the table.

reporting-example/resources/sql/queries.sql
```
-- :name read-employees :? :*
-- reads the list of employees
select * from employee
```

Let's run the conman/bind-connection statement to reinitialize the query functions and call the read-employees function it generates. We should see the following in the REPL console:

```
reporting-example.db.core=> (conman/bind-connection *db* "sql/queries.sql")
{:snips {}, :fns {:read-employees {:meta {...}, :fn #object[...]}}}
reporting-example.db.core=> (read-employees)
({:name "Albert Einstein",
```

```
    :occupation "Engineer",
    :place "Ulm",
    :country "Germany"}
  {:name "Alfred Hitchcock",
   :occupation "Movie Director",
   :place "London",
   :country "UK"}
   ...)
```

Notice that the result of calling read-employees is simply a list of maps where the keys are the names of the columns in the table. Let's see how we can use this to create a PDF with a table listing the employees in our database.

Generating the Reports

The clj-pdf library uses syntax similar to Hiccup's to define the elements in the document. The document itself is represented by a vector. The document vector must contain a map representing the metadata as its first element. The metadata is followed by one or more elements representing the document's content.

Let's create a namespace called reporting-example.reports and look at a few examples of creating PDF documents. We use the pdf function to create the reports and the template macro to format the input data. We also reference the reporting-example.db.core namespace so we can call the read-employees function later on.

reporting-example/src/clj/reporting_example/reports.clj
```
(ns reporting-example.reports
  (:require [reporting-example.db.core :as db]
            [clj-pdf.core :refer [pdf template]]))
```

The pdf function accepts two arguments. The first can be either a vector representing the document or an input stream from which the elements are read. The second can be either a string representing the output file name or an output stream.

Let's generate our first PDF by running the following code in the reporting-example.reports namespace:

```
reporting-example.reports=> (pdf
              #_=>    [{:header "Wow, that was easy"}
              #_=>     [:list
              #_=>      [:chunk {:style :bold} "a bold item"]
              #_=>      "another item"
              #_=>      "yet another item"]
              #_=>     [:paragraph "I'm a paragraph!"]]
              #_=>    "doc.pdf")
nil
```

As you can see, the report consists of vectors, each starting with a keyword identifying the type of element, followed by the metadata and the content. We also have a list that contains three rows followed by a paragraph. The PDF will be written to a file called doc.pdf in our project's root. The contents of the file should look like the following figure:

> **Wow that was easy**
> _____
>
> - **a bold item**
> - another item
> - yet another item
> I'm a paragraph!

Next, let's see how we can use the template macro to format the employee data into a nice table. This macro uses $ to create anchors to be populated from the data using keys of the same name.

The template returns a function that accepts a sequence of maps and applies the supplied template to each element in the sequence. In our case, since we're building a table, the template is simply a vector with the names of the keys for each cell in the row. Let's add the following template to the reporting-example.reports namespace:

reporting-example/src/clj/reporting_example/reports.clj
```clojure
(def employee-template
  (template [$name $occupation $place $country]))
```

Let's try it out in the REPL:

```clojure
reporting-example.reports=> (employee-template (take 2 (db/read-employees)))
(["Albert Einstein" "Engineer" "Ulm" "Germany"]
 ["Alfred Hitchcock" "Movie Director" "London" "UK"])
```

It looks like our template works as expected. Let's use it to generate a report containing the full list of our employees:

```clojure
reporting-example.reports=> (pdf
                   #_=>   [{:header "Employee List"}
                   #_=>    (into [:table
                   #_=>           {:border false
                   #_=>            :cell-border false
                   #_=>            :header
                   #_=>            [{:backdrop-color [0 150 150]}
                   #_=>             "Name" "Occupation" "Place" "Country"]}]
                   #_=>           (employee-template (db/read-employees)))]
                   #_=>   "report.pdf")
nil
```

The resulting report should look like the following figure:

Name	Occupation	Place	Country
Albert Einstein	Engineer	Ulm	Germany
Alfred Hitchcock	Movie Director	London	UK
Wernher Von Braun	Rocket Scientist	Wyrzysk	Poland
Sigmund Freud	Neurologist	Pribor	Czech Republic
Mahatma Gandhi	Lawyer	Gujarat	India
Sachin Tendulkar	Cricket Player	Mumbai	India
Michael Schumacher	F1 Racer	Cologne	Germany

Of course, the template we used for this report is boring. Let's look at another example. Here we output the data in a list and style each element:

reporting-example/src/clj/reporting_example/reports.clj
```
(def employee-template-paragraph
  (template
   [:paragraph
    [:heading {:style {:size 15}} $name]
    [:chunk {:style :bold} "occupation: "] $occupation "\n"
    [:chunk {:style :bold} "place: "] $place "\n"
    [:chunk {:style :bold} "country: "] $country
    [:spacer]]))
```

Let's create a report using employee-template-paragraph by running the following:

```
reporting-example.reports=> (pdf
  #_=>    [{}
  #_=>     [:heading {:size 10} "Employees"]
  #_=>     [:line]
  #_=>     [:spacer]
  #_=>     (employee-template-paragraph
  #_=>       (db/read-employees))]
  #_=>    "report.pdf")
nil
```

Our new report should look like the figure on page 412.

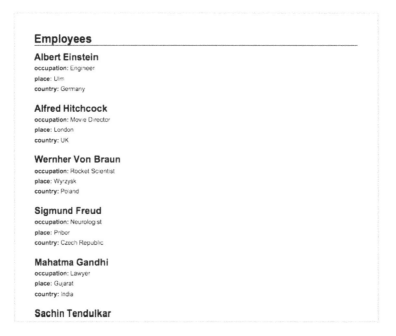

Displaying the Reports

Now that we've created a couple of reports on our data, let's see how we can serve them from our application. Let's write the functions to create the list and the table reports using the preceding examples:

reporting-example/src/clj/reporting_example/reports.clj

```
(defn table-report [out]
  (let [data (db/read-employees)]
    (pdf
     [{:header "Employee List"}
      (when-not (empty? data)
        (into [:table
               {:border false
                :cell-border false
                :header [{:backdrop-color [0 150 150]}
                         "Name" "Occupation" "Place" "Country"]}]
              (employee-template (db/read-employees))))]
     out)))

(defn list-report [out]
  (pdf
   [{}
    [:heading {:size 10} "Employees"]
    [:line]
    [:spacer]
    (employee-template-paragraph (db/read-employees))]
   out))
```

We update our page to provide links to both types of reports.

reporting-example/resources/html/home.html
```
{% extends "base.html" %}
{% block content %}
<div class="row">
    <div class="span12">
        <h1>Select report type:</h1>
        <ul class="nav nav-pills">
            <li class="btn btn-default">
                <a href="/report/list">List reports</a>
            </li>
            <li class="btn btn-default">
                <a href="/report/table">Table reports</a>
            </li>
        </ul>
        {% if error %}
        <h2>An error has occurred while generating the report:</h2>
        <div class="alert alert-danger">{{error}}</div>
        {% endif %}
    </div>
</div>
{% endblock %}
```

Next, we navigate to reporting-example.routes.home and add some references needed to create the report route.

reporting-example/src/clj/reporting_example/routes/home.clj
```
(ns reporting-example.routes.home
  (:require
   [reporting-example.layout :as layout]
   [reporting-example.db.core :as db]
   [clojure.java.io :as io]
   [clojure.tools.logging :as log]
   [reporting-example.middleware :as middleware]
   [ring.util.http-response :as response]
   [reporting-example.reports :as reports]))
```

We also update the home function to serve the page without passing it any parameters.

reporting-example/src/clj/reporting_example/routes/home.clj
```
(defn home-page [request]
  (layout/render request "home.html"))
```

Now we write a function to generate the response. We create an input stream using a supplied byte array and set it as the response. We also set the appropriate headers for the content type, the content disposition, and the length of the content.

```
reporting-example/src/clj/reporting_example/routes/home.clj
(defn write-response [report-bytes]
  (with-open [in (java.io.ByteArrayInputStream. report-bytes)]
    (-> (response/ok in)
        (response/header "Content-Disposition" "filename=document.pdf")
        (response/header "Content-Length" (count report-bytes))
        (response/content-type "application/pdf"))))
```

Next, we write another function to generate the report. This function creates a ByteArrayOutputStream that's used to store the report. Then it calls one of our report-generation functions with it. Once the report is generated, we call write-response with the contents of the output stream.

```
reporting-example/src/clj/reporting_example/routes/home.clj
(defn generate-report [{:keys [path-params] :as request}]
  (try
    (let [report-type (:report-type path-params)
          out (java.io.ByteArrayOutputStream.)]
      (condp = (keyword report-type)
        :table (reports/table-report out)
        :list  (reports/list-report out))
      (write-response (.toByteArray out)))
    (catch Exception ex
      (log/error ex "failed to render report!")
      (layout/render request "home.html" {:error (.getMessage ex)}))))
```

Last but not least, we create a new route to serve our reports.

```
reporting-example/src/clj/reporting_example/routes/home.clj
(defn home-routes []
  [""
   {:middleware [middleware/wrap-csrf
                 middleware/wrap-formats]}
   ["/" {:get home-page}]
   ["/about" {:get about-page}]
   ["/report/:report-type" {:get generate-report}]])
```

You should now be able to navigate to http://localhost:3000 and select a link to one of the reports. When you click the link, the corresponding report is served.

What You've Learned

This covers the basics of working with relational databases. You've now learned how to do the basic database queries and manage the connection life cycle, and you've written a reporting application that serves binary content in action. As we've covered in this chapter, database records are easily mapped to Clojure data structures. So the Clojure community largely sees object-relational mapping libraries as unnecessary.

Writing RESTful Web Services with Liberator

In this appendix, we'll cover how to use the Liberator library to generate our application endpoints.[1]

Using Liberator

Liberator is a Clojure library for writing RESTful services modeled after webmachine,[2] a popular service framework for Erlang. Its primary feature is that it puts a strong emphasis on decoupling the front end from the back end of your application.

Conceptually, Liberator provides a clean way to reason about your service operations. Each request passes through a series of conditions and handlers defined in the resource. These map to the codes specified by the HTTP RFC 2616, such as 200 OK, 201 Created, 404 Not Found, and so on.

This approach makes it very easy to write standards-compliant services and to group the operations logically. It also means that your services will automatically use the appropriate HTTP codes associated with a particular response.

Due to its focus on the separation of the front-end and back-end logic, Liberator is a natural choice for writing many types of web applications. These include general-purpose services, single-page applications, and applications that might have nonweb clients, such as mobile applications.

---

1. http://clojure-liberator.github.io/liberator/
2. https://github.com/basho/webmachine

In this section we'll cover how to create a simple application that serves static resources, provides basic session management, and handles service operations.

We first create a new application called *liberator-service* using a Leiningen template called *reagent-template*. This template is less opinionated than the Luminus template, and therefore it provides a better starting point for Liberator-based applications.

```
lein new reagent liberator-service
```

Once the application is created, we need to add Liberator, Cheshire, and cljs-ajax dependencies to our project.clj dependencies vector:[3]

```
:dependencies
[ ...
  [cheshire "5.10.0"]
  [liberator "0.15.3"]
  [cljs-ajax "0.8.0"]]
```

Cheshire is a fast and easy-to-use JSON parsing library. We'll use it for parsing the requests from the client and generating the responses.

The application generated by the template contains a file called src/clj/liberator_service/handler.clj that contains the routes for the application. The home-page function generates the HTML using the Hiccup HTML templating library. The syntax is the same as the Reagent HTML templating syntax we covered previously.

Defining Resources

Liberator uses the concept of resources to interact with the client. The resources are simply Ring-compliant handlers that can be used inside your Reitit routes. These resources are defined using the resource and the defresource macros. We need to reference these functions in the liberator-service.handler namespace to start working with Liberator.

```
(ns liberator-service.handler
  (:require ...
    [liberator.core :refer [defresource resource]]))
```

Now we can update our route handler to use a Liberator resource to serve the HTML page:

liberator-snippets/home.clj
```
(defn loading-page [request]
    (html5
        (head)
```

---

3.   https://github.com/dakrone/cheshire

```
        [:body {:class "body-container"}
         mount-target
         (include-js "/js/app.js")]]))
(def app
  (reitit-ring/ring-handler
    (reitit-ring/router
      [["/" {:get (resource
                     :handle-ok loading-page
                     :etag "fixed-etag"
                     :available-media-types ["text/html"])}]])
    (reitit-ring/routes
      (reitit-ring/create-resource-handler {:path "/" :root "/public"})
      (reitit-ring/create-default-handler))
    {:middleware middleware}))
```

This allows the Liberator resource to handle the request type. Let's start the app by running the following command and navigating to http://localhost:3000/ in the browser. We should see the home page displayed, advising us to start Figwheel to compile ClojureScript.

```
lein run
```

Say we want to name the resource handler; we can use defresource instead:

liberator-snippets/home.clj
```
(defresource home
               :handle-ok loading-page
               :etag "fixed-etag"
               :available-media-types ["text/html"])

(def app
  (reitit-ring/ring-handler
    (reitit-ring/router
      [["/" {:get home}]])
    (reitit-ring/routes
      (reitit-ring/create-resource-handler {:path "/" :root "/public"})
      (reitit-ring/create-default-handler))
    {:middleware middleware}))
```

The request in the preceding route is simply a map that's described in What's in the Request Map, on page 33.

A set of keys defined by the Liberator API represents each resource type for different types of actions that follow. A key can fall into one of four categories:

- Decision
- Handler
- Action
- Declaration

Each key can be associated with either constants or functions. The functions should accept a single parameter that is the current context and return a variety of responses.

The context parameter contains a map with keys for the request, the resource, and optionally the representation. The request key points to the Ring request. The resource represents the current state of the resource, and the representation contains the results of content negotiation.

Let's take a close look at each category and its purpose.

Making Decisions

Decisions are used to figure out how to handle the client request. The decision keys end with a question mark (?) and their handler must evaluate to a Boolean value.

A decision function can return a Boolean value indicating the result of the decision, or it can return a map or a vector. In the case where a map is returned, the decision is assumed to have been evaluated to true, and the contents of the map are merged with the response map. If a vector is returned, it must contain a Boolean indicating the outcome, followed by a map to be merged with the response.

When any decision has a negative outcome, its corresponding HTTP code is returned to the client. For example, if we wanted to mark as unavailable the route we defined earlier, we could add a decision key called service-available? and associate it with a false value.

liberator-snippets/home.clj
```
(defresource home
             :service-available? false
             :handle-ok loading-page
             :etag "fixed-etag"
             :available-media-types ["text/html"])
```

If we reload the page, we'll see the 503 response type associated with the Service Not Available response.

Alternatively, we could restrict access to the resource by using the method-allowed? decision key along with a decision function.

liberator-snippets/home.clj
```
(defresource home
  :method-allowed?
  (fn [context]
    (= :get (get-in context [:request :request-method])))
  :handle-ok loading-page
```

```
:etag "fixed-etag"
:available-media-types ["text/html"])
```

Since checking the request method is a common operation, Liberator provides a key called :allowed-methods. This key should point to a vector of keywords representing the HTTP methods.

liberator-snippets/home.clj
```
(defresource home
  :allowed-methods [:get]
  :handle-ok loading-page
  :etag "fixed-etag"
  :available-media-types ["text/html"])
```

We can also combine multiple decision functions in the same resource:

liberator-snippets/home.clj
```
(defresource home
  :service-available? true

  :method-allowed? (request-method-in :get)

  :handle-method-not-allowed
  (fn [context]
    (str (get-in context [:request :request-method]) " is not allowed"))

  :handle-ok loading-page
  :etag "fixed-etag"
  :available-media-types ["text/html"])
```

Creating Handlers

A handler function should return a standard Ring response. Handler keys start with the handle- prefix. We saw a handler function when we used the handle-ok key to return the response in our resource.

You'll find other handlers as well, such as handle-method-not-allowed and handle-not-found. The full list of handlers can be found on the official documentation page.[4] These handlers can be used in conjunction with the decisions to return a specific response for a particular decision outcome.

For example, if we want to return a specific response when the service is not available, we do the following:

liberator-snippets/home.clj
```
(defresource home
  :service-available? false
  :handle-service-not-available
  "service is currently unavailable...")
```

---

4.   http://clojure-liberator.github.io/liberator/doc/handlers.html

```
  :method-allowed? (request-method-in :get)
  :handle-method-not-allowed
  (fn [context]
    (str (get-in context [:request :request-method]) " is not allowed"))

  :handle-ok loading-page
  :etag "fixed-etag"
  :available-media-types ["text/html"])
```

Our resource now has custom handlers for each decision outcome.

Taking Actions

An action represents an update of the current state by the client, such as a PUT, POST, or DELETE request. The action keys end with an exclamation point (!) to indicate that they're mutating the application's internal state. Once an action occurs, we can return the result to the client using the handle-created handler.

Writing Declarations

Declarations are used to indicate the resource's capabilities. For example, our resource uses the available-media-types declaration to specify that it returns a response of type text/html. Another declaration we saw is etag, which allows the client to cache the resource.

Putting It All Together

Let's look at an example of a service that has a couple of resources that allow the client to read and write some data. The application will display a list of to-do items and allow the user to add additional items to the list.

The client will be implemented in ClojureScript and use Ajax to communicate with the service. The client code will consist of a few functions to retrieve, render, and save to-do items. Let's look at each of these in turn.

The first function renders the items in our list.

liberator-service/src/cljs/liberator_service/core.cljs
```
(defn item-list [items]
  (when (not-empty items)
    [:ul
     (for [item items]
       ^{:key item}
       [:li item])]))
```

Next we add a function called get-items to grab the items from the server as a string, and a function called parse-items to parse it into a list. The parse-items

function expects to receive data as a newline-separated string, generating a
vector from nonempty items.

liberator-service/src/cljs/liberator_service/core.cljs
```
(defn parse-items [items]
  (->> items
       clojure.string/split-lines
       (remove empty?)
       vec))

(defn get-items []
  (GET "/items"
    {:error-handler
     #(session/put! :error (:response %))
     :handler
     #(session/put! :items (parse-items %))}))
```

Note the function is calling session/update-in! to store the result. This function
is provided by the reagent-utils library. The session namespace contains a
Reagent atom and provides several utility functions for managing its state.

The session provides a way to represent the global state for the application,
such as the user information. It should not be used for any component-spe-
cific data, however. Since our application is extremely simple, it's a convenient
way to track the to-do items.

If we receive an error, the :error-handler is invoked and it populates the :error key
in the session.

We also need to add a function for adding new items to the list. Let's call this
function add-item!; its code looks as follows:

liberator-service/src/cljs/liberator_service/core.cljs
```
(defn add-item! [item]
  (session/remove! :error)
  (POST "/items"
    {:headers {"x-csrf-token"
               (.-value (.getElementById js/document "__anti-forgery-token"))}
     :format :raw
     :params {:item (str @item)}
     :error-handler #(session/put! :error (:response %))
     :handler #(do
                 (println "updating")
                 (session/update-in! [:items] conj @item)
                 (reset! item nil))}))
```

This function looks for the anti-forgery token on the page and sets it as the
header, as we've done before. It also sets the :format key to the :raw value,
indicating that we don't wish to do any processing on the data we send and
receive. The success handler updates the session to conj the value to the list

and resets the item atom to nil. Errors are handled the same way as for the previous component.

To use the add-item! function, we have to create a UI component; let's call it item-input-component and put the following code in it:

liberator-service/src/cljs/liberator_service/core.cljs
```
(defn item-input-component []
  (let [item (atom nil)]
    (fn []
      [:div
       [:input
        {:type :text
         :value @item
         :on-change #(reset! item (-> % .-target .-value))
         :placeholder "To-Do item"}]
       [:button
        {:on-click #(add-item! item)}
        "Add To-Do"]])))
```

The component creates a local state to hold the value of the item as it's being typed in by the user and then calls the add-item! function to send it to the server.

Finally, we create the error-component that displays itself whenever the :error key is present in the session.

liberator-service/src/cljs/liberator_service/core.cljs
```
(defn error-component []
  (when-let [error (session/get :error)]
    [:p error]))
```

Let's update the home-page component to display the components that we just created.

liberator-service/src/cljs/liberator_service/core.cljs
```
(defn home-page []
  [:div
   [:h2 "To-Do Items"]
   [error-component]
   [item-list (session/get :items)]
   [item-input-component]])
```

Now let's update the init! function to fetch the initial list of to-do items from the server when the page loads.

liberator-service/src/cljs/liberator_service/core.cljs
```
(defn init! []
  (clerk/initialize!)
  (accountant/configure-navigation!
   {:nav-handler
```

```clojure
   (fn [path]
     (let [match (reitit/match-by-path router path)
           current-page (:name (:data  match))
           route-params (:path-params match)]
       (reagent/after-render clerk/after-render!)
       (session/put! :route {:current-page (page-for current-page)
                             :route-params route-params})
       (clerk/navigate-page! path)
       ))
   :path-exists?
   (fn [path]
     (boolean (reitit/match-by-path router path)))}})
 (accountant/dispatch-current!)
 (mount-root))
```

Now we'll create corresponding resources to handle each of the operations. Let's start by adding a reference to clojure.java.io to read and write the to-do file and to ring.util.anti-forgery for handling CSRF.

```clojure
(ns liberator-service.routes.home
  (:require ...
            [clojure.java.io :as io]
            [ring.util.anti-forgery :refer [anti-forgery-field]]))
```

Next let's change the home-page and add the anti-forgery-field to it. This is necessary to ensure that a fresh anti-forgery value is generated for each session. We also have to update the home resource accordingly.

liberator-service/src/clj/liberator_service/handler.clj
```clojure
(def mount-target
  [:div#app
   [:h2 "Welcome to liberator-service"]
   [:p "please wait while Figwheel is waking up ..."]
   [:p "(Check the js console for hints if nothing exciting happens.)"]])

(defn head []
  [:head
   [:meta {:charset "utf-8"}]
   [:meta {:name "viewport"
           :content "width=device-width, initial-scale=1"}]
   (include-css (if (env :dev) "/css/site.css" "/css/site.min.css"))])
```

```clojure
(defn loading-page [request]
  (html5
   [:html
    (head)
    [:body
     (anti-forgery-field)
     [:p (str (anti-forgery-field))]
     mount-target
     (include-js "/js/app.js")]]]))
(defresource home
  :allowed-methods [:get]
  :handle-ok loading-page
  :etag "fixed-etag"
  :available-media-types ["text/html"])
```

Let's create a resource that responds to GET requests and returns the contents of the items file found in the root directory of the project. Note that when we're working with mutable resources such as files, we don't wish to place them in the resources folder. Once the application is packaged as a JAR, then the resources become read-only. Therefore, we need to reference these from an external location.

liberator-snippets/home.clj
```clojure
(defresource items
  :allowed-methods [:get]
  :handle-ok (fn [_] (io/file "items"))
  :available-media-types ["text/plain"])
```

In the resource, we use the :allowed-methods key to restrict it to only serve GET requests. We use the available-media-types declaration to specify that the response is of type text/plain. The resource then reads the items file from disk and returns its contents to the client.

Next, we update the resource to support POST requests that will allow adding an item contained in params to the list of items on disk.

liberator-snippets/home.clj
```clojure
(defresource items
  :allowed-methods [:get :post]
  :handle-ok (fn [_] (io/file "items"))
  :available-media-types ["text/plain"]

  :post!
  (fn [context]
    (let [item (-> context :request :params :item)]
      (spit (io/file "items") (str item "\n") :append true)))
  :handle-created (io/file "items"))
```

The updated resource checks that the method is either GET or POST and uses the post! action to update the existing list of items. We then use the handle-created handler to return "ok" upon success.

You'll notice that nothing is preventing us from adding a blank item. Let's add a check in our service to validate the request to add a new item:

liberator-service/src/clj/liberator_service/handler.clj

```clojure
(defresource items
  :allowed-methods [:get :post]
  :handle-ok (fn [_] (io/file "items"))
  :available-media-types ["text/plain"]

  :post!
  (fn [context]
    (let [item (-> context :request :params :item)]
      (spit (io/file "items") (str item "\n") :append true)))
  :handle-created "ok"

  :malformed? (fn [context]
                (-> context :request :params :item empty?))
  :handle-malformed "item value cannot be empty!")
```

Now, if the value of the item parameter is empty, we'll be routed to handle-malformed to inform the client that the item name cannot be empty. Next time we try to add an empty user, we'll see a 400 error in the browser:

```
POST http://localhost:3000/add-user 400 (Bad Request)
```

If you click the Add To-Do button without filling in the item field, you'll see the following error:

As you can see, Liberator ensures separation of concerns by design. With the Liberator model, you'll have small, self-contained functions, each of which handles a specific task.

Leiningen Templates

Once we create a particular type of application, such as our guestbook app, we may want to write other applications that use the same structure. It would be nice to be able to create a skeleton app template that could be used for this task. This is precisely what we can do with Leiningen templates.

Throughout this book we've been primarily using the Luminus template for starting new projects.[1] Here we'll cover how a template works and how to make templates of our own.

What's in a Template

A Leiningen template is a collection of assets that are used to generate a particular project. The templates use the Stencil library to inject dynamic content, such as the name of the project, into the asset files when they're rendered.[2]

We'll take a look at a template project called *compojure-template* to see how it works.[3]

Since templates are Leiningen projects, they each contain a project.clj file.

compojure-template/project.clj
```
(defproject compojure/lein-template "0.4.7"
  :description "Compojure project template for Leiningen"
  :url "https://github.com/weavejester/compojure-template"
  :eval-in-leiningen true
  :license {:name "Eclipse Public License"
            :url "http://www.eclipse.org/legal/epl-v10.html"})
```

---

1. https://github.com/luminus-framework/luminus-template
2. https://github.com/davidsantiago/stencil
3. https://github.com/weavejester/compojure-template

It looks like a regular project file, except for the eval-in-leiningen key that prevents Leiningen from launching a separate process for the given project during the build time.

The template itself is found at src/leiningen/new/compojure.clj, and it looks like this:

```
compojure-template/src/leiningen/new/compojure.clj
(ns leiningen.new.compojure
  (:require [leiningen.core.main :as main]
            [leiningen.new.templates :refer [renderer year project-name
                                             ->files sanitize-ns name-to-path
                                             multi-segment]]))

(def render (renderer "compojure"))

(defn compojure
  "Create a new Compojure project"
  [name]
  (let [main-ns (sanitize-ns name)
        data    {:raw-name   name
                 :name       (project-name name)
                 :namespace  main-ns
                 :dirs       (name-to-path main-ns)
                 :year       (year)}]
    (->files data
      [".gitignore"  (render "gitignore")]
      ["project.clj" (render "project.clj" data)]
      ["README.md"   (render "README.md" data)]
      ["src/{{dirs}}/handler.clj"       (render "handler.clj" data)]
      ["test/{{dirs}}/handler_test.clj" (render "handler_test.clj" data)]
      "resources/public")))
```

The compojure function is where all the fun happens, and it's what gets called when we run lein new compojure myapp to create an application using this template. The function declares a map called data with some useful variables, such as the sanitized project name, that's used to render the assets.

The leiningen.new.templates/render function is used to generate the resulting files at the specified path. Each resource is represented by a vector where the first element is the name of the file to be generated and the second is a call to the render function with the name of the template file. The {{dirs}} tag is replaced by the value of the :dirs key from the data map.

We find the template files at the resources/leiningen/new/compojure path. These files don't need to have the same folder structure as the resulting project. As you can see in the preceding code, we specify the target path explicitly when we render each asset.

The template files use tags that match the keys in the data map, such as the {{namespace}} anchor, whenever dynamic content needs to be injected. This anchor is replaced with the value specified at that key when the resource is generated. Let's look at the handler.clj template file as an example:

compojure-template/resources/leiningen/new/compojure/handler.clj

```
(ns {{namespace}}.handler
  (:require [compojure.core :refer :all]
            [compojure.route :as route]
            [ring.middleware.defaults :refer [wrap-defaults site-defaults]]))

(defroutes app-routes
  (GET "/" [] "Hello World")
  (route/not-found "Not Found"))

(def app
  (wrap-defaults app-routes site-defaults))
```

Note that since Stencil uses {{ and }} delimiters, it can end up interpreting the contents of the template as tags. To avoid this, it's possible to temporarily change the delimiters as follows:

```
{{=<% %>=}}
(let [{{:keys [foo bar]} :baz} m]
  (println foo bar))
<%={{ }}=%>
```

Now that we've seen what a Leiningen template looks like, let's create a fresh template project by running the following command:

```
lein new template my-template
```

The resulting project contains the following files. Note that the package structure matches the name of the template that we supplied.

```
____.gitignore
|____.hgignore
|____CHANGELOG.md
|____LICENSE
|____project.clj
|____README.md
|____resources
| |____leiningen
|   |____new
|     |____my_template
|       |____foo.clj
|____src
  |____leiningen
    |____new
      |____my_template.clj
```

Once we've created our template, we can install it locally by running lein install. Then we can start using it instead of having to write the boilerplate for this kind of project. If we wish to make our template available to others, we can publish it to Clojars by running lein deploy clojars.[4]

---

4.   https://clojars.org/

Index

Thank you!

How did you enjoy this book? Please let us know. Take a moment and email us at support@pragprog.com with your feedback. Tell us your story and you could win free ebooks. Please use the subject line "Book Feedback."

Ready for your next great Pragmatic Bookshelf book? Come on over to https://pragprog.com and use the coupon code BUYANOTHER2021 to save 30% on your next ebook.

Void where prohibited, restricted, or otherwise unwelcome. Do not use ebooks near water. If rash persists, see a doctor. Doesn't apply to *The Pragmatic Programmer* ebook because it's older than the Pragmatic Bookshelf itself. Side effects may include increased knowledge and skill, increased marketability, and deep satisfaction. Increase dosage regularly.

And thank you for your continued support,

The Pragmatic Bookshelf

Kotlin and Android Development featuring Jetpack

Start building native Android apps the modern way in Kotlin with Jetpack's expansive set of tools, libraries, and best practices. Learn how to create efficient, resilient views with Fragments and share data between the views with ViewModels. Use Room to persist valuable data quickly, and avoid NullPointerExceptions and Java's verbose expressions with Kotlin. You can even handle asynchronous web service calls elegantly with Kotlin coroutines. Achieve all of this and much more while building two full-featured apps, following detailed, step-by-step instructions.

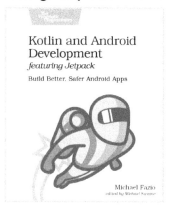

Michael Fazio
(444 pages) ISBN: 9781680508154. $49.95
https://pragprog.com/book/mfjetpack

Learn to Program, Third Edition

It's easier to learn how to program a computer than it has ever been before. Now everyone can learn to write programs for themselves—no previous experience is necessary. Chris Pine takes a thorough, but lighthearted approach that teaches you the fundamentals of computer programming, with a minimum of fuss or bother. Whether you are interested in a new hobby or a new career, this book is your doorway into the world of programming.

Chris Pine
(230 pages) ISBN: 9781680508178. $45.95
https://pragprog.com/book/ltp3

Intuitive Python

Developers power their projects with Python because it emphasizes readability, ease of use, and access to a meticulously maintained set of packages and tools. The language itself continues to improve with every release: writing in Python is full of possibility. But to maintain a successful Python project, you need to know more than just the language. You need tooling and instincts to help you make the most out of what's available to you. Use this book as your guide to help you hone your skills and sculpt a Python project that can stand the test of time.

David Muller
(140 pages) ISBN: 9781680508239. $26.95
https://pragprog.com/book/dmpython

Modern CSS with Tailwind

Tailwind CSS is an exciting new CSS framework that allows you to design your site by composing simple utility classes to create complex effects. With Tailwind, you can style your text, move your items on the page, design complex page layouts, and adapt your design for devices from a phone to a wide-screen monitor. With this book, you'll learn how to use the Tailwind for its flexibility and its consistency, from the smallest detail of your typography to the entire design of your site.

Noel Rappin
(90 pages) ISBN: 9781680508185. $26.95
https://pragprog.com/book/tailwind

Essential 555 IC

Learn how to create functional gadgets using simple but clever circuits based on the venerable "555." These projects will give you hands-on experience with useful, basic circuits that will aid you across other projects. These inspiring designs might even lead you to develop the next big thing. The 555 Timer Oscillator Integrated Circuit chip is one of the most popular chips in the world. Through clever projects, you will gain permanent knowledge of how to use the 555 timer will carry with you for life.

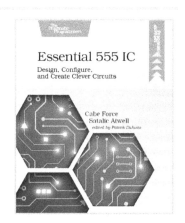

Cabe Force Satalic Atwell
(104 pages) ISBN: 9781680507836. $19.95
https://pragprog.com/book/catimers

Resourceful Code Reuse

Reusing well-written, well-debugged, and well-tested code improves productivity, code quality, and software configurability and relieves pressure on software developers. When you organize your code into self-contained modular units, you can use them as building blocks for your future projects and share them with other programmers, if needed. Understand the benefits and downsides of seven code reuse models so you can confidently reuse code at any development stage. Create static and dynamic libraries in C and Python, two of the most popular modern programming languages. Adapt your code for the real world: deploy shared functions remotely and build software that accesses them using remote procedure calls.

Dmitry Zinoviev
(64 pages) ISBN: 9781680508208. $14.99
https://pragprog.com/book/dzreuse

Apple Game Frameworks and Technologies

Design and develop sophisticated 2D games that are as much fun to make as they are to play. From particle effects and pathfinding to social integration and monetization, this complete tour of Apple's powerful suite of game technologies covers it all. Familiar with Swift but new to game development? No problem. Start with the basics and then layer in the complexity as you work your way through three exciting—and fully playable—games. In the end, you'll know everything you need to go off and create your own video game masterpiece for any Apple platform.

Tammy Coron

(504 pages) ISBN: 9781680507843. $51.95

https://pragprog.com/book/tcswift

Design and Build Great Web APIs

APIs are transforming the business world at an increasing pace. Gain the essential skills needed to quickly design, build, and deploy quality web APIs that are robust, reliable, and resilient. Go from initial design through prototyping and implementation to deployment of mission-critical APIs for your organization. Test, secure, and deploy your API with confidence and avoid the "release into production" panic. Tackle just about any API challenge with more than a dozen open-source utilities and common programming patterns you can apply right away.

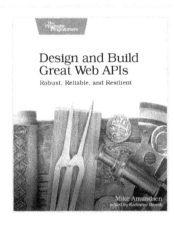

Mike Amundsen

(330 pages) ISBN: 9781680506808. $45.95

https://pragprog.com/book/maapis

The Pragmatic Bookshelf

The Pragmatic Bookshelf features books written by professional developers for professional developers. The titles continue the well-known Pragmatic Programmer style and continue to garner awards and rave reviews. As development gets more and more difficult, the Pragmatic Programmers will be there with more titles and products to help you stay on top of your game.

Visit Us Online

This Book's Home Page
https://pragprog.com/book/dswdcloj3
Source code from this book, errata, and other resources. Come give us feedback, too!

Keep Up to Date
https://pragprog.com
Join our announcement mailing list (low volume) or follow us on twitter @pragprog for new titles, sales, coupons, hot tips, and more.

New and Noteworthy
https://pragprog.com/news
Check out the latest pragmatic developments, new titles and other offerings.

Save on the ebook

Save on the ebook versions of this title. Owning the paper version of this book entitles you to purchase the electronic versions at a terrific discount.

PDFs are great for carrying around on your laptop—they are hyperlinked, have color, and are fully searchable. Most titles are also available for the iPhone and iPod touch, Amazon Kindle, and other popular e-book readers.

Send a copy of your receipt to support@pragprog.com and we'll provide you with a discount coupon.

Contact Us

Online Orders:	*https://pragprog.com/catalog*
Customer Service:	*support@pragprog.com*
International Rights:	*translations@pragprog.com*
Academic Use:	*academic@pragprog.com*
Write for Us:	*http://write-for-us.pragprog.com*
Or Call:	+1 800-699-7764